# THE CAROLINA BACKCOUNTRY
# ON THE EVE OF THE REVOLUTION

# THE CAROLINA BACKCOUNTRY ON THE EVE OF THE REVOLUTION

*The Journal and Other Writings of Charles Woodmason, Anglican Itinerant*

EDITED WITH AN INTRODUCTION BY

*Richard J. Hooker*

PUBLISHED FOR THE

*Institute of Early American History and Culture at Williamsburg, Virginia*

BY THE UNIVERSITY OF NORTH CAROLINA PRESS
*Chapel Hill, 1953*

© 1953 The University of North Carolina Press
All rights reserved
Manufactured in the United States of America
ISBN 0-8078-4035-1
Library of Congress Catalog Card Number 53-13218

00   99   98   97   96      7   6   5   4   3

*To My Mother and Father*

## *Part Three*

# Introduction

IN THE AUTUMN of 1766 a newly ordained Anglican minister named Charles Woodmason left the culture and wealth of Charleston, South Carolina, to work in the back settlements of the province. Before him lay the great adventure of his life in a turbulent frontier region among motley, and often primitive, immigrants who for varying reasons had found their way to this distant land.

Woodmason remained in the Backcountry for six years. During this time he traveled over three thousand miles a year, organized more than thirty widely scattered congregations, and rode constantly from one settlement to another exhorting, marrying, baptizing, and advising the settlers on all their problems. He found himself in a new world in which civilized standards of conduct sometimes seemed inverted, and where primitive living conditions had loosened all social and family ties. He eventually came to know well a large part of the interior settlements. From Camden, his headquarters, he itinerated northward to the upper Wateree and Catawba Rivers, northeastward to the settlements on Lynches River, and eventually northwestward even to the Cherokee towns beyond Saluda River.

This energetic, curious, and intelligent man became the recorder and chronicler of the vast Backcountry region. Herein lies his singular importance. His writings present to modern view the daily life, the thoughts, the hopes and fears of colonial frontier peoples. It is fortunate that his private journal, three of his sermon books, some of his letters, together with miscellaneous but important papers, have been preserved in manuscript form. These are now collected and published for the first time because they provide a remarkably detailed and vivid picture of a region, a time, and a personality.

The writings of Woodmason reveal the swift settlement of a forest region, the conversion of wilderness into small farms, the strife among national and religious groups, and the imprint of frontier conditions upon them all. His is probably the fullest extant account of any American colonial frontier.

The picture is of course not perfect. Although an honest and conscientious man, Woodmason's strong convictions and prejudices pervade every page he wrote. He did not undertake his work as an unformed youth, but rather as a man who brought with him the experiences of a life passed in his native England, in the Parish of Prince Frederick Winyaw, South Carolina, and in the city of Charleston. Although he entered the Anglican ministry with immense zeal, in background he was a man of affairs—planter, merchant, and parish and provincial official. In fact, perhaps the most remarkable circumstance of his mission—and one that may never be fully explained—is the religious impulse that led him late in life from the luxuries of Charleston to the savage simplicities of the frontier.

About Woodmason's life in England there remain only scattered bits of information. He was certainly of the gentry class and an Anglican, brought up to reverence his church. He was probably born about 1720,[1] but his writings say nothing about parents, brothers, sisters, or more distant relatives. There is a brief, bitter, and enigmatic reference to a wife for whom he "sacrificed all he had in Life," together with affectionate mention of a son from this marriage.[2]

Wherever he might have been born, London probably became his home. He certainly knew the city and, later, was to wonder how its citizens would have looked upon the uncouth interior settlers of South Carolina. In London he admired the services of St. Paul's Cathedral, delighted in the singing of the girls in Magdalen Chapel, listened with curiosity to a Baptist preacher in

1. Careful search has failed to reveal the date of either Woodmason's birth or death. However, he left a wife and son behind when he emigrated about 1752, described himself as "old" in 1771, and could perform the strenuous work of his ministry in South Carolina as late as 1772.

2. See pp. 193, 198.

Clerkenwell, and made friends who later became his correspondents when he was in America.[3]

It was probably in 1752 that Woodmason took ship to South Carolina.[4] He no doubt intended that his family should follow later, but this was never to be. At some time in the following years a kick from a horse rendered him unfit for "Nuptial Rites," whereupon his wife chose to remain in England.[5] And Woodmason's stated purpose in emigrating to America, to discover an "opening" for his son, failed to develop, and the younger Woodmason remained in England.[6]

Soon after his arrival in Charleston, Woodmason rode northward beyond Peedee River in search of plantation sites or the location of a country store. His explorations finished, he began an almost feverish accumulation of lands. He purchased eighteen slaves and took advantage of the South Carolina bounty to obtain two tracts of land totalling nine hundred and fifty acres.[7] During the next seven years he acquired more than 1200 additional acres in the Peedee River region.[8]

Woodmason remained among the "sober, sensible and Literate"

3. See pp. 23-25, and Sermon Book, II, 30, 232, [488].

4. In March, 1752, Woodmason was in Gosport, Hampshire, England, where he had already waited some time for favorable winds in order to sail for South Carolina. Woodmason to Dr. Ward, Gosport, March 19, 1752, Additional Manuscripts 6211, f. 234, British Museum. Woodmason stated that he crossed the Peedee River shortly after his first arrival in South Carolina about the time of the sale of a deceased gentleman's belongings, "(I think it was Mr. Ouldfield)." The will of John Ouldfield was proved Dec. 30, 1752. Wills, Charleston County, 1752-1756, 54, typescript in Caroliniana Library, University of South Carolina. In late 1765 Henry Laurens wrote that he had known Woodmason for "some 13 or 14 Years past." Letter Book of Henry Laurens, Oct. 30, 1762, to Sept. 10, 1766, Historical Society of Pennsylvania.

5. See p. 198.    6. See p. 193.

7. The province gave fifty acres of land for the head of the household and the same amount for each member of his family, white or Negro. Woodmason asked for one tract of land in the Santee region and another tract on Lynches Creek or the waters of the Peedee. Journal of the Council, Oct. 1, Nov. 5, 1754, Office of Historical Commission of South Carolina, Columbia, S. C. Hereinafter cited as Council Journal. Mortgage Book ZZ, 210-11, Office of Historical Commission of S. C.

8. Council Journal, Jan. 3, Aug. 1, 1758; May 1, Sept. 4, 1759; Nov. 10, 1761; Memorial Book, VII, 268; XIV, 125, Office of Hist. Commission of S. C.; Mortgage Book ZZ, 208-9. The plats for many of the grants to Woodmason are in the Office of the Hist. Commission of S. C.

inhabitants of lower Prince Frederick Winyaw Parish for nearly a decade. To what extent his plantations throve is uncertain, though a mortgage of 1758 shows that he lived in some elegance, despite his lonely state, for he used as partial security "One Burse and Book Case with about 100 Vol. of Books One Chest of Drawers two Mahogonny Tables Six Mahogany Chairs twelve other Chairs two Beds with Bedsteads Quilts Blankets and furniture One Watch one fowling Piece a Silver milk Pot and Tongs eight Silver Spoons" together with other items.[9]

Now, as later, ambition and restlessness drove him into other activities. As early as 1754 he described himself as both "Planter and Merchant."[10] Several years later he refused two proposals to establish Backcountry stores, being "intimidated" by fear of the Cherokee and Catawba Indians.[11] In 1757, however, he began a store on Black Mingo Creek,[12] the northern branch of Black River, where he possessed the double advantage of being close to his plantations and far from hostile Indians. Three years later he petitioned the Assembly for permission to construct a "substantial Floating Bridge" across Black Mingo Creek, but if the Assembly took action it left no record of it.[13]

9. Mortgage Book ZZ, 210-11. On numerous occasions Woodmason borrowed money or mortgaged his property, but whether through necessity or to finance an expansion of his activities is not clear. See Mortgage Book ZZ, 208-13; Mortgage Book XX, 350-51, 452-53; VV Copy Jan. 1759-July 1760, Nos. 262, 682, Office of Register of Mesne Conveyances, Charleston, S. C.; Miscellaneous Records Charleston County 1758-1763, 810, typescript in Charleston Free Library, Charleston, S. C.; Mortgage Book 1753, 361-63.

10. *Ibid.*, 361.    11. See pp. 140-41.

12. In 1760, in a petition to the Assembly, Woodmason stated that he had been in business on the Black Mingo for three years. Journal of the Commons House of Assembly, May 2, 1760, Office of Historical Commission of S. C. Hereinafter cited as Commons Journal. In 1760, Colonel Pawley's Battalion impressed goods from "Charles Woodmason & Company." *Ibid.*, Feb. 14, May 19, 1760. If the "& Company" indicates that Woodmason had a partner, it was probably one John Baxter who, in 1763 and 1764, was co-plaintiff with Woodmason in suits for non-payment of loans. Record, Court of Common Pleas 1763-1769, May 11, 1763, May 9, 1764, typescript in Charleston Court House; Summons, Oct. 4, 1763, Judgment Rolls, 1764 (A to C), Charleston Court House.

13. Commons Journal, May 2, 1760.

Even more striking in their variety and number were Woodmason's activities on behalf of church and state. In 1756 he was
named church warden for the Parish of Prince Frederick Winyaw.
Since the parish lacked a rector—the notoriously immoral Reverend Michael Smith having left by request—the vestry asked him
to read prayers and a sermon each Sunday, a task he undertook
and continued for the next six years.[14] He also visited all parts of
the parish as collector of the poor tax for the vestry.[15] In 1757
Woodmason was elected a vestryman himself, contesting sixth
place among the fifteen candidates.[16] In this office, as when
church warden, he kept the vestry minutes and acted as correspondent in the search for a resident minister.[17]

Other offices followed. In 1757 he was chosen lieutenant, under
Captain James Crokatt, of the Black River Church militia company.[18] The following year he was appointed justice of the peace
by Governor and Council,[19] an office he held and diligently
served, in Craven County and in Charleston, for seven years.[20] In
1759 the governor made Woodmason a constable,[21] and in 1761
he was both coroner [22] and collector of the general tax.[23] Each
office added to his knowledge of local government and prepared

14. Register for Prince Frederick, Winyaw, Apr. 19, 1756, South Carolina
Historical Society, Charleston, S. C.; Rev. Charles Martyn to Bishop of Lon-
don, Charleston, Dec. 20, 1765, Fulham Palace Transcripts, S. C., No. 90,
Library of Congress. Hereinafter cited as Ful. Trans.

15. Commons Journal, Apr. 29, 1761.

16. Register for Prince Frederick, Winyaw, Apr. 11, 25, 1757.

17. The minutes of the Register for Prince Frederick, Winyaw, are in the
handwriting of Woodmason from Apr. 27, 1756 through June 28, 1757. See
letter to Bishop of London, May 1, 1756, *ibid.*, May 1, 1756 (also Ful. Trans.,
S. C., No. 25); Charles Woodmason to Rev. John Andrews, Black River, June
28, 1757, *ibid.*

18. Council Journal, May 4, 1757.      19. *Ibid.*, Feb. 16, 1758.

20. *South Carolina Gazette*, Oct. 13, Dec. 8, 1758; Jan. 19, 1759; Feb. 2,
July 5, 1760; Mar. 28, 1761; Mortgage Book ZZ, 205. His activities as magistrate
in Charleston appear in *S. C. Gaz.*, Dec. 31, 1764; July 13, Aug. 24, 1765;
Commons Journal, Jan. 15, Mar. 5, 1765.

21. *Ibid.*, Jan. 19, 1759.           22. *Ibid.*, May 25, June 23, 1761.

23. *Ibid.*, Apr. 29, June 3, 1761, and notice to former collectors of the general tax in *S. C. Gaz.*, Sept. 22, 1766.

him for his later role of adviser to the Backcountry and penman of the Regulators.

The planter-merchant period of Woodmason's career ended abruptly in 1762. Strong, though entirely circumstantial, evidence shows that about July of this year he returned to England.[24] Quite possibly his wife had died (for within a few years he was to begin his fruitless search for a new one), and he found it necessary to settle her estate and to provide for his son. His own affairs in South Carolina must have been left in a tangled state, for during his absence the provost marshal seized his lands and sold them for debt.[25]

Woodmason returned to South Carolina in late 1762 or early 1763 to begin a quite different life. Planting and storekeeping behind him, he now became a resident of Charleston and gave his full time to civic duties.

Proud and luxurious Charleston was the political, economic, and social center of the colony, but located far to the southeast of its geographical center. In the city and its nearby coastal parishes were concentrated South Carolina's wealth, political power, slavery, and the strength of the Anglican Church. Charleston, wedged between the Ashley and Cooper Rivers, was the funnel of export and import for the colony. Its citizens—"So rich, so luxurious, polite a People!" Woodmason was to describe them [26]—owed their privileges to rice, indigo, slavery, law, and trade. Planters, merchants, and lawyers controlled the Assembly and were close-

24. Although Woodmason left many traces of his activities in South Carolina, there is nothing to indicate that he was in the province during the second half of 1762. Again, in a "Memorial" to the Bishop of London, Sept. 16, 1776, written in England, Woodmason states that he has "thrice crossed the Ocean," a number of voyages that can be accounted for only by an unrecorded two-way crossing. Memorial of Charles Woodmason to the Bishop of London, Wells, Sept. 16, 1776, William Stevens Perry, ed., *Historical Collections relating to the American Colonial Church* ([Hartford, Conn.], 1870), I, 535, with corrections in Ful. Trans., Va., Box 2, No. 201.

25. Advertisement of provost marshal, *S. C. Gaz.*, Nov. 20, Dec. 4, 1762. It is possible that Woodmason was writing autobiographically some years later when he discussed the case of a man who left the province, was supposed to have had no intention of returning, and whose property was seized and sold for debt in his absence. See p. 125.    26. See p. 60.

knit by similar interests and intermarriage, and all three groups usually owned not only plantations but summer homes in Charleston.[27] The plantations were the colony's principal source of wealth, and a visitor from New England marvelled at how closely conversation in Charleston held to slaves and the prices of indigo and rice.[28]

Woodmason quickly found a place for himself in this city. Egerton Leigh, a member of the Council, got that body to transfer Woodmason's commission as justice of the peace from Craven County to Berkeley County.[29] Well-placed friends were probably responsible for his appointment as clerk of two Assembly commissions: the Commissioners of Pilotage for the Bar and Harbour of Charleston,[30] and the Commissioners of Streets.[31] That his public services exceeded the requirements of his offices appeared when the Charleston Grand Jury, upon his information, presented "Mary M'Dowell, in *Pinckney-Street* in *Charles-Town*, for keeping a most notorious Brothel, and a receptacle for lewd women, to the great annoyance of the inhabitants of said street."[32] Vice, it seems, was a concern of his even before he became a minister. He did not ignore the pleasures of society, however, and as secretary of the charitable and social St. George's Society of Charleston[33] he no doubt found the literate companionship and "Converse" he so greatly missed later in the interior.

By the summer of 1765 Woodmason had become a popular and successful figure in Charleston. It was to be said that he had acquitted himself "in a most irreproachable and becoming Manner" as "the principal acting Magistrate" of the city,[34] and he

27. For the interrelationships of planters and merchants see Leila Sellers, *Charleston Business on the Eve of the Revolution* (Chapel Hill, 1934), 146-47.

28. Mark Antony De Wolfe Howe, ed., "Journal of Josiah Quincy, Junior, 1773," Massachusetts Historical Society, *Proceedings*, 49 (1915-16), 456.

29. Council Journal, Sept. 23, 1763.    30. *S. C. Gaz.*, May 11, 1765.

31. *Ibid.*, Jan. 19, Feb. 9, May 25, 1765.    32. *Ibid.*, Nov. 12, 1764.

33. *Ibid.*, Sept. 7, 28, 1765. The Society, whose members were of English origin, had been founded in 1733. See Frederick P. Bowes, *The Culture of Early Charleston* (Chapel Hill, 1942), 120.

34. Rev. Charles Martyn to Bishop of London, Charleston, Dec. 20, 1765, Ful. Trans., S. C., No. 90.

himself was to write that "I was greatly caressed, and ev'ry ones favriter." [35]

A swift fall from favor took place when Woodmason, apparently unable to resist a new office, applied for the post of stamp distributor.[36] Like many others, he may not have anticipated the sharp popular reaction to the Stamp Act when its full implications were known. Chief Justice Charles Shinner may already have been his patron, as he was later. If so, this association would have increased the unpopularity which now overtook Woodmason. Shinner, an Irish placeman, refused to open the courts prior to official notice of repeal of the Stamp Act.[37] On him was focused a great part of the popular anger which anyone close to him would have shared. As late as 1771 Woodmason's feelings still rankled from the recollection that he "was deem'd (and am still) a private Spy and Correspondent of the Ministry—a faithless fellow—one that is a betrayer of the Country, and of the Rights and Priveleges of America." [38]

Late in 1765, the would-be stamp distributor made a decision that was to change the course of his life. Suddenly, and perhaps without consulting his friends, he applied for the position of itinerant Anglican minister in the upper part of St. Mark's Parish.

Why should Woodmason have come to such a radical resolution? His worldly Charleston friends may well have been puzzled, and Woodmason later remembered that he had exposed himself to the "Laughter of Fools" and ridicule of the licentious.[39] His income in Charleston was not endangered, for his name had just reappeared in the commission of the peace.[40] The itinerant position, on the other hand, paid but little and required arduous duty on the distant frontier. His bitter experience in the Stamp Act crisis may have precipitated this decision.

What neither friends nor "Fools" could understand was that Woodmason sincerely wished to serve his Church and his fellow men and for ten years had worried about the lack of Anglican ministers in the Backcountry. As church warden, vestryman, and lay reader, nearly ten years earlier, he had written to the Bishop

35. See p. 193.    36. See pp. 49, 193.    37. See p. 295.
38. See p. 193.    39. See p. 25.    40. S. C. Gaz., Oct. 31, 1765.

of London and to a minister about to visit England to urge that ministers be dispatched to defend the interior settlements against the hordes of dissenters.[41] In 1757, too, he had noticed with pleasure the Assembly's authorization of the itinerant post for which he now applied.[42]

Although Woodmason had not visited the back settlements he had had full opportunity to inform himself about them. His store on Black Mingo Creek had been frequented by travelers and cattle drovers from the Yadkin, Indian Town, and the Cheraws, and as tax collector he had gone himself as far inland as the Welsh Tract.[43] He had become anxious about the great conquests of the revivalistic New Light Baptists in North Carolina, and he knew that they were entering the South Carolina Backcountry. In a report on the Southern Anglican churches, which as a candidate for the ministry he now composed for the Bishop of London, he proposed to "disperse these Wretches." In a deplorably inaccurate prophecy he said that he expected them to "fly before Him as Chaff." [44]

Since there were no Anglican bishops in America to ordain ministers, Woodmason now prepared for a voyage to England. He left well recommended. The Reverend Charles Martyn, Rector of nearby St. Andrew's Parish, wrote the Bishop of London that the candidate's only motive seemed to be that of "being serviceable" to the back settlers. He regretted Woodmason's "Misfortune, of not being very conversant in the learned Languages," but thought that his frontier location might obviate the need.[45] In a separate testimonial, Martyn and two other Anglican ministers testified to Woodmason's irreproachable life and doctrines during

41. Vestry and Church Wardens of Prince Frederick, Winyaw, to Bishop of London, May 1, 1756, Register for Prince Frederick, Winyaw; Charles Woodmason to Rev. John Andrews, Black River, June 28, 1757, *ibid.*

42. *Ibid.* The creation of St. Mark's Parish and the act authorizing an itinerant minister in the upper part of that parish are in Thomas Cooper, ed., *The Statutes at Large of South Carolina* (Columbia, S. C. 1838), IV, 20-21, 35-37. Hereinafter cited as *Stat. at Large of S. C.*

43. Petition of Woodmason to Assembly, Commons Journal, Apr. 29, June 3, 1761.

44. See p. 78.

45. Rev. Charles Martyn to Bishop of London, Charleston, Dec. 20, 1765, Ful. Trans., S. C., No. 90.

his three years in Charleston.[46] Lieutenant-Governor William Bull, a native South Carolinian and always a friend to the Back-country, presented the candidate's name to the church commissioners, under whose jurisdiction the appointment lay. These gentlemen, though not unanimously, agreed to appoint him provided he could return ordained from England within six months.[47]

By December 21, 1765, Woodmason had boarded the ship *Jenny,* which was preparing to sail for Hull, England, under Captain James Yeoman.[48] Repercussions of his decision followed him even on shipboard, and in an exchange of letters with the wealthy merchant Henry Laurens, whom he had known since he first came to South Carolina, he charged that friend with having called him an "unsettled creature," of having withheld confidence, aid, and pity from him, and of having persecuted him while in distress. Did he refer to his Stamp Act troubles? Laurens emphatically denied the accusations. Had Woodmason visited him he would have received him "as a Christian and a Gentleman." And had Woodmason asked his advice, as he had often done in the past, he would have given it "freely and without flattery." It was perhaps fear of just such advice, Laurens thought, which had deprived him of a visit.[49] Two days later the *Jenny* sailed.[50] There is nothing to show whether or not Woodmason had answered the reproachful letter of Laurens.

During Woodmason's visit in England he was ordained and licensed to work in the Parish of St. Mark's.[51] As he left the coast of England on his return voyage he began a Journal to record the events of his new life. He solemnly recorded his failure to

46. Testimonial of Rev. Charles Martyn, Rev. Alexander Keith of St. Stephen's, and Rev. James Harrison of St. James' Goose Creek, Dec. 13, 1765, Colonial Letters of Orders 1765-1767, Office of Church Commissioners, London.

47. Extract from Register of the Board of Church Commissioners of South Carolina, Dec. 14, 1765, *ibid.*

48. *S. C. Gaz. (Revived),* June 2, 1766.

49. Letter Book of Henry Laurens, Oct. 30, 1762, to Sept. 10, 1766, Historical Society of Pennsylvania.

50. *S. C. Gaz. (Revived),* June 2, 1766.

51. Woodmason was licensed Apr. 28, 1766. Licensed to Plantations, Fulham Palace Manuscripts, Office of Church Commissioners, London.

bring the ship's company to prayer for a prosperous voyage and, all unconsciously, revealed that during the voyage everyone but himself had a wonderful time. In Charleston, he waited impatiently until the Church Commissioners signed his commission, and then left the same day to take up his duties. Four days later he arrived at Pine Tree Hill and for the first time saw the Backcountry where he was to work.[52] The experience came as a shock, and the Journal, heretofore consisting largely of routine record, became increasingly the description of a new and strange world.

The Backcountry, as Woodmason discovered, was separated by a wide gulf from the coastal plantation strip that looked to Charleston as its center. In every sense the back settlers were underprivileged inhabitants, looked upon by the coastal planters as a distant and barbaric population forming a convenient buffer against Indian attack.

Geographical differences underlay the division of the province. The low country, which extended more than a hundred miles from the shore line, consisted near the ocean of sand, swamps, and pine barrens, and along the river valleys of the combination of soil and water needed for rice plantations. Westward appeared waste lands of sand and pines, only lightly settled before the Revolution or used for cattle ranges.

The "Sand Hills," until recent geologic times the coast, marked the fall line. Here began the higher lands of the Piedmont which swelled into hills as they approached the mountains a hundred miles distant. The Piedmont was interlaced with clear rivers and innumerable creeks, and the earth was covered by forests of oak, hickory, and pine. Fertile soils appeared along the courses of the rivers and larger creeks and on some of the plateaus between the river valleys.[53]

The Backcountry of Woodmason's day included more than the Piedmont. Much of the country below the fall line, though still distant from the coastal plantations, was recently settled and underprivileged. Relative poverty, lack of social organization, and

52. See p. 6.

53. Robert L. Meriwether, *The Expansion of South Carolina 1729-1765* (Kingsport, Tenn., 1940), 113-14. Hereinafter cited as Meriwether, *Expans. of S. C.* Sellers, *Charleston Business*, 25-26.

an exclusion from most of the benefits of the provincial government created the state of mind that characterized the back settlers.

In part the back settlements owed their existence to the fears of Charleston and the coastal plantation region. In the colony's beginning there were "external" enemies, the Spanish to the southward and the Indian tribes that ringed the English settlements. Even as Spanish power began to decline there was no relief, for from the west came the growing influence of the French among the Indians.

When rice, and later indigo, became staple crops, the Carolina planters awoke to the presence of a growing "internal" danger, the Negro slaves. Lieutenant-Governor William Bull stated the problem: the few white inhabitants of the maritime settlements had a "numerous domestic Enemy . . . thick sown in our plantations, and [they] require our utmost attention to keep them in order." [54]

The rulers of the colony became adept at a sort of chess game whereby the human pieces that inhabited or bordered South Carolina might be moved to give security to the planters. An early move was to encourage white, Protestant immigrants to settle frontier regions. These could absorb the shock of Indian, Spanish, or French attack and thus permit coastal planters to remain vigilantly watchful over their slaves at home. Or, should a slave uprising take place without a concurrent external danger, frontiersmen might be "brought down" to help quell the revolt. Even friendly Indians might be used to terrorize the slaves and keep them submissive. [55]

54. William Bull to Lord Hillsborough, Charleston, Sept. 10, 1768, Records of the Province of South Carolina, Sainsbury Transcripts from the British Public Record Office, XXXII, 40, Office of Historical Commission of South Carolina. Hereinafter cited as P.R.O. Trans.

55. Dr. George Milligen-Johnston wrote in 1763 that the Indians should never be extirpated, for their lands would soon be occupied by runaway Negroes who would soon become more formidable enemies than the Indians could ever be. [Dr. George Milligen-Johnston], *A Short Description of the Province of South-Carolina . . .* (London, 1770), in *Colonial South Carolina; Two Contemporary Descriptions,* ed. by Chapman J. Milling (Columbia, 1951), 136. In 1766 Catawba Indians were brought to coastal swamp lands to hunt out runaway slaves who were thought to be planning some "dangerous conspiracy

Under Governor Robert Johnson, appointed in 1729, South Carolina undertook an ambitious settlement scheme. Not only were eleven frontier townships authorized, most of them in the "middle country" below the fall line, but in succeeding decades the Assembly passed other acts to encourage settlement on the exposed edges of the colony.[56]

The Piedmont, the scene of Woodmason's principal work, was little settled except for Indians, fur traders, and a scattering of intrepid settlers, until the 1750's. Then, especially after the defeat of Braddock exposed the Pennsylvania and Virginia frontiers to Indian attack, frontiersmen from these colonies moved southward to the South Carolina Backcountry. After the Cherokee War of 1760-1761 and the French and Indian War, the flow of immigrants swelled. Many of these were encouraged by a grant of one hundred acres of land, free of quitrents for a decade, which Governor Boone was authorized to make in 1761. The Assembly provided additional funds for the passage, tools, and provisions of immigrants.[57]

---

and insurrection." A. S. Salley, "The Boundary Line between North Carolina and South Carolina," Historical Commission of South Carolina *Bulletin No. 10* (Columbia, 1929), 27. An illustration of the manipulation of peoples appeared in 1776 when the British were a new "external" enemy. It was suggested that Creek Indians be allowed to kill runaway slaves on Tybee Island. This would prevent their being captured and sold for money, "the sinew of war," by the English, would discourage other slaves from deserting, and would establish a hatred between the Indians and Negroes. Col. Stephen Bull to H. Laurens, Savannah, Mar. 14, 1776, Robert W. Gibbes, ed., *Documentary History of the American Revolution* ... (Columbia and New York, 1853-57), I, 268. The preceding year, the Rev. William Tennent, on a Backcountry mission to convert the back settlers to war against England, claimed to have found a Tory plot to expose the low country to Creek and Cherokee Indian attack: "I am in possession of an affidavit by which it appears that the malcontents on the frontiers expect to gather into forts, and suffer the savages to pass on and massacre the associated Inhabitants." Rev. Wm. Tennent to Council of Safety in Savannah, St. Mathew's Parish, Sept. 10, 1775, *ibid.*, 169. See also David Duncan Wallace, *The History of South Carolina* (New York, 1934), I, 368, 374; Sellers, *Charleston Business*, 110.

56. Verner W. Crane, *The Southern Frontier* (Durham, 1928), 291-94; Wallace, *Hist. of S. C.*, II, 41-42; Sellers, *Charleston Business*, 111-12. For contemporary reports of immigration to Long Canes and Ninety-Six, see the *Georgia Gazette*, Apr. 21, July 7, 1763, Nov. 22, 1764.

57. Sellers, *Charleston Business*, 29. After 1760, many of the immigrants

INTRODUCTION

The back settlers came from Europe, the British Isles, the older settlements of South Carolina, and from the frontiers of more northern colonies. They came as groups, as families, and as individuals. German settlers built cabins in the fork between the Broad and Saluda Rivers, at Saxe Gotha south of the lower Saluda River, on the upper Salkehatchie, and in the Ninety-Six District. Welsh settlers from Pennsylvania took up land along the upper Peedee River. French Protestants settled near the upper Savannah River in Hillsborough Townships, while the Ulster Irish penetrated nearly every part of the Piedmont and dominated the Waxhaws District along the North Carolina—South Carolina border.[58]

Religious differences outnumbered even the variety of nationalities, as Woodmason discovered. There was a scattering of Anglicans, immigrants from coastal South Carolina, from England, or from Pennsylvania, Virginia, and Maryland. German-speaking settlers usually followed the teachings of the Lutheran and Reformed Churches. The Scots and Ulster Irish imported Presbyterianism, and here and there appeared individuals or small settlements of Quakers, Huguenots, Dunkards, Seventh Day Baptists, Regular Baptists, a growing number of New Light Baptists, and what Woodmason described as "an hundred other Sects." [59]

But there were also the immigrants from northern frontiers who had grown up almost untouched by religious influences. Such people retained only tattered remnants of the religious and social disciplines that their parents or grandparents had left behind in more settled parts of the world. What one generation may have saved from the ravages of near-wilderness living conditions it may have failed completely to pass on to the next.

With little more than hungry emotions to bring to religion, these children of the forest offered a challenging mission to adven-

from more northern colonies came by way of the Great Philadelphia Wagon Road. See Carl Bridenbaugh, *Myths and Realities; Societies of the Colonial South* (Baton Rouge, [1952]), 129-30.

58. See Meriwether, *Expans. of S. C.* for a thorough painstaking reconstruction of Backcountry settlement through 1765.

59. See Leah Townsend, *South Carolina Baptists 1670-1805* (Florence, S. C., 1935). See also *infra.*, p. 13.

turous ministers or to inspired men among themselves. Lieutenant-Governor William Bull characterized the Christian
denominations as "subdivided ad infinitum in the back parts, as
illiterate enthusiasm or wild imagination can misinterpret the
Scripture," while "every circle of Christian knowledge grows
fainter as more removed from the center."[60] Woodmason described the process of de-Christianization even more explicitly.
"It is very few families whom I can bring to join in Prayer," he
wrote, "because most of them are of various Opinions the Husband a Churchman, Wife, a Dissenter, Children nothing at all."[61]

Law and order, morality, family integrity, and knowledge of
the outer world were also weakened by exposure to the frontier.
Visitors to the interior settlements had been astonished well before Woodmason. An Anglican minister in St. Bartholomew's
Parish reported that all but two or three of the women he married
were pregnant. When he asked if this was according to custom,
those questioned gave joking answers or were angry.[62] Governor
James Glen, while on a visit to Ninety-Six in 1753, observed that
though children abounded their parents did not "bestow the least
Education on them, they take so much Care in raising a Litter of
Piggs, their Children are equally naked and full as Nasty, The
Parents in the back Woods come together without any previous
Ceremony, and it is not much to be wondered at that the Offspring
of such loose Embraces should be little looked after." Should the
back settlers wish to become Christians, he acknowledged, they
could not, for there was no clergyman within a hundred miles.
The Governor compared the people's manners to those of Indians,
and he found one man fifty years of age who had never seen a
church, a minister, a ship, or a "great Gun."[63]

60. Bull to Hillsborough, Charleston, Nov. 30, 1770, P.R.O. Trans., XXXII,
370.

61. See p. 52.

62. Charles Boschi to the Society for the Propagation of the Gospel, St.
Bartholomew's Parish, Apr. 7, 1746, in Florence Gambrill Geiger, ed., "St.
Bartholomew's Parish as Seen by its Rectors, 1713-1761," *South Carolina
Historical and Genealogical Magazine,* 50 (1949), 191.

63. Gov. Glen to Lords of Trade, Ninety-Six, Oct. 25, 1753, P.R.O. Trans.,
XXV, 350-51. For similar reports of the influence of the frontier see George
Howe, *History of the Presbyterian Church in South Carolina* (Columbia, 1870),

Woodmason often met such people. At Granny Quarter Creek he saw settlers who were "Neither English, Scots Irish, ór Carolinian by Birth—Neither of one Church or other or of any denomination by Profession." [64] Following his service at Flatt Creek, shortly afterwards, his audience "went to Revelling Drinking Singing Dancing and Whoring—and most of the Company were drunk before I quitted the Spot—They were as rude in their Manners as the Common Savages, and hardly a degree removed from them." [65] He estimated that 94 per cent of the young women he married were already pregnant, and that nine-tenths of the back settlers suffered from venereal disease.[66] At times, however, he rejoiced to discover "a very genteel and polite Congregation." [67] He found it necessary to adjust the character of his sermons frequently: what suited a "vile disorderly Crew" was unfit for a "serious Moral Community." [68]

There is clear evidence that many of the inhabitants of the interior were industrious. Many individuals kept large herds of cattle and hogs, and from the back settlements came an increasing surplus of indigo, flour, ship biscuit, hemp, tobacco, beef, tallow, wax, and other items for the Charleston market and export.[69] The only transportation was by lumbering, four-horse wagons, and as many as three thousand of these crossed the ferries approaching Charleston each year.[70]

---

I, 287; J. Adam de Martel to Bishop of London, Purrysburg, July 13, 1769, Ful. Trans., N.C., S.C., Ga., No. 12; Gilbert P. Voigt, "The Germans and the German-Swiss in South Carolina, 1732-1765: Their Contribution to the Province," South Carolina Historical Association, *Proceedings,* 1935, 22.

64. See p. 23.          65. See p. 56.      66. See p. 100.
67. See p. 20; see also pp. 17, 49.       68. See p. 41.

69. *S. C. Gaz.,* Nov. 14, 1768; Bull to Hillsborough, Charleston, June 7, 1770, P.R.O. Trans., XXXII, 282-83; same to same, Nov. 30, 1770, *ibid.,* 395-96, 399; Bull to Lords of Trade, Charleston, Dec. 17, 1765, *ibid.,* XXX, 300; *South Carolina Gazette and Country-Journal,* July 15, 1766. Hereinafter cited as *S. C. Gaz. and C-J.*

70. Bull to Hillsborough, Charleston, June 7, 1770, P.R.O. Trans., XXXII, 283; [Lord Adam Gordon], "Journal of an Officer in the West Indies who travelled over a part of the West Indies, and of North America, in the Course of 1764 and 1765," in Newton D. Mereness, ed., *Travels in the American Colonies* (New York, 1916), 399; Sellers, *Charleston Business,* 34-35.

Charles Woodmason was a man of firm purposes and strong convictions. His life in the Backcountry, furthermore, was largely spent in combat—against immorality, irreligion, the Baptists and Presbyterians, and the apathetic attitude of the powerful men who in Charleston determined the fate of the back settlers. In short, an overwhelmingly large proportion of Woodmason's activities and thoughts were partisan.

Many of his statements and judgments are supported by independent witnesses. Others are not, and in such cases differences of opinion as to his accuracy will certainly arise because his writings are full of implied or overt opinions relative to institutions, affiliations, allegiances, and places. Most of these still evoke emotional reactions, and his vigorous views will give pleasure or anger on issues of race, nationality, religion, class, section, locality, or family.

Woodmason was an Englishman, an Anglican, a gentleman, and a person of some learning. In all these respects he represented a minority viewpoint on the frontier and was excluded from a full sympathy with those among whom he lived. And yet, had it been otherwise, he probably would not have so fully recorded what to him was novel or disagreeable.

As an Englishman he carried with him national prejudices and the memory of a social and political order in sharp contrast to what he found among the back settlers. With dismay and open-eyed wonder he described the Backcountry "State of Nature," or "our present unsettled Situation—When the Bands of Society and Government hang Loose and Ungirt about Us— When no regular Police is establish'd, but ev'ry one left to Do as seemeth Him Meet." [71]

As an Anglican he not only shared the denominational biases of his day, but he despaired at the failure of his church to maintain itself on an expanding frontier. It was his unhappy fate to move among myriad enemies of his beloved Church of England and to view the crumbling of a once powerful church-state establishment on the outer fringes of the British Empire. He tried to promote seemliness and order in religion and, by doing so, in-

71. See p. 226.

dulged in descriptive attacks upon the unsightly and sometimes pathological behavior of the revivalists. Tricked, thwarted, and persecuted by Presbyterians and Baptists, he fought back at them savagely.

As a gentleman, Woodmason looked at those about him with a measuring-rod that found them lacking. In great part his bitter scorn for the New Light Baptist clergy was the snobbishness of class, and his astonishingly ribald letter to John Chesnut is filled with the same spirit.

Even as a man of some learning, eager for conversation, he felt alone in a wilderness, and in 1768 he complained that he missed "Society and Converse—I have not yet met with one literate, or travel'd Person—No ingenious Mind—None of any Capacity—Only some few well dispos'd Religious Persons, but whose Knowledge is very circumscrib'd." [72] At times he encountered men who wished religious argument, and he remarked on their barren intellectual background and lack of reading. [73]

Woodmason's own broad background influenced his thought and work. When he journeyed into the Backcountry in 1766 he was a man well along in his middle years who had been merchant, planter, clerk of two Assembly commissions, and incumbent of nearly every local office. His interests inevitably extended far beyond the care of the souls entrusted to him as an Anglican priest. He assumed the office of tribune of the people. The state of morality, the plight of the poor, the lack of care and education for children, the conduct of magistrates, the clothing, food, housing, recreations, drunkenness, health, agriculture, transportation, and intellectual interests of the inhabitants all aroused his interested and often indignant attention. His past and present careers clearly intermingled when in a written sermon he warned an unruly congregation not to bring dogs to church or he would "fine" those

72. As a gentleman, Woodmason found himself handicapped in competition with the New Light Baptist clergy: "You will bear reprehensions from these Plebians," he stated in a sermon, "because You can laugh it off;—But to be told of your faults by a Gentleman, cuts to the Quick, and You hate him for it." Sermon Book, III, [700]. See p. 38.

73. See pp. 22, 52, 114.

who did so. At some point he remembered to cross out the word and to substitute "inform the Magistrate." [74]

In little more than a year after he removed to the Backcountry, Woodmason became an ardent partisan of the Regulator movement, a frontier rebellion which is discussed at length in an introduction to the third part of this book. On behalf of the back settlers who joined in this revolt against the self-centered Assembly, Woodmason wrote the "Remonstrance" of 1767 and, thereafter, produced a stream of pleading, satirical, or eloquent petitions and protests. In this work he found a perfect use for the accumulated experiences of his former careers. With his full knowledge of coast and back settlements together with his interest in virtually every aspect of society, Woodmason could express Regulator grievances clearly and forcibly. He was prepared and anxious to speak with authority on every possible complaint, from the scarcity of Bibles on the frontier to the loathsome state of the Charleston jail.

From a defender of his Church and winner of souls Woodmason became a missionary of English civilization. He was aware that he deviated from a strict construction of priestly duties, and writing to an English friend in 1771 about the Regulator movement he anticipated an objection that "you may think that I am out of my Proper Sphere." His *apologia* revealed that he had adopted a social gospel: "But Sir, if acting for the Good of Mankind in General The Right and Liberty of the Subject—the Relief of the Poor, the Needy the distress'd—the Stranger—the Traveller—the Sick and the Orphan—If the Advancement of Religion—Good of the Church, Suppression of Idleness, beggary, prophaneness, Lewdness and Villany—If banishing of Ignorance Vice and Immorality, promoting Virtue and Industry, Arts and Sciences, Commerce and Manufactures, and ev'ry Public Work, be Characteristic of a Christian I hope that I have not . . . deviated from what my Great Master came into this World to establish—Glory to God Peace on Earth—and Good Will among Men." [75] A few months later, in an address to some of the Regulators, he stated

74. For a discussion of Woodmason's role in the Regulator movement, see pp. 172 ff.     75. See p. 212.

that "Public Evils, in ev'ry Shape, are to be laid Open—other wise, how will they be redress'd? Ministers are as much Watchmen in these Respects, as Magistrates." [76]

The Backcountry influenced Woodmason in still another way. During his fourteen years among the coastal inhabitants he had found friends and patrons and, for three years, had been a "favriter" of the Charlestonians. As for the Anglican clergy, he had reported in 1765 that they were the "best Sett of Men, that Carolina were ever blest with at one Time." [77]

Among the impoverished and underprivileged back settlers his attitude changed. He berated those who looked upon the inhabitants of the interior "in a Meaner Light than their Black Slaves, and care less for them." [78] He attacked the "overgrown Planters who wallow in Luxury, Ease, and Plenty," [79] and lamented that South Carolina should be under "an *Aristocratic* Government instead of a *Royal* and *Free*." [80] For the coastal inhabitants who cried out against English invasions of their rights his scorn knew no limit: "Lo! such are the Men who bounce, and make such Noise about Liberty! Liberty! Freedom! Property! Rights! Priveleges! and what not; And at the same time keep half their fellow Subjects in a State of Slavery." [81] The Anglican clergy of the coast fared little better. He lamented their "Inattention and Indolence" and accused them of "Cringing and fawning to the Great Ones." [82]

Woodmason did not indulge in Utopian dreams. The sight of a country in near-wilderness condition, struggling to develop an ordered society, did not awaken in him thoughts of a new order of things. If he saw the Backcountry in a "State of Nature," it was not one tinged with sunrise colors; his highest ambition was to mold the raw materials of a frontier into patterns of respectability and to create, as quickly as possible, a replica of a stable, tranquil, law-abiding English countryside. Vice and immorality must be suppressed; thieves and vagrants must be eliminated; towns, bridges, roads, and ferries must be built; the land must be made to bloom by industry; and schools must be founded to render the next generation literate, "polite," and sensible. He would import

76. See p. 127.          77. See p. 75.          78. See p. 60.
79. See p. 121.          80. See p. 288.         81. See p. 262.
82. See pp. 44, 193-94.

to the wilderness all the apparatus of English stability, including whipping posts. In his phrase he wished to "New Model and form the Carriage and Manners, as well as Morals of these wild Peoples," and to "bring about a Reformation" in their lives.[83]

As an advance agent of English culture, Woodmason was impatient. He displayed all the fervor of a prophet and he dismissed those in his path with angry and contemptuous words. Indignation and vivid rhetoric fill his pages, and his swift-paced writings are heavily sprinkled with strong words, irony, sarcasm, and satire. He was quick to attribute to his enemies sordid designs and malicious motives. Too often, one suspects, he interpreted their behavior as directed against himself as an individual.

In the face of implacable opposition from Baptists, Presbyterians, and many of the irreligious, Woodmason, thwarted and lonely, sought comfort in martyrdom. "Whom but an Heart of Oak could bear up Firm against such Torrents of Malice, Bigotry, and Impudence!" he exclaimed. He tried to sustain their "Calumnies" with "Christian Meekness and Compassion," and "the Contempt and Derision befitting a Gentleman," but found this difficult.[84] "I am exactly in the same situation with the Clergy of the primitive Church, in midst of the Heathens, Arians, and Hereticks," he concluded.[85]

Aging, ill, and his congregations largely submerged by the sweep of the New Light Baptists, Woodmason finally decided to leave South Carolina. In 1772 he accepted an offer of Bromfield Parish, in Culpeper County, Virginia. But because he conscientiously awaited the arrival of an expected minister for St. Mark's Parish, Bromfield Parish was given to another to prevent its lapse into the governor's patronage. The towns of Falmouth and Fredericksburg, Virginia, however, raised a "liberal subscription" to make him their lecturer.[86] It is not clear whether he accepted this appointment, though he did preach at the Upper Chapel, Brunswick Parish, Virginia, on February 21, 1773.[87]

Late in the same year he moved to Maryland to which, he

83. See p. 61.    84. See p. 47.    85. *Ibid.*
86. Memorial to Bishop of London, Wells, Sept. 16, 1776, in Perry, ed., *Historical Collections*, I, 534, with corrections in Ful. Trans., Va., Box 2, No. 201.
87. Sermon Book, II, [322].

claimed, he was invited by Commissary General Walter Dulany. In this colony, the mecca of colonial Anglican clergymen because of the high salaries paid there, he awaited an empty benefice to which he said Governor Eden, members of the council, and other principal men recommended him.[88] From time to time he preached at St. John's Chapel in Baltimore County, and visited other churches as distant as York County, Pennsylvania.[89]

In Maryland as elsewhere, Woodmason complained, the "Sectaries" intercepted his mail. When they found that he had written essays in defense of the Anglican Church, he was publicized as a government spy and an enemy to American liberty. His position became more dangerous when he read the homily of obedience, together with the service of the day, on May 29 (Restoration Day), 1774, and refused to read the "Brief for collecting Money for relief of the poor of Boston, (but in fact to purchase Ammunition)." This last act, he remembered later, so provoked the county committee that he was advised to "consult his safety" by a return to England.[90]

Late in 1774 he did sail to England. There, for two years, he occasionally preached at St. Stephen's in Bristol and in other nearby towns.[91] In September, 1776, he wrote to the Bishop of London to ask aid as a Loyalist refugee and described himself as broken both in fortune and in health.[92] On the following November 17, he preached at a small town near Bristol, and this fact is the last he ever noted in his sermon books.[93] Thereafter the record is blank; of his later years, if any, and of his death nothing is known.

88. Memorial to Bishop of London, Wells, Sept. 16, 1776, in Perry, ed., *Historical Collections*, I, 535, corrected in Ful. Trans., Va., Box 2, No. 201.

89. Sermon Books, II, [28], [258], [322], [481]; III, [808]; IV, [236]. Woodmason is said to have been the curate of Mr. Deans, in St. James Parish, Maryland. Ethen Allen, Historical Notices of St. James Parish, 4. Maryland Diocesan Library, Baltimore, Md.

90. Memorial to Bishop of London, Wells, Sept. 16, 1776, in Perry, ed., *Historical Collections*, I, 535-36, corrected in Ful. Trans., Va., Box 2, No. 201.

91. Sermon Book, II, [118], [322].

92. Memorial to Bishop of London, Wells, Sept. 16, 1776, in Perry, ed., *Historical Collections*, I, 536, corrected in Ful. Trans., Va., Box 2, No. 201.

93. Sermon Book, II, [322].

The Journal is in many ways the most reliable of all the writings of Charles Woodmason. Although a few phrases suggest that it may have been written for the eyes of another, it generally maintains the tone of a private record. Some entries were made a week or more after the events described, but on the whole it is a fresh account of the author's earliest impressions of the Backcountry and its people.

The letter of 1766 to the Bishop of London, the letter of 1771 to an unnamed correspondent in England, together with the "Remonstrance" and the appended writings which relate to the Regulator movement are mainly self-explanatory in their character and the circumstances surrounding their composition. The voluminous notes to many of these seem to have been written as aids to the English correspondent to whom they were sent.

The contents of the Sermon Books—the sermons themselves, the letter to John Chesnut, and the several memoranda—are varied in nature. Within the three volumes of Sermon Books are fifty sermons, twelve of which were prepared for the second half of a morning-afternoon service. Like many a minister before and since his time, Woodmason borrowed from his predecessors in the ministry. With few exceptions his sermons were those of seventeenth- and eighteenth-century English churchmen. Notations at the beginning of the sermons show that he ranged widely to find suitable discourses. The family of Captain Matthew Singleton listened to a sermon which Woodmason gave at the High Hills on the death of their child, quite unaware that it had been used by one Thomas Cheesman on November 24, 1706.[94] Two sermons delivered by Woodmason at the High Hills, and later on the Congaree River, were understandably subjected to "several Omissions and Modifications" from the version written by William Lyford in 1646.[95] Remarkably interdenominational were the adventures of a sermon first preached by Father Philip Ellis Monk Benedic before James II and his Queen at Whitehall, February 24, 1685. "Alter'd and adapted to the Meridian of Charleston" it was given by the Anglican Woodmason in the Lutheran Church of that city on Ash Wednesday, 1768.[96]

94. *Ibid.*, [28].        95. *Ibid.*, IV, [1].        96. *Ibid.*, II, [513].

These sermons pilfered from the past would be of little interest to students of the American colonial scene were it not for the additions which Woodmason made to them. When he met problems that his predecessors knew nothing of he fell back upon his own devices. Long doctrinal discourses were interrupted while Woodmason applied religious precepts to immediate and pressing Backcountry problems. What he said on such subjects, it is worth noting, was delivered to congregations who were usually in a position to check on the general accuracy of his remarks and who at times were challenged to deny the truth of the facts.

The amazing letter to John Chesnut also appears in the Sermon Books. There is no way of knowing whether this is a copy of a letter actually sent to Chesnut or whether it was no more than a catharsis for the author's high anger.

Whatever its purpose, the letter provides a study of the Backcountry community of Camden, with particular emphasis on three of its leading figures: Joseph Kershaw, the storekeeper; John Chesnut, his protégé and partner; and John Canty, the tavernkeeper. The picture is certainly a hostile one. Not only is Camden the "little Sodom," but its leading citizens are described in terms that recall that Woodmason was contemporary with another Anglican minister, Laurence Sterne.

The tone of derisive raillery is maintained in the "Burlesque" sermon appended to the Chesnut letter. Again, one cannot be sure why it was written. Is it an exercise in mockery of the ill-educated frontier clergymen? Is it primarily an attack upon that "fiend from Hell," Chesnut's mother? Or is it only, as it purports to be, intended to simplify for "Mother Chesnut" a sermon that in its original form was beyond her understanding. Most likely it is all of these.

The Sermon Books also contain "Memoranda" on William Richardson, Chief Justice Charles Shinner, and the Regulator movement. These are definitely the least reliable of Woodmason's writings, even though they were apparently written only as aids to memory. The first two depend heavily upon hearsay evidence, and all three were written many years after the events described and show a confusion of chronology together with a fair degree of factual error.[97]

In general, however, Woodmason's writings maintain a high level of consistency in statements of fact when, at different times, for different purposes, and for different audiences, he repeats himself. His accounts of events or descriptions of Backcountry life differ only in emphasis and detail, whether appearing in the Journal, the sermons, the rhetorical pieces, or the "Memoranda."

But it is not simply as authentic and highly informative historical documents that Woodmason's Journal and other papers will be read today. His writings will hold the reader and lure him on because their author was something more, as well as something less, than a perfectly accurate recorder of the life around him. He was, though unconsciously for the most part, a literary artist of distinguished ability. His pleas on behalf of the poor back settlers are fervent, powerful, and moving, and his narratives of such commonplace incidents as crossing a swollen creek or spending the night in the woods are vivid to a degree attained by few writers in colonial America. His addiction to strong language on every subject he treats suggests that he probably exaggerated the hardships that he endured (great as they were) and that he overemphasized the brutish and nasty aspects of frontier life (ugly as they were). This extravagance of language evidently proceeded from an habitual extravagance of feeling. Like a much more famous Anglican clergyman of the same century, Jonathan Swift, Woodmason worked, thought, and felt with peculiar intensity.

The parallels between the two men are indeed striking. Both considered themselves exiles—Swift in Ireland and Woodmason in the Carolina Backcountry—from all that they cherished. Both displayed the same ambivalence toward their kind—an indefinable compound of contempt and benevolence that, on the one hand, made them almost pathologically aware of man's vile nature and ways but, on the other hand, led them courageously and effectively to champion the misguided wretches among whom their lot

97. Because the "Memorandum" on the Regulator movement is largely repetitive of other, earlier documents in this present volume, it is not included. Where, however, it includes material not found in the other documents, this information is supplied in footnotes scattered throughout the book.

was cast. In a word, both worked passionately to promote rational ideals, and the resemblances between their styles are not accidental, for the two men proceeded from the same philosophical premises. With a less powerful intellect than that of the Irish Dean, Woodmason shared his vehement moral earnestness and in some measure his gifts of irony, sarcasm, and invective. He is a lesser Swift on the American frontier, and it is from this combination of man and place that arise observations both trenchant and unfailingly lively.

## Treatment of the Text and Acknowledgments

The writings of Woodmason are to be found in two libraries. In the Library of Congress are the Transcripts of the Fulham Palace Manuscripts, which include the letter of Woodmason to the Bishop of London of 1766, the description of the Southern Anglican Church in 1765, the long letter of 1771 to an English friend, and the enclosures that went with this letter. Although these have been collated with the original manuscripts, formerly in the Bishop of London's Fulham Palace but now in the office of the Church Commissioners in London, the references are to the easily available and wonderfully accurate transcripts made for the Library of Congress.

The manuscript Journal and the three manuscript volumes of Sermon Books are in the Library of the New-York Historical Society. All four items were presented to the Society in January, 1894, by Daniel Parish, Junior. A clipping from an unidentified book catalog, pasted on the wrapper of the Journal, lists both Journal and Sermon Books for sale at a price given in English currency, indicating the probability that Mr. Parish had purchased the manuscripts from a British dealer.

The Journal, unbound and uncovered, measures $7\frac{3}{8}$ by $8\frac{13}{16}$ inches. On the first page is the title, "Journal of C. W. Clerk. Itinerant Minister in South Carolina 1766. 1767. 1768," in Woodmason's handwriting, and the entries continue to the bottom of the last page. The leaves are sewn together, and there is nothing to show that there was ever a cover.

The three volumes of sermons are in identical calf bindings

and measure approximately 4¾ by 7½ inches. The bindings contain neither titles nor lettering, but inside the front covers the volumes are numbered 2, 3, and 4, indicating that there was originally a volume 1. On the inside front cover of the fourth volume is inscribed, in Woodmason's hand, "Occasional Discourses in South Carolina." The paper used for the various sermons differs in quality and size. The Sermon Books are without page numbers, and the pagination in the present volume is supplied by the editor in brackets.

In transcribing the writings of Woodmason no changes have been made in grammar, spelling, or capitalization. Where Woodmason's spelling or capitalization is not clear, modern practice is followed except in those cases where the author normally followed English eighteenth-century practice different from that of today. The punctuation of the original manuscripts is kept, including the lavish use of dashes. The only exceptions occur where both a dash and a period are used to end a sentence, in which case the dash is omitted, and where a dash concludes a paragraph, in which case a period is substituted. The brackets of Woodmason are changed to parentheses in order to prevent their being confused with editorial insertions.

At times Woodmason crossed out words and phrases in his manuscripts and substituted others. In nearly every instance these changes are purely stylistic and do not alter the meaning. In such cases the crossed-out words are not given. Where, however, there resulted a change in meaning or emphasis or where the first terms revealed a psychologically interesting slip, the first version is given in a footnote.

Abbreviations have been expanded in nearly every case, and raised letters have been lowered. The ampersand has been spelled out, although "&c." is retained as a form commonly used in eighteenth-century printing. The thorn is always rendered as "th." Contractions of words which employ the apostrophe are left in their original form. Abbreviations and contractions of proper names are kept as in the original, except for the lowering of superscript letters. Where such forms are not clear the expanded form is given in brackets.

Since I first developed an interest in the writings of Charles

Woodmason, nearly ten years ago, my work has been made pleasant and easier by the aid of many people. I received only courtesy and kind attention from the staffs of the principal libraries where research was done: the Library of Congress, the New-York Historical Society, the University of Chicago, the Newberry Library of Chicago, the Office of Church Commissioners in London, the Historical Commission of South Carolina, the Caroliniana Library of the University of South Carolina, the Charleston Library Society, the South Carolina Historical Society, the Charleston Court House, and the Historical Society of Pennsylvania. Part of my research was made possible when, in 1947, I received a Grant-in-Aid of Research from the Social Science Research Council.

It gives me pleasure to remember the assistance of some individuals. Miss Dorothy C. Barck, Librarian of the New-York Historical Society, granted me permission to publish the Journal and extracts from the Sermon Books and was helpful in other ways. In England, Mr. T. G. Woodmason of Bigbury, South Devon, had the goodness to make a careful, though fruitless, search of the Bigbury Parish Church Register for a record of the birth, marriage, or death of Woodmason. Mr. W. R. Savadge of Twickenham, Middlesex, made a similar effort among the records of Bristol and vicinity, again without success. In South Carolina, Miss Helen G. McCormack, of the Charleston Museum, was remarkably kind in leading me to out-of-the-way sources. Mr. Robert L. Meriwether, of the University of South Carolina, guided me in the use of the Caroliniana Library which he directs. Mr. F. M. Hutson, in the Library of the Historical Commission of South Carolina, aided me during my repeated trips to Columbia, S. C. In Chicago, especially helpful were Miss Winifred Ver Nooy and Miss Katherine Hall of the University of Chicago Library.

In the arrangement and editing of this book the editor benefitted from the experience of Mr. Lester J. Cappon, Editor of Publications of the Institute of Early American History and Culture at Williamsburg, Virginia. Two other members of the Institute's staff, Mr. Lyman H. Butterfield, Director, and Mr. Douglass Adair, Editor of the *William and Mary Quarterly,* made wise and useful suggestions during the later stages of the work.

My wife Nancy, herself an historian, helped me greatly by a careful and critical reading of the manuscript and by aid in reading the proof.

RICHARD J. HOOKER

*Roosevelt University*

✝✝✝✝✝✝✝✝✝ PART ONE ✝✝✝✝✝✝✝✝✝

# The Journal of the
# Rev. Charles Woodmason

✝✝✝✝✝✝✝✝✝✝✝✝✝✝✝✝✝✝✝✝✝✝✝✝✝✝✝✝✝✝✝✝✝✝✝✝✝✝✝✝

# Journal of C. W. Clerk

## ITINERANT MINISTER IN SOUTH CAROLINA

## 1766 · 1767 · 1768

### *1766 · June 10*

Sail'd down to Gravesend, and embark'd on board the Portland, a Snow, G. H.[1] Master, and same Evening went down the River.

The Passengers were, 3 London Bucks—5 or 6 Tradesmen, and some Ladies of Pleasure, seeking a Retreat.

### *June 11*

Came to Anchor in the Downs. 12th Went on Shore at Deal, 13th Sail'd down Channel: Address'd the Passengers to join in Prayer for a prosp'rous Voyage. Refus'd.

### *12th*

Pass'd by the Isle of Wight. 13th off Plymouth. 15th Clear'd Channel, and bid adieu to Old England.

From this Time to the 21t the Passengers Sea-Sick and on

### *Sunday 22d*

Collected them together at Divine Service—Refus'd attending in the afternoon. Captain and Londoners went to Cards.

### *Sunday 29*

All the Ships Company attended Sermon—save two Scotsmen —Captain and Gentlemen invited the Ladies in the afternoon to drink Tea—Would not suffer them to come into the Cabbin: Which affronted the Bucks.

---

1. The master of the "Portland" was George Higgins. *S. C. Gaz. and C-J,* Aug. 19, 1766.

A Criminal Commerce enter'd into between the Gentlemen and Ladies—Read them Lectures of Continence and Temperance. Laughed at and Ridiculed.

### Sunday July 6th

Ships Company attended—Behaved ludicrously.

### Sunday July 13th

Not half the People attended—One of the Bucks absented.

### Sunday July 20th

The Commen People attended—Captain and Women to themselves.

### Sunday July 27th

All the passengers at Divine Service—Captain and Women behav'd indecently.

### Sunday August 3d

Refus'd to officiate any more, as they turn'd both the Sermon and Service to Raillery.

### August 12th

Landed in Charlestown: A dangerous Fever in the Place carries off 8 or 10 persons ev'ry Day—Carried by Gentleman to his Country Seat on Ashley River.

### August 17th

Officiated at St. Andrews Church. Weather excessive hot and Sultry, and Country very Sickly—Multitudes of New Imported Irish People die daily.

### August 24

The Ministers of St Andrews, St James', St John's, and other Parishes down in the Fever. Officiated at St Andrews. Received Intelligence of the Death of 4 Episcopal Ministers, and 3 of the Kirk of Scotland. About 40 Persons in these Churches, which is more than usual.

### August 31

Continued at the Gentlemans Seat, and pray'd with them most days, they being of the Baptist Congregation—Did Duty this Day at St. James Church—Two other Ministers died this Week, and all in the Country very ill of the Fever. The Clerk of the Board of Church Commissioners sick—No Board as yet met to receive my Credentials, and give me my Commission.

### September 7

Officiated at St. Andrews—On the 12th the Board of Commissioners (25 in number) met at the Council Chamber, and sign'd my Commission. Left me to move as I thought proper without any Restrictions but would not allow my Salary to commence from the Day of my Landing (as the Law expressly appoints) but from the day of my Commission. Deliv'd Mr. Broughtons Letters and Parcel of Books to the Reverend Mr. Hart.[2] Miles rode to St Andrews and St James.——50 [miles traveled] *

### September 12th

Sett off from Charlestown to enter on my Mission—Wet to the Skin in several claps of Thunder—and greatly fatigu'd thro' Horses failing during this hot Weather.

### Sunday 14th

Officiated at St Marks Church 80 Miles from Town—70 in Congregation—which is double the Number in Common——80 [miles]

The Roads hot and Sandy—and Weather excessive Sultry.

2. The Rev. Oliver Hart, minister of the Baptist Church in Charleston, was born in Bucks County, Pennsylvania, in 1723 and came to Charleston in 1749. William Rogers, *Sermon Occasioned by the Death of the Rev. Oliver Hart* ... (Philadelphia, 1796), 20-21.

* The number of miles which Woodmason traveled was recorded in the right-hand margin of the MS Journal and occasionally he inserted the total mileage up to a certain point. This information has been transferred to the end of the paragraph opposite which the original marginal note occurred. Hereafter [miles traveled] will appear simply as [miles], and [total miles traveled] will be [total miles].

*16th*

Arriv'd at Pine Tree Hill and Centre of my Distric.[3] This Week employ'd in riding the Environs and baptizing.——50 [miles]; 40 [miles]

*Sunday 21st* [4]

Officiated in the Presbyterian Meeting House to about 200 Hearers, Cheifly Presbyterians. Offer'd to give Sermon twice on ev'ry Sunday. Rejected.

Beside this Meeting House, there is another of Quakers with a large Congregation [5]—But they have neither Pastor or Teacher or Speaker at Either.

The People around, of abandon'd Morals, and profligate Principles—Rude—Ignorant—Void of Manners, Education or Good Breeding—No genteel or Polite Person among them—save Mr. Kershaw an English Merchant settled here.[6] The people are of all Sects and Denominations—A mix'd Medley from all Countries

---

3. By an act of 1756, a salary of £700 (or about £100 Sterling) was provided for a clergyman to preach at "Fredericksburgh, Pine Tree Creek, or such other centrical part in the Waterees as the said commissioners shall direct and appoint, and six times a year at least, at the most populous places within forty miles of the same." *Stat. at Large of S. C.,* IV, 21.

4. Woodmason first wrote "28th," then corrected it to "21st." The change could have resulted either from error or from the delay of a week in making the entry.

5. A small immigration of Irish Quakers came to the Waterees in October, 1751, and took up land on both sides of the Wateree River above and below the future town of Pine Tree Hill, later Camden. A Quaker meeting was organized as early as 1753. Meriwether, *Expans. of S. C.,* 103-5; Thomas J. Kirkland and Robert M. Kennedy, *Historic Camden* (Columbia, S.C., 1905), 11-12, 73-74.

6. Joseph Kershaw, an Englishman and an Anglican, was a man of great importance in the entire region of the Wateree River. He was the son of Joseph Kershaw of Sowerby, Yorkshire, England, and emigrated to Charleston about 1750 with two brothers. Joseph Kershaw served as a clerk for James Laurens and Company and later worked for the firm of Ancrum, Lance and Loocock. In 1758 the latter firm sent him to establish a country branch on the Wateree River. Sellers, *Charleston Business,* 89-90. Woodmason had known Kershaw earlier, when the latter was still a clerk in Charleston. See the letter to John Chesnut, pp. 140 ff.

and the Off Scouring of America. Baptized 20 Children this Week and rode about 40 Miles——Miles Brought over 220.

### September 28

Officiated in the Meeting House—Promoted a Petition to the General Assembly to have a Chapel built, which ev'ry one of ev'ry Class and Sect sign'd. About 150 persons present at Service.

Received Great Civilities from Mr. Samuel Wyly,[7] an eminent Quaker in the Neighbourhood—who kindly rode about with me to make me known to the People.

Not a House to be hir'd—Nor even a single Room on all this River to be rented, fit to put my Head or Goods in—The People all new Settlers, extremely poor—Live in Logg Cabbins like Hogs—and their Living and Behaviour as rude or more so than the Savages. Extremely embarrassed how to subsist. Took up my Quarters in a Tavern—and exposed to the Rudeness of the Mobb. People continually drunk.

The Country being very Sickly, Mr. Kershaw would not permit me to move abroad much as this Week. Married a Couple—for the 1st Time—Woman very bigg.——20 [miles]

My English Servant Man whom I brought over, taken with the Fever. Excessive hot Weather for the Season.

### October 5th

The Season very dry—and people in Great distress for want of Provisions—Greatly relieved by the Kindness of Mr. Kershaw, who open'd all his Stores to them.

Offer'd to take 20 Boys and educate them Gratis would they fit up a Room for a School, which they promis'd to do.

About 100 People this day at Service—Offer'd to catchecise

7. Samuel Wyly, one of the Irish Quakers, had come to the Waterees in 1752. He became a leader among the Quakers, established a store, became a justice of the peace, was placed in charge of the nearby Catawba Indians, and in January, 1766, attempted to take his seat in the Assembly to represent St. Mark's Parish. Since as a Quaker he refused to take the election oath, it was resolved that he could not be seated. Wyly died February 13, 1768, at the age of forty-six. Meriwether, *Expans. of S. C.*, 104-5; *S. C. Gaz.*, Dec. 22, 1759; Kirkland and Kennedy, *Historic Camden*, 51; Commons Journal, Jan. 25, 1766; *The South Carolina and American General Gazette*, Mar. 4, 1768.

their Children in the Afternoon, but none brought—Do not find but one religious person among this Great Multitude.

The Weather comes more moderate. But my Horse quite worn down for want of Grass.——25 [miles]

### October 8th

Received a Subpena from C. T. [Charles Town] to attend Court to give Evidence in a Suit at Law; Went down the Country. Preached at the High Hills of Santee. Met here with some serious Christians But the Generality very loose, dissolute, Idle People—Without either Religion or Goodness—The same may be said of the whole Body of the People in these Back Parts.——[total] miles 305

Received at St Marks by Col Richardson [8]—a Worthy sensible Gentleman and Pious Christian.—Once more in a Christian family.——50 [miles]

### Sunday October 12

Did Duty at St. Marks Church—This Church has been destitute of a Minister these 3 Years—And so little do they care for Religion, that they'l not send to England for a Minister tho' this Church is on the Establishment.[9]

Their late Minister is remov'd to Pon pon—At his first Sermon 50 Persons attended—But they fell off to about 7 or 8 the Communicants only—Often when he gave Notice to celebrate None attended—At other times, No Elements provided—Wearied out, and vex'd at their Indifference, he quitted them.

8. Richard Richardson, born in Virginia about 1704, became a leading South Carolinian. As early as 1757 he was named colonel of militia, and during the Cherokee wars of 1760-1761 he commanded a regiment. Richardson was repeatedly elected to the Assembly to represent St. Mark's Parish, and on the outbreak of war with England he played an important part in both political and military affairs. Joseph S. Ames, "The Cantey Family," *S. C. Hist. and Gen. Mag.*, 11 (1910), 225-26.

9. St. Mark's Parish had been established in 1757 by dividing the Parish of Prince Frederick. Richard Richardson was named as one of the commissioners to build the church and parsonage and to manage the affairs of the church. *Stat. at Large of S.C.*, IV, 35-37; James M. Burgess, *Chronicles of St. Mark's Parish, Santee Circuit, and Williamsburg Township, South Carolina, 1731-1885* (Columbia, S.C., 1888), 12-13.

The people solicited me to fill this Vacancy—but I declin'd, as could not to accept it with out leave of my Diocesan and it would be annulling the Orders of the Church Commissioners. Withal, I came to this Wild Country to support the Interests of the Church of England and the People of our Communion, trodden under foot by the Herds of Sectaries.

### Sunday 26 [10] October

Returned from C. T. My Journey being thrown away—The plaintiff suffering a Nonsuit. My English Servant seduc'd from my Service.——210 [miles]

### Sunday 19

Officiated at the parish of St Matthew on the upper part of Santee at Solicitation of the Inhabitants—A vast Congregation— In the Evening was carried down the Road to another Congregation who met at a Gentleman's where I preach'd and baptiz'd— Made it late (by our long singing) e're Service was over—Quite fatigued.——110 [miles]

### Monday 20

The Minister of St John's being Sick, went down to that parish—and baptiz'd. But no Congregation assembled there not being an House wherein hardly a well person. All in the fever. ——[total] miles 695
The same at St Andrews and St James—Went down with a party of Friends to the Sea Islands for fresh Air—Courteously and genteely treated by a very rich Gentleman of the Baptist Communion who promis'd to make handsome provision for me.——100 [miles]

### October 29

My Friend, the Gentleman above, bit by a mad Dog—and died in four Days—A very Great Loss, and much Grief to Me. Invited to Charlestown by the Cheif Justice, the Honorable Charles Shinner Esquire who treated me with Great Kindness and

10. This entry is out of chronological order. The day and date are apparently correct.

Humanity—Promis'd to be my Friend and to take me under his protection.[11]

Accordingly he prepar'd to accompany me into the Country and to look out for a place to build me an House and Chapel at his own Expense, till public Affairs (now very fluctuating) were settled, and the Country in some Quiet—which was up in Arms thro' a Gang of Theives and Robbers that laid the province under Contribution.——10 [miles]

Mean time rode up to St Marks, and did Duty there on Sunday November 9. and returned to the Cheif Justice,—whom I found in Great afliction thro' loss of his two Sons, who died after few Hours Illness of a flux and fever.——160 [miles]

Suffer'd great fatigues this Journey thro' bad and tir'd Horses walk'd 60 Miles on foot thro' the hot burning Sands and Sun. Obliged to lay by for a fortnight to recover Strength, and take Rest, till the Weather came cooler.

### December 6

The Cheif Justice set off with me (with his attendants) for the Country. On Sunday the 7th preached at St Jame's before him and some other Gentlemen of the Council, and from Charlestown.——16 [miles]; [total] miles 981

### December 8

Sett off for St Marks, and received with great kindness at Col. Richardsons.——64 [miles]

### December 14

Officiated at St Marks Church—and on the 18th arrived at Pine Tree Hill. Mr. Kershaw took me to his House, till Lodgings could be fitted up for me.——50 [miles]

The Cheif Justice busied in concerting Measures to suppress the Gangs of Horse Theives—Depressing Vice, and bringing about a Reformation of Manners—As most of the low People around had Connexions with these Theives, this gave them the Alarm. The Robbers gather'd in a Body and stood on their defence.

11. For the background and character of Chief Justice Charles Shinner see pp. 289-96.

### December 21

Officiated in the Meeting House. By Influence of the Cheif Justice, had a Congregation, and preach'd in the Afternoon.

Found the School Room that was intended for me, turn'd by the Tavern Keeper into a Stable. Only 3 Boys offer'd, out of 2 or 300 that run wild here like Indians—But as their Parents are Irish Presbyterians, they rather chuse to let them run thus wild, than to have them instructed in the Principles of Religion by a Minister of the Church of England.

### 25. Christmas Day

Officiated as usual in the Meeting House, and would have celebrated with the C. J. but could raise no Communicants—Withal, the Elders would not consent to it, as to have in their Phrase, Mass said in their House. About 100 People, cheifly Church People from distant Parts—None of whom would consent to receive the Communion in a Meeting House. Hereby the Poor lost 100£ which the C. J. intended to give the Poor.

### December 26

The Cheif Justice attempted to raise the Militia, and to attack the Gang of Theives—But the officers were too cowardly—All afraid to venture—Nor could he enlist any Volunteers.[12]

His intention was to cross the Country, to take me with Him, and to make a Circle back to C. T.—The Robbers hearing of his Intent laid in wait for to attack Him and his Retinue. So by perswasion he returned by the Road which he came up.[13]——1095 [total miles]

Could not purchase in Fee Simple a Piece of Ground for a

12. In his "Memorandum" on the Regulator movement, written long after the events he described, Woodmason said that no one would "turn out or obey" Shinner "because he brought not Orders from the Governour." Sermon Book, IV, [372].

13. This incident played a part in the charges against Shinner which preceded his removal from office in 1767. According to Shinner, Govey Black, a notorious outlaw, and eleven men had lain in wait for him as he was "very credibly informed by many persons of good repute." Shinner's opponents appeared to disbelieve the story. Commons Journal, Apr. 9, May 27, 1767.

Chapel or Dwelling House. Received a Petition from the People to the Assembly for to settle a fine Tract of 460 Acres of public Land on me, for a Glebe. This Land worth 500 Guineas

### Sunday 28

Officiated as usual at Pine Tree. Congregation about 80 people Tho' they are so populous around, that 500 might attend if they would.

### January 1, 1767

Gave them a Sermon suited to the Day—and set off to accompany the Cheif Justice in his Return—The Tavern Keeper [14] (who is a Rich fellow, and Who has made an Estate by encouraging Vice and Idleness) affronted at my Discourse against Immorality as if aim'd against Him—He cryed out like Demetrius that the Craft was in Danger—And (but behind our Backs) abus'd both my Self and Cheif Justice, vowing Vengeance on both.

Jan. 3) Took leave of my Hon'd Friend—and on Jan. 4.) assembled the People at the High Hills, and gave them Service.—25 [miles]

Had a large Congregation—but according to Custom, one half of them got drunk before they went home.

Next Day cross'd the River (Wateree) into the Fork to baptize several Children—A Shocking Passage. Obliged to cut the Way thro' the Swamp for 4 Miles, thro' Canes, and impenetrable Woods—Had my Cloaths torn to Pieces—After meeting some Religious People return'd back the same Way: and went down to St Marks Church w[h]ere I officiated on Sunday Jan. 11. and then returned back to Pine Tree Hill.——25 [miles]; 75 [miles]

Jan. 18) Officiated as usual at Pine Tree—and received an Invitation from the people on Pedee River to visit them—With Man and Horse to carry me, where (after many Difficulties,—much fatigue, and suffering Hunger, Cold, and no Bed to lye on, but only the Ground) I arrived the 22d—80 [miles]; 1300 [total miles]

14. The tavernkeeper was John Canty. See p. 138 and notes.

*Sunday January 25 • 1767*

A Congregation at the Cheraws of above 500 People. Baptiz'd about 60 Children—Quite jaded out—standing and speaking 6 Hours together and nothing to refresh me, but Water—and their Provisions I could not touch—All the Cookery of these People being exceeding filthy, and most execrable.

Next Day, I returned and preached the 27th in my Way back at Lynch's Creek to a great Multitude of People assembled together, being the 1st Episcopal Minister they had seen since their being in the province—They complain'd of being eaten up by Itinerant Teachers, Preachers, and Imposters from New England and Pensylvania—Baptists, New Lights, Presbyterians, Independants, and an hundred other Sects—So that one day You might hear this System of Doctrine—the next day another—next day another, retrograde to both—Thus by the Variety of Taylors who would pretend to know the best fashion in which Christs Coat is to be worn none will put it on—And among the Various Plans of Religion, they are at Loss which to adapt, and consequently are without any Religion at all. They came to Sermon with Itching Ears only, not with any Disposition of Heart, or Sentiment of Mind—Assemble out of Curiosity, not Devotion, and seem so pleas'd with their native Ignorance, as to be offended at any Attempts to rouse them out of it.——40 [miles]

I was almost tir'd in baptizing of Children—and laid my Self down for the Night frozen with the Cold—without the least Refreshment—No Eggs, Butter, Flour, Milk, or anything, but fat rusty Bacon, and fair Water, with Indian Corn Bread, Viands I had never before seen or tasted.——1340 [total miles]

I set off next day for Pine Tree, glad to be once more under the Roof of the good Samaritan, Mr. Kershaw, who poured Wine and Oil into my Wounds, and would have prevented my moving from him for a Space: But I was obliged to travel upwards—having engaged my Self for next Sunday at the Settlement of Irish Presbyterians called the Waxaws, among whome were several Church People.——40 [miles]

This is a very fruitful fine Spot, thro' which the dividing Line between North and South Carolina runs—The Heads of P. D. [Peedee] River, Lynch's Creek, and many other Creeks take their Rise in this Quarter—so that a finer Body of Land is no where to be seen—But it is occupied by a Sett of the most lowest vilest Crew breathing—Scotch Irish Presbyterians from the North of Ireland—They have built a Meeting House and have a Pastor, a Scots Man among them [15]—A good Sort of Man—He once was of the Church of England, and solicited for Orders, but was refus'd—whereon he went to Pensylvania, and got ordained by the Presbytery there, who allow him a Stipend to preach to these People, who (in his Breast) he heartily contemns—They will not suffer him to use the Lords Prayer. He wants to introduce Watts' [16] Psalms in place of the barbarous Scotch Version—but they will not admit it—His Congregation is very large—This Tract of Land being most surprisingly thick settled beyond any Spot in England of its Extent—Seldom less than 9, 10, 1200 People assemble of a Sunday—They never heard an Episcopal Minister, or the Common Prayer, and were very curious—The Church people among them are thinly scatter'd but they had a numerous Progeny for Baptism—rather chusing they should grow up to Maturity without Baptism than they should receive it by the hands of Sectaries—So in Compliance with their Request to visit them, I appointed Sunday the 31st to go up to them—and the Presbyterian Minister was to come down to this Meeting House in my Absence.—1380 [total miles]

He came down on the Friday. I stay'd till Saturday till I moved—when there arose such a Storm of Wind, Rain, Hail and Storm, as I think I hardly ever before saw. I could not stir out of the House, and was obliged to keep close Quarters.

But above, it was Fair Weather, and more than a thousand people assembled to attend my coming—and returned greatly vex'd and disapointed—Whereon I sent them Word, I would attend them very soon.

Accordingly I wrote them (and enclosed advertisements) that I

15. The Rev. William Richardson, Presbyterian minister at the Waxhaws. See pp. 132-35 and n. 42.

16. Isaac Watts (1674-1748) was an English theologian and hymn writer. Among his works are the *Hymns* (1707), and *The Psalms of David* (1719).

would be with them (if Health and Weather permitted) the last Sunday in February.[17]

Mean time went down to the High Hills where I officiated and baptiz'd on Sunday the 7th. Next day at St Marks—giving the people Sermons and Lectures, in various Places, and at different Houses as I went along—For I found it here, the same as at Lynch's Creek and the Cheraws—Wherever you went to a House to marry or baptize, a Multitude would assemble, and desire a Discourse; which I was more ready alway to give, than they to ask.

At all these Places I've been at, I read the King's Proclamation against Vice and Immorality,[18] which has had very good Effects. For thro' want of Ministers to marry and thro' the licentiousness of the People, many hundreds live in Concubinage—swopping their Wives as Cattel, and living in a State of Nature, more irregularly and unchastely than the Indians—I therefore made Public Notice ev'ry where be given, that whoever did not attend to be legally married, I would prosecute them at the Sessions—and that all who had liv'd in a State of Concubinage on application to me, I would marry Gratis—Numbers accepted of my Offer, and were married, and then I baptiz'd their Children—Several who were Episcopal, and who had been married by Itinerant Dissenting Ministers desir'd to be re-married by the Liturgy, as judging such their former Marriage invalid.——[total] Miles 1380

As there are no Clergy in North Carolina, the Magistrates are there permitted to Marry—and many of this Province travel over there for to be join'd—Several Couple married by them apply'd likewise to be re-married, as judging such their former Marriage temporary only.

From St Marks I returned to Pine Tree Hill, where my Good Samaritan had finish'd off two upper Rooms in a House belong-

17. Woodmason never preached in the Waxhaws. Although he prepared a sermon to give there, some of the elders of the Waxhaw Presbyterian Church were opposed to his coming. See p. 93, n. 23.

18. The Royal Proclamation "For the encouragement of piety and virtue, and the preventing and punishing of vice, prophaneness, and immorality" was issued October 31, 1760. *Bibliotheca Lindesiana, Vol. VIII. Handlist of Proclamations Issued by Royal and Other Constitutional Authorities 1714-1910 George I to Edward VII* (Wigan, 1913), col. 97.

ing to an Old Widow Dutch Woman—And about this Time the Waggons with my Goods and Library came from C. T. the Carriage of which cost me Seven Guineas.——50 [miles]

### Sunday Feb. 14

Officiated at Pine Tree—Find my Congregation here to be at a medium about 60 or 70 Persons—But no Clerk or Singing—none to make the Responses—they sit all the Time of Prayer and Sermon, and I have but one person (as yet) offer as a Communicant.

Friday 19. Journey'd upwards to Lynch's Creek, and did Duty there on Sunday the 21. A Crowd of People assembled, the Major Part Episcopals—Married several Couple on the Proclamation and Baptized 30 or 40 children and 2 Adults—A Great Number of Adults present—but all of them totally ignorant of the first Principles of things—So cannot baptize them—And what is worse, being oblig'd to be in perpetual Motion, I cannot have Time to instruct them, which is great Grief to me. In this Congregation was not a Bible or Common Prayer—None to respond. All very poor and extremely ignorant—Yet desirous of the Knowledge of God and of Christ. Their Case is truly pitiable, but out of my power to amend and the Legislature turn a deaf Ear to all Remonstrances on this Subject, and like *Gallio* care for none of these things.[19]——40 [miles]

From the lower part of Lynch's Creek I proceeded to the upper—and from the Greater to the Lesser; The Weather was exceeding Cold and piercing—And as these People live in open Logg Cabbins with hardly a Blanket to cover them, or Cloathing to cover their Nakedness, I endur'd Great Hardships and my Horse more than his Rider—they having no fodder, nor a Grain of Corn to spare.——[total] miles 1470

I had appointed a Congregation to meet me at the Head of Hanging Rock Creek [20]—Where I arriv'd on Tuesday Evening—Found the Houses filled with debauch'd licentious fellows, and Scot Presbyterians who had hir'd these lawless Ruffians to insult

19. Acts 18:12-17.
20. Hanging Rock is a hundred-foot cliff overhanging the branch of Little Lynch's River. Meriwether, *Expans. of. S. C.*, 145.

me, which they did with Impunity—Telling me, they wanted no D——d Black Gown Sons of Bitches among them—and threatning to lay me behind the Fire, which they assuredly would have done had not some travellers alighted very opportunely, and taken me under Protection—These Men sat up with, and guarded me all the Night—In the Morning the lawless Rabble moved off on seeing the Church People appear, of whom had a large Congregation. But the Service was greatly interrupted by a Gang of Presbyterians who kept hallooing and whooping without Door like Indians.——30 [miles]

From this Place I went upwards to Cane Creek where I had wrote to the Church People for to assemble—But when I came I found that all my Letters and Advertisements had been intercepted. I trac'd them into the hands of one John Gaston, an Irish Presbyterian Justice of Peace on Fishing Creek, on other Side the River. However, at a Days Notice, about 80 Church People were brought together on Sunday the 27th who behav'd very decently and orderly. One Elderly Gentleman stood Clerk—He brought 6 Sons and 4 Daughters with Him, all excellent Singers, so that the Service was regularly perform'd—Baptiz'd 27 Children.——20 [miles]

Here came Deputies from Camp Creek and Cedar Creek two adjoining Settlements—and Indeed, I was glad to get away from this starved place, where have lived all this Week on a little Milk and Indian Corn Meal, without any other Sustennance but Cold Water—and hardly any Fire to warm me tho' the Season bitter Cold indeed. Wood is exceeding plenty (for the Country is a Forest and Wilderness) but the people so very lazy, that they'l sit for Hours hovering over a few Embers, and will not turn out to cut a Stick of Wood.——1520 [total miles]

I preach'd and baptiz'd at these two Settlements and returned to Pine Tree, where officiated as usual on Sunday March 1.——55 [miles]

In my Absence, found that my Lod[g]ings had been robbed. About 30 Volumes of my Books—much Linen, my Letter folder Port Folio, Key of Desk, and many little Articles taken away. It appear'd to me that Search had been made after my private

Papers—and MSS. But they were secur'd. This was some Device of the Presbyterians. By their hurry, they took what Books they first laid hands on, whereby several of my Setts are spoiled.

Set off this Week for St Marks Church and officiated as usual. The Weather very wet and Cold and Road intolerably bad. Gave Sermon at the High Hills both going down and coming up.—— 100 [miles]

Sunday 15) Officiated for the 1st time at Rafting Creek where married many agreeable to my Summons, and baptiz'd a Number of Children.

Proceeded from Pine Tree to Lynch's Creek, enduring the same hardships as before and more—The Creeks being full of Water and almost impassable—Obliged to swim both Self and Horse over Lynchs Creek, and Black Creek—The Swamps full of Water—Bridges carried away, and riding for Miles to the Skirts in Mud and Water—So that the Horse gave out.

Obliged to stay a day in a dirty smoaky Cabbin without Sustenance.——50 [miles]

When I came to Thompsons Creek, found it so swelled and so exceeding Rapid, that I waited 2 days for subsiding of the Waters—Mean time the people collected together, and brought their Children for Baptism, and had Sermons. They entertained me very hospitably and took good Care of my Horse.——1680 [total miles]

Saturday came, and the Creek still very deep and rapid—I got a Sailor to make a Raft, on which he was to venture over and inform the People that I was come and could not get to them. The Man ventur'd on the Raft, but no sooner put off, but the Torrent ingulph'd him in a Moment, and both him and Raft were carried to the Bottom—I never was so frighten'd, sweat at ev'ry Pore, thinking that the Man was drowned, and my Self the occasion of his Death. But he rose again, and got hold of a Tree floating in the Stream—We threw him Ropes, by which we pull'd him on shore unhurt—and he was as unconcern'd and merry, as if nothing had happen'd to Him.

I then mounted Horse, and rode to and fro up and down the Creek to endeavor to find some narrow place, where to fall some

Great Trees, and mount over by them—But the Stream was ev'ry where too Broad. So waited till Sunday Morning.——40 [miles]

When the Neighbours came again—and a Bold Man brought a very large strong and High Horse. We found a place where the Waters were not very rapid—and he made trial if he could swim it on his Horse, and happily effected it.

He then recross'd the Stream, took my Saddle and Baggage at Times on his Head, and carried them safe and dry to the opposite Bank.

The Women then stript me Naked, and gave Him my Cloaths which he carried on his Head in like Manner—They put their aprons around me—and when he returned, I got behind Him, and the Horse carried us both over very safe—but I never trembled more in my Life. The People placed themselves at Places below, to take me up if I slipt off, or that the Horse sank under me. The Man afterward brought over my Horse—but I was almost stiff and torpid with the Cold, and being in the Cold Water—the Wind blowing very sharp at N. E. and Ground cover'd with Ice.——2020 [total miles]

It was now but 12 Miles to Pedee River to the place of Rendezvous. Found the People not assembled—for they could form no Imagination that I could get to them—because none but those within the two Rivers could meet—All above and below were hinder'd—Yet in an Hours Time, I had 100 People in the Congregation.——10 [miles]

In the Afternoon, I drew up for them a Petition to the Legislature for this Part of the Province to be rais'd into a Parish which petition was cheerfully sign'd. The Weather grew mild and Clear.

On Monday I returned to Thompsons Creek, and found it fordable and on Tuesday gave Sermon to another Congregation assembled there.——10 [miles]. From hence I set off across the Country for Hanging Rock—but for want of Guides and thro' not knowing the Country nor understanding their Directions, I lost my Self in the Woods for here are no Roads—only small paths, in many places grown up with Grass or cover'd with Leaves and undiscernable. I got to a Cabbin at Night, and sat up by the Fire— The poor Woman had nothing but Indian Corn Bread and Water. In the Morning I pursu'd my Journey, and after wand'ring the whole Day, and riding 30 Miles to and fro out of my Way, arriv'd at Hanging Rock at 3 in the afternoon. But the greater Part of the Congregation were gone—However I gave them Service and baptiz'd 6 Children.——80 [miles]; 2120 [total miles]

In the Morning came a large Body of people, 2/3 of them Presbyterians—They had prepared a Band of Ruffians as before to make disturbance—But a Neighbouring Magistrate came to Service and officiated as Clerk, bringing with Him a party of the Catawba Indians—These poor Wretches behaved more quiet and decent than the lawless Crew—who kept (as before) a great Noise without Door; The Indians resented their affronts and fought with several of them, which only made more Noises. I went home to the Magistrates House, and from thence next day to visit the Presbyterian Minister according to an Invitation made me when he was at my House at Pine Tree—We address'd some of the Elders, and represented the Insolence of some of their Congregation. They disown'd all Proceedings and the authors of them—tho' twas very visible that they set them on. I threatned them so severely that never afterward had any more disturbances in these Parts.——20 [miles]

Returned to Pine Tree, and gave Sermon as usual on Sunday April 5th. The Reason why my Congregation here is not larger, am told is That there are a Gang of Baptists or New Lights over the River to whom many on that Side resort—And that on Swift Creek 10 Miles below, a Methodist has set up to read and preach ev'ry Sunday—Both of them exceeding low and ignorant persons—Yet the lower Class chuse to resort to them rather than to hear a Well connected Discourse.——50 [miles]

All this obliges me to repeat the Liturgy by Heart and to use no Book but the Bible, when I read the Lessons. I have the whole Service and all the Offices at my fingers Ends. I also give an Extempore Prayer before Sermon—but cannot yet venture to give Extempore Discourses, tho' certainly could perform beyond any of these Poor Fools. I shall make Trial in a short time.

Received an Invitation from the People on other Side the River to visit them—who sent a pilot to conduct me on Sunday April 12. The Path an entire Bogg and deep Swamp—Had a very genteel and polite Congregation; 50 Young Ladies all drest in

White of their own Spinning—Many of them Baptists.——30 [miles]

From thence recross'd the River thro' a long deep miry Swamp, and on the Thursday gave Service at the High Hills—on Good Friday some Miles below, and on Easter Sunday administered the Holy Communion at St Marks Church—about 80 persons attended. Most of them Gentry from distant Parts—but had only eight Communicants—the most ever known here.——2220 [total miles]

Attended the next day at their Vestry, and drew up for them a Letter to my Lord of London to supply them with a Pastor—but could not prevail with them to sign it [21]—They seem'd to be all inclined to turn Baptists—and shewed no Regard for or to the Church.——40 [miles]

Received News that Mr. Shinner the Cheif Justice was suspended from his Office, by desire of the House of Assembly, who had an Implacable Resentment against Him on Account of his Endeavours to enforce the Stamp Act—In Him I lose a good Benefactor and the Poor, the Church and Religion, a strenuous and valuable Friend.

Employ'd this Week in going to different Houses to baptize Children—Preached a fine Sermon at Pine Tree to a large Congregation. Went back over the River again into the Fork and gave Service on Sunday April 26. Had a smart Congregation.—— 20 [miles]; 50 [miles]

Sunday May 3. Officiated at Pine Tree. 10th at Hanging Rock, where (being Sunday) had no Presbyterians or any Disturbance, on the 17th over the River in the Fork—on the 21st at Lynch's Creek, and the 24th on Pedee River.——30 [miles]; 60 [miles]; 80 [miles]

At P. D. The Sheriff and people of Anson County in North

21. This petition, dated April 20, 1767, was sent to the Bishop of London without signatures. It informed the Bishop that St. Mark's Parish had been without a minister for two years, since the Rev. Mr. Evans had moved to St. Paul's Parish and asked a replacement. The duties would be "very easy, as the laborious Part is executed by an Itinerant Minister [Woodmason] plac'd about 50 Miles above us by the Church Commissioners." Ful. Trans., S.C., No. 44.

Carolina attended and conducted me up thither, and treated me with great Civility.——30 [miles]

A numerous Body of People attended at the Court House where I celebrated Divine Service and baptiz'd about 60 Children. A great Dinner was prepared by the Sheriff for the Company. They had ne'er seen an Episcopal Minister before. A Number of Well dressed people here—seem'd more an English than Carolina Congregation—A large Body of Baptists and New Lights with their Teachers attended—Wanted to preach before me, and to enter into Disputes—found them exceeding Vain and Ignorant— They rode down the Road 10 Miles with me to escort me, asking Questions on Divinity all the Way. I found their Reading to be of no greater Extent than the Pilgrims Progress and Works of John Bunyan.——50 [miles]

Tuesday gave Sermon to a Congregation of Baptists, Quakers, and a mix'd Multitude, at head of Thompsons Creek and baptiz'd several Children—and on Wednesday at Black Creek.——2380 [miles]

Holy Thursday the 21. Gave Sermon and baptized at Lynchs Creek. A large Body of people attended—But not a Bible among them. Married several Couple.

Crossed the Country to Hanging Rock, and on May 29th gave Service and Sermon speaking to a mix'd Company—Baptiz'd a Number of Children—Several Adults, and many whole families. A Great Many Presbyterians attended, who did not disturb me. Some Women attempted it, but were soon silenc'd—Many of the Men withdrew—Had no Clerk—Nor could raise a psalm. The next Day gave Sermon to a small Congregation on Camp Creek. ——30 [miles]; 20 [miles]

In Consequence of an Appointment and Invitation, went over the River to Rocky Mount, w[h]ere was kindly received by the younger Mr. Kershaw.—10 [miles]

Rocky Mount is an Hill on the West Side Wateree River, about 20 Miles below the Province Line. It is very elevated, and a fine Situation. The Land is good, and plowed to the Summit, bringing Wheat Rye Indian Corn and all kind of Grain and Fruit Trees—This is [a] most delightful healthy part of this Country— No Bogs, Marshes, Swamps, Fogs, Insects to annoy you. Its but newly settled. But the People are already crowded together as thick as in England.

On the 31. (Sunday) I gave Service to about 400 people among whom a great Number of Baptists and Presbyterians. I had here a good Clerk, and excellent Singing. The Women sing as well or better than the Girls at the Magdalene Chapel, London—They all came from Virginia and Pensylvania—Not an English person or Carolinian among them—I baptiz'd 4 Children and promised to visit them Monthly.

Returned to Pine Tree and by the way, gave Sermon to another Body of People on Beaver Creek—on the 7th at Pine Tree—14th at Pine Tree the 21st St Marks, the 26. at Beaver Creek, the 28th Rocky Mt.——35 [miles]; 135 [miles]; [total] miles 2610

July 2. Returned from Rocky Mount—3d Gave Sermon at Beaver Creek and Baptiz'd several Negroes and Mullatoos. Married several Couple on the Proclamation—5th Gave Service at Pine Tree and 12th at Rafting Creek—the 19th at Lynch's Creek—where received an Invitation to preach to a Congregation on Granny Quarter Creek, which I attended next Day, and found about 100 people assembled together—More rude ignorant, and void of things, than any Circle hitherto among. Not a Bible or Prayer Book—Not the least Rudiments of Religion, Learning, Manners or Knowledge (save of Vice) among them.——65 [miles]; 60 [miles]

Such a Pack I never met with—Neither English, Scots Irish, or Carolinian by Birth—Neither of one Church or other or of any denomination by Profession, not having (like some of the Lynchs Creek people) ever seen a Minister—heard or read a Chapter in the Scriptures, or heard a Sermon in their days.——15 [miles]

Went down to Pine Tree, and on the Saturday following was accompanied up to Rocky Mount by several Gentlemen and Ladies—not from Motives of Religion, or Respect—But thro' Curiosity, and Itching Ears. My appearance among them being a Novelty—and none in the World so fond of Novelties, as the Carolinians—The difference between them and the Londoners, is, That the former are quickly tir'd of any thing, even what pleases their fancy—The latter never think they can have enough of what pleases them—Of the two, the Carolinians are the most fickle—and there is not a more fickle trite, superficial people in the World.[22]——15 [miles]

The 26. I gave Sermon at Rocky Mount to a numerous Audience, of various degrees, Countries, Complexions and Denominations—Baptiz'd 36 Children—and was quite exhausted thro' the Great Heat of the Weather and Length of the Service.

When we came from Sermon, My Company found two of their Horses carried off—While we were at Sermon, the Gang of Horse Theives paid a Visit to the Creatures—Their Intent was to carry off my Horses, by Way of Reprisal [I] having stirr'd up the Country against them, and brought up the Cheif Justice to raise the Country: But unluckily for my Friends, they carried off two of their Horses instead of mine, so that their Scheme of Pleasure was greatly disconcerted.——35 [miles]; [total] miles 2800

Tuesday following we proceeded downward, and gave Sermon and baptiz'd; and married many Rogues and Whores on Beaver Creek.——35 [miles]

Next day went down and gave Sermon at Rafting Creek and on August 2d at Pine Tree. Quite jaded and almost worn out thro' heat of the Weather, and dullness of the Horse, travelling over the hot Sands this dry Season.——15 [miles]; 15 [miles]

Went down this Week to St Marks Church, and from thence by Invitation to Santee River—where the Gentry assembled to hear me—but more out of Curiosity than Religion.——50 [miles]; 20 [miles]; 20 [miles]

Gave Sermon the 16th at Lynchs Creek. 17th at Granny's Quarter. 18th at Beaver Creek. 21 at Dutchmans Creek on the West Side of the Wateree. Lost my Self in the Woods in going from thence to Rocky Mount and stayed in the Woods the whole Night, quite famished and fatigued—Could find no Water—Would have given all the Mines of Peru (if had them) for a drop

22. Such sweeping characterizations as this are not convincing. But for what it is worth, it may be mentioned that Henry Laurens wrote to a friend, the Rev. Mr. St. John, on November 11, 1747, "The people of this province are generally very fickle, especially as to Governors spiritual or temporal, soon pleased and soon disgusted." David D. Wallace, *The Life of Henry Laurens* (New York, 1915), 95.

of Water.—In the Morning, found the right Path, and pursu'd my Journey.——8o [miles]; 35 [miles]

The 24. preached at Rocky Mount from whence the People carried me up the Country to Fishing Creek, settled cheifly by Presbyterians, but several worthy Church People among them.— Had a crowded Audience—but obliged to drive some of the Presbyterians away, who wanted to be Insolent. Returned to Rocky Mount.——10 [miles]; 10 [miles]

From Fishing Creek, the People conducted me to Sandy River, near Broad River—Gave Service the 30th to above 500 persons who had never seen a Minister before. Baptiz'd 50 Children and several Adults. Met with many serious and Religious persons— The Service perform'd this Day with as much pomp as if at St Pauls. Married several Couples—Quite exhausted with the heat of the Weather and Crowds of People—Went down from hence to Pine Tree.——30 [miles]; 65 [miles]; 3185 [total miles]

I forgot to set down that in the last Excursion from Lynchs Creek to the Cheraws, my Horse fail'd and was obliged to stay in the Woods, in the Night when he got from me and I got lost— wandering a Day and Night in the Wilderness, not knowing where I was, famished, and without any Sustenance.

Thus You have the Travels of a Minister in the Wild Woods of America—Destitute often of the very Necessaries of Life— Sometimes starved—Often famished—Exposed to the burning Sun and scorching Sands—Obliged to fight his Way thro' Banditti, profligates, Reprobates, and the lowest vilest Scum of Mankind on the one hand, and of the numerous Sectaries pregnant in these Countries, on the other—With few Friends, and fewer Assistants —and surmounting Difficulties, and braving Dangers, that ev'ry Clergyman that ever entered this Province shrinked even at the thoughts off—Which none, not even the meanest of the Scotch Clergy that have been sent here, would undertake, and for which he subjected himself to the Laughter of Fools and Ridicule of the Licentiousness [sic] for undertaking.

| Number of Persons married this Year about | | 40 Couple |
|---|---|---|
| Children baptized about | 760 | 782 |
| Adults | 10 | that took a |
| Negroes and Mullatoes | 12 | Register off. |

Beside many others, whose Names were not given in, or attended too.

No other Clergyman of the Church of England from the Sea to the Mountains, on the North Side of Santee River to the Province Line. Number of Miles rode this year (All perform'd by one Horse) 3185. May say, full four thousand Miles.

Observe that not above 2 or 3 out of any family can attend Divine Service at one Time, thro' want of Horses and Saddles— otherwise each Congregation would be doubled. They therefore come by turns.

Congregations rais'd, and attended occasionally. 1767

| [Miles from Camden] | | | | auditors more or less communicants |
|---|---|---|---|---|
| 80 | A | 1 | Great Swamp of Santee | 80— 2 |
| 50 | A | 2 | St. Marks Church | 70— 6 |
| 26 | A | 3 | High Hills of Santee | 300— 1 |
| 18 | B | 4 | Rafting Creek | 200— 1 |
| | C | 5 | Pine Tree Hill (The Centre) | 200— 2 |
| 16 | B | 6 | Granny Quarter Creek | 90— |
| 30 | B | 7 | Hanging Rock Creek | 50— 2 |
| 28 | B | 8 | Little Lynchs Creek, Flat Creek &c | 150—15 |
| 33 | B | 9 | Great Lynch's Creek (2 Places) | 100— 3 |
| 70 | D | 10 | Thompsons Creek (2 Places) | 150 |
| 96 | E | 11 | Cheraws, on Pedee River | 400— 2 |
| 125 | D | 13 [23] | Anson Court House, North Carolina | 300 |
| 36 | F | 14 | Camp Creek, and Cedar Creek | 40— 2 |
| 26 | F | 15 | Beaver Creek, White Oak &c | 120 |
| 32 | F | 16 | Dutchmans Creek | 50 |
| 34 | B | 17 | Rocky Creek, Wateree Creek &c | 300— 4 |
| 40 | F | 18 | Fishing Creek | 60— 2 |
| 42 | F | 19 | Waxaws | 70 |
| 96 | E | 20 | Sandy River (near Broad River) | 300 |
| 40 | E | 21 | Fork of the Wateree and Broad River | 100— 3 |

A—Attended ev'ry 2 Months.     D—Once a Year.
B—Once ev'ry Month.            E—Twice a Year.
C—Ev'ry other Sunday, by Law.   F—Once a Quarter.

23. Woodmason skips from number 11 to number 13.

Could all these Congregations be regularly attended ev'ry Sunday, the Number set against each (say treble the Number) would attend. But it would employ 20 Ministers. The figures set before the Letters express the Number of Miles each Place is distant from my Centre.

These Congregations being settled—their Children Baptiz'd, and the people rouz'd from their Insensibility—A New System of Things, and an entire Alteration in the Minds of Individuals, seem'd to take place from this Period.

I will wave all Political Matters (leaving it to another Paper— which I have mention'd) [24] and proceed in my Journal just to set down Facts, and Occurences respecting my Self—and the State of Religion in this Country.

The fatigue and Pain—the Toil and Expense I have sustain'd in these Peregrinations are beyond Description—Few beside me could have born them. The Task deterr'd ev'ry one—None to be found to enter on it.

But [25] the people wearied out with being expos'd to the Depredations of Robbers—Set down here just as a Barrier between the Rich Planters and the Indians, to secure the former against the Latter—Without Laws or Government Churches Schools or Ministers—No Police established—and all Property quite insecure— Merchants as fearful to venture their Goods as Ministers their Persons—The Lands, tho' the finest in the Province unoccupied, and rich Men afraid to set Slaves to work to clear them, lest they should become a Prey to the Banditti—No Regard had to the numberless petitions and Complaints of the people—Thus neglected and slighted by those in Authority, they rose in Arms—

24. Woodmason has made no mention of a paper on political matters in his Journal. This reference to such a paper may be an error, or it could be evidence that Woodmason intended this Journal for the eyes of someone with whom he was in correspondence.

25. This paragraph and those that follow up to the entry of September 6 were clearly added later, and out of chronological order, by Woodmason. The reference to the Remonstrance and to the sermon of November 20 would suggest that Woodmason wrote this passage in late November or early December, 1767. He probably erred in believing that the blank space in his Journal came at the end of the calendar year. Actually, it came at the end of his first year as clergyman on the South Carolina frontier.

pursued the Rogues, broke up their Gangs—burnt the dwellings of all their Harbourers and Abettors—Whipp'd and drove the Idle, Vicious and Profligate out of the Province, Men and Women without Distinction and would have proceeded to Charlestown in a Regular Corps of 5000 Men, and hung up the Rogues before the State House in Presence of Governor and Council.

For the Mildness of Legislation here is so great and the Clemency of the Cheif in Authority has been carried to such Excess that when a notorious Robber was with Great Pains catch'd and sent to Town, and there try'd and Condemn'd he always got pardon'd by Dint of Money, and came back 50 times worse than before. The fellows thus pardon'd form'd themselves into a large Gang, ranging the province with Impunity.

It was with great Pains that I prevail'd with the Multitude to lay aside desperate Resolutions. I wrote to all in Authority—and received for answer, that if they would apply in a Constitutional Way, their Greivances should be redressed.

I drew up for them a Remonstrance, which was presented to the House. Many articles of a Civil Nature were granted. But those of a Religious remain as they were—save the raising of a large Distric big enough for 6 Parishes into one Parish, because they want not to increase the Number of Members of Assembly. But the Regulators (so the Populace call themselves) will not long be passive—If the next Sessions do not relieve them, they are determin'd to surround the Metropolis.

I now proceed in my Journal for the second Year. (but forgot to Note, that on the 20th November) I was at Beaver Creek where gave Sermon to a Body of about 2000 arm'd persons, of the Populace call'd Regulators—and it was happiness for many that I went there as I sav'd many Homes from being burnt and stopped the Outrages of the Mobb—No Lives were lost nor Blood spilt.

### September 6 • 1767

Officiated at Pine Tree Hill—On the 9th went up to Fishing Creek and returned to Pine Tree.——40 [miles]; 40 [miles]

The 13th Gave Sermon at Rafting Creek—the 20th at Little Lynch's Creek. The 21 at Grannys Quarter.——36 [miles]; 40 [miles]

The 25th at Beaver Creek—Next day in my Way up fell into an Ambuscade of the Horse Theives who lay in wait for me. They carried me to their Gang, who received me with Great Civility, and promis'd to restore the Horses they had Stollen.—Desir'd I would give them a Sermon which I promis'd to do as next Monday. By this Detainer Great Part of the Congregation dispers'd, imagining, that I was sick and could not come.——33 [miles]

On Monday I went to the Rendezvous according to Promise— But the Militia having Notice, took to arms intending to surprise the Rogues—As they have Spies ev'ry where, they had early Intelligence, and moved off—leaving their Wives, Whores and Children. So I gave Sermon to the Militia instead of the Banditti.[26]——33 [miles]

October 3d) Officiated at Pine Tree—During Sermon the Rogues beset several Houses and robbed them, stripping both Houses and all in them of ev'ry thing they could carry off. The Congregation after Sermon took to Arms and pursu'd them and at 15 Miles end came up with them at 25 Mile Creek, and fir'd on them—One Man was wounded whom his Companions carried off. They recover'd several Horses, and much Goods. October 10 Officiated at Rafting Creek—17 Lynchs Creek—19 at Grannys Quarters—25th Rocky Mount—26th Beaver Creek from whence I was conducted over the Wateree River (across the Wild Woods where had never before been) to Little River, where I officiated the 31. to about 300 Persons.——18 [miles]; 18 [miles]; 60 [miles]; 64 [miles]; 24 [miles]; 30 [miles]

Here a large Body of People met me—I baptized several Adults, and of them 3 or 4 Quakers, who conform'd to the Church.——36 [miles]

Returned to Pine [Tree] and preach'd there the 1st being All

26. In another version of this incident, written many years later, Woodmason states that about forty thieves appeared for the sermon with about twenty-five of their "fine Girls." The attack took place about mid-sermon, and some of the girls were captured together with apparel and other "Goods." Woodmason also states that the attack was not to have taken place until after the sermon and his departure, and that by coming early "He was expos'd to be shot by them as an Informer and it was a Mercy he escap'd." "Memorandum" on the Regulator Movement, Sermon Book, IV, [373].

Saints but the Presbyterians disliked the Service and Sermon of the Day saying it was Popish &c.——50 [miles]

I assembled them on the 5th in the Meeting House, w[h]ere came the Magistrates, Elders, &c and several of the principal Quakers—The Days Service and Sermon (being of Popery) gave Satisfaction [27]—This the 1st Sermon ever preached on this Day in this Province out of Charlestown.

On the 8th preached at Rafting Creek—9th at the Hills—15. Lynchs Creek. 16 Grannys Quarter. 22d Rocky Mount. 24 Dutchmans Creek—and on the 29th at Little River.——50 [miles]; 60 [miles]; 45 [miles]; 63 [miles]

### December 1767

The 6th at Pine Tree. 8th at Grannys Quarter. The 13th at Rafting Creek—the 17th the Weather so Wet and Cold could not Journey, so officiated at Pine Tree—the 20th at Great Lynchs Creek.—32 [miles]; 36 [miles]; 30 [miles]

The Church Warden below came up, and with some other Serious Christians accompanied me to Little Lynch's Creek, where had a very religious Congregation of 70 persons—had 15 or 16 Communicants—In afternoon rode 5 Miles to another Congregation and gave Service to them—Spending the Evening in singing Psalms and Hymns.——30 [miles]; 5 [miles]

This Day we had another Specimen of the Envy Malice and Temper of the Presbyterians—They gave away 2 Barrels of Whisky to the Populace to make drink, and for to disturb the Service—for this being the 1st time that the Communion was ever celebrated in this Wild remote Part of the World, it gave a Great Alarm, and caus'd them much Pain and Vexation. The Company got drunk by 10 oth Clock and we could hear them firing, hooping, and hallowing like Indians. Some few came before the Communion was finish'd and were very Noisy—and could I have found out the Individuals, would have punish'd them.—— 837 [total miles]

They took another Step to interrupt the Service of the Day.

27. November 5 is "Guy Fawkes' Day," in celebration of the discovery of the Gunpowder Plot in 1605.

The Captain of the Corps of Militia on this Creek being a Presbyterian, order'd the Company to appear as this day under Arms to Muster—The Church People refus'd. He threatn'd to fine—They defy'd Him: And had he attempted it, a Battle would certainly have ensu'd in the Muster field between the Church folks and Presbyterians, and Blood been spilt—His Apprehension of Danger to his person made him defer it till the 26th.

Some of the New Lights and Baptists would have communicated as to day, but I did not approve it, till I knew them better—had some proofs of their Sincerity, and could judge whether Motives of Curiosity, not Religion, prompted them.

Cross'd the Country, and the Wateree River to Rocky Mount—was in Great Danger of my Life—the Stream being so rapid that it carried away the Boat down the River and stove us on the Rocks—We threw the Horses over, and they swam to shore and we were taken out by Canoos that came off. I was quite spent with Toil and Sweat—Wet to the Skin, and all my Linen and Baggage soak'd in Water.——25 [miles]; 862 [total miles]

### December 27

Officiated at Rocky Mount. Had but a small Congregation and 5 Communicants—The Name of the Holy Sacrament frightened them all away. Returned with the Church Warden down the Country.——33 [miles]

### 1768

January 1) Preached at Granny Quarter Creek to a mix'd Multitude of People from various Quarters—But no bringing of this Tribe into any Order. They are the lowest Pack of Wretches my Eyes ever saw, or that I have met with in these Woods—As wild as the very Deer—No making of them sit still during Service—but they will be in and out—forward and backward the whole Time (Women especially) as Bees to and fro to their Hives—All this must be born with at the beginning of Things—Nor can be mended till Churches are built, and the Country reduc'd to some Form. How would the Polite People of London stare, to see the Females (many very pretty) come to Service in their Shifts and a short petticoat only, barefooted and Bare legged—Without Caps or Handkerchiefs [28]—dress'd only in their Hair, Quite in a State of Nature for Nakedness is counted as Nothing—as they sleep altogether in Common in one Room, and shift and dress openly without Ceremony—The Men appear in Frocks or Shirts and long Trousers—No Shoes or Stockings—But I should remember that I am talking of my Self, and Religious Matters, Not the Customs of the Country.——36 [miles]

January 3) Officiated at Pine Tree—The Weather now set exceeding Cold. Hard Rain all this Week. Could not stir out the ensuing Sunday, being a Great Storm, which did much Damage. ——931 [total miles]

17) Wind, Rain, Cold, Frost, Storm, alternately—No going any Journeys, the Rivers and Creeks being swelled, and the Country all under Water. so officiated this Day at Pine Tree Hill.

The 24th went up to Rocky Mount—but got exceeding Wet by swimming the Creeks—I contracted a very Great Cold and Cough. From thence cross'd the Country, and gave Sermon at Grannys Quarter the 28th so down to P. T. [Pine Tree]——33 [miles]; 33 [miles]; 36 [miles]

February 7. At Pine Tree 14th Grannys Quarters not being able for the floods to go further—And 'twas with hazard of my Life, and with great Pains and Difficulty that I got over this Creek.—36 [miles]

17th Being Ash Wednesday, I officiated and gave Sermon but had a very small Congregation. Could not get the Church People to attend. The 21. Got over the Creeks by Riding 30 Miles about and heading them, and reach'd my Congregation on Little Lynchs Creek. over which was obliged to swim. The Water and Weather very Cold. This gave me a severe Sore Throat.——60 [miles]

The 28th got up to Rocky Mount but had not above 30 persons. All the Creeks being full, and impassable; for no Bridges

28. Governor Dobbs of North Carolina visited the families on his lands on Rocky River, along the North Carolina-South Carolina border, and noted that the children went barefoot "in their shifts in the warm weather, no woman wearing more than a shift and one thin petticoat." Gov. Dobbs to the Board of Trade, Newbern, Aug. 24, 1755, William L. Saunders, ed., *The Colonial Records of North Carolina* (Raleigh, 1885-90), V, 356-57.

are yet built in the Country—Nor are there any ferries or Boats—
We pass at the Fords when the Waters are low—and when up, all
Communication is cut off.——66 [miles]

March 6) Weather exceeding Cold. Hard Frost, and a Great
Snow fell which drove my Auditors to the Tavern Fire, which
they would not quit to come to Service—Sat 2 Hours in the
Pulpit waiting till almost perishd.——1295 [total miles]

March 8) Preached at Beaver Creek to a vast Concourse—on
the 13. at Grannys Quarter—20th Lynchs Creek—but almost
perish'd in these Journeys—the Weather sharp and cold. Their
Cabbins quite open and expos'd. Little or no Bedding, or anything to cover them—Not a drop of anything, save Cold Water
to drink—And all their Cloathing, a Shirt and Trousers Shift and
[one word illegible] Petticoat. Some perhaps a Linsey Woolsey.
No Shoes or Stockings—Children run half naked. The Indians
are better Cloathed and Lodged. All this arises from their Indolence and Laziness.——1295 [total miles]; 40 [miles]; 36 [miles];
56 [miles]

The 27. officiated at Pine Tree. and tho' the Weather was Cold
prevailed with some to stay Evening Service—The Days too short
and Weather too severe to enter on any long Journey.

April 1. Officiated again at P. Tree, Being Good Friday—Had
but very few at Service—The Sectaries deeming it savour'd of
Popery.

Next day set off with my Baggage to visit the distant Congregations and gave Sermon at Grannys Quarters. On Easter Sunday
at Lynchs Creek, w[h]ere had a very devout Congregation and
some New Communicants 18 Received—16 could not come thro'
the Waters.——30 [miles]

Easter Monday) Set off with Guides for the Province Line.
Married and Baptiz'd all the Way—Tuesday preached at Brown's
Creek to a New Congregation—Many came from Thompsons
Creek, Black Creek and great Distance,—Some to be married
others Baptiz'd others out of Curiosity.——40 [miles]; 1497
[total miles]

Tuesday—proceeded along the Line across the Province baptizing all the Way—Wednesday it rain'd hard—Could not procure
Guides for Money—Lost my Self amidst the various Cattle Tracts

and Winding Paths—No Sun to steer by, Nor knew the Course
of the Country—In this plight wet to the skin rode to and fro till
Night came, when got to the Cabbin of a poor Old Dutch
Woman, who inform'd me that I was got into the Waxaw Distric
among a Tribe of Presbyterians.——30 [miles]. She had no Refreshments. Not a Grain of Corn for the Horse, nor the least Sub-
sistance. We left the Horse to shift for himself and to feed on the
twigs and Bushes—Her Son was from home—She dry'd my
Cloaths, and I sat up all Night by the Fire, quite tired and spent,
having not made what could be called a Meal for some days—
Nothing but Indian Corn Meal to be had Bacon and Eggs in some
Places—No Butter, Rice, or Milk—As for Tea and Coffee they
know it not. These people are all from Ireland, and live wholly on
Butter, Milk, Clabber and what in England is given to the Hogs
and Dogs. In the Morning I sat off, the Weather being fair. Call'd
at several Houses to hire Guides and paid them—but they no
sooner found that I was a Church Minister than they quitted me
—I hir'd 3 or 4 in this Manner—What was still worse, they would
direct me wrong, and send me quite out of the Way—I learn'd
however, that there was a rich Man among them, who had plenty of
Corn fodder, Meat, Liquors and Necessaries, and that he kept
Tavern. I Procur'd a Boy to conduct me, and got there after riding
30 Miles instead of 12. I found many People there. When I told
my Necessity—how sick I was with long fasting—Horse jaded and
tir'd—My Self Weary and faint thro' fatigue and Cold, and took
out Money to desire Refreshments He would not comply nor sell
me a Blade of fodder, a Glass of Liquor (tho' he own'd he had 2
Barrels of Rum in House) nor permit me to sit down nor kindle
up a Fire—All my arguments were in vain. He looked on me as an
Wolf strayed into Christs fold to devour the Lambs of Grace.
Thus did this rigid Presbyterian treat me. At length I got a
little Indian Corn for my Horse paying treble Price. Such was
the Honesty of the Saint.——30 [miles]; 1557 [total miles]. I proceeded along thro' the Country knowing that if I steered a due
West Course I should strike the Great Road leading down to Pine
Tree,[29] and after crossing several Creeks, and getting very wet I

29. A petition from the Waterees in 1752 asked for a road from Beard's
Ferry on the Santee northward to the Catawba nation. The Assembly ap-

struck it, not far from the Province Line about 2 in the afternoon being about 10 Miles too far North of my intended Rout[e].——— 15 [miles]

Here I waited for Passengers, and got Information that some Church People lived about 10 or 12 Miles off whom I at length found, and was kindly received—But they had nothing to give save a little Milk—My Concern was for my Horse who held out to Admiration—I got dry'd and shifted, and had a dry, but cold Lodging—In the Morning, the Man conducted me forward on my Journey.——10 [miles]

I call'd at the House of the Presbyterian Pastor, who knew me. But they denyed being at home—Not being willing to give offence to his flock in entertaining a person who was drawing off the People from them.

From hence I was carried to the House of the principal Church Man in these Parts, but he was from home. His Son piloted me to the River—and after swimming Rocky Creek and Fishing Creek got to Rocky Mount soon after Night but wet to the Skin—My Horse worn out and my Self quite exhausted. Here we both got some Refreshment but Mr. Kershaw being from home, our fare was but indifferent.——35 [miles]

Next day the People in Fishing Creek came to wait on me and told me that they expected me as last Sunday agreeable to my Advertisement—and that a Multitude met from distant Places and above 30 Children brought for Baptism—This surpriz'd me as I had sent up no such advertisement—So resolved to search into this Presbyterian Trick.——1587 [miles]

Proceeded on my journey upwards—and on the 10th gave Sermon to the Congregation at Little River—I found the Scarcity of Provisions here, greater than on other Side of the River, and not a Bushel of Corn to be had for Money—Nor Necessaries of any Kinds and the poor People almost starving—I was supplied with Bacon and Eggs—but having liv'd a fortnight on this my Stomach became quite Sick—No Bread, Butter, Milk or any thing else to be had.——25 [miles]

---

proved, and the road was finished as far as Pine Tree Hill by 1755 and to the Waxhaws by about 1760. Meriwether, *Expans. of S. C.*, 106-7. See Robert Mills, *Atlas of the State of South Carolina* (Philadelphia, 1825).

Here I baptiz'd a very sensible, and agreeable Young Woman who in Name of her family and Neighbours invited me to come to head of the Wateree Creek, to baptize her Brothers Sisters, and many Others.

I proceeded to Sandy River—and on the 17th my large Congregation there assembled. I proposed crossing of Broad River to go among the Episcopalians at Fair Forrest, and so on to the Cherokee Country—But Deputies arrived from them acquainting me with their Scarcity and Want of all Provisions and Necessaries, desiring I would defer my Journey.——35 [miles]

Wednesday I went to the family on the Wateree Creek a most romantic Situation—a fine farm, and neat decent People. Here my Horse was took good Care off, and I got some Milk, and a fowl broil'd—the 1st fresh Meat had tasted for some time. I was very weak and reduc'd in flesh, Yet made a long Discourse, on the Subject of Baptism and Regeneration—The Congregation was the best drest, and wellbehav'd sensible religious People that have met with in these Parts. I baptized 5 Adults and 10 Infants—and at their Desire appointed a Day when I would return and administer to them the Holy Sacrament—The Evening was spent in Singing.

I had a good Bed and warm Lodging—which much refresh'd me—but the weather being very Cold and Moist I wanted something better than cold Water to support me under my fatigues.— 1647 [total miles]

The next Day it rain'd hard, and I had a Congregation downward to attend the Day following—They undertook to show me a shorter Path than by the Common Road and sent a Guide with me. I set off in midst of the bad Weather as they told me I had but 15 Miles to go.

The Guide went with me but 3 Miles—when being very wet, he quitted me and returned back—nor could be persuaded to advance. He gave me directions—but they were quite wrong, and I found that he was quite Ignorant, and had imposed both on my Self and the People.

Here I was left to wander amidst Bogs, Rocks, Defiles, Swamps, Thickets and Morasses—Not knowing which way to steer, as the Sun did not shine—I passed two Creeks up to my Waist in Water, and at length got into the proper Path—But when I came to Side of the Creek, it was so swollen by the Rains, so deep and rapid, that it was impossible to cross it: Night came on—My Self and Horse were spent, and the Creature dying for Hunger—Never was so backward or Cold a Spring known in this Clime. Not a Blade of Grass or Leaf on the Trees, tho' at this Season the Country is generally in Verdure—On the Banks of this Stream I was obliged to pass the Night in my Wet Cloaths it raining hard all Night, and freezing in the Morning—When Day Light appear'd I rode back 8 Miles to a Cabbin to get Assistance—The People came back with me, and felled Trees across the Stream and got over to the other Side, where they made my Situation known to Captain Dougharty.[30]——40 [miles]; 16 [miles]; 1703 [total miles]

This Good Man with his People ventur'd their Lives and brought me over on fallen Trees—They took the Horse and carried him lower down to an Island, where was Eddy Water, and so swam him over—The Captains family dryed my Cloaths and warm'd me but I was so stiff, and so spent as to be unable to move—I sent to the Congregation that I could not attend but desir'd they would come on Sunday to Rocky Mount where I desir'd the People to convey me as quick as possible lest I should grow too sick and weak to be remov'd. They accordingly got Horses ready and carried me across the Country to Rocky Mount —But the Motion of the Horse brought on my Sickness Having fasted so long, nor had any Refreshments and enduring so much Cold, A Pleurisy seized me—I had most severe Vomitings and Sickness, and had such severe Pains and Spasms that ev'ry Step of the Horse, was as if a Stab in the Vitals.——10 [miles]

Having undergone Great Misery, I was brought to Mr. Kershaws in this sad State, where I lay till End of the Month, when I was so far recovered, as to get down by slow Movements to Pine

---

30. This may have been Cornelius Dougharty, formerly a fur trader with the Cherokee Indians during the 1750's. John H. Logan, *A History of the Upper Country of South Carolina* (Charleston, 1859), 383, 434-35; Edward McCrady, *The History of South Carolina under the Royal Government 1719-1776* (New York, 1899), 271; Meriwether, *Expans. of S. C.*, 132, 192; Chapman J. Milling, *Red Carolinians* (Chapel Hill, 1940), 268-69.

Tree—but reduc'd to a Skeleton, and as weak as any Infant.——
36 [miles]

I made shift however to give Sermon the 1st May tho' could
hardly speak, as I did on the 8th when growing tir'd of Confinement and having no Company or Conversation I went up to
Lynch's Creek, and married and baptized there.——30 [miles]

Here I bargain'd for a pleasant Hill to build me a small House
on, and to retire from Pine Tree.[31]

How dismal the Case—How hard the Lot of any Gentleman in
this Part of the World! No Physician—No Medicines—No Necessaries—Nurses, or Care in Sickness. If You are taken in any
Disorder, there You must lye till Nature gets the better of the
Disease, or Death relieves You, Tis the fashion of these People to
abandon all Persons when Sick, instead of visiting them—So that
a Stranger who has no Relatives or Connexions, is in a most Terrible Situation! [32]——1779 [total miles]

The same as for Society and Converse—I have not yet met with
one literate, or travel'd Person—No ingenious Mind—None of
any Capacity—Only some few well dispos'd Religious Persons,
but whose Knowledge is very circumscribed.

From Lynchs Creek I crossed the Country by Way of Beaver
Creek and gave a Sermon there to the New Imported Irish, who
behav'd very reverently, and were very thankful.[33] The Weather
comes on Mild, and the Leaves and Grass appear. The Waters
begin to retreat and the Creeks become fordable. So that I got
over them all without Danger, and on the 22d gave Sermon at
Rocky Mount.——30 [miles]

From thence I crossed over toward Broad River to Jacksons

31. In Sermon Book, II, [358] the ground plan of a house is superimposed
upon the manuscript sermon.

32. In a sermon given at the High Hills, July 8, 1770, and at Rafting
Creek, July 15, 1770, Woodmason urged that attention be paid to those
who were ill: "And let me exhort You to visit one another when sick, and to
render all Kind and neighbourly offices each to the other in these Cases: Do
all You can to comfort and relieve them—Give them good Advice—and exhort
them to Repentence and Amendment of Life, should it please God they
recover." Sermon Book, II, [433], [454].

33. These may have been all or part of the 270 Irish who arrived in Charleston on two ships on February 10, 1768. McCrady, Hist. of S. C., 593.

Creek, where a large Body of People met me on
to whom I preach'd twice and baptis'd their Childr
many serious and religious Persons, and promis'
again in July and administer to them. From hen
the Country and after baptizing at several Places returned to
Pine Tree.——25 [miles]; 60 [miles]

In all these Excursions, I am obliged to carry my own Neces-
saries with me—As Bisket—Cheese—A Pint of Rum—Some Sugar
—Chocolate—Tea, or Coffee—With Cups Knife Spoon Plate
Towels and Linen. So that I go alway[s] heavy loaded like a
Trooper. If I did not, I should starve. Never will I be Out again
from home for a Month together to take the Chance of things—
As in many Places they have nought but a Gourd to drink out off
Not a Plate Knife or Spoon, a Glass, Cup, or any thing—It is
well if they can get some Body Linen, and some have not even
that. They are so burthen'd with Young Children, that the
Women cannot attend both House and Field—And many live by
Hunting, and killing of Deer—There's not a Cabbin but has 10
or 12 Young Children in it—When the Boys are 18 and Girls 14
they marry—so that in many Cabbins You will see 10 or 15
Children. Children and Grand Children of one Size—and the
mother looking as Young as the Daughter.[34] Yet these Poor
People enjoy good Health; and are generally cut off by Endemic
or Epidemic Disorders, which when they happen, makes Great
Havock among them.——1894 [total miles]

June 4. being the Kings Birth Day, all the People round me got
drunk so that had but 40 Persons to attend Service on the 5th they
being all laid up—A Presbyterian fellow carried off the Key of the
Meeting House, whereby made it 12. o'th Clock Service began.
On the 8th went over the River to baptize and marry.——30
[miles]

34. Out of the thirty or more families Governor Dobbs of North Carolina
saw on his Rocky River lands near the undefined border between North
Carolina and South Carolina he found "not less than from 5 or 6 to 10
children in each family." Gov. Dobbs to the Board of Trade, Newbern,
Aug. 24, 1755, *Col. Recs. of N. C.*, V, 355. In the above passage Woodmason
is apparently referring to two generations in "many Cabbins" with "Children
and Grand Children of one Size."

The 12th went to the Lower Congregation at Lynchs Creek. Weather exceeding hot but Country delightfully pleasant. Rather too wet for the Season. Having a long Service and many Children to baptize. Got a Great Hoarseness and Sore throat by my Long and Loud Speaking.——40 [miles]

Monday the 13th Went down to St Marks Church to meet the Vestry there, in order to draw them up a Letter to the Bishop to send them over a Minister, but they (according to Custom for 3 Years past) could not make a Board.——100 [miles]

It seems, that one of them was Contractor for building the Church and Parsonage—and has not yet fulfilled his Contract. When a Minister comes, he will be obliged—therefore he staves it off, as long he can, and the Interests of Religion the Church, and People suffer—Corruption and Jobbing are as well understood here, as in the Old Country: All is Venial—Moral Honesty is hard to be found: and Vital Christianity, not at all.——2064 [total miles]

Returned Home very jaded—and find my Self too weak and too greatly reduc'd to take Long, or many Journeys—And shall never be the Man, as before, am so lowered. I have sent to Town for Refreshments having had nothing but Tea and Coffee by me, these 12 Months. Spirituous Liquors, none save what my Good Samaritan will now and then put in my Bags, when I travel. And my Stipend, has not yet paid the Expence of my Outset here, and the many Articles provided for the Poor, and raising the different Congregations, and my travelling Charges.

I have unravelled the Mystery of the Advertisement set up at the Waxaws. 'Twas done by one John Gaston a Justice of Peace among these Presbyterians, to have a Laugh at the Church People. He has also set up to marry People, and has actually married Several Couple, tho' his own Pastor lives but few Miles from Him—There is a strict Law against all this—And altho' I have got Depositions against this Wretch, I can find none to serve. And We are so far from the Supream Court, as not to be able to obtain Writs from thence, and make Return, within the Time prescrib'd.[35]

35. In 1770, Woodmason finally wrote to Justice Rawlins Lowndes to complain that John Gaston "formerly a Justice of Peace" had created disorder

I have obtain'd Account how many Children—and how many Couple, the Dissenting Teacher married this last Year. Married 140 Couple—All of whom ought to have come to me, add to which those married contrary to Law by the Magistrates here, and in North Carolina maybe 140 Couple more (at least) He baptiz'd 303 Children Not all of this Province. So that with the Magistrates, this Teacher—Itinerant Ministers, and my Self, about 300 Couple was married in my Distric this last Year, and about 1200 Children baptiz'd—By which You may judge of the Multitude committed to my Care.

But instead of having more Ministers to do Duty, their Number lessen daily—The Itinerant station'd to the Southward of me having made about 1000 Guineas clear, is retir'd home. The Ministers of St James's and St Stephens Santee, are remov'd elsewhere—Those of St Andrew's St Philips and others, gone to England for Health, or on Business—and 2 or 3 lately come over, do not relish the Climate, and are gone back—We have not now more than 10 or 12 Clergymen in this large, and rich Province. So that my Duty grows heavier and more weighty ev'ry Day— While I am wearing away, and almost destroyed by the Great Burden on my Shoulders.

You may ask how it is that I imagine to compose, or compile Discourses? This is an hard Task on me, as what suits one Congregation and Sett of People, will not another. One Class shall be a vile disorderly Crew. The Address to them will not suit a serious Moral Community—It is this Midnight Work of Study and Writing that much impairs me—for when I come off a Journey of 100 Miles jaded, sweated, and exhausted, Instead of resting and refreshing I must go to the Desk, and write for the next Sunday, or meeting of some particular Congregation—Or, as the Season calls.

As to Itinerant Ministers) You must understand that all (or

---

by performing marriages. With his complaint he submitted an affidavit of one James Adams who had attended such marriage ceremonies. The letter was brought to Council by Lieutenant-Governor Bull, who was advised "to referr the Papers to the Attorney General to form such a Prosecution on them against the said John Gaston as might be proper on this Occasion." Council Journal, Sept. 4, 1770. There is nothing to show the outcome of this referral.

greatest Part) of this Part of the Province w[h]ere I am, has been settled within these 5 Years by Irish Presbyterians from Belfast, or Pensylvania and they imagin'd that they could secure this large Tract of fine Country to themselves and their Sect. Hereon, they built Meeting Houses, and got Pastors from Ireland, and Scotland. But with these there has also a Great Number of New Lights and Independants come here from New England, and many Baptists from thence, being driven from, and not able to live there among the Saints—Some of these maintain their Teachers. But to keep up their Interests, and preserve their People from falling off to the Church established, and to keep them in a Knott together, the Synods of Pensylvania and New England send out a Sett of Rambling fellows Yearly—who do no Good to the People, no Service to Religion—but turning of their Brains and picking of their Pockets of ev'ry Pistreen the Poor Wretches have, return back again, with double the Profits I can make—for tho' the Law gives me 12/6 Currency for ev'ry Baptism, I never yet took one farthing—and of near 100 Couple that I've married, I have not been paid for 1/3. Their Poverty is so Great, that were they to offer me a fee, my Heart would not let me take it.

'Tis these roving Teachers that stir up the Minds of the People against the Establish'd Church, and her Ministers—and make the Situation of any Gentleman extremely uneasy, vexatious, and disagreeable. I would sooner starve in England on a Curacy of 20£ p ann, than to live here on 200 Guineas, did not the Interests of Religion and the Church absolutely require it—Some few of these Itinerants have encountered me—I find them a Sett of Rhapsodists—Enthusiasts—Bigots—Pedantic, illiterate, impudent Hypocrites—Straining at Gnats, and swallowing Camels, and making Religion a Cloak for Covetuousness Detraction, Guile, Impostures and their particular Fabric of Things.

Among these Quakers and Presbyterians, are many concealed Papists—They are not tolerated in this Government—And in the Shape of New Light Preachers, I've met with many Jesuits. We have too here a Society of *Dunkards*—these resort to hear me when I am over at Jacksons Creek.[36]

36. Some Dunkers, originally from Pennsylvania, settled near Beaver Creek about 1748 and associated for religious purposes by July, 1759. Jackson's Creek

Among this Medley of Religions—True Genuine Christianity is not to be found. And the perverse persecuting Spirit of the Presbyterians, displays it Self much more here than in Scotland. It is dang'rous to live among, or near any of them—for if they cannot cheat, rob, defraud or injure You in Your Goods—they will belye, defame, lessen, blacken, disparage the most valuable Person breathing, not of their Communion in his Character, Good Name, or Reputation and Credit. They have almost worm'd out all the Church People—who cannot bear to live among such a Sett of Vile unaccountable Wretches.

These Sects are eternally jarring among themselves—The Presbyterians hate the Baptists far more than they do the Episcopalians, and so of the Rest—But (as in England) they will unite altogether—in a Body to distress or injure the Church establish'd.

Hence it is, that when any Bills have been presented to the Legislature to promote the Interests of Religion, these Sectaries have found Means to have them overruled, for the leading Men of the House being all Lawyers, those People know how to grease Wheels to make them turn.

If Numbers were to be counted here, the Church People would have the Majority—But in Point of Interest, I judge that the Dissenters possess most Money—and thereby they can give a Bias to things at Pleasure.[37]

The Grand Juries have presented as a Greivance, the Shame and Damage arising from such Itinerant Teachers being suffer'd to ramble about—They have even married People under my Eye in defiance of all Laws and Regulations—And I can get no Redress—I do all the Duty—take all the Pains. If there is a Shilling to be got by a Wedding or Funeral, these Impudent fellows will endeavour to pocket it: and are the most audacious of any Sett of Mortals I ever met with—They beat any Medicinal Mountebank.

Such is the General State of Religion in these Parts delegated to me, and yet, when it is laid out into Parishes, and all Ferments

was a short distance westward of Beaver Creek. See Townsend, *S. C. Baptists*, 167.

37. It is not clear whether Woodmason is speaking of South Carolina or of the Backcountry.

subside, I query if I get a Parish or Settlement among them—for, so far from being thanked for my Labours, many, even of our Clergy, say, I do too much—My Activity displays their Indolence. None yet among them ever went out of his Parish, nay not even round his Parish to baptize—and I have seen in Charlestown, Children brought to the font to be baptized, and the Minister put them off till another Day, because he was going to Dinner, or Tea, or Company. If such cannot forgo a Meal for an Hour, how would they go without any Sustenance save Indian Meal and Water, or Bacon and Eggs for a Month, and that but once in 24 Hours? Or taste nothing better than Water for 6 Months together, and ride 200 Miles ev'ry Week, or Month?

I must freely say, that it has been owing to the Inattention and Indolence of the Clergy, that the Sectaries have gain'd so much Ground here. While they could sit down Easy and Quiet, enjoying the Delicacies of Life, they thought no more of the Church, or of her Interests than of the Empire of Japan.

I have not as yet been over above half my District—Have not been able to get over Broad River, where never yet a Church Minister has been seen—and for want of whom, they are devour'd by Swarms of different Teachers. A very large Body of People lye East of me, whom I've never as yet seen—There are 50 or 60 Adults to baptize, and 3 or 400 Children—Between them and me lyes a sandy barren Desart 40 Miles over, without Tree, Bush, Water, House or Inhabitant—So that without a Guide I should be utterly lost and perish—I sent a Poor Man over to them last Summer, to desire them to send over Horses and a Guide—He got lost in this Wilderness, and was found with his Saddle under Him— We knew his Loss by his Horse coming home. This Syrtes cannot be travelled in the Summer on Account of the Flies, and Muskettos, which are so numerous, they would sting Man and Horse to Death—It is only passable Spring and Fall.[38]

They have now got a Schoolmaster at this Place. An old Presbyterian fellow, or between that and a Quaker—They send their Children to him readily, and pay him, tho' they would not to me,

---

38. Woodmason here describes the sand hills, apparently from hearsay information. These hills are now wastes of sand covered with scrub oak or pine trees. See Meriwether, *Expans. of S. C.*, 3, 9, and map, p. 2.

who would have educated them Gratis. Such is their atachment to
their Kirk:—Some call me a Jesuit—and the Liturgy the Mass—
I have observ'd what Tricks they would have play'd on Christ-
mas Day, to have disturbed the People. I will mention another.

Not long after, they hir'd a Band of rude fellows to come to
Service who brought with them 57 Dogs (for I counted them)
which in Time of Service they set fighting, and I was obliged to
stop—In Time of Sermon they repeated it—and I was oblig'd
to desist and dismiss the People. It is in vain to take up or commit
these lawless Ruffians—for they have nothing, and the Charge of
sending of them to Charlestown, would take me a Years Salary—
We are without any Law, or Order—And as all the Magistrates
are Presbyterians, I could not get a Warrant—If I got Warrants
as the Constables are Presbyterians likewise, I could not get them
serv'd—If serv'd, the Guard would let them escape—Both my
Self and other Episcopals have made this Experiment—They
have granted me Writs thro' fear of being complain'd off, but
took Care not to have them serv'd—I took up one fellow for a
Riot at a Wedding, and creating disturbance—The people took
up two others for entering the House where I was when in Bed—
stealing my Gown—putting it on—and then visiting a Woman
in Bed, and getting to Bed to her, and making her give out next
day, that the Parson came to Bed to her—This was a Scheme laid
by the Baptists—and Man and Woman prepared for the Purpose.
The People likewise took up some others for calling of me Jesuit,
and railing against the Service—The Constable let them all
loose—No bringing of them to Justice—I enter'd Informations
against some Magistrates for marrying—but cannot get them out
of the other Justices Hands till too late to send to Town for a
Judges Warrant.

Another Time (in order to disapoint me of a Congregation,
and to laugh at the People) they posted a Paper, signifying, That
the King having discovered the Popish Designs of Mr. Woodmason and other Romish Priests in disguise, to bring in Popery
and Slavery, had sent over Orders to suspend them all, and to
order them to be sent over to England, so that there would be
no more preaching for the future. This was believed by some of
the Poor Ignorants, and kept them at home.

The Quakers have not been silent any more than their Brethren. This Place was laid out as an Asylum for them. But being unsupported from home, they are come to Nothing—They posted a most virulent Libel at the Meeting House—ridiculing the Liturgy particularly the Absolution—Blessing, and Cross in Baptism—calling me by Name an old Canting Parson—I keep the paper by me, and would have sent it over to Dr. Fotheringall [39] and the Friends at their Yearly Meeting but for the earnest Intreaty of Mr. Wyly, who begg'd that I would not detriment the whole Body, for sake of a few Individuals—I complied for Peace sake, tho' I knew him to be privy to it. The Reason why these People are not much regarded from home is, that they are a vile, licentious Pack—Absolute Deists unfit the Title of Christians— and I know but of one Person of a serious sober Cast among them.

What I could not effect by Force—or Reason—I have done by Sarcasm—for at the Time when they sent the fellows with their Dogs, one of the Dogs followed me down here—which I carried to the House of one of the principals—and told Him that I had 57 Presbyterians came that Day to Service, and that I had converted one of them, and brought Him home—I left the Dog with Him—This Joke has made them so extremely angry that they could cut my Throat—But I've gained my Aim, having had no disturbance from them since—for if a Presbyterian now shews his face at Service, our People ask him if he is come to be *Converted*. So Shame has driven them away.[40]

39. This is almost certainly a reference to Samuel Fothergill (1715-1772), a prominent English Quaker. During the years 1754-1756, Fothergill traveled extensively in the American colonies where he visited Quakers in widely scattered places. In 1760 he was appointed a member of a committee to visit all the quarterly and other meetings in England. "Samuel Fothergill," *Dictionary of National Biography*, VII, 508-9.

40. In a note appended to an anti-Presbyterian sermon, Woodmason lists a number of examples of the "Insolencies and Audacity" of the Irish Presbyterians and New Light Baptists. From the contents, it is apparent that the note was written as a brief memorandum, probably some years after the incidents described: "At the Congaree Chapel, they enter'd and partly tore down the Pulpit—At St Marks a Sett of Waggoners got round the Church with their Whips, and oblig'd the Minister to quit the Service. On Whitsunday following after the Communion was ended, they got into the Church and left their Excrements on the Communion Table, and at Lynchs Creek they

Whom but an Heart of Oak could bear up Firm against such Torrents of Malice, Bigotry, and Impudence! Sustain their Calumnies and bear with their Insolence—Which I pass over with that Christian Meekness and Compassion becoming my Function—and the Contempt and Derision befitting a Gentleman.

I am exactly in the same situation with the Clergy of the primitive Church, in midst of the Heathens, Arians, and Hereticks—and endeavour like them to make my Life and Converse agreeable and unexceptionable (tho' its next to an impossibility) and to be all things to all Men that I may gain some; and yet I cannot please All. To engage the Dissenters I give an extempore prayer before Sermon, and sometimes an extempore Discourse—but this disgusts the Church People, and made severals with draw.——2064 [total miles]

June 16. Came up from St. Marks to Pine Tree, and next Day went down to Swift Creek, where married 2 Couple and baptiz'd several Adults and Young Children—Sunday the 19th at the Meeting House at Pine Tree—The Presbyterians carried off the Key—But some Persons got in and open'd the Doors—The Magistrate attended—but had but a small Congregation the Principal People generally riding abroad ev'ry Sunday for Recreation.——20 [miles]

The open profanation of the Lords Day in this Povince is one of the most crying Sins in it—and is carried to a great height—Among the low Class, it is abus'd by Hunting fishing fowling, and Racing—By the Women in frolicing and Wantoness. By others in Drinking Bouts and Card Playing—Even in and about Charlestown, the Taverns have more Visitants than the Churches.[41]

---

oblig'd the People to desist from building a Chapel. At Congarees, the Baptist Teacher entered at head of his Gang, and began preaching when the Minister had ended. They built a Meeting House close to the Chapel, and obliged the Minister to quit his Residence. But the Insults and Vexations which private Persons sustain'd in their Property and Business is not to be expressed." Sermon Book, III, [742].

41. A visitor from New England wrote similarly of Charleston in 1773: "The Sabbath is a day of visiting and mirth with the rich, and of licence, pastime and frolic for the negroes. The blacks I saw in great numbers playing pawpaw, huzzle-cap, pitch penny, and quarrelling round the doors of the Churches in service-time; and as to their priests—Voltaire says 'always speak

Friday the 24th Set off for the Wateree Creek, and pass'd up on the Western Side of the River where had never befor been—Very graciously received by People of all Denominations, who were very earnest and solicitous that I would come over and give them Sermons—But I need have a Royal Stud of Horses, and a Constitution of Iron and Brass to repair to all these Places—More especially as I can seldom get Provisions to eat—for did I not carry Victuals with me, I absolutely should starve. The Poor People are now getting in their Wheat and Barley which brings them Bread but hundreds have not a Mouthful of Meat—But are reduc'd to the sad Necessity of gathering Apples Peaches &c green from the Trees, and boiling them for food.

Sunday 26. Gave Sermon at Captain Doughartys to about 400 Persons—Baptiz'd 24 Infants—2 Adults and married a Couple—Numbers of Bastard Children brought from Time to Time to be baptized.——36 [miles]

### Congregations rais'd in 1768.

| | | | Communicants |
|---|---|---|---|
| 22.[42] | Little River. 50 Miles N.W. from Pine Tree | 200 Auditors | 10 |
| 23. | Browns Creek. 70 Miles N.E. | 300 | 6 |
| 24. | Jackson's Creek. 50 Miles W. | 200 | 16 |
| 25. | Lower Part of Wateree Creek. N.W. 36 Miles | 100 | 9 |
| 26. | Lower Part of Little Lynchs Creek. N.E. 30 Miles | 80 | 2 |
| 27. | Grave's Ford and Sawneys Creek N.W. 12 Miles | 150 | |

### Journal Continued.

June 27. [total] miles 2120. Came to Rocky Mount on the 28th Pass'd the Wateree Rivers and when on Cedar Creek taken in the Greatest Storm of Rain Thunder and Lightning ever was in—Wet

---

well of the prior.' The slaves who don't frolic on the Sabbath, do all kinds of work for themselves on hire." "Journal of Josiah Quincy," Mass. Hist. Soc., *Procs.*, 49 (1915-16), 455.

42. The numbers of the congregations continue the list of those raised in 1767. See p. 26.

to the Back Bone. Got to a Planters, where shifted and dry'd—In Afternoon set off for Hanging Rock—Next day visited the Congregation at Granny Quarter Creek and returned to Pine Tree. Disapointed in receiving Necessaries from Charlestown—No Waggons going down at this Season—Reduc'd to live on Dry Bisket and Water. No Meat to be bought for Money—Wherefore try to catch Fish, and Boil Rice, and eat it with Milk.——30 [miles]; 25 [miles]

July 3. Officiated at Pine Tree (now to be call'd Camden [43] in Honor of Lord Cambden (the Americans being very fond at present of all who declar'd in their favor against the Stamp Act. As I was intended for a Distributor, I thereby lost their Affections, and shall never more regain them.)

July 6th. Went to upper Lynchs Creek, and back next day to Cambden. The People in Great distress for want of Meat and Meal. They have had a good Wheat Barley and Oat Harvest, but the Upper Brooks are dry, and the Mills stand Still, having no Water to grind.——65 [miles]

July 17. Officiated in the Meeting House at Cambden. Found a Paper stuck in the Pulpit, signifying that they should lock up the Meeting and admit no Preachers but their own. Had a large Congregation to hear me for the last Time the People being preadvis'd of it, but I knew not their Intention till this Morning.——[total] Miles 2240

Am told that this Meeting House was built by 4 persons at their private Cost, for the whole Body, and they were to be paid by Sale of the Pews. Now while I officiate they'l not buy the Pews, nor subscribe to their expected Teacher—and the Owners resolve not to suffer any Duty to be done there by any one, till they are reimbursed. But the Pews are too high for these Poor Bigots to purchase being 10 Guineas each Pew, and the House not yet ceil'd or finish'd.

Their Teacher is expected in September. He demands 100£ Sterling P annum—This they cannot raise—So their Meeting will be shut up forever.

43. The change of name, attributed to Joseph Kershaw, occurred some time between February 13 and April 12, 1768. Kirkland and Kennedy, *Historic Camden*, 12, 94-95.

One of the Undertakers offer'd to sell me his 4th Part for 30£ Sterling. If our late Cheif Justice had liv'd he determin'd to purchase the whole Fabric, and to have routed this Crew. For altho' he was a Gentleman of Ireland, yet he abominated these Northern Scotch Irish and they are certainly the worst Vermin on Earth.

After Service the Episcopalians waited on Mr. Kershaw the Proprietor of this Village to know if he would build a Church or Chapel, or hire a Room for Performance of Divine Service—but he declined—fearful of giving offence to his Good Customers the Presbyterians: Whereon the People sign'd me a Certificate to the Governor and Council, testifying that I could not do Duty at this Place thro' Want of a Room to assemble the People in.

Thursday 21. Went over the Wateree River with a Horse loaded with Provisions and Necessaries—and went to the House where Guides were to be provided to conduct me to Broad River but they disapointed me.——[total] Miles 2240

22. An excessive hot sultry Day. Rode to Graves' Ford where a midling Congregation attended, they not having had due Notice. I expected a Great Number of Baptists and New Lights here, as they are numerous in this Quarter so gave a suitable Discourse.

Hir'd 3 Men to carry my Baggage, and to guide thro' the Woods cross the Country—Set off after Sermon, intending to ride all Night for Coolness—Rode 20 Miles in this Wilderness (where never had before been) before Night—When my Guides after they had drank out my Liquor, left me to shift for my Self.

Travell'd alone in a dreary Forrest—Lost the Path travers'd the Woods all Night, and in Morning found my Self just where I was at Sun Set. Excessive thirsty and weary—Walk'd near 30 Miles this Night in the Woods.

Altho' I could scarce stand, yet led my loaded Horse 12 Miles, to my appointed place on Jackson's Creek where I almost expired with faintness—Was put to Bed, and took Great Care off. ——80 [miles]

Sunday 31) A handsome Congregation attended—Had but 9 Communicants, tho' 20 had given in their Names. Baptized several Children and married several. What with the Weddings Christianings 2 Sermons—Long prayers—Catechising—Singing—

and the Communion, I was on my Legs from 8 to 6—quite spent—
and so faint and wearied, that could take no Sustenance.

Monday August 1. Stomach too weak to eat. Tho' very weak,
and the Weather hot, rode across the Country down the Wateree
Creek, to attend the Congregation as next day. Rested well this
Week, and taken great Care off by the People, a great many being
gather'd to bid me Welcome.——20 [miles]; [total] miles 2340

Tuesday) A large Congregation and baptized sundry Children.
Married a Couple, who imprudently (or impudently) left the
Service and staid not to Sermon, carrying with them 1/2 the
Congregation to frolic and dance. After Sermon rode 12 Miles
to give the Communion to a Sick and dying Person, and then
went to Rocky Mount.——20 [miles]

Wednesday) Baptiz'd a family of New Lights, whom I have
been lab'ring these 12 Months to reclaim: Went forward to Beaver
Creek.——25 [miles]

Thursday 4. Gave Service and Sermon at Beaver Creek to a
mix'd Multitude. Went cross the Country to Hanging Rock Creek,
and took a Surveyor with me.——15 [miles]

Friday) Surveyed 100 acres of Land, intending to build and live
on it—Petitioned the Governor and Council for it to be settled
on such Church, or Chapel as may be founded in these parts.

Saturday) Went up the Country to the Province Line, and very
hospitably received by the People.——40 [miles]

Sunday) Had a large Audience—Many came 20, 30 Miles out of
North Carolina—Baptiz'd Children till was weary. My discourse
pleas'd so well, they said I was inspired. Monday—Went down
Great Lynchs Creek: and on Tuesday gave Sermon to a mix'd
Congregation of Dissenters, and Strangers.——20 [miles]

It having been a common Taunt by the Dissenters, that the
Church Ministers could not preach or pray Extempore as their
Teachers did &c. &c. the Episcopalians begged me to preach
Extempore to convince these Gainsayers to the Contrary, whose
Request I complied with—My Prayer and Sermon was an Hour
and a Quarter. This the 1st time of attempting any thing of this
Sort and I acquitted my Self greatly to their Satisfaction. The
Dissenters were confounded and astonished and the Church
People, pleas'd and delighted. An Old Gentleman (a Capital Per-

son among them) took me home to his House—treated me very
genteely (in their Way) introduc'd me to his Daughter (an agreeable Girl) and offer'd her in Marriage—But I declin'd the offer—
she being too Young for me—Next day I returned to Cambden.——15 [miles]; [total] Miles 2475; 35 [miles]

In this Circuit of a fortnight I've eaten Meat but thrice, and
drank nought but Water—Subsisting on my Bisket and Rice
Water and Musk Melons, Cucumbers, Green Apples and Peaches
and such Trash. By which am reduc'd very thin. It is impossible
that any Gentleman not season'd to the Clime, could sustain this—
It would kill 99 out of 100—Nor is this a Country, or place where
I would wish any Gentleman to travel, or settle, altho' Religion
and the State requires a Number of Ministers—Their Ignorance
and Impudence is so very high, as to be past bearing—Very few
can read—fewer write—Out of 5000 that have attended Sermon
this last Month, I have not got 50 to sign a Petition to the Assembly. They are very Poor—owing to their extreme Indolence for
they possess the finest Country in America, and could raise but
ev'ry thing. They delight in their present low, lazy, sluttish, heathenish, hellish Life, and seem not desirous of changing it. Both
Men and Women will do any thing to come at Liquor, Cloaths,
furniture, &c. &c. rather than work for it—Hence their many
Vices—their gross Licentiousness Wantonness, Lasciviousness,
Rudeness, Lewdness, and Profligacy they will commit the grossest
Enormities, before my face, and laugh at all Admonition.

Last Sunday I distributed the last Parcel of Mr. Warings Tracts
on Prayer. It is very few families whom I can bring to join in
Prayer, because most of them are of various Opinions the Husband a Churchman, Wife, a Dissenter, Children nothing at all.
My Bibles and Common Prayers have been long gone, and I
have given away to amount of £20 of Practical Books, besides
those I received of the Society—Few or no Books are to be found
in all this vast Country, beside the Assembly, Catechism, Watts
Hymns, Bunyans Pilgrims Progress—Russells—Whitefields and
Erskines Sermons. Nor do they delight in Historical Books or in
having them read to them, as do our Vulgar in England for these
People despise Knowledge, and instead of honouring a Learned
Person, or any one of Wit or Knowledge be it in the Arts, Sciences,

or Languages, they despise and Ill treat them—And this Spirit prevails even among the Principals of this Province.——[total] Miles 2510

Now will come on their Season of Festivity and Drunkenness— The Stills will be soon at Work for to make Whisky and Peach Brandy—In this Article, both Presbyterians and Episcopals very charitably agree (Viz.) That of getting Drunk.

Saturday August 6th) Set off to Beaver Creek—Overtaken by heavy Thunder Storm, and Wet to the Skin. Obliged to stay at White Oak Creek, at a Cabbin, for to dry my Self and Cloaths.

This was a lucky Circumstance for a Poor Woman just by, who was in Labour, and could get but two Women, and no Midwife to attend her. By my Care and Skill she was happily deliv'd, and I had innumerable Blessings bestowed on Me.——25 [miles]

Sunday 7th) Pursu'd my Journey, conducted by several Persons. Had a very numerous Congregation—Deputies came from the Places above offering to build me an House and Chapel if I would come and reside with them. To which could give no Answer, till their Request was laid before the Governor and Council—However I promised to visit, and give them a Sermon.——10 [miles]

About 10 Miles from this Creek, on East and West Side of the Wateree River, live a Number of Seventh Day Baptists.[44] I read the Laws in force for due Observance of the Lords Day and sent to them to forbear Working, Planting, Riding Carting and other Avocations and not to give Offence to their Christian Brethren by such Illegal Practises or I should carry the Laws into Execution. In Return for my Admonitions, they sent a Message That if I offer'd to come into their Parts for to preach they would give me Corporal Punishment—To such heights of Insolence are these Sectaries grown.——[total miles] 2535

The Congregation desir'd my permission to take them up and commit them to Prison, but I would not suffer it.

Service Ended, I concluded to return home, there being neither Lodging for Self or Horse, nor a Mouthful of Sustenance to be had. And I found my Self very faint thro' the Journey, and

44. A group of Sabbatarians from Pennsylvania had settled in the vicinity of the Broad and Wateree Rivers. John Pearson acted as lay preacher. Meriwether, *Expans. of S. C.,* 157-58; Townsend, *S. C. Baptists,* 172-74.

extream heat of the Weather—Getting Wet—and the Great Length of the Service, having many Children to baptize and People to marry—(All Gratis) and having had neither Supper or Breakfast. I was directed to return by a different Road from which I came up, and found it extream pleasant and Romantic—beautifully diversified with the Paintings of Nature—But about 5 at Night the Sky thickned—Thunder Clouds broke all Around—And I was again wet to the Skin and Bones All my Cloaths and Linen being spoil'd. I got home at 9. in a sad Trim—where went to bed supperless having nothing to comfort me but a little Tea and Brown Sugar wrapped my Self up in my Blanket but could not sleep. It continued thundering and Raining all the Night—Next Day at Noon I visited my Good Samaritan and got some Refreshment and received from Him some Papers and Letters from England.——25 [miles]

Heavy Rains all this Week—Many Applications made to me for Advice in the Physical Way—But for want of Medicines could give no Assistance to the Poor People.

The Schoolmaster of this Villa (altho a Presbyterian) having been drunk for some days past—I gently chid Him for such Misdemeanour—for which he gave me such horrid abuse, that but for the Bystanders, I should have caned Him—and was about to whip a Strumpet whom he keeps for her Lewdness and Prophaneness—but was prevented. And yet there is a Magistrate here [45]—but he is a Presbyterian—So are these Wretches. Instead of this Magistrate punishing these worthless Sinners he protects them—and he had the Assurance to write to me to make them Satisfaction for my Admonitions to them (they not being of my Church he said) or he should indite me for an Assault—This dirty fellow I must report to the Governor and Council: How can Ministers suppress Vice, thus openly countenanc'd and protected?——[total] Miles 2570

Great Insolencies are now committed by those fellows who call themselves *Regulators*—They are [ever ?] wanton in Wickedness and Impudence—And they triumph in their Licentiousness. Its said that above two thousand Presbyterians from North Carolina

45. John-Newman Oglethorpe was justice of the peace in Camden. *S. C. and Amer. Gen. Gaz.*, Dec. 12, 1768.

are coming down to join them—We have but 2 or 3 Magistrates who are Episcopalians in this Vast Back Country—And these they have threatened to Whip for issuing Writs against some of their Lawless Gang. They have actually whipped all the Constables and Sheriffs officers took and tore the Kings Writs—and Judges Writs. Silenced the Constables—Stopp'd payment of all Public Taxes—and We are now without Law, Gospel, Trade, or Money. Insulted by a Pack of vile, levelling common wealth Presbyterians In whom the Republican Spirit of 41 yet dwells, and who would very willingly put the Solemn League and Covenant now in force—Nay, their Teachers press it on them, and say that [it] is as binding on the Consciences of all the Kirk, as the Gospel it Self, for it is a Covenant enter'd into with God, from which they cannot recede.[46]

Wednesday 10) Experienc'd the Effects of getting Wet last Saturday and Sunday, being this day seized with a fever—Sickness at Heart, Extream Lassitude—Griping, Purging—Pain in my Right Side, and Great faintness—Yet move about striving to shake it off. My only Physic being Fasting and Exercise—I attribute this spasmodic Disorder as much to Night Dews as to the Rain and to my Lying about in their open Cold Cabbins—unfloored and almost open to the Sky—These Dews are very pernicious, are vastly, searching, and penetrate to the Vitals—I had last Week Experience of the Velocity and force of the Air—By smelling a Barbicu dressing in the Woods upwards of six Miles—I have made many Remarks and Experiments here both on the State of the Air, and Percussion of Sounds. I can hear a Cannon fir'd from this Place, 10 Miles further than any Thunder in the Horizon. The Nature of the Air here, is but little known, or attended too by the Natives—and yet much depends on it—for Many noxious Damps and Exhalations arise that generate putrid fevers and other Disorders, of which they seem not sensible, nor can be brought to any belief of it.——2570 [total miles]

46. This passage would indicate that Woodmason, like others in the Backcountry, was shocked at the overt defiance of the authority of the Charleston courts. He was also very likely outraged by the activity of the Presbyterians in the Regulator movement. Later, as prominent Anglicans took over some of the leadership, he felt better.

Friday 12) Having promised a Congregation at Grannys Quarter to attend them, I attempted to fulfil my Word, tho' very weak and full of Pain—but was 6 Hours in going 16 Miles—The People almost gave me out—Here I baptiz'd a family of New Lights, and several Children—Married some Whores and Rogues (Gratis) and thro' want of Time to compile a suitable Discourse gave them Dr. Bradfords on Baptism and Spiritual Regeneration.——16 [miles]

Saturday Afternoon I ventur'd to go up to Lynchs Creek tho' extream Weak—and went thro' the Sundays Service—Baptized 10 Children—Married 2 Couple—Publish'd 6 more Couple.—14 [miles]

Solicitations from various Quarters to baptize and preach. The Poor People are hungry after the Word, and ready to devour Me. In the Evening I pass'd to the Spot of Land laid out for my future dwelling, and slept on it for the 1st Time. The People very kind in nursing and attending of me.——6 [miles]

Monday) My Horse got loose and run down to Pine Tree, but the People returned with Him (tho' with loss of Bridle and Housing) in the Evening. Found the fever gone off, and my Strength return'd.

Tuesday August 16. In Consequence of a Promise made, set off this Morning with a Guide for Flatt Creek—Here I found a vast Body of People assembled—Such a Medley! such a mixed Multitude of all Classes and Complexions I never saw. I baptized about 20 Children and Married 4 Couple—Most of these People had never before seen a Minister, or heard the Lords Prayer, Service or Sermon in their Days. I was a Great Curiosity to them—And they were as great Oddities to me. After Service they went to Revelling Drinking Singing Dancing and Whoring—and most of the Company were drunk before I quitted the Spot—They were as rude in their Manners as the Common Savages, and hardly a degree removed from them. Their Dresses almost as loose and Naked as the Indians, and differing in Nothing save Complexion—I could not conceive from whence this vast Body could swarm—But this Country contains ten times the Number of Persons beyond my Apprehension.——[total] Miles 2606

Returned in the Evening to a Gentleman's House 10 Miles

distant and stayed the Night. Next Day went down to Pine
Tree.——25 [miles]; 25 [miles]

Here I found a Packet from the Lieutenant Governor enclos-
ing some Proclamation lately issued for the Rioters to disperse on
Pain of Proscription—with a pardon for all who would remain
Quiet for the future.[47] This I am directed to publish thro' the
Country, and to accompany it with suitable Exhortations.

Tho' vastly fatigu'd—almost famished, and very weak thro'
Heat of the Weather and Pain of traveling (having several Boils
broke out on me and my Skin full of Seed Ticks) Yet I set to
Work to draw up a Discourse suitable to the Subject enjoin'd
Me.[48]

Thursday) Went up the Wateree River to marry and baptize
according to Notice given—Here I published the Proclamation.—
2656 [total miles]

The Licentious Gang of Presbyterians stopt the Governors
Messenger—broke open my Packet to see the Contents and would
have whipp'd the Man, if not prevented: for some among them
fear'd, that if they took this Step, I would leave off preaching

47. This refers to two proclamations issued by Lieutenant-Governor Bull.
The first of August 3 commanded "all the Justices the Provost Marshall and
all other the Peace Officers" to use every legal means to suppress all "Tumults
and unlawfull Assemblys" and to execute the laws, and that all aiding should
have the support of law "as they shall answer at their Peril for the neglect
thereof." Council Journal, Aug. 3, 1768. On August 5, the Lieutenant-Governor
issued a second proclamation which stated that many of those "Concerned in
the said Acts of Violence have unwarily been drawn in and were Provoked
thereto by the Great and repeated Losses they have sustained," and that he
therefore promised "his Majestys most gracious Pardon for the Misdemeanours
by them Committed at any time before the date hereof." This proclamation
was dated August 6. Council Journal, Aug. 5, 1768. See S. C. Gaz., Aug. 8, 22,
1768.

48. This sermon is in Sermon Book, IV, [197-235]. The text is I Thessalon-
ians 4:11, "And that ye study to be quiet." Following the sermon is the nota-
tion, "Preached by Order of Lieutenant-Governor Bull of South Carolina."
The following places are listed, without dates, as those where the sermon
was delivered: "St. Marks Church, Hanging Rock Creek, Lynch's Creek, Rocky
Mount on Wateree River, and John Graves House on the Wateree." Shortly
before Woodmason left Maryland as a Loyalist, the sermon was delivered "At
the Chapel of St. John, Baltimore County, Md. Nov. 1774." Sermon Book, IV,
[236].

and retire to Town, and then the Church People would whip them.——10 [miles]

Sunday 21) A Day appointed for a General Meeting of the people on 25 Mile Creek to hear the Proclamation and my Discourse on the State of Public Affairs—To hinder which the Presbyterians sent up to the Waxaws and brought down their Teacher from thence to the Meeting House at Pine Tree—Where was a General Assembly of the Sectaries of all Kinds round about and many Church People some out of Curiosity—Others, because they would not hear the Proclamation—The Provost Marshal was to come up from Town to publish it—But the Regulators got Intelligence and arm'd 500 Men, threatening to whip, or shoot Him—So it was sent to Me. Another was sent to St Marks to Col. Richardson for him to draw out his Regiment and publish it. He indeed came up, but was afraid to do—To such pass are Things come here—and so weak are the Hands of Government.

I had not above 50 Auditors—but they were so well pleas'd with my Sermon, as to desire me to print it—I intend to send a copy to Charlestown.[49]

The Congregation confirm'd to Me the Report, that the Anabaptists should threat to whip me, if I came any more on that Side the River to preach, or publish Proclamations—Excited thereto by some of the principal of the Presbyterians—Returned in the Evening to Pine Tree alias Cambden, to my Lodgings.—— 20 [miles]

Monday the 22d. The People tell me that the Regulators being exasperated, at my publishing the Governors Proclamation some of their Head Men brought their Children as Yesterday to the Meeting to be baptized, altho' they are Members of the Church. ——2686 [total miles]

Wednesday the 24. Hearing of an Assembly at Hanging Rock Creek I sat off for that place with my Horse heavy loaded with Provisions and Necessaries—Weather exceeding dry and Hot. The Creature gave out, and was obliged to tarry in the Wild Wilderness all Night—I ty'd the Horse to a Tree, Wrapp'd my

49. Following the sermon Woodmason wrote: "A Copy of this Sermon was deliver'd to the Honorable Othniel Beale Esq President and to the Gentlemen of the Council for to be printed." *Ibid.*

Self in my Cloak—took my Saddle for my Pillow, and (like Charles the 12th) slept in my Boots very comfortably—I had no Fire—But I am under no dread of Wild Beasts or Snakes—Thousands Would have been scar'd—I had a fine warm Night. But had it rain'd, I should have been in an dismal Situation.——30 [miles]

Thursday) Attended the Multitude, which consisted wholly of Irish Presbyterians and lawless Persons—so that I dar'd not to read the Proclamation as my Life would have been endangered.

Friday) Hearing that another Multitude was to assemble as this day on Lynch's Creek, I sent the Proclamation to the Heads of them—fearing to go my Self, lest I should be torn in Pieces for not one of the Magistrates dare do as I do—and 'tis a Mercy that they pay some Regard to my Gown.

Set off for the Waxaws, to consult with some Persons about building of a small Chapel in those Parts, Met on the Road with a Presbyterian Teacher, who travelled with me the Day. The People subscribed to a General-House—i.e. Neither Church, or Meeting—but open for Ministers of all denominations. My Horse greatly jaded thro' heat of the Weather and Great drought and my Self greatly tormented with Seed Ticks, by my lying in the Woods. Seed Ticks are a small Insect not bigger than the Point of a Needle with which ev'ry Leaf and Blade of Grass is covered at this Season of the Year—they bite very sharp—get into the Skin cause Inflammations—Itchings, and much torment.——20 [miles]; 2736 [total miles]

Saturday—Crossed the River—and came to Rocky Mount very weary and hungry—having eaten nought but a little Rice these 4 days.——20 [miles]

Sunday 28) Went to the Wateree Creek to attend the Congregation there—Many People assembled. Read the Proclamation—and in afternoon my late Sermon, which pleas'd them—And they too desired that I would print it.——10 [miles]

In the Evening attempted to ride up to Jacksons Creek to attend a Congregation on Tuesday—But the Horse being very Sick and tired, gave out. So put up at a Cabbin on the Road.

Monday) Finding the Horse unfit for Travel, walk'd back to the Wateree Creek, and from thence led the Horse down to Pine

Tree where I came on Tuesday very weak and very Weary—the Weather being very hot and dry, and having had no Sleep for some Nights, my Skin being full of Seed Ticks.——30 [miles]

Employ'd this Week in answering the Governor's Letter—Writing to the Council—Board of Church Commissioners and in filling up Petitions from the Peoples.

The Seditious Multitude refuse to embrace the Governor's Proclamation.[50]

Saturday September 3) Rode down the Country on the West Side the Wateree River into the Fork between that and the Congaree River—This is out of my Bounds—But their having no Minister, and their falling (therefrom) continually from the Church to Anabaptism, inclin'd me to it—The People received me gladly and very kindly. Had on Sunday 4—a Company of about 150—Most of them of the Low Class—the principal Planters living on the Margin of these Rivers.

Baptiz'd 1 Negroe Man—2 Negroe Children—and 9 White Infants and married 1 Couple—The People thanked me in the most kind Manner for my Services—I had very pleasant Riding but my Horse suffered Greatly. The Mornings and Evenings now begin to be somewhat Cool, but the Mid day heat is almost intolerable— Many of these People walk 10 or 12 Miles with their Children in the burning Sun—Ought such to be without the Word of God, when so earnest, so desirous of hearing it and becoming Good Christians, and good Subjects! How lamentable to think, that the Legislature of this Province will make no Provision—so rich, so luxurious, polite a People! Yet they are deaf to all Solicitations, and look on the poor White People in a Meaner Light than their Black Slaves, and care less for them. Withal there is such a Republican Spirit still left, so much of the Old Leaven of Lord Shaftsbury and other the 1st principal Settlers still remains, that they seem not at all disposed to promote the Interest of the Church of England—Hence it is that above 30,000£ Sterling have lately been expended to bring over 5 or 6000 Ignorant, mean, worthless, beggarly Irish Presbyterians, the Scum of the Earth, and Refuse of Mankind, and this, solely to ballance the Emigra-

50. In its issue of Aug. 22, 1768, the *S. C. Gaz.* admitted that neither proclamation was "likely to produce the desired effects."

tions of People from Virginia, who are all of the Established Church.——50 [miles]; [total] Miles 2846

It will require much Time and Pains to New Model and form the Carriage and Manners, as well as Morals of these wild Peoples—Among this Congregation not one had a Bible or Common Prayer—or could join a Person or hardly repeat the Creed or Lords Prayer—Yet all of 'em had been educated in the Principles of our Church. So that I am obliged to read the Whole Service, omitting such Parts, as are Repetitious, and retaining those that will make the different Services somewhat Uniform— Hence it is, that I can but seldom use the Litany, because they know not the Responses.

It would be (as I once observ'd before) a Great Novelty to a Londoner to see one of these Congregations—The Men with only a thin Shirt and pair of Breeches or Trousers on—barelegged and barefooted—The Women bareheaded, barelegged and barefoot with only a thin Shift and under Petticoat—Yet I cannot break [them?] of this—for the heat of the Weather admits not of any [but] thin Cloathing—I can hardly bear the Weight of my Whig and Gown, during Service. The Young Women have a most uncommon Practise, which I cannot break them off. They draw their Shift as tight as possible to the Body, and pin it close, to shew the roundness of their Breasts, and slender Waists (for they are generally finely shaped) and draw their Petticoat close to their Hips to shew the fineness of their Limbs—so that they might as well be in Puri Naturalibus—Indeed Nakedness is not censurable or indecent here, and they expose themselves often quite Naked, without Ceremony—Rubbing themselves and their Hair with Bears Oil and tying it up behind in a Bunch like the Indians—being hardly one degree removed from them—In few Years, I hope to bring about a Reformation, as I already have done in several Parts of the Country.——284[6?] [miles—MS torn]

Received Letters from England—One acquaints me with death of the Reverend Mr. Crallan, 10 days after his Embarking.[51] This

---

51. The Rev. James Crallan became assistant minister of St. Philip's Church, Charleston, October 14, 1767. According to one source he was "occasionally deranged in his mind" and had tried to throw himself out of a window. He resigned from St. Philip's on April 25, 1768, to return to England. In pas-

is the 13th or 14th of the Clergy dead or gone here within these 2 Years—This Gentleman grew insane before his departure. He was a Saint—An Angel in his Life and Manners—A most pious and devout Young Man, and yet he could not escape the Censure of these flighty, Proud, Illprincipled Carolin[i]ans. They are enough to make any Person run Mad—And they crack'd the Brain of one Young Man Mr. Amory the Year before.[52] We have two now in the same Condition—And others, whose Situation is so uneasy, that Life is a Burden to them—I would not wish my worst Enemy to come to this Country (at least to this) Part of it to combat perpetually with Papists, Sectaries, Atheists and Infidels— who would rather see the Poor People remain Heathens and Ignorants, than to be brought over to the Church. Such Enemies to Christ and his Cross, are these vile Presbyterians.

Tuesday 6th) Officiated at Sawneys Creek; I expected at least 3 or 400 People, but had not half the Number—They refus'd to listen to the Governors Proclamation—But readily subscribed My Petitions drawn up for Churches and Chapels—Even several of the Anabaptists subscrib'd. There being very Great Enmity between these Sects. They begg'd Pardon for [MS torn, one word missing] Indiscreet Speeches of some of their People, laying the blame on some of the Church People, who had threatned to whip some of their Teachers if they offered to harangue the Multitude.——20 [miles]; 2866 [total miles]

My Horse being jaded, I borrowed one of a Gentleman for this Days Duty, who proved restif and unmanageable—and in my Return run away with me into the Woods amidst the Bogs and Marshes, where at last he stuck—And I was obliged to wade thro' a large Morass to get to dry Land—After which he became more

sage he jumped overboard to his death. Frederick Dalcho, *An Historical Account of the Protestant Episcopal Church, in South Carolina* (Charleston, 1820), 198-99; *S. C. and Amer. Gen. Gaz.*, Aug. 26, 1768.

52. The Rev. Isaac Amory, A.M., became rector of St. John's Church on John's Island in November, 1764. The particular attention he paid to some Negroes in his parish brought remonstrances from his congregation and led, finally, to his resignation in September, 1765. Minutes of Vestry of St. John's, Colleton, 1734-1817, 1, 75, typescript in S. C. Hist. Soc.; Dalcho, *An Hist. Account of the P. E. Church in S. C.*, 361-62.

governable, and brought me home safe, tho' I sweated thro' fear of passing the Night in that Bogg.

The River is now very low, and fordable in many Places, so that I cross it with Safety, tho' always with Fear and trembling—the Bottom being rough Rocks and Sharp Stones, and the Water rolling over the Rocks makes beautiful Cascades, but what is terrifying to Horses. Mine is now used to it. There are but 3 Boats on this Long River of 150 Miles but they are about opening of Roads, and making of Ferries.

Thus You have a Journal of two Years—In which have rode near Six thousand Miles, almost on one Horse. Wore my Self to a Skeleton and endured all the Extremities of Hunger, Thirst, Cold, and Heat. Have baptized near 1200 Children—Given 200 or more Discourses—Rais'd almost 30 Congregations—Set on foot the building of sundry Chapels Distributed Books, Medicines, Garden Seed, Turnip, Clover, Timothy Burnet, and other Grass Seeds—with Fish Hooks—Small working Tools and variety of Implements to set the Poor at Work, and promote Industry to the amount of at least One hundred Pounds Sterling: Roads are making—Boats building—Bridges framing, and other useful Works begun thro' my Means, as will not only be of public Utility, but make the Country side wear a New face, and the People become New Creatures. And I will venture to attest that these small, weak Endeavours of mine to serve the Community, has (or will) be of more Service to the Colony, than ever Mr. Whitfield's Orphan House was, or will be. On which he has [Ms. torn, one word missing] Twelve Thousand Pounds Sterling (by [Ms. torn]) from which Mankind has not been twelve pence benefitted.

It is the greatest Stretch of Folly and Madness, for any Man (much less such a sensible Man as Mr. Whitfield) to think of founding a College or Academy on the Scite of the Orphan House—which stands in a barren sandy unhealthy Soil and Situation—Where Youth must continually combat with all the Diseases of this Clime, and which is one of the hottest Spots on the Globe 6 Months in the Year—Youths may languish there, and have their Stamina destroyed—It would be Death and inevitable Destruction to send Children there from healthful Places. They cannot raise Wheat there, nor any of the European Fruits or

Plants. The Back Parts of this Country or of North Carolina would be more su[itable?] Especially the Place which Whitfield sold to the Moravians, which is now a very fine thriving Settlement—Where Health and Plenty abounds, and ev'ry thing denotes the Salubrity of the Air, and temperature of the Clime. Here he should have founded his Orphan House, and made it an House of Industry, not a Seminary for to train up Preachers and Teachers in the Principles of Methodism and Libertinism— And then by giving them the Orphan House, they would have dy'd there like Rotten Sheep and the Sect become extinguished.

This attempt of Mr. W. to convert the Orphan House (or Whitfields Folly as tis called) into a College, has lower'd Him entirely in the Minds of the Americans, who think that he has other Designs than he pretends—some Venial Views, some particular Scheme to answer—As the Place has not the least Article to recommend it for a Public Academy—Charles Town has far superior Advantages and here is a large Fund—a Good Library— and all Requisites for establishing a College—And yet on mature Deliberation the Scheme was dropt, this Clime being thought too relaxing for either the Body or Mind of Students—Which is evident, from the Bad Health, and quick Deaths of most of the Clergy, and Literate Persons that settle here—Except they pursue Methods of Living, inconsistent with, or opposite to: the Regulari[ty] of Things.

## PART TWO

# Society and Institutions
# of the Backcountry

# A Report on Religion in the South:

*"The* New Lights *now infest the whole Back Country."* [1]

An Account of the Churches in South Carolina, Georgia, North Carolina, and the Floridas, 1765

Number 1

A List of the Parishes laid out in the Province of South Carolina with the Names of the Incumbents, and Number of Members each Parish sends to the General Assembly

| Titles of the Parishes | Incumbents Names | Members in Assembly |
|---|---|---|
| **Berkley County** | | |
| St. Philips Charlestown | Rev. Robert Smyth. Rector Joseph Dacres Wilton, Lecturer | 3 |
| St. Michaels Charlestown | Robert Cooper Rector Harte. Lecturer | 3 |
| St. Andrews—Ashley River | Charles Martyn. Rector | 3 |
| St. George—Dorchester | Serjeant | 2 |
| St. John | Hockley | 3 |
| Christ Church—Wando | Drake | 2 |
| St. Thomas and St. Dennis | Alexander Garden (Missionary | 3 |
| St. James—Goose Creek | James Harrison (Missionary | 4 |
| **Colleton County** | | |
| St. Paul | Evans | 3 |
| St. John | Dawson | 3 |
| St. Bartholemew | Vacant | 4 |
| St. Matthew | Mr. Paul Turquand, Recommended. | 2 |

1. Ful. Trans., N.C., S.C., Ga., No. 67. This "Account" of the Southern churches was written by Woodmason some time in 1765, after his decision to apply for the position of itinerant in St. Mark's Parish. It was probably intended for the use of the Bishop of London, but there is no way of telling whether it was the result of Woodmason's initiative or by request of the Bishop. The "Account" and the "Notes" which follow have been checked for accuracy with the original manuscripts, now in the Office of Church Commissioners, London. The portions relating to North Carolina, both of the "Account" and the "Notes," are published in *Col. Recs. of N. C.*, VII, 283-88.

| Titles of the Parishes | Incumbents Names | Members in Assembly |
|---|---|---|
| **Granville County** | | |
| St. Helena or Port Royal say Beaufort Town | Vacant. | 3 |
| St. Peters. Purrysburgh | Vacant. | 1 |
| Prince Wiliam | Reverend Mr. Frink | 2 |
| **Craven County** | | |
| St. James Santee | Warren Rector | 2 |
| St. Stephen | Alexander Keith Rector. | 1 |
| Prince Frederick | Skeyne. | 2 |
| Prince George, alias Georgetown | Offspring Pearce. | 2 |
| St. Mark | Vacant | 2 |
| **Extra Parochial Distric's** | | 50 Members in the House of Assembly |
| August | Vacant | |
| Congarees | Reverend Mr. Imber, late of Purrysburgh | |
| Warterees [Waterees] (or Fredericksburg) | Charles Woodmason Recommended | |
| 20 Parishes, which send Members | Number of Clergy in the Provinc (if all Vacancies filled). 25 Besides, A Clergy- | |
| 3 Extra-Parochial, send no Members | man (the Reverend Mr. Crawling is Master of the Provincial Free School | |

Verte

## No. 2.

A List of the Parishes in the Province of Georgia, with the Names of the Incumbents, and Numbers of Members which each Parish sends to form their General Assembly

| Titles of the Parishes | Incumbents | Members |
|---|---|---|
| Christ's Church (or Savannah Town | Reverend Mr. Zubberbuler | 8 |
| St. Matthew's | | 4 |
| St. George's | | 2 |
| St. Paul's | | 3 |
| St. Philips | | 2 |
| St. John's | | 3 |
| St. Andrews | | 2 |
| St. James's | | 1 |
| | Total | 25 Members |

## No. 3

A List of the Counties in North-Carolina, with the Number of Members each sends to their General Assemblies—Which Counties (by a late Act) are rais'd into Parishes, and endowed with 100 £ Sterling P Ann for an Incumbent charg'd on the Publick Treasury, and under the Patronage of the Lord Bishop of London

| Names | Taxable Persons in each County (i.e. White Men above 16 capable of bearing Arms) | No of Members |
|---|---|---|
| Anson | 800 | 2 |
| Beaufort | 742 | 2 |
| Berke | 1634 | 3 |
| Bladen | 1244 | 2 |
| Brunswick | 186 | 2 |
| Bute | 200 | 2 |
| Carteret | 541 | 2 |
| Chowan | 745 | 5 |
| Craven | 1175 | 2 |
| Cumberland | 652 | 2 |
| Curriticuck | 709 | 5 |
| Dobbs | 954 | 2 |
| Duplin | 1085 | 2 |
| Edgecumb | 1207 | 2 |
| Granville | 2882 | 2 |
| Hallifax | 2029 | 2 |
| Hartford | 1393 | 2 |
| Hyde | 604 | 2 |
| Johnston | 899 | 2 |
| Mecklemburgh | 791 | 2 |
| New Hanover | 446 | 2 |
| Northampton | 1169 | 2 |
| Onslow | 978 | 2 |
| Orange | 2699 | 2 |
| Pasquotank | 850 | 5 |
| Pitt | 741 | 2 |
| Rowan | 1486 | 2 |
| Tyrrill | 996 | 5 |
| Towns | 29706 which at 4 to a family (deducting | |
| Bath | the Heads or Taxables) are 119,164 | 1 |
| Brunswick | Souls, but one or two Clergy of the | 1 |
| Edenton | Church of England among them [2] | 1 |
| Hallifax | | 1 |
| New Bern | | 1 |
| Salisbury | | |
| Wilmington | | 1 |
| Tarborough | | |

Total 75 Members

2. The English transcriber was correct in his following note: "These figures are not clear but in any case they do not work out properly."

No. 4

| | East Florida | |
|---|---|---|
| Towns and Parishes | Ministers | Members of Assembly |
| Saint Augustine | Reverend Mr. Forbes | None yet convened |

No. 5

| | West Florida | |
|---|---|---|
| Towns | Ministers | Members of Assembly |
| Mobille | An Idle debauchd person who pretends to be in Orders, and who came there from Jamaica, takes on Him to do Duty | None |
| Pensacola | No Minister | |

## Notes and Remarks.[3]

### No. 1.

*St. Philips Charlestown*   This Church is allow'd to be the most elegant Religious Edifice in British America—It is built of Brick. Length 100 feet Breadth 60 Height 40, with a Cupola of 50 feet, with two Bells, and a Clock and Bell. It has 3 Portico's before the West, North and South Doors. It was built from the Model of the Jesuit Church at Antwerp. Having Gallerys around, exceeding well plann'd for Sight and hearing. In this Church is a Good Organ, the Great Organ has 16 Stops—the Choir Organ 8. It is well Ornamented. Has rich Pulpit Cloths, and Coverings for the Altar and a very large Service of Plate. A Lecturer (or Assistant is maintain'd here by the Publick—His Salary 200 £ Stg P Ann, as is also the Rectors; and his fees full as much. Divine Service is perform'd here with Great Decency and Order: both on Holidays and Week Days.

*St. Michaels*   Is a New built Church from the Model of that of Greenwich being Truss'd—Roof[e]d and no Pillars. Is 80 feet by

3. These "Notes" are to be found in Ful. Trans., S.C., Nos. 300, 298, 299. The "Notes" are endorsed: "Mr. Woodmason's Account of South Carolina, North Carolina, Georgia &c 1766."

60. Has a Tower and Steeple 196 feet high, and a Ring of 8 Bells lately hung. In this Church is a small Organ, but a large and Noble One is now in Hand, to be sent over. The Plate and Ornaments of this Church are superb. Divine Service is regularly perform'd here on Sundays Holidays and Week Days as at St. Philips—The Rector and Assistant's Salaries are the same as theirs but the Fees are not above 100 £ Stg P Ann.

*St. Andrews* Was lately consum'd by Fire, but is rebuilt, and is a pretty Edifice It has an Organ.—This parish has also a Chapel of Ease.[4]

*St. George's* Is a very handsome Brick Church, with a Steeple, 4 Bells, and an Organ. An Endowd free School is in this Parish.

*St. Johns Berkley County* Was burnt about 7 Years ago, and not yet rebuilt, tho' the Money for it has been long collected. Here is a pretty Chapel of Ease A handsome School, well endow'd, and a House for the Master.

*Christ Church* Is a pretty Brick Building—but very plain.

*St. Thomas* Is a Good Church—Has a Chapel of Ease, and a Publick School well endow'd.

*St. James's Santee* This Church fell to decay some Years ago, and has not been since rebuilt. Service is perform'd at (what was formerly) a Chapel of Ease.

*St. James's Goose Creek* This is one of the best Country Churches in the Province, and both it and the Parsonage stand close by the Bridge, over which is the Greatest Flux and Reflux of People, in the Province, which makes it very troublesome and expensive to the Minister, as he is daily and hourly pester'd with Travelers calling for Lodging or Entertainment.

*St. Matthew* Is a Parish just laid out—Has as yet no Church built, or Parsonage House or Glebe laid out.

*St. Helena* This Church is in the Town of Beaufort, Port Royal, which altho' the second Town in the Province, boasts the very meanest Church in it.

---

4. Chapels of ease were established in large parishes, where many people lived at a distance from the parochial church. They had the parochial rights of baptism and burial but were without either rector or endowment. Celebration of the great festival days was reserved for the parish church. See Dalcho, *Hist. of the Prot. Episc. Ch. in S. C.*, 267-68.

*Prince William*   This is the second best Church in the Province, and by many esteem'd a more beautiful Building than St. Philips. It is far more elegant than St. Michaels, and is beautifully pew'd and Ornamented.

*Prince George*   This Church is in the Town of Georgetown—is 80 feet by 50 has 3 Isles, but no Galleries as yet—The Pulpit and Pews are well Executed, but the Altar Piece is not yet up. Here is a free School.

The other Parish Churches are all Timber Buildings—But the Parsonage Houses of most of them are of Brick, and Good Structures. The Glebes of several are Valuable; Particularly St. Andrews St. Georges and St. Stephens.

In Charlestown, is a Public Provincial School, endowed with 100 £ Stg P Ann, besides Bye Scholars, which makes it a profitable Place   The Free Masons, and other Public Societies, maintain Charity Schools So that there is not a Beggar in the Province —Ev[e]ry Parish maintains its own Poor—But there are few, or none, out of Charlestown.

As the Province has undertaken to add 30 £ Stg P Ann to the Salaries of the Clergy, whereby their Stipends are now 110 £ Stg. beside their fees, House and Glebe; It is almost a Sin for any of the Parochial Clergy longer to recieve the Mission Money—Nor are there but two who choose to continue on the Old foot, receiving only 80 £ Stg from the Treasury and 30 £ from England—This Money could be better employ'd in Georgia.

*Augusta*   Is a Town high up on the River Savanna, and a Place of Great Resort for Trade with the Indians—It is a frontier Settlement. The Society maintains a Missionary here a[t] 75 £ Stg Salary. It is almost scandalous for the Rich Province of South Carolina to receive the Societys Money, or to suffer them to maintain their Clergy—But the Reason why no more Parishes are laid out arises from Political Motives, as it would encrease the Number of Assembly-Men; which Place is so troublesome and expensive, that few are to be found at an Election to undertake it.

*Purrysburgh*   Is a Town on Savanna River, between *Savanna* and *Augusta;* The Inhabitants cheifly *Switzers* and *Saltzburghers.* The Reverend Mr. Imber, who lately come over with the French

Protestants, was establish'd at this Place, But differing with the People, he now is among those he come over with, and *Stumpels* Germans.[5]

Altho' the Country Parishes in South Carolina, are on one and the same Establishment, Yet some are more lucrative, others more desirable than the Rest. Hence, it is not uncommon when Vacancies happen, for Ministers to remove from one Parish to another. For Instance—St. Helena and Prince George, being Towns, are more pleasant and profitable, than St. Jame's or St. Stephen, which are inland. St. Andrew and St. George, by being near the Sea, and inhabited by Rich Planters, are more agreeable than Prince Frederic or St. Mark, which are inhabited by poor and illiterate People. While St. Mark and St. Matthew, tho' very undesirable on Account of the want of sensible and literate Persons to make an Incumbents Hours pleasing, are, on another Account preferable to all the Rest; for what they enjoy as to *Wealth,* these possess in respect to *Health,* no Part of England being better, and none in the Province so good as to this Particular.

Beside the two Episcopal Churches in Charlestown, there are those other Places for Religious Worship.

1 A Presbyterian Meeting, the Minister of the Kirk of Scotland, and acting by the Model of the Directory.
2 An Independant-Meeting, in Alliance with those of New England.
3 A Baptist Meeting—in Harmony with those of Pennsylvania.
4 A Quakers Meeting—Ditto
(N. B. There are but 2 or 3 Quakers in Town, so no Congregation of them)

5. A Prussian officer named Stümpel brought over five hundred Germans to England. There, without resources to conduct them to America, he deserted them. Through government aid and private donations, they were sent to South Carolina. Here Governor Boone, in 1764, provided for their settlement on Hard Labor Creek in what was to become Abbeville County. G. D. Bernheim, *History of the German Settlements and of the Lutheran Church in North and South Carolina* (Philadelphia, 1872), 161-65; McCrady, *Hist. of S. C. under the Royal Govt.,* 367-68.

5  An Arian Meeting, acting on *Whistons* [6] System and Principles—There are but few Members, but it is Well endow'd
   (N. B. All the Teachers of these Meetings wear Gowns, and
   have Good Salaries paid them by their respective Congregations.)

6  A Dutch Lutheran Church. Service is perform'd here in the
   German Tongue; It has an Organ—The Pastor officiates in his
   Surplice and Cope, after the Manner of the Danish Church in
   Wellclose Square.

7  A French Calvinist Church—Service is perform'd here in the
   French Tongue, after the Geneva Pattern. It has but a small
   Congregation, but is Rich, and well endow'd.

8  A Jews Synagogue.

In the Country are 8 Presbyterian Meetings, supply'd with
Ministers from Scotland, who form a Presbytery, and govern their
Members after the Plan of the Scotch Kirk. Most of these Congregations are in decay tho' strongly supported from Home. And
in Charlestown, most of the rising Generation incline to the
Church Establish'd, and will join it in Time. This is owing to our
having of late Years, Good and Worthy Clergymen sent over:
A Matter of most serious Concern: For the Church has greatly
suffered through default herein. But the Parishes will not now
accept unworthy Persons but will reject them as they lately did
two. One at *Beaufort*,[7] the other *P. Frederick;*[8] which rotten Mem-

6. William Whiston (1667-1752), an English divine, was an Arian in doctrine. His principal work, *Primitive Christianity Revived,* was published in
1711, and four years later he organized a society for promoting primitive
Christianity. See "William Whiston," *Dict. of Nat. Biog.,* XXI, 10-14.

7. The Rev. William Peasely, clergyman at Beaufort in St. Helena's Parish,
was charged with immorality by the vestrymen and discharged in 1756. The
bitter controversy which preceded his discharge may be followed in A. S.
Salley, ed., *Minutes of the Vestry of St. Helena's Parish, South Carolina
1726-1812* (Columbia, S. C., 1919), 71, 73-86.

8. The Rev. Michael Smith, ousted from the Prince Frederick Church where
Woodmason served afterwards as church warden and vestryman, had obtained
a parish in North Carolina. Here the church wardens of Hanover County and
a Mr. Benjamin Heron wrote letters in defense of Smith's character. The letter
of Heron defended Smith from one he believed Woodmason to have written.
Heron questioned Woodmason's rank as a gentleman and charged, also on
hearsay evidence, that Woodmason was frequently out of his senses. Church

bers are now roving about *North-Carolina* in a starving Condition.

Methodism has been endeavour'd to be introduc'd in Carolina, but has made no Progress: They run to hear *Whitfield* out of Curiosity only, as an Orator, but will not adopt his Principles, or admit his Pupils  He intended the Orphan House in Georgia, as a Seminary of Disciples to be entirely devoted to Him, and sent out as his Emissaries around: Some of them have appear'd in Publick—but were such Lame Tools, that their Master was as much asham'd of them, as the People despised them. He has now given up the House to the Publick of Georgia, to serve as a Publick College for that Colony.

The Greatest Harmony subsists between these Sectaries, and the Establishment—owing to the Candour, Prudence, and regular demeanour of the present Clergy, who are the best Sett of Men, that Carolina were ever blest with at one Time.

The People of South Carolina in General, may be said to be a sensible and Moral People. Divine Service is perform'd in the Country Churches on Sunday Mornings only. All the Churches have a Service of Plate—Surplices worn only in the three Towns. Great Regard to Decency and proper Deference is observ'd by these Provincials, as to Externals—As to Internal Righteousness, Holiness, and Purity, it lyes in small Compass. There are but very few Communicants, in any Congregation: Which is partly owing to the false Zeal of the Presbyterians, who by *forcing* their people indiscriminately to the Holy Ordinance, have made more *Deserters,* than *Volunteers* in the Cause of Religion.

Messrs. Smith—Cooper—Martin—and Keith—have acquir'd Genteel Fortunes since being in the Province.

### Notes on No. 2.

The Province of Georgia have laid out their Colony into Districs or Parishes—And this is All—The Provincial Allowance to their Clergy is but 25 £ Stg P Ann, which would not pay for Cloathing. There are no Churches or Parsonages yet built—

wardens of Hanover County to S.P.G., Oct. 1, 1759, *Col. Recs. of N. C.,* VI, 58-60; Benjamin Heron to S.P.G., Portsmouth, Sept. 17, 1760, *ibid.,* 312-13. The Rev. Michael Smith had gained a remarkably unsavory reputation while in Prince Frederick Parish. See Wallace, *Hist. of S. C.,* I, 421.

Glebes however are reserved and very Good Land There only wants a Governor or Man of Spirit who has the Cause of Religion at Heart, to bring forward these Matters and set the Wheel of Things going, Which wou'd move with the greatest Velocity, if but once put in Motion—This first Mover is wanting—Messrs. Westly and Whitfield has thrown a Damp on all Religious Matters in this Colony: They strain'd the Cord, till it broke—And it will require half an Age to repair the Damages they did in a short Space.

The Church in *Savanna* Town, is but mean: As indeed, is the Town it Self However, it is a genteel Living for a Clergyman, and not worth less (all Matters laid together) than 300 £ Stg P Ann. The present Incumbent (Mr. Zourbylyber [*sic*]) is now retiring with a Fortune of 5 or 6000 Guineas accumulated there: Cheifly by making of Bricks. He waits only for a Successor. The People of Georgia, are greatly below those of South Carolina both in Manners, Morals, and Wealth—But they are far beyond, and much superior in all Respects, to those of North Carolina: Here are great Openings for the Clergy—And this Province (if properly attended too) can be kept wholly in the Interests, Principles, and dependant on the Church of England.

## No. 3

As to North Carolina, the State of Religion therein, is greatly to be lamented—If it can be said, That there is any Religion, or a Religious Person in it. A Church was founded at Wilmington in 1753. Another at Brunswick in 1756, the Walls of each are carried up about 10 or 12 feet and so remain. Governour Dobbs us'd Great Endeavours to get these Buildings finish'd, and to lay out Parishes—But lived not to effect it—But the present Governour has got an Act pass'd, for a Church to be built in each Parish or Distric, and Church Matters to be settled on the Plan of South Carolina. He has given Public Notice hereof to the Clergy—Inviting of them to come abroad Promising of them his Protection Encouragement and Support: At the same time mentioning what Numbers of Sectaries overspread the Country, and the Danger that not only the Church Established, but even Religion it Self will be totally lost and destroyed if not quickly attended too.

Here is an opening—A large Harvest for all that are sincerely dispos'd to act for the Glory of God and the Good of Souls— How many thousands who never saw, much less read, or ever heard a Chapter of the Bible! How many Ten thousands who never were baptized or heard a Sermon! And thrice Ten thousand, who never heard of the Name of Christ, save in Curses and Execrations! Lamentable! Lamentable is the Situation of these People, as to Spirituals, Even beyond the Power of Words to describe.

There are 2 or 3 Itinerant Ministers in the Northern Part (or Lord Granvills Division) of the Province, and several Small Chapels are built in that Distric—But not a Church or Minister in any one Town of their Province, Maritime or Inland.

In the Back Part of this Country between the Heads of Pedee and Cape Fear Rivers, is a Distric of 12 000 Acres, formerly granted to Whitfield, and by Him sold to Count Zinzendorff—It is very rich Land—scituated just at foot of the lower Hills, and where the Springs take their Rise, that form these Great Rivers above mentioned. The Spot is not only Rich, fertile, and luxuriant, but the most Romantic in Nature  Sir Philip Sidneys Description of Arcadia, falls short of this *real* Arcadia Georgia, Circassia, Armenia, or whatever Region it may be compared too. To this Spot Zinzindorff transplanted his Hernhutters; who being join'd by others from Pensylvania, and Elsewhere now form a very large and numerous Body of People, Acting under their own Laws and Ordinances, independent of the Community, Constitution or Legislature in and over them. They are a Set of *Recabites* among the People of *Israel*—Forming a Distinc[t] Body, different in all things from All People. Here they have laid out two Towns—*Bethelem* and *Bethsada;* [9] delightfully charming! Rocks, Cascades, Hills, Vales, Groves, Plains—Woods, Waters all most

9. These are probably descriptions of Bethabara, settled in 1753, and Bethania, settled in 1759, by Moravians in North Carolina. Bernheim, *Hist. of Germ. Settlements,* 158-59. See Adelaide L. Fries, ed., *Records of the Moravians in North Carolina* (Raleigh, 1922-25), I, II. The detail and enthusiasm of Woodmason's account of these towns suggest that he might have visited them. He did visit in North Carolina, probably when he was living in Craven County. See pp. 21-22.

strangely intermixt, so that Imagination cannot paint any thing more vivid  They have Mills, Furnaces, Forges, Potteries, Founderies All Trades, and all things in and among themselves—Their Manners are not unlike the *Dunkers* of *Pensylvania:* Like them, they have All things (save Women) in Common; and receive to their Community Persons of all Nations, Religion and Language. They are seated near some valuable Copper Mines, from which they draw Great Advantage; And having all things free, setting all Hands at Work according to their Ability (for they are all *Bees, not a Drone* suffer'd in the Hive) What they do not consume they sell in the Adjacent Territory, Receiving for their Meal, Flour, Earthen Ware, Peach-Brandy, Whisky—Tools of Iron and Utensils of Copper, Wood and Turnery Wares &c. &c. Deer Skins, Fox, Otter, Raccoon, and other Furs and Peltry—These they send off into Virginia on the one Hand, and into South Carolina on the other—Receiving in Return Rum, Sugar, Linen and Woollen Goods—Pewter and Tin Wares, and other Necessaries.

Africk never more abounded with New Monsters, than Pensylvania does with New Sects, who are continually sending out their Emissaries around. One of those Parties, known by the Title of *New Lights* or the *Gifted Brethern* (for they pretend to Inspiration) now infest the whole Back Country, and have even penetrated South Carolina. One of C. W's [Charles Woodmason's] strongest Endeavours, must, and will be, to disperse these Wretches Which will not be a hard Task, as they will fly before Him as Chaff. Some of them lately kill'd a Travelling Person, and cut Him into Atoms singing Hymns, making Processions and Prayers, and offering up this inhuman Sacrifice to the Deity, as an acceptable Oblation—Six of them were secur'd and brought down to Charlestown, where they were kept six Months—During which Period, not all the Expostulations, Reasonings and Remonstrances of our Gentry and Clergy could make any Impression on their Diabolical Minds, or bring them back to Reason or Reflection. One of the Principal was hang'd—And that made Impression on them, and after some Months Confinement, they (shewing Marks of Penitence and Contrition) were banish'd the Province.[10]

10. This refers to the murder of two men in the Congarees in February, 1761. Seven men were brought to trial, four were convicted, and one, Jacob

Lately they took another extraordinary Step. For, after deluding
a Rich Planter, wasting his Substance, and perverting his Understanding One of their Teachers pretended to work Miracles, and
declared that He had Power equal with *Christ,* and that *God* had
given Him Authority even to raise the Dead—And that to evince
his Assertion, He would raise the first Dead Body they should
meet with. The bigotted Planter had not such strong Faith, but
that he called on Him to realise His Assertions. This Nonplus'd
the Villain, and put Him on a Scheme, how to deceive his Votary
and bring Himself off. So one of the Fraternity was procur'd, and
properly tutored to counterfeit Himself Dead, and to revive on
certain Prayers and Breathings being utter'd over Him. Accordingly this abominable Farce was play'd. The fellow lay as Dead—
The Pretended Prophet, prays, anoints, exercises, and calls on
the seemingly inanimate Wretch to *Arise*—But whether the fellow
kept his Breath so long as to suffer Suffocation, or the Exorcist
made his Conjurations too long, Certain it was, That the Wicked
Wretch was really gone, and (by playing the Fool too well) was
with Great difficulty recover'd. The Person thus impos'd on, was
one Mr. *Skinking Moore*,[11] of Little-River the Boundary between
the two Carolina's. This Moore was alway reckon'd a sensible
Man—Nor was his Senses so far darkened by these Fascinations,
but for Him to perceive some Gross Delusions some Great Decep-
tions—These Children of Satan gave out that the Party was in a
Trance—and they would have perswaded the unhappy Victim,
to have utter'd Blasphemies and Prophecies, as Matters revealed
to Him, while his Soul had left the Body, and till her reentering
her House of Clay. But the Poor Sinner's Pain had been so great
and the Sense of his Guilt bore so heavy on his Mind, as to make

---

Weber, **was** hanged. Weber seems to have called himself the "most High"
and to have stated that one of the men murdered was the "old Serpent" without whose death the world could not be saved. The accounts of the Weberites,
of their character and crimes, are all secondary, but none of them seem to
lack in weird details. See William Bull to William Pitt, Charleston, Apr. 26,
1761, P.R.O. Trans., XXIX, 80-82; *S. C. Gaz.,* Apr. 25, 1761; Wallace, *Hist. of
S. C.,* I, 348; Bernheim, *Hist. of the Germ. Settlements,* 195-205.

11. This probably refers to Schenking Moore, who is listed in the militia re-
turns as captain of the New Hanover Foot Company for 1754. *Col. Recs. of
N. C.,* XXII, 306, 388.

Him confess the whole Cheat to Mr. Moore, and thereby recover Him from his Lethergy, but not to his Estate, which he had so foolishly lavish'd on them.

The most zealous among the Sects, to propagate their Notions, and form Establishments, are the Anabaptists. When the Church of England was established in Carolina, the Presbyterians made Great Struggles; but finding themselves too weak, they determin'd to effect that by Cunning (the Principles they work by, for they are all Moles) which Strength could not effect. Wherefore, as Parish Churches were built only along the Sea Coast, they built a Sett of Meeting Houses quite back behind in the Interior Parts—Imitating the French—who by making a Chain of Forts from Canada to Louisiana endeavour'd to circumscribe the English, and prevent the Extension of their Trade. So did the Presbyterians with our Church—If they could not *suppress,* they would *cramp* the Progress of the Liturgy and Church Establish'd. And accordingly did, erect Meeting Houses as before said. None of the Church oppos'd Them—And the Almighty (by taking these People in their own Craft) have suffer'd them to fall into the Nett they spread for others. For, the Anabaptists in Pensylvania, resolving themselves into a Body, and determined to settle their Principles in ev[e]ry vacant Quarter, began to establish Meeting Houses also on the Borders—And by their Address and Assiduity, have worm'd the Presbyterians out of all these their strong Holds, and drove them away—So that the Baptists are now the most numerous and formidable Body of People which the Church has to encounter with, in the Interior and Back Parts of the Province And the Antipathy that these two Sects bear each other, is astonishing. Wherefore, a Presbyterian would sooner marry ten of his Children to Members of the Church of England than one to a Baptist. The same from the Baptists as to the Presbyterians— Their Rancour is surprizing—But the Church reaps great Good by it—And thro' their Jealousies, gains Ground on them very fast.

But these Baptists have great Prevalence and footing in North Carolina, and have taken such deep Root there that it will require long Time and Pains to grub up their Layers.

The Manners of the North Carolinians in General, are Vile and Corrupt—The whole Country is a Stage of Debauchery Dissoluteness and Corruption—And how can it be otherwise? The People are compos'd of the Out Casts of all the other Colonies who take Refuge there. The Civil Police is hardly yet establish'd. But they are so numerous—The Necessaries of Life are so cheap, and so easily acquir'd, and propagation being unrestricted, that the Encrease of People there, is inconceivable, even to themselves.

Marriages (thro' want of Clergy) are perform'd by ev'ry ordinary Magistrate. Polygamy is very Common—Celibacy much more—Bastardy, no Disrepute—Concubinage General—When'will this *Augean* Stable be cleans'd!

## No. 4

### East-Florida

Consists only of one Town—*St. Augustine*—

It is tolerable Well built after the Spanish Manner—And the Woods for two or three Miles being clear'd away Augustine is accounted, and may be said to be one of the healthiest Places in North America.

Everything there is very dear—for it receives all its supplies from Charlestown There are two Chapels—but quite Naked—Void of all Embellishments; The Spaniards having stripped them of ev'ry thing.

Here are few Traders or Inhabitants beside the Garrison, Sutlers, Publick Officers, and others dependant on them. The Governour [12] is a Single Man, keeps a Concubine, and the other Officers copy the Example—So that no Face or Appearance of Religion is there to be seen.

### West Florida

Has two Divisions—*Pensacola,* and *Mobile*—

The former is a Fort, scituate at Bottom of a large and capacious Bay. Here the Governour [13] resides—No Civil Jurisdiction is as

12. James Grant, Governor of East Florida, was popular with people of every class. See Charles Loch Mowat, *East Florida as a British Province 1763-1784* (Berkeley, 1943), 32-33.

13. George Johnstone, a Scot, was appointed Governor of West Florida on November 20, 1763, and was recalled to England in early 1767.

yet settled Which has drove all the People away that came there to settle   A Chaplain ought to be here with the Troops—but alas! None. The Governour is a Single Person, keeps a Concubine, has a Child by her and the Infection rages, and is copied. Greatly is it to be lamented (on the Side of Vertue and Religion) that Immoral and reprobate Persons are sent out as Governours of Provinces, and more especially New, and to be cultivated Provinces. One such Person, at the beginning of Things does more Damage to the Nation, more Mischief to Mankind, more Hurt to Goodness than twenty Succeeding Him can repair. He Spreads the Contagion—Lays the Principles of Things in Vice and Evil, Gives Rotteness to the Constitution, and propagates Disease where he should establish Health, Strength and Vigour.

Mobile is a Fort, seated on a River of that Name, distant (at its Mouth) 60 Miles from Pensacola, and lyes about 40 Miles from the Rivers Mouth. Here is a Chapel in the Fort, but no Chaplain. The Inhabitants (copying after the Pattern set them by their Principal) are Strangers to the Paths of Vertue, and sunk in Dissoluteness and Dissipation. No Forms of Government yet fix'd on, or carried into Execution—Whereby Numbers who went there to settle, have been ruined, or retreated to the French Settlement of New Orleans.

A Person, who calls Himself a Clergyman, patrolls about this Place, and officiates occasionally—But if He is One, They say, that He is such a Disgrace to the Character that they (bad as they are) hold Him in Detestation.

This was the Place, to which Mr. Harte (now Lecturer of St. Michael, Charlestown) was destin'd—And which he visited. But he found both Place and People too disagreeable to be preferr'd to so agreeable a Situation as He now enjoys. Mr. Harte was there, when the General Congress with the Indians was held [14]—And at

14. The Congress of the Choctaw and Chickasaw Indians took place at Mobile, March 26 to April 4, 1765. According to Governor Johnstone, two thousand Indians were present. The Congress opened with the ceremony of smoking the calumet and with prayers by the Reverend Samuel Hart. Cecil Johnson, *British West Florida 1763-1783* (New Haven, 1943), 39. The Reverend Samuel Hart had been licensed to West Florida on May 5, 1764. Licensed to Plantations, Ful. MSS., Church Commissioners' Office, London.

their departure, he gave them a Sermon—the Interpreter, explaining his Words to them Sentence by Sentence. The Indian Chief was very attentive and after Dinner ask'd Mr. Harte, where this Great Warriour God Almighty, which he talk'd so much off, liv'd? and if He was a Friend of His Brother George over the Great Water? Mr. Harte then expatiated on the Being of God, and his Attributes—But could not instil any Sentiment into the Indian, or bring Him to any the least Comprehension of Matters—And dwelt so long on his Subject as to tire the Patience of the Savage, who at length, took Mr. Harte by the Hand, with one of his, and filling out a Glass of Rum with the other, concluded with saying "Beloved Man, I will alway think Well of this Friend of ours God Almighty whom You tell me so much off, and so let us drink his Health—and then drank off his Glass of Rum.

# A Letter to the Bishop of London:

## "I have a wide field before Me!" [15]

Charlestown Oct 19. 1766

My Lord

It is my Duty to acquaint Your Lordship, that I arrived here August 12. last—after a Passage of 9 Weeks—I found the Season hotter than ever known, and both Town and Country exceeding sickly, owing to a most inclement Spring and Summer more Rain having fallen from March to August last than in 7 Years preceeding—Since which it has been exceeding hot and dry, and likely to continue . . . Sept. 5. The Church Commissioners met, and gave me Induction to my Settlement . . . The next day I set off— and (after officiating at St. Andrews, St. James, and St. Marks) arrived at my Station of Fredericksburg the 16th—The People instantly fram'd a Petition to the Assembly for a Church and House to be built which will be granted—And I have carried the Liturgy and the Bible, 50 Miles further than ever yet read in these Parts—Not a House could I set foot in but found some sick, some dead so that have had a melancholy Progress. I've baptiz'd Numbers of Children. Have been among the Sectaries call'd *New-Lights* and rode above 500 Miles around through the hot burning Sun and Sands; I bless God without Injury to my Health—but with much fatigue and Expence.

There being a Tract of rich Land of 640 Acres (or a Mile square) originally laid out for the Town of Fredericksburg, but abandon'd as too low for a Settlement—the People have petitioned for it, as a Glebe and to be settled on the Church—Its now worth 500 Guineas—I hope to carry this Prize—In 10 Years

15. Ful. Trans., S. C., No. 91.

it will be worth 2000 £—And if I succeed I shall think my Self a Good Son of the Church.

As most of my flock are Sectaries of various Denominations and Countries, and a mix'd Multitude, and not a School or School-Master among them, I have taken 20 Poor Children to educate Gratis in Writing, Arithmetic, Psalmody, and the Principles of Religion and Things—These I make attend Divine Service regularly—and thro' their Sides I hope to make Impressions on their Relatives.

But I have a wide field before Me! My Distric is 150 Miles in breadth and 300 Length: And as this Country ever was the Grave of the Clergy, it has been bitterly so this Summer.

For, In May, landed Mr. Lonsdale his Wife, 5 Children and Servants who went to Prince William Parish, where they were soon cut off by the Endemic Fever that rages here, and not one now left.

Mr. Tonge of St. Pauls and his Wife were taken in July—She is since dead—His Recovery is doubted.

In August dy'd
Mr. Imer—at Saxe Gotha
Mr. Pridereau—St. Helena
Mr. Glassoniere—Orangeburg
Mr. Dawkins—Johns Island
And a Dutch Minister—and a Presbyterian Minister from Ireland for Williamsburgh Township, few days after his Landing.

In October dyed Mr. Alexander Skeene Minister of P. Frederic. Mr. Alexander [16] (who was ordain'd with me) embark'd 12 days before and arrived here about 10 days after Me—In his Journey to Sunbury the Fever overtook Him, and carried him off.

Mr. Hockley of St. Johns has been down these 5 Months—Mr. Martin of St. Andrews—Mr. Pierce of Prince George—Mr. Dawson of John's Island, and Mr. Keith of St. Stephen, are now all down, and I doubt of their Recovery.

Mr. Amory of Purrysburgh, and Mr. Drake of Christ Church are returned home.

16. In his letter of March 26, 1771, Woodmason admitted that this report of the death of the Rev. Mr. Alexander was based upon false information. See below, p. 192.

Thro' these Removals, and this Great Mortality, 8 or 10 Parishes are now vacant.

And tho' the Back Country fills fast with New Settlers, yet our Assembly will not lay out New Parishes, lest by increasing the Number of Assembly Men, they lessen the Town Interest, which is opposite to the Country, I should say to the Public Interest— Thus Religion, Learning, and the Public Good, are sacrific'd to the Interests of Private Persons.

The Ship with the Box of Books from the Society, is arriv'd— Also Mr. Turquand for St. Matthews Parish.

The Salaries of our Town Clergy are double to those of the Country, tho' they do less Duty—for I perform more in one Month, than they in a Year. This Partiality was lately attempted to be remedied, and the Corps put on an equal foot And a Bill was order'd into the Assembly for that Purpose; but miscarried thro' the Precipitancy of the Clergy, who push'd it unreasonably when Peoples Minds were inflam'd about the Stamp Act—We must now wait 3 Years before it can be resumed.

I really find not the People seemingly the same as formerly. The Stamp Act has introduc'd so much Party Rage, Faction, and Debate that the ancient Hospitality, Generosity, and Urbanity for which these People were celebrated is destroyed, and at an End: Malevolent Minds greatly injur'd Me in my Absence, by insinuating that I corresponded with, and was a Spy of the Ministry—and gone home, not for Orders, but with Information, and Anecdotes—By which I was exposed to all the Load of Abuse, Detraction, and Infamy, as an innocent Person may be supposed to suffer from Infernals, and the Rage of Demons. Not a Soul have they spar'd whom they thought were Advocates for the Act.

I am not yet settled, nor yet got my Goods up into the Country the Carriage is so tedious and Expensive—Many Articles, its impossible to transport, and therefore am obliged to dispose off— St. Matthews Church is not yet built—for ev'ry thing lay suspended till the Repeal of the Stamp-Act—for they seem'd resolv'd to starve themselves, to starve their Mother Country.

Our Legislature is very intent on annihilating their Public Debt, which is almost compass'd, Whereby the future annual Taxes will be very light—They are determined alway to raise the current Supplies within the current Year, and never to anticipate the Revenue.

If more Ministers are not provided, and do not come over soon, We shall have all the late German, French, and Irish Settlers, become followers of the New Lights, or join the other Sectaries, and the Interests of the Church be entirely lost for they are already at a very low Ebb.

That Your Lordship may long live to be an Ornament to the Age and Country wherein You reside, and a Blessing to these Wild Regions, is the prayer of My Lord, Your Lordships most obliged most obedient and most dutiful Son and Servant Charles Woodmason

# On Correct Behavior in Church:

## "Bring no Dogs with You." [17]

Always contrive to come before Service begins—Which You may do, as We begin so late. 'Tis but putting and getting things in Order over Night—Whereas many will hardly set about it till Sunday Morning. Contrive too, to go as early as possible to rest on Saturday Night so that You may rise early and refresh'd on the Lords day and not be hurry'd in dressing, and ordering Matters. The coming late to Sermon discourages People, for lack of Company—and coming in after Service is begun is very troublesome—Disturb both me and ev'ry One and should be avoided as much as possible—But if it is unavoidable, pray enter leisurely—tread softly—nor disturb any who are on their Knees or are intent on their Devotions. Bring no Dogs with You—they are very troublesome—and I shall ~~fine~~ [18] inform the Magistrate of those who do it, for it is an Affront to the Divine Presence which We invoke, to be in the midst of Us, and to hear our Prayers, to mix unclean things with our Services.

When You are seated—do not whisper, talk, gaze about—shew light Airs, or Behaviour—for this argues a wandering Mind and Irreverence towards God; is unbecoming Religion, and may give Scandal and Offence to weak Christians:—Neither sneeze or Cough, if You can avoid it—and do not practise that unseemly, rude, indecent Custom of Chewing or of spitting, which is very ridiculous and absurd in Public, especially in Women and in Gods

17. Sermon Book, II, [421-32]. These extracts are from a sermon obviously designed for troublesome congregations. It was given at the High Hills, July 8, 1770, and at Rafting Creek, July 15, 1770. *Ibid.*, [454].

18. This is an interesting slip. Woodmason was still thinking as a magistrate.

House. If you are thirsty—Pray drink before you enter or before Service begins, not to go out in midst of Prayer, nor be running too and fro like Jews in their Synagogues—[19] except Your necessary Occasions should oblige You—Do You see anything like it in Charles Town or among Well bred People. Keep Your Children as quiet as possible. If they will be fractious, Carry them out at once for I will not have Divine Worship *now* consider'd by You, as if I was officiating in a private House.

Those among you who have not the tunes we do now, or shall sing, and are desirous of them, I will write them out for . . . . Many among you possibly prefer Extempore Sermons, to those which are Premeditated, and may call my Mode of Delivery, rather *Reading* than *Preaching*. 'Tis true, extempore Discourses have their peculiar Merit—but there is hardly one Man in the World, but will speak better and more useful Sense, premediately than Extempore. . . .

Ev'ry Sunday Afternoon, I purpose catechising as Many of You, Young and old, as can possibly attend. . . .

When Banns are published—Don't make it a Matter of Sport; but let it stir You up to put up a Petition to Heav'n for a Blessing of God upon the Parties.

19. The Rev. Charles Boschi reported that he had stopped a congregation in St. Bartholomew's Parish from entering and leaving the chapel in time of sermon or prayer to make punch, or to bring drinking water to those in the chapel during time of worship. Charles Boschi to the S.P.G., St. Bartholomew's Parish, Apr. 7, 1746, *S. C. Hist. and Gen. Mag.*, 50 (1949), 190.

# The Plight of the Anglicans:

### "The Stipends of the Clergy here, is not a competent Maintenance." [20]

You need not be told that ev'ry Minister has a Particular and distinc[t] Charge. He has a Circle assigned Him, in which He is to move and not stir out off. He cannot leave his Church for one Sunday without leave of the Vestry (except in one Particular Case) under Pain of a Fine—Nor can He quit the Province, on any Account whatever with out Leave of the Assembly—So that some Gentlemen have expired, because they could not go off for Change of Air—on Account of the Houses not sitting. And (I believe) none at present, are Elected, or Inducted into their Parishes—So that to act contrary to the Voice of their Vestries, would subject them to being dismissed immediately . . . .[21]

20. Sermon Book, IV, [154-84]. A postscript, p. [196], indicates that this sermon was written for presentation in the homes of Backcountry Anglicans: "At Thomas Woodwards—Broad River, At Thomas Edgehills—Saludy River, At John Lees—near the Catawba Nation, At Lewis People's—on Little Lynchs Creek, At Thomas Kinnerly—on Great Saludy, At the Congaree Chapel on Congaree River, at Lane's Mill—on Wateree River, At High Hills of Santee, and Rafting Creek, (With various Omissions and Modifications)." The date of the sermon is ca. 1769-1770.

21. Lieutenant-Governor Bull reported that once a clergyman was made rector, there was no way to get rid of him even though he gave "great cause of scandal" to the parish, and that "The People have therefore determined latterly not to elect their Clergy but keep them only quam diu se bene gesserint, for I know no instance of any Clergyman wantonly dismissed: This proceeding is founded on a clause in the Church Act impowering the Church Wardens of a vacant Parish to agree with any Minister to officiate till a Rector is elected, and they draw on the Public Treasurer for his Salary annually." Bull to Hillsborough, Nov. 30, 1770, P.R.O., Trans., XXXII, 369. See also Bull to Earl of Dartmouth, Charleston, Feb. 22, 1775, *ibid.*, XXXV, 21-22.

The Stipends of the Clergy here, is not a competent Maintenance. It hardly subsists them—and those few among Us who *Shine away* owe their Splendor to their marrying of Women of Property. Not from their Incomes . . . . I am a single Person and yet my Income hardly clears the Expences of my constant Journeys here around and among You. One fifth of my Stipend goes Yearly in Horse flesh—Another in Charity—A Third in Cloathing—A fourth in other Necessaries—And the Remainder in Contingent Expenses of Books Stationary, Wares and the Like. So that I save Nothing. Nay, I could not support myself but from the Contributions and Assistance of private Friends and Gentlemen. Because ev'ry thing is against Me and the Salary, is totally inadequate to the Expense. And yet I travel without any Attendance, or the least Appointment becoming a Gentleman—and One whom You have known, to Live and move, in a more Eligible Department, but who sacrific'd all to render You what Services, was in his Poor Power and for which Sacrifice he receives no thanks.

And as I never had the offer, so never have I ask'd or received the Value of an Apple or an Egg from You [22]—but always travelled on the foot, and with the Spirit of a Gentleman . . . .

I speak not thus from any regard to Money because its well Known, that where persons are poor I demand Nothing, and where Two pay, Three do not . . . .

For You must not imagine that ev'ry *Raw Collegian,* An unseason'd foreigner could Rough it as I do. It is by many painful Sicknesses Several Voyages—Constant Travel and Change of Air that has inur'd me to undergo the Fatigues I now do. Few, or None were Capable of it, save my Self. None could be found to

22. In a sermon of ca. 1771, Woodmason makes a similar statement: "I can safely say, that in five Years being among You, I'd not received the Value of an Apple or an Egg from any of You—And I can further safely say, and prove, that in that Space, I have scattered among You five hundred Guineas." Sermon Book, III, [611]. In a petition of 1770 asking that a chapel of ease be founded in or near the High Hills, the names of thirty men are subscribed as contributors towards the expenses of such a chapel. The largest contribution was that of the Camden merchant, Joseph Kershaw; the second largest was that of Charles Woodmason. See Virginia Eliza Singleton, *The Singletons of South Carolina* (n.p., n.d.), 5-6.

undertake this Mission, therefore I was solicited to it. And have had sufficient Reason to lament that ever I accepted of it, as You all Well know. Not an House has been provided, or Chapel built, or any Thing done . . . .

My Residence being unsettled, I have not been able to form so many settled Congregations as I could wish. Yet the Number that I have rais'd, would hardly be believ'd. Yet as fast as I build up, others pull down. Go where I will, I have half a dozen of these Wandering Stars [New Light Baptists] at my Heels. They come not near me, but when I am departed, then they all fall to *braying* and discomposing Peoples Thoughts and Minds.

# The Presbyterians Urged to Be Tolerant:

## "We should live like Brethren in Unity." [23]

I speak this [urging kind treatment to non-Presbyterians] on Account of the Infidels and Atheists around, who never will be perswaded to turn Religious, by any Rough treatment, or abusive Words—As also on Account of our Neighbours of the Reformed Churches in Germany. Severals of whom (as well as of my People) complain, that when they have brought their Children to this House of Worship for to be baptized Your Elders would not suffer the Minister to receive them, because the Parents were not in Church membership with You. Now Gentlemen I do not think this Treatment defensible—but rather reprehensible. . . . And I further hope, never more to hear of Your Inhospitality to Strangers, only because they are Episcopalians, and not of Your Kirk. . . .

2dly. There is an External Enemy near at Hand, which tho' not formidable either to our Religion or Liberties, still is to be guarded against. These are our *Indian* Neighbours. Common Prudence, and our Common Security, requires that We should live

23. Sermon Book, IV, [303], [314-15]. Woodmason appended an explanatory note to this sermon: "N. B. In the Year 1768 I was invited by Mr. Richardson, and others of the Waxaw Settlement on the Catawba River in North Carolina, to give them A Sermon in their Meeting House in that District. Mr. Richardson (their Pastor) saying That his People were very desirous of hearing an Episcopal Minister, as they never had seen or heard an English Preacher (they being all Scotch-Irish Presbyterians) And Mr. Richardson recommending Christian Love and Peace for the Subject the following Discourse was drawn up to oblige them. But some of the Kirk Elders not being agreeable, it was never deliver'd." *Ibid.*, p. [274]. Woodmason errs in the date. According to his Journal, he arranged to exchange with William Richardson in late January, 1767. See p. 14.

like Brethren in Unity, be it only to guard against any Dangers to our Lives and Properties as may arise from that Quarter.

3dly. We have an *Internal* Enemy Not less than 100 M̶ [100,000] *Africans* below us (and more are daily importing) Over these We ought to keep a very watchful Eye, lest they surprize us in an Hour when We are not aware, and begin our Friendships towards each other in one Common Death.[24]

24. Woodmason later adds that the Presbyterians and Anglicans should unite against the New Light Baptists as their common enemy. *Ibid.,* [317].

# The Baptists and the Presbyterians:

*"This is very fine* Talking: *I could wish that all the*
Doings *too, were equally Innocent."* [25]

But surely, if Persons have received more and better Edification by resorting to the Schism Shop, then by continuing constant
in Well doing at their own Chapel certainly it will display it Self
in their Lives and Manners. This is the Test by which We must
try the Validity of these Assertions—And therefore I hope it will
not be thought invidious if I enter into a few Particulars. Because
I hear so much Talk about *Conversion,* certainly there must be
some very Great Reformation of Morals among You: But I would
not have Te Deum sung before the Victory be gain'd.

You doubtless will allow, That keeping Holy the Lords day, is

25. Sermon Book, III, [465-96]. The sermon is roughly dated 1768 by the
postscript: "N. B. The Substance of the foregoing Sheets was delivered at the
Episcopal Chapel on the Congaree River in South Carolina, about the Time
when the Affair of the Episcopate was agitated in America." A subsequent
note is intended to clarify one of Woodmason's charges in the sermon:
"Memorandum—The Baptists had built a meeting House within few Rods
of this Chapel—and about a thousand persons of the dissenting Tribe, were
at that time under the Hands of Surgeons for the Vener[e]al Distemper."
*Ibid.,* [532].

The strictures against the Baptists for failing to reform the behavior of their
members are unfair. In some cases he grudgingly admits reform, although at
the same time he attempts to minimize the concessions by charges that the
reforms are only superficial or that they have given way to other forms of misbehavior.

The records of the Cashaway Baptist Church in the Peedee section show
that valiant efforts were made to reform erring members. In September, 1759,
members were forbidden to attend shooting matches or races without consent,
and in the years following many members were investigated, and sometimes
suspended, for drinking too much, and for other forms of misbehavior. See
Cashaway Baptist Church Book, Record Book 1756-1778, typescript in Caroliniana Library, Columbia.

a positive Command of God, and enjoin'd by the Laws of this Land—And that Two Years past, it was rather more profan'd than any other day of the Week—and I would enquire if it is not so still? It may be replied, That it is not—That there is not that frolicing, feasting and Rioting as formerly. But this I deny. For as my Station leads me to travel over most Parts of the Country, and ofttimes on Sundays, as well as other Days, I do aver, that there is little or no Reformation of Manners on this Head save in some few Environs of a Meeting House, or among the Cohee Settlers—For the same riding the Woods, Shooting Cattle Hunting—driving Waggons, Hogs Horses—Travelling to and fro—Fishing—Fowling—Trapping—Taverning, Swimming and Bathing, and various Field and Domestic Matters, are carried on, and followed up as usual. Nor can I perceive any Reform: So far from it, That the Sabbath is not so regularly observ'd, as when You us'd statedly to resort to Church: But since quitting of the Church, the Sabbath is but seldom observ'd—for we see none resort to any Place of Worship, but when some Itinerant Babler, or Vagrant Ignorant Bellweather comes to a Meeting House and then the Silly Herd run in Droves to listen to what none can comprehend and this for greater Edification. If therefore staying at Home, Sleeping and Lounging privately tipling and wantoning, be hallowing the Lords Day, I will acknowledge that in this Sense it is *highly* sanctified—tho' I think it would more rationally and more religiously be so, would People resort to their proper Churches to hear the Word of God solemnly read, and their Duty explain'd to them in a sober, sensible and judicious Manner.

There is one Circumstance which I cannot but thus publickly take Notice off and reprove, because it not only occasions the Non-observance of the Sabbath but is an Evil in it Self, and scandalous to the Country—and that is—The transacting of all Public Business on Saturdays. Thus We see Magistrates have their Sittings—Militia Officers their Musters—Merchants their Vendues —Planters their Sales, all on Saturdays: Is there any Shooting, Dancing, Revelling, Drinking Matches carrying on? It is all begun on Saturday, and as all these Meetings and Transactions are executed at Taverns, Not a Saturday in the Year, but some one or other of them (and at more than one Tavern) are statedly repeatedly carried on—So that at these Rendezvous there is more Company of a Saturday, than in the Church on Sunday: And these Assemblies are not only carried on under Eye of the Magistrates, but even by them—Most of them being Store or Tavern Keepers. Thus Vice and Wickedness is countenanc'd by those whose Duty it is to suppress it—but their Interest to promote it. And yet several of these Magistrates are Heads of these New Congregations: Consequently, all this tends to Edification. It tends to all Kinds of Debauchery: For of those who may quit the Tavern and return home, they are so heavy, sleepy drunk and stupid, as to be unable, utterly unfit to attend Public Worship on Sunday. Herefrom they stay at home to sleep off their Dose, and thereby confine their families likewise: And herefrom arises the Evil of so few assembling here at Divine Service ev'ry Lords Day: Saturday being chosen as a day whereon they may fully indulge themselves in Drink, and so sleep it off on Sunday, to be fit to attend Business on Monday, and so not two days lost to them in the Week. (But this Subject I shall consider more fully in a future Discourse.)

It may be reply'd to me, That altho' People do stay at home, and not come to Chapel on those Sundays when there is no Sermon at the Meeting Yet that they employ themselves in Religious Exercises, and Works of Edification: What Works?—In Singing of Hymns and Spiritual Songs—whereby their Hearts are greatly inflam'd with Divine Love and Heav'nly Joy, and makes the H[oly] G[host] be shed abroad in their Hearts. This is very fine *Talking:* I could wish that all the *Doings* too, were equally Innocent. But let me say, that these Assemblies at Private Houses for Singing Hymns, is very reprehensible. First because People may assemble in this Place, and Sing, and then no Scandal would arise, and 2dly The Hymns commonly sung, had far better be thrown into the Fire. I have seen many of them—Which are not only execrable in Point of Versification, but withal full of Blasphemy Nonsense, and Incoherence. No Edification therefore can spring from such Singing. Withal should it be said, that they thus meet because these Hymns and Tunes are not permitted in the Church—I answer That as to the Tunes, the Clerk is the Person concern'd Who is both able and willing to gratify any in Choice of Tunes; And as for Hymns We do not disallow of them, provided they be Solemn, Sublime, Elegant and Devout—Fit to be offer'd up to the Throne of Grace—And such can be furnish'd to any Religious Society, desirous of them.

The best Things are most liable to Abuse—And these Singing Matches lie under the Imputation of being only Rendezvous of Idlers, under the Mask of Devotion. Meetings for Young Persons to carry on Intrigues and Amours. For all Classes of Villains, and the Vicious of both Sexes to make Assignations; and for others to indulge themselves in Acts of Intemperance and Wantoness, So that these Religious Societies are Evil spoken off, and therefore ought to be abolished conformable to what was done in the Primitive Times. The first Christians us'd to assemble at Nights, at the Tombs of the Martyrs, and there sing Hymns and perform Prayers. But as this gave Offence to the Heathens, and occasion'd the whole Body to be censur'd for the Irregularities of a Few it was judged proper to abolish these Nocturnal Meetings: And this Act of the Primitive Church ought to be a Rule to us at present: For it is rather better to decline an Innocent Duty that may be productive of some Good, rather than to have it perverted by base Minds to many Purposes of Evil:

But let us go on, and examine if in the General Corruption of Manners these New Lights have made any Reform in the Vice of Drunkenness? Truly, I wot not. There is not one Hogshead of Liquor less consum'd since their visiting us, or any Tavern shut up—So far from it, that there has been Great Increase of Both. Go to any Common Muster or Vendue, Will you not see the same Fighting, Brawling Gouging, Quarreling as ever? And this too among the Holy ones of our New Israel? Are Riots, Frolics, Races, Games, Cards, Dice, Dances, less frequent now than formerly? Are fewer persons to be seen in Taverns? or reeling or drunk on the Roads? And have any of the Godly Storekeepers given up their Licences, or refus'd to retail Poison? If this can be made appear, I will yield the Point. But if [it] can be made apparent that a much greater Quantity of Rum is now expended in private families than heretofore—That the greater Part of these religious Assemblies are calculated for private Entertainments, where each brings his Quota and which often terminates in Intemperance and Intoxication of both Sexes, Young and Old: That one half of those who resort to these Assemblies Go more for sake of Liquor, than Instruction, or Devotion. That if it be proven that Liquor has been top'd about even in their very Meeting Houses, and the Preachers refreshed with Good Things, and after the Farce ended Stuff'd and Cramm'd almost to bursting, then it must be granted that little or no Reform has been made among the Vulgar in Point of Intemperance save only among some few Persons in some Places where the Mode only is chang'd, and drinking in Public wav'd for the Indulgence of double the Consumption in Private.

The horrid Vice of Swearing has long been a reproach to the Back Inhabitants, and very justly—for few Countries on Earth can equal these Parts as to this greivous Sin. But has it ceas'd since the Admission of rambling Fanatics among us? I grant that it has with and among many, whom they have gain'd to their Sect. Yet still it too much prevails. But the Enormity of this Vice, when at the Highest, produc'd no Evils, Jarrs, disturbances Strifes, Contentions, Variance, Dissimulations, Envyings, Slanders, Backbitings and a thousand other Evils that now disturb both the Public Places and repose of Individuals. So that where they have cast out one Devil, Seven, and twice Seven others have enter'd In and possess the Man. For never was so much Lying, Calumny, Defamation, and all hellish Evils and vexations of this Sort that can spring from the Devil and his Angels, so brief so prevalent, so abounding as since the Arrival of these villanous Teachers, Who blast, blacken, Ruin, and destroy the Characters, Reputations, Credit and Fame of all Persons not linked with them to the Ruin of Society, the Peace of families, and the Settlement of the Country.

We will further enquire, if Lascivousness, or Wantoness, Adultery or Fornication [are] less common than formerly, before the Arrival of these *Holy* Persons? Are there fewer Bastards born? Are more Girls with their Virginity about them, Married, than were heretofore? The Parish Register will prove the Contrary: There are rather more Bastards, more Mullatoes born than before. Nor out of 100 Young Women that I marry in a Year have

I seen, or is there seen, Six but what are with Child? And this as Common with the Germans on other Side the River, as among You on this Side: So that a Minister is accounted as a Scandalous Person for even coming here to marry such People, and for baptizing their Bastard Children as the Law obliges Me to register All Parties who are Married, and all Children Born. This occasions such Numbers (especially of the Saints) to fly into the next Province, and up to the German Ministers and any where to get Married, to prevent their being register'd, as therefrom the Birth of their Children would be trac'd: And as for Adulteries, the present State of most Persons around 9/10 of whom now labour under a filthy Distemper (as is well known to all) puts that Matter out of all Dispute and shews that the Saints however outwardly Precise and Reserved are not one Whit more Chaste than formerly, and possibly are more privately Vicious.

And nothing more leads to this Than what they call their Love Feasts and Kiss of Charity. To which Feasts, celebrated at Night, much Liquor is privately carried, and deposited on the Roads, and in Bye Paths and Places. The Assignations made on Sundays at the Singing Clubs, are here realized. And it is no wonder that Things are as they are, when many Young Persons have 3. 4. 5. 6 Miles to walk home in the dark Night, with Convoy, thro' the Woods? Or staying perhaps all Night at some Cabbin (as on Sunday Nights) and sleeping together either doubly or promiscuously? Or a Girl being mounted behind a Person to be carried home, or any wheres. All this indeed contributes to multiply Subjects for the King in this frontier Country, and so is wink'd at by the Magistracy and Parochial Officers but at same time, gives great Occasion to the Enemies of Virtue, to triumph, for Religion to be scandalized and brought into Contempt; For all Devotion to be Ridicul'd, and in the Sequel, will prove the Entire banishment and End of all Religion—Confusion—Anarchy and ev'ry Evil Work will be the Consequence of such Lewdness and Immorality.

But certainly these Reformers have put some Stop to the many Thefts and Depradations so openly committed of late Years?—To answer this Question recourse must be had to the Magistrates and Courts of Justice, who are ready to declare, that since the

Appearance of these New Lights, more Enormities of all Kinds have been committed—More Robberies Thefts, Murders, Plunderings, Burglaries and Villanies of ev'ry Kind, than ever before. And the Reason hereof, Is, That most of these Preaching fellows were most notorious Theives, Jockeys, Gamblers, and what not in the Northern Provinces, and since their Reception and Success here have drawn Crowds of their old Acquaintances after them; So that the Country never was so full as at present of Gamesters Prostitutes, Filchers, Racers, Fidlers and all the refuse of Mankind. All which follow these Teachers, and under the Mask of Religion carry on many detestable Practises. In short, they have filled the Country with Idle and Vagrant Persons, who live by their Criminalities. For it is a Maxim with these Vermin of Religion, That a Person must first be a Sinner e're He can be a Saint. And I am bold to say, That the Commonality around, do not now make half the Crops nor are 1/4 so Industrious, as 3 Years ago. Because half their Time is wasted in traveling about to this and that Lecture—and to hear this and that fine Man, So that they are often a Month absent from their families. . . .

For only draw a Comparison between them and Us, and let an Impartial Judge determine where *Offence* may cheifly be taken, At our Solemn, Grave, and Serious Sett Forms, or their Wild Extempore Jargon, nauseaus to any Chaste or refin'd Ear. There are so many Absurdities committed by them, as wou'd shock one of our *Cherokee* Savages; And was a Sensible Turk or Indian to view some of their Extravagancies it would quickly determine them against Christianity. Had any such been in their Assembly as last Sunday when they communicated, the Honest Heathens would have imagin'd themselves rather amidst a Gang of frantic Lunatics broke out of Bedlam, rather than among a Society of religious Christians, met to celebrate the most sacred and Solemn Ordinance of their Religion. Here, one Fellow mounted on a Bench with the Bread, and bawling, *See the Body of Christ,* Another with the Cup running around, and bellowing—*Who cleanses his Soul with the Blood of Christ,* and a thousand other Extravagancies—One on his knees in a Posture of Prayer—Others singing—some howling—These Ranting—Those Crying—Others dancing, Skipping, Laughing and rejoycing. Here two or 3 Women falling on their Backs, kicking up their Heels, exposing their Nakedness to all Bystanders and others sitting Pensive, in deep Melancholy lost in Abstraction, like Statues, quite insensible— and when rous'd by the Spectators from their pretended Reveries Transports, and indecent Postures and Actions declaring they knew nought of the Matter. That their Souls had taken flight to Heav'n, and they knew nothing of what they said or did. Spect[at]ors were highly shocked at such vile Abuse of sacred Ordinances! And indeed such a Scene was sufficient to make the vilest Sinner shudder. Their Teacher, so far from condemning, or reproving, them, call'd it, the Work of God, and returned Thanks for Actions deserving of the Pillory and Whipping Post. But that would not have been *New* to some of them. And if they can thus transgress all bounds of Decency Modesty, and Morality, in such an Open Public Manner, it is not hard to conceive what may pass at their Nocturnal Meetings, and Private Assemblies. Is there any thing like this in the Church of England to give Offence?

But another vile Matter that does and must give Offence to all Sober Minds Is, what they call their *Experiences;* It seems, that before a Person be dipp'd, He must give an Account of his Secret Calls, Conviction, Conversion, Repentance &c &c. Some of these Experiences have been so ludicrous and ridiculous that *Democritus* [26] in Spite of himself must have burst with Laughter. Others, altogether as blasphemous Such as their Visions, Dreams, Revelations—and the like; Too many, and too horrid to be mention'd. Nothing in the *Alcoran* Nothing that can be found in all the Miracles of the Church of Rome, and all the Reveries of her Saints can be so absurd, or so Enthusiastic, as what has gravely been recited in that *Tabernacle* Yonder—To the Scandal of Religion and Insult of Common Sense. And to heighten the Farce, To see two or three fellows with fix'd Countenances and grave Looks, hearing all this Nonsense for Hours together, and making particular Enquiries, when, How, Where, in what Manner, these Miraculous Events happen'd—To see, I say, a Sett of Mongrels under Pretext of Religion, Sit, and hear for Hours

26. Democritus, born ca. 470 B.C., was one of the leading Greek physical philosophers, an older contemporary of Socrates.

together a String of Vile, cook'd up, Silly and Senseless Lyes, What they know to be Such, What they are Sensible has not the least foundation in Truth or Reason, and to encourage Persons in such Gross Inventions must grieve, must give great Offence to ev'ry one that has the Honour of Christianity at Heart.

Then again to see them Divide and Sub divide, Split into Parties—Rail at and excommunicate one another—Turn out of Meeting, and receive into another—And a Gang of them getting together and gabbling one after the other (and sometimes disputing against each other) on Abstruse Theological Question—Speculative Points—Abstracted Notions, and Scholastic Subtelties, such as the greatest Metaph[ys]icians and Learned Scholars never yet could define, or agree on—To hear Ignorant Wretches, who can not write—Who never read ten Pages in any Book, and can hardly read the Alphabett discussing such Knotty Points for the Edification of their Auditors, is a Scene so farcical, so highly humoursome as excels any Exhibition of Folly that has ever yet appear'd in the World, and consequently must give High offence to all Inteligent and rational Minds.

If any Thing offensive beyond all This to greive the Hearts and Minds of serious Christians presents it Self to view among them, it is their Mode of Baptism, to which Lascivous Persons of both Sexes resort, as to a Public Bath. I know not whether it would not be less offensive to Modesty for them to strip wholly into Buff at once, than to be dipp'd with those very thin Linen Drawers they are equipp'd in—Which when wet, so closely adheres to the Limbs, as exposes the Nudities equally as if none at All. If this be not Offensive and a greivous Insult on all Modesty and Decency among Civiliz'd People I know not what can be term'd so. Certainly a few chosen Witnesses of the Sex of the Party, and performance of the Ceremony in a Tent, or Cover'd Place, would be equally as *Edifying,* as Persons being stript and their Privities expos'd before a gaping Multitude who resort to these Big Meetings (as they are term'd) as they would to a Bear or Bullbaiting.

It must give Great Scandal and Offence to all Serious Minds thus to see the Solemn Ordinances of God become the Sport, Pastime and Derision of Men—and to view them marching in

Procession singing Hymns before the poor wet half naked Creature—Very edifying this! Just as much as I saw lately practis'd
at Marriage of one of their Notable She Saints around whom
(the Ceremony ended) they march'd in Circles singing Hymns,
and chanting Orisons, with a vast Parade of Prayer Thanks giv-
ings and Religious Foppery; Which had such marvellous Effect
on the virtuous Devotee as to cause her to bring a Child in five
Months after, as a Proof that their Prayers for her being fruitful
was answer'd.

This Devotee was highly celebrated for her extraordinary Illu-
minations, Visions and Communications. It is the same who in
her Experience told a long Story of an Angel coming to visit her
in the Night thro' the Roof of her Cabbin—In flames of Fire
too! It was very true that she was visited in the Night, and that
the Apparation did jump down upon her Bed thro' the Shingles
by an opening she had made for the Purpose—and that it came
to her all on Fire. Yes! But it was in the Fire of Lust; And this
Angel was no other than her Ghostly Teacher, to whom she
communicated a Revelation that it was ordain'd He should caress
Her; And He Good Man, was not disobedient to this Heav'nly
Call—He afterward had a Revelation That it was the Will of
God such a Man was to take her to Wife Which the Poor unthinking Booby did, in Conformity to the Divine Will express'd
by his prophet—Little dreaming that He was to Father the
Prophets Bastard. All this (and much more) the Woman has con-
fess'd to Me. But You see hereby that Revelations now a days,
are not strictly to be depended On—and that those who have
such extraordinary Gifts of the Spirit given, are apt to fall into
Mistakes, as did a Neighbouring Teacher lately in the Night
Poor Man Mistaking another Woman for his Wife—and the
Spirit in her making no resistance. . . .

But not Content with alledging the Vile falsities of Non Edification, and Offence as Extenuations of their quitting the Church
in which they were Born, and Baptiz'd in order to be baptiz'd
over again, and to be Pure from all Sin—(Save that of Schism
and Lying) Another Company has given out, That it was against
their Conscience to stay any longer among us—That they had
Scruples of Conscience about Kneeling, and Bowing, and other

Ceremonies enjoin'd by our Liturgy and therefore to *quiet their Consciences* they were under necessity of quitting us.

Well, who can but Pity and compassionate such tender Consciences, Such delicate Minds!—Who would wound such refin'd Organs as their exquisitely form'd Angelic Souls carry about them. I have been told that Your late worthy Pastor quite inverted the Nature of Things to comply with these over Nice Gentry, and to quiet the Qualms of their uneasy Consciences. This Chapel where We now are, was built agreeable to their Humour. No Pews, Font, Communion Table, or any thing resembling a Place of Worship saving this Pulpit, so that it may serve either for a Conventicle, Chapel, Dancing Room, Hall of Justice, Barn or any Thing. Yet this did not Content—Their *poor Consciences* were so very Clamorous, That a New Barn must be built with 4 Doors instead of Two, and no Pulpit at All, in Order that ev'ry one may dance In and Out ev'ry Minute like Jews at their Synagogue, or Wasps in their Nest. Mr. Rowand would dispense with the Ring in Marriage—Yet this did not prevent *tender Consciences* from running to *unknown* Magistrates, to get Married. He retrenched the Service—omitted 2 or 3 Repetitions of the Lords Prayer—Gave an Extempore Prayer before Sermon—Preach'd Extempore—Wore no Surplice—Officiated in a Coat—Put his Band in his Pocket—Wore a Blue instead of a Black Coat—Never call'd for God fathers or God Mothers:—Nor us'd the Sign of the Cross excepted desir'd—Or read the Nicene or Athanasian Creeds, but by desire—Left it to People to receive Standing, or Kneeling at receiving the Communion—Varied several Passages in the different Offices, and endeavoured to make himself All Things to All Men, to quiet their rebellious Consciences. Yet All would not Do—*Conscience* must be obey'd, and after all his Endeavours to gratify their Humours at Expence of *his* own Conscience, They had the Conscience to quit Him, tho' a most Pious, Just, Upright, and Holy Man. But he was no Orator. A Matter that doubtless must give Great Offence to weak Consciences from the Self same argument That He was not with all his other Good Qualities, Ten feet high. . . .

Some of our qualmish Neighbours whose Consciences keep them in perpetual Disquiet cannot bear the Thought (without

Shuddering and Sweating) of Bowing at the Name of *Jesus*. But their *tender* Consciences will never upbraid them or fly in their faces, for bowing down upon a Strumpet, and committing fornication.

Others, will not admit of the Cross in Baptism but their Consciencies have not the least Objection to the Stealing of my Horse, or killing my Cattle and Hogs, and saying a Long Grace over their Flesh when cook'd up to their Table.

Again, Others have Scruples of Conscience in respect to use of the Ring in Marriages but have not the least Scruple of running away with other Mens Wives—Of committing adultery, of breaking the Laws of the Land by being named by Lay Men, and marrying of Others, by No Form, or, any Ceremony, or before any Witnesses, so that none know if they are, or are not married, or of turning away this Wife, and taking another of having 2 or 3 Wives or Concubines at the same Time.

Others more Reighteous over much than these, and whose Consciences rise up in Judgment against them for receiving the Holy Commandment Kneeling, feel no Scruples at not paying of their Just Debts, and cheating and overreaching whomsoever they can deceive under the Mask of Piety.

Others, whose Consciences torment and trouble them for having made use of Prayer printed in a Book, make no Scruple of promising Marriage to a Young Ignorant Maiden. Then debauching her—and after a Time, then exposing her weakness—sacrificing her to the Lust [of] Others, and then abandoning her as a Wanton Hussey, though made so by his own conscientious Acts and Contrivances.

Others are so exceeding Conscientious That in taking of an Oath they would not lay their Hand on the Bible, or Kiss the Book. No! that is Popish—that is abominable—But they would make no Scruple to kiss their Neighbours Wife.

Some others Consciencies are very nice in respect to Hats—Buttons—Lace, and Ornaments of Dress—Their Consciencies would condemn them as Great Sinners in having more than Ten Buttons on their Coat. But they feel no Remorse in drinking Ten Bottles of Wine or Ale, and getting as drunk as Beasts.

So Conscientious are Others that sooner than come over the

Threshold of that Door to hear the Word of God read or
preached by a Man drest in a White Garment, That they will
swim in the River, Bathe in the Creeks, Men and Women publickly together Stark naked in the Stream on Sundays, without
any Qualms of Conscience for such Indecent and Immodest Practises.

It must be very Painful and Uneasy to any Person, doubtless
to be troubled with such excessive a Tender Conscience those
more especially whose Consciences would cause them to faint at
Sound of an Organ in a Church, but whose Conscience never
accuse them of utterring ten thousand Lyes, Scandals, Defama-
tions and falshoods against their Neighbours. Such are much of
a Piece with some before mention'd who will not wear a Button
on their Hats—Yet have the Conscience to cheat his Rector and
defraud Him of his Dues and Emoluments established by Law. . . .

But let me not forget some other scrupulous Conscientious
Souls, who reside somewhat Northerly of Us [the Presbyterians
of the Waxhaws] and who exclaim against our Burial Service—
Calling it the Mass Praying for the Dead, to the Saints &c. Happy
for us, that we are not made to pray to the Devil. However these
conscientious Good Christians have no Scruple of Conscience to
Entertain the Horse Theives—to accomodate them with their
Daughters To receive Presents (I mean permitting the Girls to
receive Presents) and rigging themselves out in the Spoils taken
from Others To buy Bargains of Horses and Cattle: For to be
sure, there is no Text in Scripture that prohibits a Man from
buying a Good Bargain even should He go out of the Congregation in midst of Prayer, to secure, and bind it. Nor does the
Scripture add after the 8th Commandment *Thou shalt not
Swopp:* For there is a wide Difference between Stealing and Swopping. His Stealing the Horse from another is a Sin, and Breach
of the Commandment—But his swopping Him with me (after
his being Stollen) is no Sin—because there is no Prohibition.
What excellent Casuists we have among us!—What need to repair
to *Rome* for resolving Doubts and nice Cases of Conscience,
when they can be so nicely solved within 100d Miles. Do you
think Sir I would take (I mean) Steal Sir, another's Horse! No
Sir! But if He runs away from You, I will stop Him, Hide Him

in the Woods—plow with Him till He is a Skeleton, and then bring Him home to You, and claim the Reward Promis'd in the Advertisement. Or, I will take Him (I dont say Steal Him) out of Your Field—Ride, and Work Him—and then advertize Him at some distant Place—and Ride him perhaps to Virginia, or Georgia and wear him down as much as possible till Claim'd and Worn out—for the Law does not say I must *feed* Him, but only *keep* Him—and herein I fulfill the Royal Law, in doing by others, as others would by me. Such is the Causistry of the *Waxaws*.

I was giving Sermon at Flatt Rock 20 Miles above P. T. [Pine Tree] when a Conscientious Gentleman loos'd the Bridle from my Horse, who instantly ran down the Road home, and stopped at some Cabbin on the Path. The Owner secur'd the Saddle, and then carries the Creature to the next Magistrate and Tolls Him for a Stray, instead of bringing Him back to the Assembly, or leaving Him at my own House, by which He pass'd, and from whence I saw Him, and recover'd my Property. Property which was in a fair Way of being work'd for a Month, or otherwise dispos'd off. Many other Horses, with Womens Cloaks and Garments on them have these Conscientious Persons let loose during Sermons, in these Parts—and then shar'd the Spoils, because it was very Sinful in People to assemble and hear Mass said by a Jesuit in Disguise.

Another Act of Conscience practis'd by the Holy and Devout Members of their Kirk, was To take down the Advertisements for calling our People together, and nicely erasing the Name of the Month, and inserting some other: By this Means, I had Journeys to no Purpose. When I came, there were no People— and on other days, the People would meet, and no Minister: Thus we were perplexed for a while by our Over Righteous, Scrupulous, and Tender Consciens'd Sectaries, whom but few Years before We had deliver'd from Goals and Bridewells Poverty and Nakedness, and all the Miseries of Human Nature, and for whom, I had made very large Collections to relieve their extreme Necessity and Sicknesses, on their first arrival.

# The New Light Baptists:

## "Peoples Brains are turn'd and bewilder'd."[27]

INSTEAD OF having any fix'd Place of Abode, they [the New Light Clergy] are continually ranging from River to River devouring the fastings [?] of the Land. When one is gone, comes another and another. The wont is, That they don't all agree in one Tune. For one sings this Doctrine, and the next a different— So that Peoples Brains are turn'd and bewilder'd. But You may depend that they'l bring Scripture for all that they assert. As one lately did in Excuse for a Woman who had robbed her Husband to give to Him. He [said] she had a Right to the Money the same as God has to ev'ry thing. And as God bad[e] the Israelites to borrow of the Egyptians with out any Intention of repaying them, so this Woman was equally justifiable. The taking that Money from Him with which He was to pay the Merchant for Goods credited Him, was borrowing from the Egyptians to give to the Israelites. Rare Doctrine this, for benefit of the Merchants. But I observe, that among all these gifted and spiritualized Persons—all their Quotations and Metaphors, are drawn entirely from the O. T. And we never hear one Passage from our Lords Divine Sermon on the Mount. The first Article they begin with is to set the People against their several Ministers be they of whatever denomination. But especially the Established Clergy, against

27. Sermon Book, IV, [109-18]. This sermon is prefaced by Woodmason as follows: "Having received lately several Public Papers from *Pensylvania* wherein the Utility of an *American* Episcopate is freely debated—and others, wherein the Divine Institution of Episcopacy is openly attacked and denied ... I am desir'd by the Gentlemen of the Vestry of this Parish ... to vindicate the Honour of the Priesthood." *Ibid.*, [85-86]. This should date the sermon as some time in 1768 or 1769.

whom they utter all the vile and abominable Speeches, their rank Hearts can devise. Altho' there are not a more regular and Serious Body of Men on this Continent. The Common Prayer is run down—and the several Modes of Administration of Divine Offices. Then they begin with the Neighbourhood. Some are consigned to Damnation, others to Salvation—That is—Such as are Sensible and valuable Persons, Lovers of Peace and Order, and of the Church of England, and whom they are sensible they can make no Impression on—they are Reprobated—But the Giddy, and the Ignorant the Enthusiastic and Superstitious, whom they judge they may draw round them, such are *decreed* to be sav'd— And their Names are wrote in the Lamb's Book of Life—because they read it there. I ask'd some of those deluded Persons, thus infatuated, thus impos'd on, How these Persons, and when, and where they read and saw this Book of Gods decrees when at same Time, they could not read the *Psalter* when laid before them?— And what Language it was In? Because A *Dutchman's* Name would certainly be wrote in *Dutch* and as they could not read *Dutch* How could they tell that the Dutchmans Name was there?—The Answer given, was,—That the finger of God pointed it out to them.

Such are the Proceedings of these Men and in this Manner as they beguile poor unthinking, illiterate Creatures. But this Finger that pointed, was the finger of Satan—That this and that Man had a Good Fat Beef, or Porker, to be Kill'd for the next Assembly of the Saints at his House. This the Poor Wretch takes as a favour little imagining that they come to devour that Bacon, which Himself and family must subsist on in the Winter. And its observable That You never hear of any Preachments at Houses that are too Poor to feed Gods Lambs. . . .

I am sorry, very sorry, that I should ever be driven to utter public Invectives against any Man, or Sett of Men whatever, and especially from the Pulpit, a Place dedicated, and sacred to Divine Matters only. But the Insolence and Presumption of these Incendiaries, is intolerable. They oblige me to break thro' all bounds of Decorum. Not content with vilifying the Common Prayer, the Articles, the Canons and Homilies of our Church (which I dare aver not one of these fellows ever saw or read) But they have made open and publick attacks on me in their Several Congregations. One of them lately to shew his Wit, went quibbling and quirking on my Name. He told the Audience there were various Kinds of *Masons* in the World (and so went on) but that I was a Mason who built on rotten foundations and rais'd Buildings only of Straw and Strubble, and daub'd with untemper'd Mortar, and would never make any Strong buildings for Christ of such Carnal Ordinances—and that tho' I was an Wood Mason, He queried if I was a *Good* Mason—but as Wood was a perishable Matter, and serv'd for Fewel, so that I should Perish Everlastingly and serve for fuel to Hell fire.

Here You have the Church of England call'd A Rotten foundation—The Liturgy and Discipline—Chaff and Strubble. The Sacraments, Carnal Ordinances, and her Ministers, Children of Hell. Is this to be born in a Civiliz'd State where the Laws establish a Church and Clergy. But its not my Self only that these Wretches thus abuse; They call'd Mr. Turquand [28] A Turkey Cock (because he has a rosy Complexion) and Mr. Richardson [29] (who is a *Pale* Man) The Pale or White Horse of Death, for his People to ride on to Hell. . . .

If I give out to be at such a Place at such a Time, three or four of these fellows [New Lights] are constantly at my Heels— They either get there before me, and hold forth—or after I have finish'd, or the next Day, or for days together. Had I an hundred Tongues, or as many Pairs of Legs, I could not *singly* oppose such a Numerous Crew. . . .

How is it possible that I can visit the Sick—Or exhort, or reprove, or admonish When the People are told That I am a Jesuit in disguise—To others that I am a Presbyterian—To the Presbyterians—That I am an Independant—To the Independants That I am a Methodist?—This is done, in order to unsettle me where ever I Go—So that I am determin'd to resign my Commission as this next Week to the Board of Church Commissioners.

28. Paul Turquand had been licensed to work in South Carolina on the same day as Woodmason, April 28, 1766. He had been recommended by Lieutenant-Governor Bull to work in St. Matthew's Parish which, like St. Mark's, was in the Backcountry. Licensed to Plantations, Ful. Ms., Office of Church Commissioners, London; Bull to Bishop of London, Charleston, Feb. 1, 1766, Ful. Trans., No. 169. See also, Minutes of the Vestry of St. Matthew's Parish 1767 to 1838, typescript in Caroliniana Library, Columbia.

29. William Richardson, Presbyterian clergyman in the Waxhaws. See p. 14.

# The New Light Baptists:

*"And yet twelve months past most of these People were very zealous Members of our Church."* [30]

BUT THAT such a Charge [of Baptist hypocrisy and depravity] should be brought, levelled, or thought off, as to the whole Body, God forbid! As I know, and greatly respect, many worthy Persons among them and I wish that there were many more such. . . . For it is very plain that the Errors of some of our Neighbours do not so much proceed from a bad Heart (as is the Case with another Sect) as from a wrong Head. . . .

Would any Mortal three Years past have dreamd or imagin'd that such a Person as the infamous *Mulchey*,[31] who came here lately in Rags, hungry, and bare foot can now, at his beck, or Nod, or Motion of his finger lead out four hundred Men into the Wilderness in a Moment At his speaking the Word—Without asking any Questions, or making the least Enquiry for what or for why. . . .

And yet twelve months past most of these People were very zealous Members of our Church—and many of them Communi-

30. Sermon Book, III, [594-96], [623-26]. From a reference in this sermon to the "five Years being among You" [611], the date of this sermon must be 1771. It was delivered at Lynch's Creek, the High Hills, and the Congaree. *Ibid.*, [628].

31. The Rev. Philip Mulkey, a North Carolinian, moved to South Carolina about 1760. By late 1762 he had settled at Fairforest where he remained until 1776. In 1764 he began to preach in the Congaree region, near present-day Columbia. His highly effective preaching is credited with having led to the founding of other Baptist churches in the Congaree region. In later life he was excommunicated and the churches warned against him for adultery, perfidy, and falsehood. See Floyd Mulkey, "Rev. Philip Mulkey, Pioneer Baptist Preacher in Upper South Carolina," South Carolina Historical Association, *Proceedings* (1945), 3-12; Townsend, *S. C. Baptists*, 125-26, 142-43.

cants. What Man amongst all the Beaus and fine Gentlemen of the Land has such Influence over the Women as *Joseph Reez?* [32] It was but few Sundays past, That to make display of their Veneration for Him, and shew the Power He had over them, that He made them strip in the Public Meeting House, quite to their Shifts, and made them all walk home bare footed and bare legged. And had He only said it, they would have stript off their Smocks, and gone home stark Naked. . . .

That from the Success, and rapid Progress they have made and obtain'd, They now want to be as busy in respect to the State, as they have been with the Church. The Gentlemen of the Law, seem now to engage their Attention: Like *Straw* and *Tyler*,[33] of old, they want for to demolish all the Learned Professions. Human Learning being contrary to the Spirit of God.

32. The Rev. Joseph Reese was born in Pennsylvania and grew up an Anglican. He came to the Congaree region in 1745 where, like Philip Mulkey, he became an eloquent preacher with great command over the passions of his hearers. See Townsend, *S. C. Baptists,* 143-44; Morgan Edwards, Materials towards a History of the Baptists in South Carolina, 32-34, typescript in S. C. Hist. Soc.

33. John Rackstraw and Wat Tyler, associated in the English Peasants' Revolt of 1381.

# The New Light Baptists:

## "They apply to the Passions, not the Understanding of People." [34]

BUT OUR *unholy* Apostles, taking the Expression [the "New Tongues of the Apostles"] [35] in the Literal Sense, absolutely do speak or Sing or rehearse (or whatever it may be called) in New Tongues—In a barbrous Dialect—A constant Menotomy A squeaking, untuneable, unintelligible Jargon. Neither Verse or Prose, Singing or Speaking. And when one of them lately was reprimanded for this, and asked—Whether he sung, or spake, He answered in this blasphemous Strain *It is not I that speak—but the Spirit of God that dwelleth in me.* Yet this Spiritual Wretch had a Wench at that Time with Child by him of which she is lately deliv'd, and has made full Confession of this Villains Practices. . . .

For in respect to Him, who harangu'd the Crowd Yesterday, its well known, that two Years ago, he knew not one Letter of the Alphabet. And indeed the Man must have taken Great and extraordinary Pains (much to his Commendation) to acquire the Knowledge he has gain'd in so short a Space—for he read to me a Chapter tolerably well, tho' with great Stammering and Hesitation. And as for any other Book he frankly acknowledged he had never seen or read. . . .

However, one of them [Baptists] lately was deceiv'd—and

34. Sermon Book, III, [676-89], [700], [707]. These are extracts from a sermon "Wrote by desire of Mrs. Stark July 8. 1771. but never delivered to any Audiance." *Ibid.,* [714]. The "Mrs. Stark" may have been the wife of Robert Stark, an Anglican who was commissioned justice of the peace on July 30, 1771. Council Journal, July 30, 1771.

35. Mark 16:17. "And these signs shall follow them that believe; In my name shall they cast out devils; they shall speak with new tongues."

grossly too—For being in the Woods, to wait the Company and an Appearance of Angels—The Angels at length appear'd (Miss M. and Miss R———ts) The former of whom is now with Child but whom I married last Week, and whose Nuptials were celebrated with many Prayers and Hymns) and soon after a Legion of Devils (for wicked Spirits will alway trouble the Saints) and these in Shape of Col. R. Shoats. Immediately the Holy Man had a Revelation for one of the Angels said it was written in Scripture, *Resist the Devil, and he will flee from You;* And instantly without his making any Resistance (or even crossing himself which shew'd he was a bad Catholic) the Devils all fled—He follow'd after—and fortunately kill'd six of them which (by assistance of the Angels) he convey'd to his Tent where Abraham bad[e] Sarah make ready quickly some Cakes upon the Hearth, that the Angels might be feasted before their Departure. But as Murder will out—Unluckily this Owner of the Devils in Shape of Swine happening to traverse that Part of the Woods early in the Morning (a thing very unusual with Him) chanc'd to spy Blood on the Ground, and tracing it, it brot Him to the Patriarchs Tent, where he found his Shoats not hung up by the Head, but the Heels, by way of Punishment for disturbing the Solitude of the Saint and the Angels.

And the Primate I just now spoke off (who I hope and believe is a reform'd Man) has been a most notorious Offender in this Particular, as well as the Article of Horses. He frankly confesses his Crimes, and promises Retribution.

But of all Your Modern Apostles I think Him that went up at the 9th Hour to Pray in Neighbour R.———gs. Corn Cribb and whom R———s met returning home with a Bagg of his Corn, deserves the first Place in the Calender: Because this Vile Wretch had the Insolence but few days past, to hold forth on this Text— *All whom are in J.C. must suffer Persecutions.* But what Persecution *for Righteousness sake* hath He suffer'd. The Good Col. R. and W. R. never mention'd these Injuries done them, lest Wicked Infidels should therefrom take Occasion to blaspheme that Holy Name by which We are call'd—They suppress'd all Prosecution, and accepted of their Oaths and Promises to be honest for the future—Nor would it ever have come to the Knowledge of any one, had not one of the Angels (as before mention'd) prov'd with

Child—And this bringing on a Quarrel among themselves (altho'
the Preacher had the Wit to get one of his followers to marry her)
the Secrets of the Fraternity were disclos'd—and the Elders inhibiting him from Preaching, the fellow hereon fell a bellowing—
*Persecution.*

Indeed I must confess, That such harsh treatment of one of his
Dear Brethren, was a little unkind in Mr. *Thomas Blunt,* the
Patriarch, and Prince of this College of New Apostles on *Dan*
River in *North Carolina,* tho' his Application of that Passage in
the Epistle to the Romans, to Mr.          was very Just, and
strictly applicable—Thou that teachest another teachest Thou
not thy Self? Thou that sayest. A Man should not Steal, dost Thou
Steal? Mr. Blunt, from my own Knowledge is a Gentleman of
Great Wit and Ingenuity—and he display'd his lively Genius, the
Quickness of his Parts, the Latitude of his Understanding when
he squar'd Timber for repair of our Church of *Prince Frederick*
where, being entertain'd in the Plantation of the Church Warden,
he was so Generous, so Charitable so Public Spirited, Meek and
humble Christian as not to take, or demand or accept of one
Penny for all his Labour bestow'd on the Church. No! He scorn'd
it! He read a Chapter Morning and Evening in the Church
Bible;—and was not that very Good Pay? Withal, he was a Man
that hated Ceremonies—had a little Quakerism in Him, and
therefore, to avoid the formality of taking Leave of his Com-
rades, Bowing, Shaking hands, and other Such frivolous Matters, He very early, one Morning set off for N. C. without Beat of
Drum. It is suppos'd that the last Chapter he read, was about the
Israelites borrowing of Things from the Egyptians. Therefore
considering us in that Light, He borrow'd a Horse, and as many
Blankets and Cloaths belonging to the Workmen who were
asleep, as the Horse could carry. These Jewels of Woollen and
Jewels of Linen amounted to more than fifty Pounds! A Poor
Recompence to an Israelite for squaring four Sills for an Egyptian Temple!—But Mr. Blunt forgot all this when he repudiated
Mr.          from the Ministry of the Saints—and from his commencing *Turner of Souls,* reducing Him again to his former Occupation of Turning of *Platters* and *Bowls!* . . . But can You think

that the Spirit of God ordain'd Mr. Thomas Blunt to steal my
Horse, and rob my Negroes and Workmen. . . .

But pray does Your assembling together to see a few worthless
Wretches dipp'd in Water, and viewing their Nakedness (which
some have purposely expos'd to your view) tend to Edification?
Or bathing together promiscuously, stark naked in The Streams
and Rivers (as I myself have seen many of You) tend to Edification? . . .

You will bear reprehensions from these Plebians [the New
Light Baptist clergy] because You can laugh it off;—But to be told
of your faults by a Gentleman, cuts to the Quick, and You hate
him for it. . . .

I have this to say of them [the New Light Baptist clergy] That
I verily believe some few among them mean Well—But they are
[un]equal to the Task they undertake. They set about effecting
in an Instant, what requires both Labour and Time—They apply
to the Passions, not the Understanding of People.

# The Need for Education:

*"Speak O Ye Charlestown Gentry, who go in Scarlet and fine Linen and fare sumptuously ev'ry day."* [36]

N.B.

The Back Parts of S. C. not being laid out into Parishes, and no provision made for the Poor, The Country in General was cover'd with Swarms of Orphans,[37] and other Pauper vagrant vagabond Children to the Great Increase of all Manner of Vice and Wickedness. I therefore excited the People to petition the Legislature for the Establishment of some Public Schools, where these Children

36. Sermon Book, IV, [473-512]. Woodmason describes this sermon as "A Charity Sermon as intended to be delivered at the House of Mr. Thomas Edgehill on Saludy River, and other Places in the Back Settlements of South Carolina. 1769." It is impossible to tell when this prefatory note was written. The date of the sermon should probably be 1770. On January 29 of that year Lieutenant-Governor Bull sent the Commons a message urging schools at the Waxhaws, Camden, Broad River, Ninety-Six, New Bordeaux, Congarees, "or any other places." The Commons House eventually considered a bill providing for schools at eight different locations, each to have twenty poor children, and also decided that a college should be founded. Trouble which developed over the Wilkes' Fund prevented passage of the bill. See Commons Journal, Jan. 30, Feb. 28, Mar. 1-3, 31, Aug. 14, 1770; Laurens to James Habersham, Charleston, Mar. 4, 1770, Laurens Letter Books, 1767-1771, 477; same to same, Apr. 10, 1770, *ibid.*, 492; Bull to Hillsborough, Mar. 6, 1770, P.R.O. Trans., XXXII, 203; J. H. Easterby, ed., "The South Carolina Education Bill of 1770," *S. C. Hist. and Gen. Mag.*, 48 (1947), 95-111. There is nothing to show that the schools provided for in the bill considered by the Commons were either intended for fifty students each or were to be for a fourteen-year period. This may be Woodmason's error, or he may be speaking of the bill as it existed during a particular stage in its development.

37. A petition from the Backcountry in 1754 spoke of the orphans of deceased immigrants who "being deserted, must Perish, or go a begging." Enclosure in Gov. Glen to Board of Trade, Aug. 26, 1754, P.R.O. Trans., XXVI, 124-25.

might be taught the Principles of Religion, and fitted to become useful Members of Society. The Commons House of Assembly adopted the Petition, and made Provision for Six Schools of fifty Children each, at six different Places, to be on foot for 14 Years. But when the Bill was sent up to the Council, The Honorable Othneil Beale (President, and a New England Independent) made several Alterations—At which the House took such Offence, that the Bill was never reconsidered, and thereby miscarried. The Bill directed That all the Children should be Educated in your Proffession of the Church of England. Mr. Beale in his Bigotted Zeal for Independency would have left Matters at Large: and Grammar and the Languages taught in them. Such a Latitude, would rather have encreas'd, than rem[ed]ied the Evil it was intended to Cure: For as the Children were Orphans, and destitute of Friends, they had no Connections, and were Children of the Public, Who doubtless had the best Right to frame both their Civil and religious Principles.

A Rumour having prevail'd that the Bill had pass'd into a Law, The People met to draw up an Address of Thanks And sent for me to officiate at that and some other Public Meetings, when this Sermon was propos'd being deliver'd but postpon'd till the Act took Place, and now, will never be revived. . . .

Not many Years past [this beautiful country was] A Desert, and Forrest, overrun with Wild Beasts, and Men more Savage than they, but now Peopled and Planted to a degree incredible for the Short Space of Time—And which I never could make them [in Charleston] believe, nor could I my Self have believ'd without Ocular Demonstration. . . . And next to the Almighty, We are in a dutiful and respectful Manner to thank the Legislature for this their Patriotic favour and investing us with this Blessing of our Birth Right, *Liberty* and the *Laws*. So that now We may call our Selves Free Men.

But the Legislature wisely considering That Evils are much easier prevented than Eradicated—And convinc'd, That the Num'rous Troops of Banditti and Freebooters and Unsettled, Profligate Persons of both Sexes, originally sprung from the Great Number of Orphan and Neglected Children scatter'd over these

Back Countries, who live expos'd in a State of Nature, and were oblig'd almost to associate with Villains and Vagabonds for Subsistence They (very judiciously) have ordered Six Schools to be founded among You for training up 50 Poor Children in each, in the fundamental Principles of the Christian Religion, and first Elements of Learning to qualify them for Business, and train them up to become useful and Valuable Members of Society. So that hereby, the Ax is laid to the Root of Licentiousness, and We have a Prospect before us of seeing some Stop put to that deluge of Vice and Impiety which now overflows this Land. Let me congratulate You my Dear fellow Christians hereon—Let me say, this is the Happiest, the most blessed Day I have seen since in these Parts! Long have I labour'd to bring these Public Blessings to Good Effect. My Zeal has been Great tho' my Interest and Applications Weak. And I care not who takes the Honour so You but enjoy the Profit of the Good Intentions of the Public in Your favour. And my enlarg'd Hopes are, that the Name of God will in due Time spread from hence across this Great Continent to the Bounds of the Western Ocean, or South Sea—And that from the rising of the Sun even unto the going down of the Same *the Gospel of Christ will be great among the Gentiles, and in every Place Incense be offer'd unto His Name and a Pure Offering* (Mal 1.

This Satisfaction I can carry with me at my Return to England, That I am the first Episcopal Minister ever seen or heard in these Parts; and that I have carried the Holy Bible, and read the Liturgy of our Church, in Places, and to Persons, who never before heard a Chapter, or had heard the Name of God or of Christ, save in Oaths and Curses. I am oblig'd to severals among You (and especially to the Good People of this House) for their Pilotage and Assistance in these my Travels, and for carrying of me over Indian Creek, Reedy River, and other Waters, quite over the Line to the Stragglers in the Cherokee Country—And I take this Public Opportunity of returning You my thanks As You have been Witnesses that my Text has been verified in this Wild Region and that as far as the *Cherokee* Hills and to the *Catawba* Nation, the Poor have had the Gospel preached unto them. . . .

The Benefits [of the proposed schools] may not only result to

the present Age but likewise extend to future Generations—As it
may prove a Means of lessening the Number of Negroes that are
now employ'd as family Servants and therefrom by Degrees freeing this Land from an Internal Enemy that may one day be the
total Ruin of it. At least it may put an End to some Species of
Vice that too much prevails from the Slavery of these Poor
*Africans.* . . .[38]

Only look into the Indian Settlements near us—See there the
Poor Wretches! And where for want of due Instruction, the most
Savage Dispositions and detestable Practises contrary to the Principles of Humanity as well as of Religion, are transmitted down
from one Wretched Generation of Creatures to another—And who
for want of Knowledge are, in many Respects but one degree removed from the Brute Creation! Would we wish to see any of
our own Complexion, Descendants of Freeborn Britons in such
a State of Barbarism and Degeneracy?—And yet We began to be
almost on the borders of it. Behold on ev'ry one of these Rivers,
What Number of Idle, profligate, audacious Vagabonds! Lewd,
impudent, abandon'd Prostitutes Gamblers Gamesters of all
Sorts—Horse Theives Cattle Stealers, Hog Stealers—Branders and
Markers Hunters going Naked as Indians. Women hardly more
so. All in-a-manner useless to Society, but very pernicious in
propagating Vice, Beggary, and Theft—Still more pernicious as
We have frequently found, when United in Gangs and Combina-
tions—Such bold and dangerous Offenders as contemn all Order
and Decency—broke ev'ry Prison almost in America Whipp'd in
ev'ry Province—and now set down here as Birds of Prey to live
on the Industrious and Painstaking, Wretches, who have defy'd
all Authority, and defeated the Laws of ev'ry Country. . . . Speak
O Ye Charlestown Gentry, who go in Scarlet and fine Linen and
fare sumptuously ev'ry day. Speak O Ye overgrown Planters who
wallow in Luxury, Ease, and Plenty. Would You, Could You Can
You see or suffer Poor helpless, pretty Boys—Beautiful, un-
guarded, promising Young Girls, for want of Timely Care and
Instructions to be united with a Crew of Profligate Wretches

38. This is apparently a reference to racial interbreeding, a practice which
ministers and grand juries frequently denounced. See Wallace, *Hist. of S. C.*, I,
376.

*Whose Mouth is full of Cun[n]ing Deceit and Lyes,* from whom they must unavoidably learn Idleness, Lewdness, Theft, Rapine Violence and it may be, Murder. . . .

And I hope too, that some Attention will be paid as to learning them to sing after the Parochial Manner that so they may be useful at Church on Sundays—to carry on that Noble Part of Divine Worship quite neglected in our Congregations—and which Neglect carries many to Separate Assemblies, solely to join in Singing Hymns.

# The Justices of the Peace:

*"In my Travels, I once stopp'd at a Magistrates on his Court Day, to see the Practise of Things."* [39]

How DIFFERENT from this [40] is the Practice of some Magistrates, who instead of being backward in administering Oaths, multiply them as much as possible, for sake of the paultry fee annex'd to the Administration. In my Travels, I once stopp'd at a Magistrates on his Court day, to see the Practise of Things. Where in a Cause of 30/—17 Witnesses on both Sides were examin'd on Oath; And at the Conclusion of Things (I will be bold to affirm) that he could recollect but very little of what was sworn too on either Side—for while they were telling their Tales, he was filling up Precepts. He never sum'd up the Arguments, or cross examin'd the Witnesses, or enter'd into the Nature of Things:—but at once decided by Noses—giving Judgment in favor of Him that had the Majority of Swearers When, alas! the Truth laid quite the other Way; And the Right Claimant lost his Debt, and had a Load of Costs for to pay into the Bargain.

39. Sermon Book, IV, [410-28]. The sermon from which these extracts are taken is prefaced thus: "N. B. This Sermon delivered in the Parish Church of St. Mark in South Carolina, on Occasion of the following Patriotick Persons (vulgarly called *Regulators*) being put into the Commission of the Peace for Craven County vizt. Capt. Joseph Kirkland, Capt. Henry Hunter, Capt. Matthew Singleton, Mr. Robert Stark, Mr. Charles Culliat, Mr. Thomas Charlton All Members of the Established Church, There not being before, any Acting Magistrate in the Parish of St. Mark, of the Church of England; but all Dissenters." All but Thomas Charlton, among the above, were commissioned on July 30, 1771. Council Journal, July 30, 1771. The date of the sermon may have been a month or two later.

Another portion of this sermon, bearing directly upon the Regulator movement, is to be found on pp. 285-88.

40. Woodmason has just urged magistrates not to administer an unnecessary number of oaths.

The granting of fees [to] Magistrates was originally well intended, and design'd for Encouragement and Maintenance of sensible Men for, and In, the Administration of Justice. At that Time, few Persons were in the Commission. But what was thus plann'd for a Public Benefit, is now most sadly perverted and will hardly admitt of a Remedy, till all Fees are taken away. I knew a Magistrate that would take no fee on Administration of a simple Oath, in the Course of Pleading or to any Account for Conscience sake—as he thought the Name of God was thereby profan'd. And yet he afterward was obliged to go on in the beaten Track—as they crowded to him from all Parts, and he thereby brought the whole Weight of Business on himself; and so would it be with any Gentleman who would go about to serve the Country Gratis. Therefore as Matters now stand; the most worthy Magistrates must swim with the Stream—Or else use their endeavours with the Legislature, that Gentlemen serve the Public for Honour and not for Profit.

But 2dly Magistrates ought not to be less careful in admitting Oaths against the Estates of Deceas'd and Absent Persons than those personally Present. Nay rather they ought to be 10 M times more circumspect and Cautious—And not when ev'ry Person brings a Bit of paper, to admit him to swear to it for the sake of 5 Shillings without scrutinizing, and entering into the Merits of the Contents. This is a Great and heavy Evil, that greatly and loudly calls for Redress in this Province; For herefrom what Perjury, Fraud, Oppression Robbery, is committed! How many Widows Orphans, Creditors, and Strangers plunder'd and Injur'd! What Scenes of Villany transacted! At my 1st. Coming to this Province I chanc'd to cross P. D. [Peedee] River about the Time of Sale of a deceas'd Gentlemans Effects (I think it was Mr. Ouldfield) When stopping to dine at the ferry House—I there overheard a Knott of Villains in the next Room, contriving, and cooking up fictitious Accounts against the Estate—And they went thro' their Hellish Machinations—Each suggesting to, and writing for the other. At my departure, I imparted what I had overheard to the Gentleman at whose House I that Night lodg'd who happily was concern'd in Affairs of the Estate. He gave Notice to the Neighbouring Magistrates, who suppress'd these fictitious Accounts when presented for Attestation and thereby sav'd the Estate some hundred of Pounds: I give this as one Matter of Fact out of many such I have known, how Dead People may be robb'd who cannot speak for themselves.

The like is too often practis'd against Absent Persons—Whose Estates may be attach'd, surrender'd, or sequester'd. Of which I'll give one Instance out of many I could mention. A Gentleman in Trade here went to England to settle his Concerns on that Side the Water—And before his departure surrendered all he possessed to his Creditors which (if rightly collected, or paid) would have been more than sufficient to discharge his Debts here. It was expected that he never would return—When the [one word illegible] set about to collect his Debts, there was hardly an open Account but what the Debtor produc'd some Counter Account against, to ballance it—And they swore to these forg'd Accounts— which thereon was admitted and the Books Clos'd and Ballanced. Yet these Accounts had not the least foundation in Truth the Party never had anything from them or even any dealings with them—And some he even never saw. Hereby, when he returned from England and thought himself a clear Person, he found himself greatly indebted. And having not Money or Friends to support him in Prosecution of these Perjur'd Villains (and some not of mean Fortune) he was obliged to sit down with the Loss of his Substance Credit, and Character—and to suffer that Reproach and Infamy, due to those who had thus (under the most sacred Sanctions) so notoriously injur'd Him: But there have been Many Absentees and many Merchants in England, who have suffered in like Manner.

I have known some who were in Trade, that have sent off Quant[it]ies of Goods to their Brethren in Iniquity Northwardly and then made fict[it]ious Entries in their Books of Goods sold to deceas'd—absent, or Insolvent Persons—whom they never saw—and with Whom they never transacted Business. Then they have Fail'd—Produc'd their Book to their Creditors—and laid the blame on Persons Dead or Gone—Alledg'd the Number of Bad Debts as Cause of their Misfortunes—Have gone to Prison— Taken the Benefit of the Act—Sworn to these forg'd Books and Entries and thereby obtain'd their Discharge—and afterward been

Richer Men than Ever. I give these 3 Instances of the Great Abuse of Oaths to shew How the best and most sacred Tye, that unites Society, and devis'd for the Preservation of Property may be made a Means of destroying both. As the most wholesome food in pernicious Hands may be turn'd into Poison.

Under this Head I may mention Oaths taken *Ex Parte,* and Magistrates determining thereon, without ever hearing the Defendant A very great Abuse of Justice, and practis'd in this Parish—Also of Magistrates giving Judgment by default—and issuing Exactions thereon without hearing the Allegations of the Delinquent—Who might have never an Horse; or be Sick, or some of his family lying Dead, and many other hindrances from attending at a present'd Hour. This is great Oppression and calls loudly for Redress. And many are the injur'd Sufferers in this Case. A Wise and Equitable Magistrate, will never pronounce Sentence in such Cases, except he find the Party Perverse, Obstinate, and Audacious. With such pertinacious Contemners of the Laws, he is to deal according to Law, to make them Examples to others who may despise his Authority. The Supreme Courts lays a fine on all Jury Men and Witnesses properly summon'd that will not attend. Yet so cautious are they of not confounding the Innocent with the Guilty that on producing proper Excuse or on Oath Proof of their Incapacity of attending—the Fine shall be remitted. And certainly the Practise of the Superior Courts, ought to be a Rule to the Inferior—tho' there are some Men who think themselves Wiser than the Laws.

I will now in the 3d Place beg leave to make a few Remarks on the proper Mode of administring Oaths—In which the Honour and Reverence due to the Great and dreadful Name of God cannot be too highly consider'd. As I before observ'd, that the fewer Oaths a Magistrate administers the better—So when compell'd by the Perverseness of Parties, or Intricacy of Things, for to call the Great Judge of all the Earth to Witness between them He is then in the most Solemn Manner he can devise, to put the Word of God into their Hand, thereby not only to impress a reverential Awe of the Great Omniscience on their Minds, but to terrify, and dehort them; that in Case of their being about to swear falsely, they may stop short, and not hazard the Loss of

their Souls—And I have known this to have had very Good
Effect—by making Persons tremble and falter—and chuse to
give up the Point, rather than run such a terrible Risque.

But is this commonly done or Practis'd? Is this customary with
our Magistrates? Sorry am I in this Sacred Place, and from these
Steps of Truth, to say, that Matters are quite otherwise. How
many Justices Retail Liquor—Some in their Stores—Many in
their Houses—Several without License—And most commonly on
their Court Days, which is a Sort of *Fair*. Here have I seen, the
Bible, the Cards—the Brutes and the Laws, on one Stool—The
Magistrate sitting in his Chair, and administering Oaths—
rabbling over the Form, so as none to understand his Speech—
many in the Crowd, at the instant Cursing and Swearing—While
others intoxicated with Liquor, were calling for 'tother ½ Pint.—
Now what Reverence to God or Idea of an Oath can Magistrate
and People Entertain? With what face or Authority can such
carry the Laws into Execution against Vice and Immorality—Blasphemy and Prophaneness! No! their own bad Example would
rise in Judgment against them and condemn them and therefore
like *Gallio* they care for none of these Things—as they gain
no fees by the Sober, but the Iniquitous Part of Mankind—and
therefore will make Hay while the Sun shines—and I know one of
these who publickly have bragg'd that he made 2 Dollars a day,
ev'ry Day thro' out the Year. But this could not be if Endeavours
were us'd to prevent Litigiousness and discourage all Vexatious
Suits, instead of prompting ignorant People to bite and devour
one another.

I hope that I may obtain Your Pardon for talking like a Lay-
Man in this Place, and that what I have said (tho' it is my own
and comes from my Self) may for once be allow'd. Public Evils, in
ev'ry Shape, are to be laid Open—other wise, how will they be
redress'd? Ministers are as much Watchmen in these Respects, as
Magistrates—for whatever tends to destruction of the Soul, they
are as much bound to endeavour to root out, as the Magistrates
would any Canker that would destroy the Peace or Happiness of
Society. But one material Reason why I take this freedom for discharge of my own Conscience. I have both by Word, and in
Writing, mention'd what I here said, to the Higher Powers—and

sufficiently shewn, that much of the Immorality in the Back Country, proceeds from the Illicit Practises of venal Magistrates [in] the Abuse of Oaths; Their holding of Courts at Taverns, and retailing of Liquors in their own Houses (most of them without Licence) I have been thank'd for my Information, and what I've urg'd has been acknowledged to be just and True. Yet we see no Redress of these Evils. I therefore make bold in this open Manner (nor care who takes Offence) to discharge my Duty to my Master in my Public, as have done in my private Capacity. . . .

Wherever a Fine is impos'd by Law on Free Men—Slaves who transgress in like Manner incurr a Whipping. I just mention this, in Case of Common Swearing which is too prevalent among Negroes—and (to our Shame be it spoken) copied from their Masters. How horrid this Crime is in White Men and Christians ev'ry thinking Mind must acknowledge—but when the tremendous Name of the Almighty [is] prophan'd and abus'd by Negroes Ignorant possibly of the Crime [it] is certainly most shocking. . . .

I wish that they [the magistrates] were invested with the Powers, in respect to Drunkards, as they are over Swearers. But unhappily, the Laws of England in this Respect are not made of Force in this Province, and any drunken Person, White or Black may abuse and insult any Magistrate off the Bench with Impunity. I knew a Magistrate (an Englishman, and who imagin'd that the Laws of England in this respect extended thro' the British Dominions) that set a Man in the Stocks for 2 Hours, for prophane Swearing; for which an Action was brought—and the Magistrate could severely have suffered had not [he] proven by substantial Evidence that he was abus'd in Execution of his Office—by which Pleas, he escap'd. On this, the Gentlemen of the Law advis'd him, that for the future, to send all such Offenders to the Common Goal for 24 Hours which any Magistrate may do with those who insult him in his Duty, without assigning any other Reason.

And as to Slaves—I remember One, was try'd and punish'd by a Jury, for some flagrant Crime,—the Owner of whom made the fellow Drunk—Gave Him his Lesson, and set him on to abuse the Justice and Jurymen—Whereon, the Constable was order'd to correct Him, which he Did—But hereon, the Constable was indited, and oblig'd to pay 40/ for striking Him—As no Magistrate can of himself, without 2 freeholders duly sworn order Punishment to any Slave whatever—be he ever so saucy: Which is a wise Provision lest the Owners of the Slaves may have them maltreated, or injur'd thro Passion, or Malice or Revenge as there are too many warp'd, and rancourous Minds, that right of Spleen to the Owner whom they would illuse, if in their Power would vent their Resentment on a Poor harmless Negroe, under [one word illegible] Pretexts as Knowing that the Assertion of a Slave will not weigh against his dixit.

More sorry am I to say, That as the Laws now stand, its not worth the Pains of any Magistrate to suppress any Gaming or Lewd Houses, or tippling Cabbins, or any Persons or Places where Liquors are retail'd without Licence. For after Depositions are taken, and sent to C. T. without feeing the Attorney General they will lye quiet in the Green Bagg—And should they be preferr'd to the Grand Jury, and brought into Court—the offender will only give 10 £ to an Attorney, who moves for a Traverse—which is granted—and so the Matter rests from one Court to another and never call'd forth. So that any Person for 10 £ each Court given a Lawyer, may keep what House he pleases in Contempt of the Law. Therefore till granting such Traverses be suppress'd, and the [three words illegible] paid by the Public for Prosecutions on breach of the Provincial Laws (which is much to be wished) this crying Evil cannot be redress'd.

# Backcountry Litigiousness:

## "We see the Passions of Mortals highly inflam'd." [41]

How OFT do Mistakes and Errors arise as to Marks and Brands? I will not mention Natural Marks, which are so apt to Alter— and We all know, that the others are too frequently alter'd. In these Cases, even when Matters are Dubious, and the Alteration can't be proven to be made by the Party in Possession—When many Claimants appear, and it would puzzle a Solomon to decide, where the Property really lies, We see the Passions of Mortals highly inflam'd, and *sooner than lose my Property I'll spend a thousand Pounds!*—This is too often done, to the Injury of their Families and Creditors—whose Substance they make free to squander at Law. Not but that Imposition should be suppress'd— and Villany punish'd. But I speak, that this Passion for Law Suits and Prosecutions, does not arise so much from a Love to Justice— Regard to the Laws—or the Good of Society—but from a Corruption of the Human Heart—not from Principle, but Motives of Vexation—Too many taking Delight to vex, oppress, distress their Neighbours thro' meer Wantoness of Disposition—We should not

41. Sermon Book, II, [304-7], [317-18]. These extracts are from the sermon which angered John Chesnut, whose protests in turn provoked Woodmason's letter to Chesnut. See pp. 136-49. The sermon was evidently one of Woodmason's favorites. In South Carolina he gave it at Beaver Creek, Mar. 8, 1768; at Pine Tree Hill, June 18, 1769; at High Hills, July 22, 1770; and at Thomas Hopper's, June 28, 1771. After leaving South Carolina, he gave it once in Virginia, "At the Upper Chapel Brunswic[k] Parish, Feb. 21st, 1773," twice in Maryland, "At St. John's Chapel, Sept. 5, 1773, At Elisha Dorseys, Sept. 10, 1773," once in Pennsylvania "At House of Samuel Jones (York County) Aug. 20, 177[ ]," and three times in England, "At Congersbury, Apr. 23, 1775, At Wyck St. Laurence, June 25, 1775, At Dinder, Nov. 17, 1776, At Westbury, Sept. 1, 1776."

hear else of Persons being put to 8, or 10 £ Expence, for recovery of 40/ And altho' the Law gives the Creditor this Advantage over the Debtor it ought not to be exacted on ev[e]ry frivolous Occasion—ev'ry petty affront—As we too commonly see—for on the least Umbrage; Pique, or Misunderstanding they will *warrant* their Neighbour. . . .

What I here say, may not be strictly applicable to Any of You here about *Pine-Tree* but cannot be too forcibly urg'd to many up above, whose Spirit of Litigiousness keeps them Poor, and whose restless Minds makes them very troublesome. Would they watch over their own Concerns with that Assiduity with which they pry into, and examine the Affairs of others, they might render better Account of themselves than they Do. For examine 9 in 10 among them, they can tell You more stuff about their Neighbour, or his Transactions, than they dare declare of their Own. . . .

'Tis true, that We are here a mix'd People—of different Countries Dialects, and Denominations. But how ridiculous it is, to carry any Nationality Prejudice, or Bias about Us in these Respects. We ought to leave them all behind Us in the Ocean and consider ourselves as one Great family—pursue one General Interest and banish all Selfishness, Bigotry—Narrow Spiritedness, and Atachments, whether it arises from Motives of Religion, Custom—or Habit—for these are Great follies, and very wide of the Christian Temper.

# The Rev. William Richardson:

### "Thus fell this Poor Gentleman." [42]

### Memorandum

THE REVEREND Mr. Richardson was a Minister of the Kirk of Scotland, and sent out by the Society there for extending Chris-

42. Sermon Book, IV, [321-24]. This "Memorandum" follows the sermon which Woodmason had intended to give at the Waxhaws Church of William Richardson. It was apparently written many years after the events it describes and, like the other "Memorandums," is less reliable than the earlier writings of Woodmason. It is included here, however, because it concerns an important figure in the South Carolina Backcountry whose mysterious death caused great excitement.

William Richardson was born at Egremont, near Whitehaven, England, in 1729. He attended the University of Glasgow and then, at the age of twenty-one, emigrated to America. Here he became a student of, and resided with, the famous Rev. Samuel Davies of Virginia. Richardson was licensed in Cumberland, Virginia, January 25, 1758, and the following summer was ordained as a missionary to the Cherokee Upper Towns. He is reported to have been sent on this mission by an understanding between the Society for Propagating the Gospel in New England and the Society in Scotland for Propagating Religious Knowledge, but he was under the immediate direction of the Society in Virginia for Managing the Missions and Schools among the Indians, headed by Davies. John Martin, another student of Davies, preceded Richardson as missionary to the Cherokees. On his way to the Cherokees, Richardson presided at the ordination of Alexander Craighead at Rocky River, North Carolina. He later married Craighead's daughter, not that of "one Campbel," as Woodmason reports. Richardson found the Indians discontented with the English and, as he was refused permission to preach, he soon became discouraged and returned to South Carolina to accept a pastorate at the Waxhaws. He traveled extensively to preach to Presbyterians elsewhere, and by the time of his death was well known throughout a great part of the South Carolina Backcountry. Howe, *Hist. of the Presbyt. Church in S. C.*, I, 290-93; John Richard Alden, *John Stuart and the Southern Colonial Frontier* (Ann Arbor, 1944), 351-52. Aside from the religious motives imputed

tian Knowledge (together with another Colleague) as Itinerants in the Back Countries of America. The Presbytery of Philadelphia sent them up a Long Journey into the Cherokee Country among those Indians to try if any Impression could be made on them, or any hopes of Civilization. Being Strangers to the Language, and thwarted in their Religious Purposes by the European Traders (whose petty Interest it was that those poor Creatures should remain Savage and in darkness) after 12 Months Stay they both came down to the Back Parts of South Carolina; Mr. R. seated himself at the Waxaws, and took charge of a Congregation at that Settlement. These People were compos'd cheifly of Emigrants from the North of Ireland. He married here (in 1760) the Daughter of his Predecessor in the Meeting House, one Campbel who had bred up his Children in all the Bigotry and Zeal to the Church of Scotland, as possible—And this Zeal had infected his whole Flock. Mr. R. was a sensible, Moral, Religious and Moderate Man, but had no Children by his Wife—which added to her Melancholy and Splenetic Disposition. He wanted to introduce Dr. Watts Prayers into the Meeting House, but the Elders would not admit of it—He would use the Lords Prayer, but they annull'd it. However He would use both Watts, and the Lords Prayer in his own family, to the Great Disgust of his Wife and her Relations. Thro' these People he led a most bitter Life—and was very unhappy.

On June 1772 He was found dead on his Knees in his Study, with a Bridle round his Neck, reaching to the Ceiling. He was leaning against a Chair (as was his Custom in Prayer) and his Hands uplifted. In this Posture He was found by a female Servant. The Wife pretended Great Grief—sent for the Neighbours &c. the Elders met—and all concluded that it was an Act of his

<hr>

to Mrs. Richardson and her relatives, Woodmason's account of Richardson's death is very similiar to other existing accounts. See Howe, *Hist. of the Presbyt. Church in S. C.*, I, 416-19. The time of the death was not, as Woodmason says, June, 1772, but rather July 20, 1771. No version of the death, apparently, bothers to explain how a kneeling man could have hanged himself. A popular version of the death, based upon that of Howe, is found in Marquis James, *The Life of Andrew Jackson, Part I: The Border Captain* (Indianapolis, [1938]), 12-13.

own thro' Religious Melancholy—Therefore (to bring no disgrace on the Kirk) they called no Coroner, but buried Him as next day—the Widow following the Corps with Great Sorrow to the Grave. But some that knew the Temper of the Wife and her Relations—made this Affair Public—And it was insisted on that the Corps should be taken up out of the Grave and examined which was done. And Marks of Strangulation found on the Neck—and Bruises on the Breast. On Examination of Persons, it appeared That all the Servants were sent abroad into the Field that Morning and none left in the House but the Wife—And that her Brother had been there in Interim for a short Space. It was found too that no Man could destroy himself by the Manner in which the Bridle was found about his Neck. And it was more than probable that it was put round the Neck, and the Body plac'd in that Posture after he was strangled.

Thus fell this Poor Gentleman a Victim to Moderation—A Martyr to the persecuting Spirit that Distinguishes Superstition and Enthusiasm, from Reason and Religion.

Mr. Richardsons Colleague was station'd at Kings Tree Meeting House in the Township of Willamsburgh, but being a Man of moderate Principles could not long stay in that Quarter but removed—to another Congregation on Hobeau Neck, in the Parish of Christ Church. The People of Williamsburgh then sent for one of their own Kidney from the North of Ireland. This Gentleman stay'd about 12 Months and then Returned. They had 5 or 6 others—but none could or would stay with them except one Mr. John Rae, a learned Sensible and Good Man.[43] He was of like Moderate Principles with Mr. Richardson and labour'd to introduce the Lords Prayer but without Effect. He had no Children by his Wife and dy'd a lingering Death, given (its suppos'd) by his Wife and the Rest of her Gang—For she was in High

43. The Rev. John Rae became pastor of the Williamsburg Presbyterian Church in 1743. Rae, of the Presbytery of Dundee, Scotland, continued here until his death in 1761. On July 10, 1750, he was married to Mrs. Rachel Baird, of Prince George Parish. Meriwether, *Expans. of S. C.*, 84-85; Howe, *Hist. of the Presbyt. Church in S. C.*, I, 252, 254-55, 283-84, 323-24. The Rev. Mr. McKee, of whom little is known, is said to have succeeded Rae. After two or three years, McKee was succeeded by the Rev. Hector Alison. *Ibid.*, 325.

Spirits after his Death—and tho' so great a Bigot to her Profession that she would thot her Self polluted to have enter'd the Door of an English Church, Yet she was not so Nice in other Respects—As at Auction of her Husbands Goods and Books She courted the Writer of this to her Embrace, and wanted to Engage Him with Her on the Couch in the Study But all these People were of like Class and the most arrant Hypocrites and Rogues in Nature.

The next that Succeeded to this Meeting House was a Gentleman from Ireland—An hearty open hearted free generous Man, free from Zeal, and Bigotry. He married the Widow of his Predecessor, and she had a Child by Him or some Other. But He stay'd here but two Years. To rid them selves of Him they accus'd Him of Incontinence—So, in Resentment, he quitted them and dy'd soon after of Grief.

The next was another Scotsman who stayed only 3 Months.

The next a New Light from the Northward who stay'd but a short Space.

The next was an accomplish'd handsome Young Gentleman from Pensylvania. He had not been there above 3 Months, ere he curtailed the Long Sermons they were fond off—abridged the Prayers—Read Lessons—gave the Lords Prayer, and approach'd as near as possible to the Independants—In fall of the Year he fell Sick of the Fever,—and they absolutely starv'd him to Death For he languish'd and Expired for want of Attendance, Physic, and Necessaries.

After this they fell into Confusion and Parties—and in that ferment I left them in 1772.

# A Letter to John Chesnut:

### "Mean, degenerate Wretches, I reserve to be lashed in another form and Place, than the Pulpit." [44]

Sir

I confess, that it much surpriz'd me to be inform'd, that You took Exceptions at my last Sundays Discourse—which I imagin'd was so Catholic, of such Christian Complexion and so well received by the Audience, that not even a *North Carolina* Pettifogger could have been offended. What so fit to be deliver'd in the *Temple of Concord* (as You are pleas'd to style Your *Meeting House*) as a Sermon, pressing on all Persons then present (which were of twenty different Denominations) Unity, Peace and Concord. When I heard of Your Reflexions on Me, it occasioned, not my Resentment but Risibility—Not any Vexation, but Pity, and

44. Sermon Book, IV, [557-79]. Woodmason's title for this item reads: "Copy of a Letter wrote to Mr. John Chesnut of Pine Tree Hill. June 30. 1769." There is no evidence to show whether or not this extraordinary letter was ever sent to John Chesnut. The sermon which angered Chesnut is to be found in Sermon Book, II, [279-321], and is noted by Woodmason to have been given first at Beaver Creek on March 8, 1768, and at Camden on June 18, 1769. It may be coincidence, or it may be evidence in support of Chesnut's accusations that June 18 was the birthday of Chesnut.

According to an undocumented sketch of Chesnut's life, he was born on the Shenandoah River, Virginia, on June 18, 1743. His parents and grandparents had come together from Ireland to settle on the Virginia frontier. The father of John Chesnut died while still quite young. The widow, with three small children, married Jasper Sutton, a member of a company of frontier rangers. After the defeat of Braddock, the Sutton family moved southward. After a year or two on Fifers Creek, North Carolina, the Suttons moved to Granny's Quarter Creek in South Carolina. A year or two later, John Chesnut became an apprentice in the store of Joseph Kershaw at Pine Tree Hill. In 1763, Joseph Kershaw admitted his brother, Eli Kershaw, and John Chesnut into partnership with him. Kirkland and Kennedy, *Historic Camden*, 366-67; Sellers, *Charleston Business*, 89.

Contempt—I will appeal to Your own Memory, if Your Self, and Sam Whyly [45] prompted Me not to the fabricating the *Generous Discourse* that gave Umbrage to Your *Self Importance*. But why should You imagine that any Part of it respected You in Particular, or was aimed at Your Self Sufficiency? Did You ever hear, or know, that in my Public Orations I ever pointed at any Individual, or pointed to the life [of] one particular Person? Indeed I could hold up *many* to Public View—But I esteem'd this too mean, and beneath the Dignity of a Christian Minister in Public. Mean, degenerate Wretches, I reserve to be lashed in another form and Place, than the Pulpit. Nor would I pros[t]itude Divine Things, Times, or Places, by stooping to take particular Notice of the Vices or Virtues of any Man. Public Bodies indeed, I have attack'd and boldly dare attack—Not Covertly, but Openly not by Whispers circulated by invisible Agents but with the Word of God, Reason, and Argument—But doubtless You are conscious to Your Self of having with that Hypocrisy peculiar to a Presbyterian privately malign'd and Calumniated Me, otherwise why should You fit on a Cap upon Your Head, that no one cut out for You? Tho' I have no Great Estimation either of Your Talents or Genius, Yet I did judge [you] a somewhat wiser Person than either Your Brewer or Your Taverner. When I lately pronounced a Dehortation against Drunkenness, they both attributed to *Malice propense* in Me, to hurt the *Public-spirited* Business they were occupied in—It was well, that I did not proceed forward to declaim likewise against Adultery and Fornication Which had I done, I suppose the *Fair Virgins* his Daughters, and other Ladies of the Village would have mobbed Me as endeavouring to hurt their Occupation. I suppose that these worthy Gentlemen and Your Self, think it my Duty when I preach at the Temple of Concord, that I exhort ev'ry one to go to Your Store, buy Rum, and go home and treat his Neig[h]bours Or to order home a Good Number of Barrels of Beer from the Brewhouse, or repair to the Tavern and spend their Crop at Cards and Dice—And that these

45. Samuel Wyly, Senior, had died February 13, 1768. This reference is to his son, Samuel Wyly, Junior, about whom little is known beyond the fact that he was killed by soldiers of Tarleton during the Revolution. Kirkland and Kennedy, *Historic Camden*, 139-41.

are the especial Doctrines of Christianity. Otherwise I cannot Account for the Behaviour of the sage Captain Canty,[46] who quits the Company as soon as I name my Text. Were I a Toper I really would frequent the House of this Gentleman and call often for a Bottle or a Barel to encourage Him to stay Sermon. And doubtless it must charm me infinitely to hear as I return to my Quarters His two Modest Daughters [47] (never to be seen by Day Light) chaunting with Tom Jones [48] some doleful Psalm Tune, to let Passengers know they are Observers of the Sabbath. After which it must conduce greatly to Edification (could we be admitted to behold this sweet conscientious Captain lighting Your Honor and Ely K. [Kershaw] to Bed to his two virtuous Damsels. But I would ask why You do not blame our Good Friend Sam Whyly, the Cheif *Projector* of this unlucky Discourse as well as the *Pronouncer* of it? Why You should think me such an *Wolf in Sheeps Cloathing* (as Your *Jackalls* call me) as to profess Kindness to You in Private, Yet abuse You in Public? Is it because I would act diametrically opposite to Your Honour in point of Carriage? Who, in Public, pay me all Respect imaginable, While among Your Presbyterian Friends, You speak ev'ry Evil Thing that can enter the Mind of a Demon, and secretly urge them forward to vex and abuse me—furnishing them with Topics for their bitter Invectives—But I am afraid that the Sermon brought to Your

46. John Cantey was an early settler in the vicinity of Pine Tree Hill. He married Mary McGirt, a daughter of Colonel James McGirt. From time to time Cantey was appointed or elected to public offices and was a captain in the regiment of Col. Richard Richardson during the campaign against the Cherokee Indians in 1759-1760. In 1765 he received six acres of land in Camden, adjoining the lot of Eli Kershaw, from Joseph Kershaw. Cantey died in 1792 on his plantation a few miles from Camden. Ames, "Cantey Family," *S. C. Hist. and Gen. Mag.*, 11 (1910), 224-25; Kirkland and Kennedy, *Historic Camden*, 356.

47. John Cantey had two daughters, Mary and Sarah. Mary Cantey was born about 1749 and on November 19, 1769, married Eli Kershaw, brother of Joseph Kershaw. Sarah Cantey was born in 1753 and in 1770 married John Chesnut. Ames, "Cantey Family," *S. C. Hist. and Gen. Mag.*, 11 (1910), 225; *S. C. Gaz. and C-J*, Dec. 5, 1769.

48. A Thomas Jones of Camden is known to have made a large purchase of land in Camden in 1777, acting on behalf of Joseph Kershaw. Kirkland and Kennedy, *Historic Camden*, 97.

remembrance Your former Mean Condition of Life, a Circumstance You seem willing to forget. But by shewing that disposition [it] will, by all Parties, and in all Places, be continually brought home to Your Remembrance. If You have raised Your Self to the pitch We now see You, by dint of Merit, Genius and Application, and not by any low Arts, the Greater is Your Praise and Honour, and You need not be afraid to look the World in the face: But by being ashamed of Your Origin and Country shews a Self Consciousness of something behind the Curtain which You are afraid may meet Public Exposure and Indeed Were I disposed to do my Self Justice, and Report the many sly dark designing Tricks You have played me by Your Sectarian Emissaries, I would let the Cat out of the Bagg and publish what You would be very unwilling to hear. Were I to at[t]ack You in any Shape, it would be fighting that Hydra of Presbyterians of which You would affect to be the Head, at least private Director, and Manager. And all Recrimination on You would be stil'd Anger, Malice or Revenge against them—So I forbear.

But why should You conjecture that this Discourse was fabricated solely to point at Your Dear Self? When there are numerous Witnesses to prove their hearing it deliver'd 15 or 16 Months past at Beaver Creek at an Assembly of the *Regulators,* and others in those Parts, Many of them fill'd with Rancour and Bitterness against each Other. If a Perswasive to Amity and Good Will—If a Diswasive from Anger, Wrath, and Strife were ever necessary, it was so at that Time and (blessed by God) it had the desir'd Effect—And from the manifest Turn which the hearing of this Sermon gave to the dispositions of Many, I was induc'd to deliver it at *Pine Tree Hill,* in hopes that the like salutory Effects might be produced in that Quarter—Little imagining that it would be constru'd into a Satyr on One who I so often am in Company with at the House of Good Joseph Kershaw. If I had studied seven Years for a Passage of Scripture History applicable to You, or Him, this of *Abraham* would have been the last I should have thought off—Because there are many much more striking and applicable. But as the old Adage has it *When You are minded to beat a Dog its easy to find a Stick,* So when Persons are dispos'd to be Querulous, any thing will serve for a Pretext to Pick Holes.

Is the Character of *Lot* (as depicted in Scripture) so Vile or Atrocious, that You must not be named with Him? True! He got drunk, and lay with his own Daughters. And if You are not bely'd, You have got drunk and lain with Your own Sisters at least, many a time with Two other Sisters. Indeed You and Him differ in some Respects. He dwelt in the Great *Sodom,* So do You in a little One—He was so worthy a Person, as to be particularly delivered from the destruction of that infamous City—Whereas, You continue in Yours for the upholding of it. He was visited by *Angels;* But I believe Were We to search Your Visitants they would be found to be Devils, Devils incarnate in Human Shape. Some as foul Fiends as ever travers'd the ancient Sodom.

But what is All this to the Sermon? which it will be proper to examine, and to go over those Passages at which Exception has been taken, as Satyrical, and Reflecting on You.[49]

In the first Place, You (or Your Advocates) are pleas'd to say, that under the figure of *Abraham,* is deputed Mr. *Joseph Kershaw A Person Great in his Wealth and Honour, But greater far in his Faith and Charity.* As to the two first Articles, What degree of either Mr. K. [Kershaw] possesses, I am not to enquire into. Sufficient be it for me to remind You, That it is partly owing to the Writer of this Letter, that He Is, *What He is.* The Tender of settling at the Wateree, and there etsablishing a Store, was first propos'd to me, by Messrs. A and L.[50] I had engaged with one Mr. *Steele* [51] to carry on one at the *Congarees*—But that unfortunate valuable Man having been killed by a Party of the Cherokee Indians, I was intimidated from going up there: On which the Ground was chang'd and the Waterees marked out, At which place S. W. Mr. Millhouse and others had just sat down.[52] S. W. pressed me with earnest Entreaties Not to decline it—Pointing out the great Prospects in future, And those Advantages You now

49. This sentence suggests that Woodmason is answering a letter of protest from John Chesnut.

50. The company of William Ancrum and Aaron Loocock.

51. Robert Steill, who represented a Charleston company, settled on the Congaree River in 1749 or 1750 and engaged in trade with the Catawba Indians. Meriwether, *Expans. of S. C.,* 63.

52. This is a reference to Samuel Wyly [S. W.], Robert Millhouse, and the other early Irish Quaker settlers.

Enjoy. But I was inflexible, and dreaded the *Catawbas*. In short I trembled to hear of the Savages. Mr. K. [Kershaw] was then a Servant to Mr. Motte; [53]—Hearing me blam'd by that Gentleman for not accepting the Proposals offer'd me, The Thought of settling at Pine Tree suddenly enter'd the Mind of Mr. Kershaw who instantly waited on me, to know if I actually was resolved to give it up for that if I did, He would, with my Consent enter on the wide field. I consented, And He went forward—And He will tell You, that had I persisted, it never would have enter'd into his Imagination—And it is to this Sense of Things That I was happily the Instrument of his being pushed into a Life that He now shews me that Respect and Kindness which You so much secretly Envy and repine at.

As for *Faith* and *Charity,* I will grant Him a large Share. Much larger than I ever should have display'd had I settled at *Pine Tree*. For I hardly should have had that Faith or plac'd that Confidence In a Poor Beggars Brat, Or an herd of vile Irish Presbyterians, as He has done, In By and thro' You. Nor bestow'd my Person and Substance on a Common Trull, and an whole Tribe of Mendicants, as He has done. But there were many Reasons for such a Procedure. Your Dear Mother That Pious Zealous, Religious, devout Creature had a Daughter which she call'd Your Sister; [54] But whether You and Her were by One Father, as its hard to prove, so is it still more hard to believe; Nor can Your Mother I believe be strictly positive on that Head. This Dear Creature, the sage Duenna Your Mother then introduced at Nights to the Tent of the Good Joseph (or Abraham as You will have him Titled, and so from hence We'll call Him). And as one good Turn deserves another and oft begets another This was one of the Cheif Causes why the Good Abraham stroked Your Cheeks—Chucked You under the Chin and bad[e] You be a Good Boy: Of his building a Cabbin for Your *Good* Mother—Crediting of her with a Jugg of Rum to retail to Passengers—And to set her Husband up with a Team of Horses. Brave doings this! For which You may thank the Address of Your Parent or rather the

53. A trader named Isaac Motte lived at New Windsor until his death. Meriwether, *Expans. of S. C.,* 70.

54. Margaret Chesnut.

Young Widow [55] as she was passed for Your Sister. And here I could launch out into a wide Field of the Operations of Skill shewn by Your Pious Madona—in playing off her *angelick* Daughter to special Advantage: Indeed she was an excellent Milch Cow, and maintain'd Your family rarely well. Pity We did not know the *real* Father of the Boy she left behind her.

The Sermon said, That *Abraham* called *Lot Brother*—Which certainly must mean, That as Mr. K. has taken You into Partnership with Him, Ye are *Brothers in Trade*.

Its said too, That *Abraham* was *Lot*'s Superior—So is Mr. K. [Kershaw] to Mr. C [Chesnut]—as being Head of the Copartnership.

*Lot* was a *fatherless* Child—So was J. C. [John Chesnut] Wherefore here is plainly pointed by Abraham and Lot, K. and C. Ah, my sweet Commentators on Scripture who so readily can *spiritualize* ev'ry thing, How came Your Imaginations Now to be so dull as to *Temporalize* Things—Ye that were wont to soar above the Clouds, and bring down Heav'n to Earth, Why could You not exalt *Abraham* and *Lot,* but confer on them the Dignity of being two Country Storekeepers in the Wilderness of Carolina, amidst a Gang of Irish Bog-trotters, and the sweepings of the Jails of Hibernia! Alas poor Abraham to be reduc'd from an High and Mighty Prince (as He is styld) in the Sermon) to a Retailer of Spirituous Liquors.

Mr. J. C. too was the Son of a Man who dy'd before his Father. How oddly things will jump together oftentimes! What discerning Conjuring fellows these English Parsons are, that can thus dive into Matters, Persons, and things so mysterious So wide: so remote, And bring to Knowledge Past Events, wrapp'd up in the dark Womb of Oblivion! What diabolical Creatures! For certainly they must deal with the Devil himself. Here is a Parson come from England who never saw Ireland, nor knew a Soul in it. Nor that ever Mr. J. C. was born there, but as himself has said—And yet this strange Traveller, will tell a Man that does not know his own Father, Nor his Mother, who 'twas that begot Him—Yet, I say, will aver, that his Father dy'd before his Grand

55. According to Kirkland and Kennedy, *Historic Camden*, 368, Margaret Chesnut married a Mr. Irwin.

father! What a Necromancer this Parson is! Certainly He ought to be laid hold on for a Conjurer.

Further] *"The Conditon Lot was in when Abraham took Him into his House, was Sad and Calamitous."* Does the Sermon say so? Yes!—What a Lye! What a Scoundrel of a Parson this is, to say that when Mr. K. took Johnny C. home to look after his Horses, and put him to School to learn to Read and Write, that He was without a Hat or Shoe or Stocking, or Money, or Two Shirts or a Suit of Cloaths! His Case sad and bad indeed! Had He not on a Good Canvas Frock and a Check Shirt—and a Pair of Trowsers—and a felt Hat on? And yet he says his Case was Calamitous. What a Misrepresentation of Facts! His Case was far better than when in Ireland—There He eat nought but potatoes—but here he eat Pork, long before that Mr. K. took Notice of Him.

"Good Abraham received Him under his own Roof—made him one of his family dealt as tenderly with Him as He would have done with his own Child"—As all this happen'd to a Tittle in respect to Mr. C. Certainly it must be Him who is here described: For J. K. did indeed take him under his Roof as an Errand Boy —He had his Bed in the Garret—He din'd at the same family Table. The Book Keeper learn'd Him to write and Cypher, After which he swept Shop—Then was a Sort of Porter—Did outdoor Business; and so progressively got behind the Counter then into the Counting House; and proving a Lad of Activity, Sagacity, and that peculiar Cunning peculiar to a Presbyterian, He at length was taken into Co partnership, having an eighth allow'd him [56]—

56. There exists a copy of the articles of partnership entered into in 1763, among Joseph Kershaw, John Chesnut, Ely Kershaw, with William Ancrum and Aaron Loocock:

"The Contracting Parties Reposing Special Trust and Confidence in one another, have joined together to be Copartners in the Trade and business of Merchants and Factors, at Charles Town, in Berkley County, at Camden, at Rocky Mount, and at Chatham in Craven County in the province of aforesaid; Each party to be one fifth part Concerned during the Space of Ten years and four Months, Commencing from the first day of January, one thousand Seven hundred sixty four.

"It is agreed that the Trade at Charles Town, Shall be Carried on under the [    ] and in the name of Kershaw and Co. at Camden in the Name

And this for two Reasons, To Keep him from blabbing Secrets, or joining with any Rivals against the Store (2) To be a Spy on the Presbyterians, Penetrate their Secrets At[t]ach them to Mr. K. Interest (He being an Episcopal and an Englishman) and keep them steady to the Plan of Operations chalked out by Mr. K. One Principal End of which was—To have a Body of People ready to give Him their Votes for Member of Assembly, so as for him alway to have Place in the Senate. By whch Maneuvre, He protected Himself from Arrests Insults and Dangers—And came in for Snacks in Public Jobbs and Contracts. Especially by having the Catawba Indians consign'd to his Care and management. But this is but a small Branch of Things; one Step only of Mr. C. Ladder of Preferment. *Madona* [Chesnut's mother] was alway an useful Instrument—Well vers'd in the Art of providing Religious Chickabiddies for the use and behoof of Carnal Appetites: So that *Abraham* was never at loss for a fresh Bit.

"He furnishes Him with Flocks and Herds, with Tracts of Land and all Implements of Husbandry."—K. and C. to a Nicety— Exactly drawn! Who can't see in it? You find them figur'd out under the Names of *Abraham* and *Lot*. For has not Mr. K. given Johnny many Tracts of Land? Has He not set up his Mother in Business, Made his Father in Law a Planter, and stock'd a Place for Him? And is not his brother Jemmy [James Chesnut] Cheif Driver of his Waggons? All this is very true; But how strange is it, That this should happen in *Caanan* to *Lot* 4000 Years [ago] and afterward to one Johnny Chesnut in Carolina! But who knows but that he may be the very descendant of Lot from one of his Daughters or be the Son of Lots Wife, begotten by some Incubus upon the Pillar of Salt? Certain it is, That when Mr. M. [Mathis] kept Tavern, and Sally [Sarah Mathis] grac'd the Barr,[57] that she was a very useful Piece of Goods at *proper*

---

of Kershaw Chesnut and Co. at Rocky Mount in the name of Kershaw Chesnut and Kershaw and at Chatham in the name of Ely Kershaw and Co." Chesnut-Miller-Manning Papers, Bundle 5, folder 38, S. C. Hist. Soc.

57. Daniel and Sophia Mathis were among the Irish Quakers who settled in the Waterees prior to the founding of Pine Tree Hill. They had four children, including Sarah ("Sally") mentioned here. Kirkland and Kennedy, *Historic Camden*, 86.

Times both to Pine Tree Abraham and Lot—Its said, That *Lot* first tapped her Barrel, and finding the Taste extremely delicious could not keep his own Counsel, but must bragg of the *Excellence of Things* to Abraham who, *whetted* by the Relation, long'd for a Smack, which was readily granted, and freely indulged to as many *Tasters* as were willing to communicate one Commodity for another. But this Commerce did not please Your *Madona* as it rais'd a Rival to Your Sister [Margaret Chesnut] as to Abraham. But her Death, threw Sally into Your Mammas hands, who tutor'd her in all the Arts of Dalliance and Deception, and fram'd a raw ragged ignorant Girl fit for any Academy in Carnal Garden.

At length Your Mamma whisper'd [to] Abraham That *Sal* began to shew Signs of Pregnancy and that the Fruit must be grafted on his *Arbor Vitae.* Alarm'd and asham'd, The Good the generous *Abraham* consents to take *Sal* for better for Worse, to the Astonishment of all Mankind. Thus Abraham and Sarah made a Match [58]—in order to hide their Criminalty: A Piece of Madness and Stupidity, none, who knew [Kershaw] and his Knowledge of Life, could have suppos'd Him guilty off: Indeed He was finely taken in. For it turn'd out, That *Sal* was far from Pregnant And the Path was too oft beat for any Grass to grow except the Field could be lock'd up. Indeed after Marriage, she soon prov'd with Kid—But Abraham never did, nor ever will forgive this Trick of Your Madona, tho' He respects Sal, who turns out a notable Wife—far beyond Expectation—tho' some will not allow her Eldest Child to be really his but lay it to Your Worship. Howbeit—To prevent Your grazing any more in that field, You know that Your present Filly [Sarah Cantey]was provided for You to *break In;* And with her, a Train of her Kin equally *Tender* and Kind as her herself—So that its really amazing How You find Provender for them All. Your Magazine must be well Stock'd with Ammunition to charge so many *Mortar Pieces,* and *Howitzers.* But Your Mamma can give You Good Instructions. She is vers'd in all Arts of Gratification. To all these Mysteries of State and Private Negociations We may assign the Cause of Your Advancement to be Prime Minister in the Court of Abraham.

58. The marriage of Joseph Kershaw and Sarah Mathis took place about 1763. *Ibid.,* 380.

It is further said in the Sermon, That "Abraham was very Great and Powerful—That his very Countenance was an Honour and Support to any Man." Now this is so true of J. K. that this Expression must be meant of him: To be sure! It cannot be any one else. Because none have Merchant Mills, or Boat, or a Pack of lawless Banditti, Blackguards and Ragamuffins at their Beck, save Him. For indeed, few would chuse to be Great and Powerful In and Over such a Collection of Villains. They indeed shew him Respect and are at his Devotion: And Mr. K. may verify, That its better being the first Man at Athens, than the second at Rome. To have the favour of Mr. K is, to be favour'd by all others Around—As his frown, would subject You to Excommunication from this blessed Society: So powerful, Of such force and Prevalence is that so much admir'd desir'd and Allpowerful Article, called Rum!

It was debated lately in a brill[i]ant Assembly of Your Pine Tree Ladies, which of the 3 Monsyllables (C——Cash—and Rum) was most coveted by the Men of Valour, Learning Abilities and Skill in The District. They allow'd That All of them were highly belov'd and valu'd That both Neck and Heels would be risqued for the At[t]ainment of either—But which had most Influence Most Predominancy, most Command, was best beloved—Most Coveted, or sought after, Regard paid too &c—occasion'd high Debates—At length, one Lady by her single Voice, gain'd the Victory in favour of Rum—for to tell You the Truth Ladies, We all love it as well as the Men.

But to return to this wicked Sermon that has so lengthen'd Your Jaws, and sour'd Your Stomach. Its there said, That this Orphan Lot was "made by Abraham, A Sharer of his Fortune A Companion of his Travels—Gives Him the Privilege of his Company and of his Confidence, and takes him under his immediate Protection."—Be it so—May not all this be applied to Mr. Ch. Was He not a Poor Orphan, when He was brought by his Mother from Ireland: Did she not follow a Regiment from thence, and acted in Quality of what is call'd a *Trull?* Has not Mr. K. taken him into Partnership, and made him a Sharer in his Fortune! Does He go any where without Him? Does he not advise with Him about ev'ry thing he carries on? And is not his Opinion generally adopted? Does He not stand up for Him against ev'ry one? Defend even his most blameable and reproachable failings? Has he not made Him a Lieut. in his own Regiment of Militia and his Brother *Jemmy* an Ensign? Does he Care now for any body, so much is he lifted up? Ev'ry Passage here set down, manifestly proves, that the Preacher intended to draw a Comparison between Mr. K. and Mr. C.

Which is evident from the next Passage which is—"That Abraham was a far Greater much the better Man than *Lot* every Way— as being his Prince, and his Patron, and Benefactor. Well! its good at all times to find People acknowledge they have received Benefits. Mr. K. must certainly be an higher Man than Mr. Ch. because he is Col. or Capt. in the Regiment—and a Justice of the Quorum, and a Senator, and what Not—which Mr. Ch. is not. So far is He his Prince and above Him—And Mr. Ch. freely acknowledges him for his Patron and Benefactor—No body denies it—So there was no Occasion of mentioning of this in the Sermon.

But not Content with All this—The Preacher still goes on. "Behold, even to this Young Man To this Lot, his Pupil—to one beneath him and beholden to Him is Abraham thus Kind and Condescending! He stands not upon Punctilos Tho' High and Mighty, Generous and Munificent He yet stoops and humbles himself to be at Peace with his Inferior—To be at Peace with one bound to Him by the Laws of Kindness and Gratitude to submit to Him: And so the Good Abraham pays Respect to his Inferior Addresses himself to One who should wait upon Him, and lowers himself to the Censure of Insignificants rather than loosen the Bonds of Friendship." Now only observe what a Train of Insidious, Villanous Suggestions runs thro' all this! Who ever heard of any Quarrel between Mr. K. and Mr. C. Who ever deny'd but that Mr. K. is a Prince of a Man—Generous and Kind, and True, and Goodnatur'd and all that. It supposes that Mr. K. was giving all things out of his own hands to Mr. Ch.—Ev'ry one knows that Mr. C. is beholden to Mr. K. for what He is—But why must He be told of it in Public? Why must it be said to his face before a whole Congregation? Was it not enough to make a Man be cast down? And where is the mighty Stooping of Mr. K. to Mr. Ch? He was once a Poor Boy himself. True, He had Edu-

cation given Him, which Ch. had not. But still He was a Lad
of Parts And why should there be any Ceremony between Persons
in Trade? How ridiculous to suppose it? In short, all that this
Parson has been talking about, is only to make Mr. Ch. look little
if He could among People. Or else he wants to make Mischief
between the two Gentlemen. But that he'll not do. They too well
like one another to fall out, as this Sermon makes them for to do.
For Mr. K. never troubles his head about any Cattle or Hogs that
are brot to Store for Sale. All that is left to Mr. Ch. entirely. Who
buys, and sells, and Packs just as He thinks Proper.

Such Sir are the Reasonings of all Your Train of Attendants
and Dependants. And certainly what ev'ry One says, must be
true "That I preached a Sermon solely to abuse You, and Reflect
on You. Which has given Rise to many profound Speculations
and Cogitations, and greatly stirr'd up the Gall and Venom of
that most Peerless Pattern of Perfection, Trulla Your Mother, to
vent her bitter Reflections on All who dare call in Question
the Honour of her Family. But she forgets who once relieved her
when she begg'd her Way from Pensylvania thro' N.C.—And in
what high Rank she liv'd in on            Creek. Oh the sweet
Pumkin Bread that I eat in her Palace without a Chimney in it!
Chimney did I say—No, nor Door, or Window, or Bed or Chair.
I must insist on it, That since I've seen her this Way, and in this
her present high Exaltation (which neither She or I once dream'd
off) I have studied all in my Power to please and gratify her—
Save to the Thrusting my Money in her Hands, or spending it at
her House, or making Presents to her Daughter. But I fear that
her Anger against me proceeds from some Old Sore not yet
heal'd Up—Which was the Refusal once to take half a Bed with
Your Sister when 'twas kindly tendered to me. And rather chusing to sit up all Night by the Fire, I really must beg her Pardon
for not calling of this so Charitable an Action to Remembrance,
and expressing a due Sense of the Obligation I lye under. Indeed
she has heap'd such a Load upon me, that had I not the Heart of
a Lion, Patience of a *Job,* and a Memory very forgetful of Injuries, I certainly should have complimented Your *Madona* with
something that should make her remember me for Life. I should
do by her as Jehu did to her Sister Jezebel of famous Memory,

Give Her to the Dogs: for certainly if ever there was a fiend from Hell, on Earth, or a *Pandora* let down from Heav'n—They both (with all thats horrid and Infernal in Heav'n & Earth) meet in her Composition.

An Instance of which is her thus traducing (I will not say Translating) my Sermon into a Satyr and Parody on Your Self and Partner on purpose to inflame the Populace against me and to preclude me Your Temple of Concord A Place (without much Entreaty) I purpose never to enter again.

But for Her better being acquainted with the Contents of the Discourse, I have ventur'd to translate it into the *Quohee* Language, that when read to her, She in part may understand it, and think it at least comparable with her Mass Johns Productions.

# A Burlesque Sermon:

### *"There was an Old Man, in Old Times who was called Abraham."* [59]

### Gen. 13. v 8

AND ABRAHAM said unto Lot, Let there be no Strife I pray thee between Me and Thee, and between my Herd-Men, and thy Herd-Men, for We be Brethren.

Dear Honeys, its long Time since You sent me any Gift to the *Waxaws* and You know Honeys, that You promis'd me a Good Subscription would I come here once a Month—but Arrah my Heart not a Pistreen have I seen—And I am told, that when my Elder came down amongst You to collect for me, You went to Loggerheads, and fighting and Cursing and all about Me, Some saying, He is a Good Man, Others, That He deceiveth the People; But what I do, I do openly—I never drink with any of the Uncircumcised Philistines—Nor will I have fellowship with the deceitful. I never give a Dram but to one of the Elect. And lately We refus'd the English Parson a feed for his Horse tho' he offered 7/6 for it.

59. Sermon Book, IV, [581-604]. This "Burlesque sermon," as Woodmason entitles it on the inside front cover of the fourth volume of the Sermon Books, is really an appendage to the letter to John Chesnut. In the last paragraph of that letter Woodmason explains that he has translated the sermon that angered Chesnut and his mother into the "Quohee Language" that she might better understand it. Quohee or Cohee is of Scotch origin "Quo'he" and is also referred to as a Scotch-Irish phrase; see Mitford M. Mathews, *A Dictionary of Americanisms on Historical Principles* (Chicago [1951]), I, 386.

The sermon, for satirical and humorous purposes, is put into the form of a letter from the Rev. William Richardson of the Waxhaws. Woodmason, who knew Richardson and apparently liked him, was certainly aware that the dialect sermon was out of character with Richardson's university training. See pp. 132-34. For an extract from the original sermon, upon which the "Burlesque sermon" is based, see pp. 130-31.

But Honeys, You are too apt to make Words about Nothing; And therefore I beg You to listen to what I am going to say. And I'll tell You no Lies but the downright Truth, and what I can shew You in the Bible.

There was an Old Man, in Old Times who was called Abraham —He was indeed called Father Abraham—but not the same with Him that makes our Almanacs. This Abraham was a Great Planter—and he had more Cattel, than Gerard [?] Neilson.[60] I dare say, He branded a thousand Calfs a Year—But its not said whether he made Cheese or not. Butter, he did, and doubtless liv'd on Butter Milk as We do. He made Johnny Cakes too bak'd, as We do ours—and doubtless barrelled up abundance of *Sourings*. However thats neither Here nor there, Abraham had Milk in Abundance, and he would kill a Calf some times when a Great Man came to see Him—But that's what We poor folk can't afford to do. I question if Mr. Neilson himself does, tho' He mark'd more than 500 Calves and Yearlings last Spring—But He never kills a Creature under 3 or 4 Years. But I was going to say That this Abraham was a very Rich Man—and He had more Land than Mr. Kershaw—and He had a Kinsman they called *Lot:* He was Abrahams Brothers Son—and his Fader dy'd when He was Young and left Him without a Guardian. So Abraham administer'd on the Estate, and made the most he could of it. How much I can't tell—but I believe not a Great Deal. So *Abraham* sends for the Young Man and takes Him home to Him, and into his family Good Shoul, and makes very much of him as being a fatherless Child—as we all should do by Fatherless Children, whether they have any thing or Nothing. Well, You can't think Honey how much Abraham lov'd this Lot tho' He was a Poor barelegg'd Boy: I don't know indeed whether He wore Brogues then, or not—I fancy, they us'd *Mockasins,* as our *Indians* do— However, its of no Great Significance—Well if he'd been his own Child, He could not have been more fond of Him. I forget now whether Abraham had any Children at that Time, or not—But all this shews that He lov'd Young Children tho' none of his own.

60. Jared Neilson was a petitioner to the Assembly in 1755, together with Samuel Wyly, Robert Millhouse, and other inhabitants of the Pine Tree Hill vicinity. Commons Journal, Jan. 16, 1755.

And so I do, love them dearly, I play with my little Negroes some-times, tho' my Wife don't like it—She hates Young Children cause she has none of her own—But that's not my fault—How-ever Abraham lov'd this same *Lot* thats Certes for He furnished Him with many Herds of Cattle, and vast Tracts of Land, as much I dare say, as is from hence to *Santee.* But I don't know if the Ground was so Good, Nor do I read whether Abraham kept a Store or not, as Mr. Kershaw does. I imagine they all spun for themselves and wore Homespun, and bought their Small Wares of the *Jews* and Scotsmen that us'd to come a Hawking Goods out of Egypt. Cause in they made Good Linen, and I imagine could afford it Cheaper than Abraham's family could weave it. But by and by Dear Joy, what d'ye think? *Lot* fed his Cattle upon Abra-hams Range—and when he bid him drive off his Cattle to his own Range, he grumbled about. And Abraham's People and Lot's People went to fisty Cuffs about it, and gave one another many confounded Hard Knocks and bloody Noses and Black Eyes. Now this vex'd Abraham very much. And by my Shoul it would have vex'd any Gentleman to have his Goodnature so abus'd: And what is wont—This ungrateful Lot He takes his Servants Part—So that Abraham was oblig'd to interfere and bid them keep the Peace. And I wonder indeed He had not sent them all to Jail: For 'tis certain he could do it by Vertue of his own Authority—For every Man was Lord and King in his own House in those days. Ay, and whatever You Girls may think, Women were not then suffer'd to sit down at Table with the Men: But they were glad to eat their leavings. Well, but as to Abraham: He was unwilling to quarrel with his Kinsman and Nephew so he put up with ev'ry thing—But 'tis not every one who would have bore it so patiently. But He was a very Good natur'd Gentleman and lov'd to keep Peace in *Israel*—Tho twould have provoked any Man to have had Strangers come and eat the Bread out of one's Mouth—But as Abraham was a peaceable Man, and being a Justice of the Peace very unwilling to break the Peace, He says to Lot in the Words of my Text, Dear Honey, I pray thee now let there be no quarrel between my Servants and thy Servants for We be Brethren—We have eaten many a Peck of Salt together and why should We fall out about Trifles. Look

Yonder! Don't You see all that Great Valley—Drive all Your
Cattle down there, or into Yonder Swamp where there is plenty
of Canes—And set Your hands about clearing Land—for I hant
Room in my own Clearing for my own Creatures. My Pasture
is almost eat out—And I must be oblig'd next Winter to turn
much of it out into Old Field, and take in New Lands, So prithee
Honey Go Clear Ground for thy Self.

And what said Lot to all this?—Said? Why he mutter'd and
growled and said Nothing,—So then Abraham falls to coaxing of
Him and giving Him Sugar Words—My Dear Lot (says He) don't
be angry. Dear Shoul let me beg You to be Good humour'd—Dear
Honey dont let us fall out about a few Cows and Calves. Now
by my Shoul this was vastly kind and good in Abraham—Not
one in a thousand would have done so—But he was a very mild
inoffensive Man, and didn't chuse to have Words with folks, or
go to Law: I don't think He warranted any one Person in his
Life—He rather chose to put up with the Loss. And this made
ev'ry one impose upon his Good Nature; which oftentimes
suffer'd; and Lot He seem'd to want to take Advantage of it by
carrying Matters very high, and looking as big as Bull Beef. But
how soft and tender does Abraham speak—Let me pray thee Lot.
Now that was very obliging Honey not one in a thousand would
have borne to be impos'd upon as Lot did upon Him. And thus
He stopp'd to ask favours of Him, that should have [gone] down
on his Marrow Bones to Him he was a far better and Greater Man
every way than Lot was.

And yet Abraham was no Coward neither—By my Shoul He
was a very brave fellow. For after Lot had left Him and while
his folk were clearing Land, a Parcel of that Country Indians
Canaanightish Rascals they came Slyly one afternoon to Lot's
Tent and took Him and carried Him and his Wife and Children
away with them—So Lots People being frighted out of their
Senses runs over to Abraham and tells Him of it. He was then
just sat down to Dinner—But he didn't mind his Victuals—He
throws down Plate Knive and fork and ev'ry thing—Get me my
Horse this Minute says He—All of Ye Quoth He, come after me as
fast as You can; So they all got together in a hurry, some with
Pitchforks others with Axes—any thing that first came to Hand;

and they run like Wild Fire after Abraham and soon over took the Canaan Knights—But they no sooner heard Abraham setting up the War Hoop than they scamper'd away as if the Devil had been in them—Never once offering to look back—So Abraham releas'd Lot and got a good deal of Plunder for Him Self. But this scar'd Lot—He would not live any longer out in the Back Country, but he left Abraham and went down into the Lower Settlements to Live. He didn't like these Savage Rascals—As for Abraham He didn't care for them a Fig. No! Not He [for He] was' too powerful for them—They'd catch'd a Tartar had they medled with Him—No No, they didn't chuse to burn their fingers.

But wasn't this Honey now very kind and Good in Abraham to behave so as He did? and to a silly Young fellow too that wanted to have us'd Him Ill? Indeed He was a Prince of a Man, and he is set down in Scriptures for us to Imitate and to copy after when We are us'd ungratefully—We must not give them hard Words tho' they deserve it—But talk mildly and softly to them, as Abraham did to Lot. And I am sure tis always my Rule when any blackguard fellows abuse Me as they will somtimes—Calling me Canting Knave—Hypocritical Rascal—Presbyterian Pumpkin, and I know not what beside—But I care not a Pipe of Tobacco—and only bid them Go about their Business and mind their Cattle.

Therefore if any of You should fall out about Your Calves and Your Kine, You be sure mind and think upon Abraham—and don't abuse one another but say as Abraham did, Pray Honey let me beg You not to be Angry: Let me entreat You Brother Countryman not to be in a Passion—And so on—and not by Cussing and Swearing and [one word illegible] and Damning make bad worse—Especially when You get among any of the Virginian Crackers—for they'l bluster and make a Noise about a Turd—And they'l think they have a Right because they are American born to do as they please and what they please and say what they please to any Body. But nobody truly must talk to them. I never met with such fellows in my Life. They are so Impudent that let what be said of our Country folks (who God knows are impudent enough) they don't come up to half the height of one of these Blusterers. And theres not one of our

Old Women that can match them for Scolding—Not *Goody Sutton* [61] her Self: For set her against such a One as *Mother James* [62] and she'd silence her presently: And indeed before I came here I thought there were none to come up to our Folk, but here I find they meet with their Match.

Wherefore Dear Honies, I say again If any of this beggarly Virginian Tribe should attack You about any thing, Never come to blows or Words with them. But imitate Abraham in the Text—rather bear with some Loss or Inconvenience than go to Law with them, or to Boxing, because they'l swear any thing, and do any thing be it ever so unfair to gain their Ends—And our People are nothing to them for Lying.

And Dear Honey, let me tell You further That they are very idle extravagant People alway fidling and dancing—And if they can but get a Cow or two to give them some Milk, and make a Pound of Butter and raise a Hog or two with a little Indian Corn and a Patch of Potatoes they are as happy as Princes—They care not if they make any thing for Market, or go to Town or not—And if they do, its only with a few Deer Skins to get them some Rum. And tho' You my Dear Countryfolks are very litigious and love the Law Yet these Virginians are a Match for You—And that keeps them Poor and will ev'ry one Poor that are of such restless Minds as to make them selves troublesome to ev'ry Body. Would they watch over their own Concerns with that Assiduity with which they pry into and examine the affairs of their Neighbours they might render better Account of themselves than they can nowdo if called upon to know how they employ themselves. For examine 9 in 10 among them, they can tell You more Stuff about their Neighbours or their Transactions than they could chuse to declare of their own.

Wherefore my Dear Honies, If You would but rightly advert to Things, You need not either trouble the Courts, or the Magistrates with any of Your petty Disputes. Why, what must We do You'l say? Even Honeys, bring all Your Matters to the little House, before the Elders, and leave all Your Disputes to their Arbitration

61. "Goody Sutton" refers to the mother of John Chesnut.
62. This may refer to the wife of John James, who is recorded as inhabiting the Camden area in early 1775. Kirkland and Kennedy, *Historic Camden*, 109.

or Determination—and then Honestly and Candidly abiding by their Decisions. If You would do this, All Your Differences would soon be adjusted, Rogues detected, Villanies expos'd or punished, and Knavery stigmatized, Whereas, by employing Lawyers (whose Trade is, to put darkness for Light and Light for Darkness, and to pervert Truth) You risque both Your Money and Your Cause; And if You should chance to succeed in Your Suit, You may come off as bad or equal Sufferer with those You Litigate. Why my Dear Hones, would Ye pull out one of Your precious Eyes, to put out two of these Virginian fellows? They'l only laugh at You: But should You be oblig'd to take out a Warrant or Writ—first give Notice of Your Intentions and warn Him of the Consequences. And should You come before the Magistrate, don't abuse the Shentleman as some of these Virginian Rogues will, but behave like Good Children of St. Patrick. There's Mr. Ogelthorpe,[63] there he sits, God bless Him, I say it in his face, He's a Jewel of a Man, and strives to compose Peoples Janglings all he can, as far as he knows and no Man can do more—and yet very often instead of being prais'd and Esteem'd for admonishing and reproving offenders against the Laws He is often hiss'd or hooted at When by St. Patrick would he exert his Authorityship properly, He might commit them to the Stocks, or bind them over to their Good Behaviour. For many times when they appear before Him, they are all in a Sweat with Passion—and each overheated Party thinking himself in the Right both Parties come away discontented—Tho You must own, That there are some Wretches so Wilful and discontented—So Obstinate and opinionated, that neither Sense, Reason or Perswasion or even the Whipping Post can make any Impression on them. I need only refer You to all Public Vendues To Your Musters and Public Meetings for the Truth of this. And none are so apt to fall out about meer Trifles as the Virginians for they will abuse and vilify one another and to provoke to Anger instead of Love, be they engag'd in the most foolish Dispute. Be ye not therefore Dear Honies like unto them— for they make no Respect of Persons Nor Things, nor Times either. Sunday is the same with them, as Monday, or any other

63. See above, p. 54, n. 45.

day. And they will talk to their betters the same as to one another. Indeed they think none their Superiors. So great is their Self Conceit—And yet they know Nothing either of Learning or Religion, But will let none argue with them. Yet must it not be very provoking to see mean Persons Stubborn, Wilful and Petulant? And such, these Poor Wretches commonly be, even far beyond the meanest of our Folks. We are Civil at least. They must allow that, if they allow us Nothing Else, for We are noted for our fair Speeches. And therefore we should when it is conveniently in our Power, to teach these Clowns their Duty, and with Calmness and Gravity, with Good Words and prudent Behaviour to soften and polish Rude and ungarnish'd Minds. 'Tis the Nature of these Virginians—and it seems indeed the Distemper of the Idle and Illiterate to be quarrelsome and froward. But it is the Good, the Sensible Mans Duty (as Mr. Ogelthorpe, and Mother Chesnut knows) to help and pity them in their bad Condition. For We are not to suffer a Convulsive Man to lye in the Fire into which his angry Sickness has thrown Him, tho' in the taking up his Disease and not himselfe strike us in the face. For We are to remember that in such a Case, He will do as much even to himself—But I do not say this Shentleman to encourage any Clown in his Clownishness or the froward fretful Man in his Peevishness—But to instance That Peace and Love, Friendship and Charity are to be procur'd at any Rate—and that it is the Duty of all of us to do as Abraham did by Lot, who even parted with a Tract of Land to Lot that was well watered and on which He might set many Mills, rather than have further disputes with Him or His.

And so ought we to behave sweet Honies When We have any disputes and fallings out about our Cattle: How oft do Errors and Mistakes arise as to Marks and Brands of every Beast; I will not mention *Natural Marks,* which are so apt to alter of themselves, or to be alter'd by Rogues: And we all know that they are too frequently alter'd. In such Cases, When Matters are dubious and the Alteration can't be proven to be made by the Party in Possession—When many Claimants appear and it would puzzle a Solomon to pronounce where and with whom the Property fairly rested: In such complicated Cases, How oft do We see the Passions of Men highly inflam'd and boiling over with Rage and

Resentment venting its Violence, in opprobious Words and indecent Expressions! Says One Rather than lose my Property, I'll spend an hundred Pounds: Another threats Revenge, A third challenges to Fight, and so Blows ensue. After which comes Warrants, and Suppeneys, and Affadavers, and Recogners, and what not; and so theres Law upon Law and no end of it—And so theyl spend their Crop to the Great Injury of their families—For nobody gets any thing by it, save the Constabels. Many a time when they bring Money down here to pay Mr. Kershaw what they owe will they go to Capt. Canty's, and get adrinking (I don't speak it out of any Mislike to that *Good* Gentleman) and there get by the Head, and go to Loggerheads, and then to Justice Ogelthorpes, and so about, and so spend the little they brought to pay their Debts and yet will take up more Goods, and live on, and make free with the Substance of their Creditors whose Goods they will thus squander at Law. But still however, few Men can bear being impos'd on—And all Roguery should be suppress'd: and I wish Capt. Canty wou'd'nt let them cheat one another at Cards as they Do—for that learns them to be Sharpers, and then they go to stealing of Cattel and Horses, and so one thing begets another—For I would have all Villany punished. Only I would advise You when You do fight Not to act like Tygers and Bears as these Virginians do—Biting one anothers Lips and Noses off, and *gowging* one another—that is, thrusting out one anothers Eyes, and kicking one another on the Cods, to the Great damage of many a Poor Woman. When People do so to be sure they ought to be carried before the Justice and bound over—But what do these Virginia fellows Care? They have Nothing, so can lose Nothing. Sue a Beggar and Catch a Louse. This Passion for Law Suits and Prosecutions, I fear, don't arise so much from a Love of Justice, Regard to the Laws, or the Good of Society, so much as, Corruption of Heart and bad Blood in Your Veins; I don't think that one in Ten of You act from Principle when You do take up the Rogues. Its rather from Motives of Vexation: For too many among You, take delight to vex, oppress, and distress his Neighbours thro' meer Wantoness of Disposition. Otherwise why should We have so many Magistrates among Us, and all of them more Business than they can do. How often do we hear of Peoples being put to 8 or 10 £ Expence for recovery perhaps of Ten Shillings, only because the People couldn't raise that Money at a Moments warning without selling something to very Great Loss; And thus People take Advantage one of another; For the Moment they confess Judgment they demand Execution, and instantly sell the Peoples Goods for a Song, and will not suffer any Redemption—Such Acts of Oppression I daily hear off—Which is very Cruel from one Christian to another and from one Quohee to another Beloved Countrymen. For tho' the Law gives the Creditor this Advantage over the Debtor it ought not to be executed on ev'ry frivolous Occasion; ev'ry petty Affront as is too commonly seen—Especially among the Virginians (whom You copy too much) who will on the least Umbrage, Pique, or Misunderstanding will fly directly to the Justice, and instantly warrant their Neighbours; forgetting all those Ties of Gratitude, and the several (if not many) Instances of Kindness and Good Nature they have experienc'd from them. A Remembrance of Good Offices ought in all Cases to spring up in Your Breast, and counter ballance ev'ry little silly Provocation.

You see, in the Text, how that Abraham when He was injur'd by *Lot's* Servants did not prosecute them: And altho' their Master upheld them in their Impudence, Yet He would not quarrel with Lot about it, tho' Lot wanted to pick a Quarrel with Him. But He says to Lot, Brother Countryman, Why Should You and I be at odds about these fellows of ours. How humble and how Gentle was all this Dear Honies! Let there be no difference between us, I pray thee! What soft and meek Language is this from a Superior to an Inferior, from an Old Man, to a Young Boy! Nor was this Civil and obliging Language a fit of Courtship, or of Good Humour only for the present. No Honey! It always was customary with Abraham. It was the usual and frequent Practise of this mighty Prince; And to prove what I say, I'll tell You a Story of Him that is set down in the twenty third Chapter of Genesis— There, fold it down And You'l find there an Instance of such Courteous Behaviour as is fit to be taken Notice off, by all Proud and Morose Men. But let me tell You the Story.

Abraham was a very Old Man, and had been married a vast many Years to his Wife Sarah, who was a kind Good Woman,

and travell'd with him wherever He went—By Night, or by day—
'twas all one to Her—She stuck close to Him—And she was a very
neat housewifly Woman too—And the first We read off that made
Butter. And she was very fair too, Ruddy Cheeked and vastly
comely—from her getting up early in the Morning and milking
the Cows and drinking Butter milk. But none of us can hold out
for ever—Nor could Poor *Sarah*—for she grew old, and helpless
and Childish, as most Old Women are. Her Death happen'd very
unluckily for Abraham for 'twas when He was on his Travels.
He was got into a strange Land, among the Children of *Heth*—A
rude, heathenish blackguard Kind of People—Such as our *White
Boys,* worse than those in *North-Carolina.* However, they greatly
respected *Abraham:* As much as folks do Mr. *Kershaw* for He was
just such another Good Kind of Man. Well—Abraham, as I
said, was got among Strangers—Not a foot of Land had He there
of his own, tho' He had got so much Else where. Now He wou'dnt
send to them to tell them what He wanted. But without waiting
till the Taylor brought home his Mourning, He goes to these
Children of *Heth:* Gentlemen (Quo' He) I've lost my Poor
Wife Sarah—A Good Wife indeed she was to me! And I want
to lay her Old Bones some where, where the Wolves and Dogs
mayn't dig her up again: You know I've not any Tomb or Burying Ground here of my own, and I willingly would buy a Piece,
half an Acre or so, of some of You. And He spoke this so
friendly, so obligingly to these rude People, that they returned
his Address with such Civil and Courteous Language as was
very unusual with such Sort of Folks: So Natural *Is,* and so early
*Was* the Practise of Civil Words, and respectful Behaviour: Ay,
and Titles of Honour too, and Low Bows, and taking off the Hat
when one talks to our Betters—For it is said in the Bible (I
don't tell You a Word of a Lye) That these Men of Heth came
up to Him (But 'tisnt said, whether He rode a Camel or an
Ass) and made Him a very low Bow, quite to the Ground.
Quo' they, Sir Abraham, Thou art a Great Man amongst us.
In the best of our Sepulcheres You may lay Your Old Woman;
And then Abraham in his Turn stood up, and bow'd to *them*—
Bow'd to them all Round, and answered and said—No, Gentle-
men I thank You. I don't want Your Ground for Nothing I

have Money enough to pay for whatever I've need off: If I do accept Your favour, I'll pay duly and truly for what I have—for I don't covet or desire other Mens Goods—So let me know whose field that is Yonder, for it looks a Good Place, and as if it would answer my Purpose very well. Quo' they, Sir, It belongs to Old Mr. *Hamer,* the Father of Young Mr. *Sichem*—Well Quo' He Honies, do send for Mr. *Hamer*—Here I am, says the Old Gentleman. Quo' Abraham Sir, What will You take for Your field Yonder? Why Sir 'tis at Your Service. I've great Respect for You, and I won't take any thing—But Quo' Abraham Not so fast Sir Not so fast, I do insist to give You, what You'd sell it for outright to Another—Well, Well, Quo' Old Mr. *Hamer* if that's the Case and You will have Your own Way, You must give me 50 Dollars for it—So Abraham pulled out his Purse and counted Him out 50 Dollars—And then made a very low Bow to all the People, and invited them All to the Burying, tho' they were uncircumcis'd Philistines. But Death You know has no respect of Persons. We must all dye, and somebody must carry us to our Graves. But I was about to Observe Honies, How this Behaviour of Abraham and these Outlandish heathenish People upbraids our rude and Ill behav'd Quakers Yonder—Ay, the untaught Illmanner'd Virginians too. These Quakers will not move their Hat to any Body—Yes! You may see them Yonder in their Meeting House with their Hats off But nowhere Else—for they'l none of them move their Hat to the Governor (God bless Him) except Mr. Wyly; He's the only Gentleman among them: Tho' they say hes but Half and half neither A Wet *Quaker,* as we call them. I wish that *Haman* had hang'd that *Mordecai,* the founder of this Broad brimm'd stiffnecked Generation and then perhaps We never should have been plagu'd with them: But as Ill Luck would have it, *Haman* getting kicked up in *Mordecai's* Place, his Generation ever since, will pull off their Hats to no One.

‡‡‡‡‡‡‡‡ PART THREE ‡‡‡‡‡‡‡‡

# The Regulator Documents

‡‡‡‡‡‡‡‡‡‡‡‡‡‡‡‡‡‡‡‡‡‡‡‡‡‡‡‡‡‡‡‡‡‡‡‡‡‡‡‡‡‡‡‡

# The South Carolina Regulator Movement:

## An Introduction to the Documents

CHARLES WOODMASON arrived in the South Carolina Back-country just as a political storm, to be known as the Regulator movement, was taking shape. He remained among the frontier inhabitants until this angry and rebellious uprising, having gained its principal goal, had largely spent its force.

As Woodmason had earlier been scribe to a vestry, two Assembly commissions, and the St. George's Society of Charleston, so now he became the penman and political guide for the Regulators. He did more than simply formulate Backcountry grievances, for he knew well both the coastal and interior sections of the province and used his knowledge to benefit the latter.

At first glance it might seem strange that Woodmason, with his strong devotion to law and order, should have championed the riotous back inhabitants. But he was not one to remain a neutral observer and, when one considers his strong sense of justice and his real compassion for those who suffered, it would seem almost inevitable that he should have taken the position he did. His love of justice appears in nearly every sentence of his writings on the Regulator movement, and his humanitarianism often rises triumphant from the stern denunciations of the back settlers that he so often expressed.

The origins of the Regulator movement can be described by a simple formula: political power and the benefits of government were confined to the older and more prosperous coastal strip, while little more than the obligations of government had been extended to the people of the Backcountry. Westerners helped to bear the burdens of government, but they received few of the rewards.

Even the opportunity to protest was largely denied the back settlers. Although they were technically within parishes and had the right to vote for members of Assembly, most of them were in fact without the franchise. When the parishes were first surveyed, the lines that divided them had been extended only a short distance in a northwestwardly direction beyond the then existing area of settlement. As the western areas became populated, only theoretical, unsurveyed lines divided the parishes so that, in Woodmason's words, the settlers wandered "in the Mazes of Supposition." [1] Even settlers who knew their parish could not vote without a long trip to the parish churches near the coast, where balloting took place. The few parishes situated wholly in the Backcountry had but few representatives, and the long sessions of Assembly made it necessary that even these should live in, or near, Charleston. [2]

Early and late, the most pressing problem of the Backcountry was security for persons and for property. Frontiers attract the lawless, and the great grievance of honest back settlers was their lack of any legal means to repel or drive out the motley crew of adventurers and criminals that arrived among them.

Except for the minor jurisdiction of the magistrates, there was only one court of law in the colony, at Charleston. The distance of this court from the back settlers precluded the conveyance of prisoners to jail and the appearance of plaintiffs or witnesses against them, because of the time and expense entailed. And those who overcame these difficulties, as Woodmason pointed out, would see the case tried before a court and jury of "foreigners" who knew little of the distant interior settlements. [3]

Although the problem was an old one, efforts to remedy it had revealed little more than the Assembly's lack of concern. An act of 1721, to be sure, had created five "precinct" courts outside

1. See pp. 233, 244.
2. Bull to Hillsborough, Charleston, Sept. 10, 1768, P.R.O. Trans., XXXII, 37.
3. See pp. 220, 237-38.

Charleston.[4] Although this act was never repealed, it became inoperative within a few years, probably because the Charleston lawyers refused to attend the new courts.[5] Dissatisfaction increased as settlements were made in more distant parts of the province. But when the provincial grand jury presented the situation as a "great hardship and grievance" in 1741,[6] an Assembly committee answered only that it was "too early" and too expensive to establish county courts.[7] Seven years later an act to enable county courts to try small debt cases was disallowed in England.[8]

In 1752, sixty settlers on Peedee River, near the mouth of Lynches Creek, petitioned for a county court. The petitioners described their frontier as "a place of refuge for many evil-disposed people and those of the meanest Principles, crowding in among us—Such as Horse Stealers and other Felons, having made their escape from North Carolina, and other parts—others cohabiting with their neighbour's wives, and living in a most lascivious manner, while we have no way or means to suppress them." [9] Two years later a similar petition reached Governor James Glen and the Council from the back settlements. The "far greatest Majority" of the settlers, complained the authors, were "a Conflux out of several Nations, of the Poorest, undisciplined and ignorant sort of mankind, not used to Liberty, being therefore apt to injure each other and live without Instruction and die without Comfort." Without remedy the next generation would fall under "extreme barbarity and Disolution of manners" for lack of religion and schools. Poverty, together with the great distance to the Charleston law court, "depriveth them in great measure, of the

4. Wallace, *Hist. of S. C.*, I, 278; W. Roy Smith, *South Carolina as a Royal Province 1719-1776* (New York, 1903), 145-47.

5. Petition to Arthur Middleton and the Council, May 20, 1726, New-York Historical Society.

6. Presentments of Oct. 21, 1741, in Commons Journal, Dec. 3, 1741.

7. Commons Journal, Dec. 8, 1741.

8. *S. C. Gaz.*, Nov. 7, 1748; P.R.O. Trans., XXIII, 184-85; Smith, *S. C. as Royal Prov.*, 142-43.

9. Petition to Council, Mar. 16, 1752, in Alexander Gregg, *History of the Old Cheraws* (Columbia, S. C., 1925), 131-32. The Provincial Grand Jury in the same year mentioned the "Barbarity Impiety and Horrible Crimes practised in some of the back settlements." Council Journal, Oct. 30, 1752.

benefits and Protection of the Laws and Exposeth the weak to the Oppression of the Strong." [10]

Governor Glen asked the Assembly to act, but a bill to establish courts at Beaufort, Georgetown, and the Congarees died after one reading.[11] A few years later, petitions for county courts were reported in preparation throughout the province,[12] and in 1758 Peedee settlers asked that the dormant act of 1721 be revived and that the laws be published.[13] These and other efforts came to nothing.[14]

After the Cherokee War, a new wave of lawless men from the northward invaded the Piedmont and formed gangs. By 1765, robberies, "violences," and murders were reported from the Backcountry.[15] Lieutenant-Governor William Bull consequently asked the Assembly to consider a "Distribution of Justice" in order to "Suppress in a great degree the Idlers, and Vagabonds who now infest and injure the industrious remote Settlers too often with impunity." [16]

Early in 1766 a variety of grievances appeared in a petition to the Assembly from the inhabitants of Congaree, Ninety-Six, Saluda River, Broad River, and "Places adjacent." The petitioners listed their troubles: they were unrepresented in the Assembly, Indians and lawless whites caused hardship, their produce could reach market by "Land Carriage" only, they had neither churches nor schools, and they were annoyed by "Itinerants and Vagabonds Strollers." Pointedly, the petitioners justified their existence in terms of the coastal planters' interest: the backcountry

10. Enclosure, in Gov. Glen to Board of Trade, Charleston, Aug. 26, 1754, P.R.O. Trans., XXVI, 123.

11. Wallace, *Hist. of S. C.*, II, 50. A "Correspondent" urged county or circuit courts in the *S. C. Gaz.*, Nov. 7, 1754.

12. *Ibid.*, July 15, 1756.

13. Wallace, *Hist. of S. C.*, II, 50.

14. *Ibid.*, 48-51.

15. *S. C. Gaz.*, June 15, July 27, 1765; T. P. Harrison, ed., "Journal of a Voyage to Charlestown in So. Carolina by Pelatiah Webster in 1765," Southern Historical Association, *Publications*, 2 (1898), 146; David Ramsay, *The History of South-Carolina, From Its First Settlement in 1670, to the Year 1808* (Charleston, 1809), I, 210-11.

16. Commons Journal, Jan. 10, 1765. See also Bull to Board of Trade, Charleston, Mar. 15, 1765, P.R.O. Trans., XXX, 251.

produce benefited the trade of Charleston and they themselves formed "an useful Barrier" to the province. The main purpose of the petition was to ask that their land taxes should be less than those levied on the valuable lands of the coastal region.[17]

Petitions accomplished nothing. Not only did the Stamp Act appear a more pressing problem to the low country, but Charleston and vicinity stood to lose by the grant of relief to the interior settlements. Circuit or county courts would deprive the city of spending customers, and coastal land values might drop if the back settlements became more desirable.[18]

Yet the self-interest and lethargy which prevented aid to the Backcountry was not shared by everyone. Although there was no group sympathetic to the frontier, there were two individuals in high office who tried to help the poor back settlers.

One of these, Lieutenant-Governor William Bull, was a native of the province, the son of a former lieutenant-governor, and an able, popular, and diplomatic executive of conspicuous intelligence. Again and again Bull used his influence on behalf of the Backcountry. Twice in 1765 he urged the Assembly to establish a court system, and during the same year he tried to establish Backcountry fairs, aided the German settlements at Londonborough, near Ninety-Six, and encouraged the planting of hemp in the back settlements.[19] The following spring a new governor, Lord Charles Montagu, arrived in Charleston.[20] Thereafter, except during the governor's absences from the province, Bull could do little more than mitigate the errors of his not too intelligent superior.

Charles Shinner, the Chief Justice, was a second spokesman for the back settlers. An Irish-born placeman, Shinner had been ap-

17. Commons Journal, Feb. 27, 1766.

18. S. C. Gaz., June 15, 1766; S. C. Gaz. and C-J, Mar. 17, 1767. Woodmason says the same thing in his "Memorandum" on the Regulator movement. Sermon Book, IV, [375].

19. Commons Journal, Jan. 10, 1765; Bull to Earl of Halifax, Charleston, Mar. 1, 1765, P.R.O. Trans., XXX, 245-46; Bull to Lords of Trade, Charleston, Mar. 15, 1765, ibid., 248-51; Council Journal, Oct. 29, 1765; Bull to Lords of Trade, Charleston, Dec. 17, 1765, P.R.O. Trans., XXX, 300. In the S. C. Gaz., June 15, 1765, appeared an ardent plea for circuit courts which nearly filled the first page.

20. S. C. Gaz., June 2, 16, 1766.

pointed to his office in March, 1761.[21] Although he was honest and vigorous in his duties, his temperament and lack of legal training made him unfit for his high position. As a placeman he suffered the resentment of more competent, but unrewarded, natives of the colony.[22] In office, Shinner could do little for the back settlers. He did inspire the yearly provincial grand juries to list their grievances,[23] and in 1766 he visited the Backcountry with Woodmason in a futile effort to organize an attack upon the outlaws near Camden.[24]

Since the Assembly would not enact remedial laws, the thieves established a reign of terror that was uninterrupted until 1767. The plight of the honest settlers was described by Woodmason: "Our large Stocks of Cattel are either stollen and destroy'd— Our Cow Pens are broke up—and All our valuable Horses are carried off—Houses have been burn'd by these Rogues, and families stripp'd and turn'd naked into the Woods—Stores have been broken open and rifled by them (wherefrom several Traders are absolutely ruin'd) Private Houses have been plunder'd; and the Inhabitants wantonly tortured in the Indian Manner for to be made confess where they secreted their Effects from Plunder. Married Women have been Ravished—Virgins deflowered, and other unheard of Cruelties committed by these barbarous Ruffians." [25]

Becoming powerful and confident, the criminals sowed fear and intimidation among their victims. A gang at Long Canes was said to have sworn vengeance against anyone who interfered with their activities.[26] Threats were made against honest magistrates, constables, and private individuals, and some men were punished by the outlaws for their opposition.[27]

It was during the spring of 1767 that the back settlers, driven beyond endurance, began to strike back. Families and neighbors associated locally and spontaneously to resist the confederated

---

21. See p. 292 and n. 97.        22. See pp. 295-96, notes 101, 102.

23. *S. C. Gaz.*, Nov. 12, 1764, June 8, 1765, June 2, 1766.

24. See pp. 10-11.        25. See p. 214.

26. *S. C. Gaz. and C-J*, Aug. 4, 1767.

27. *S. C. and Amer. Gen. Gaz.*, Aug. 7, 1767; *Virginia Gazette* (Purdie and Dixon), Dec. 3, 1767.

outlaws.[28] This activity was probably encouraged when, in August, 1767, Governor Montagu offered rewards for any outlaw leaders brought to Charleston jail.[29]

In the beginning the back settlers acted only in defense of their homes and families, and without defiance of the government. By early October, 1767, however, the picture changed. On the fifth of that month Governor Montagu informed the Council that a considerable number of settlers between the Santee and Wateree Rivers had assembled and "in a Rioting Manner had gone up and down the Country Committing Riot and disturbances and that they had burnt the Houses of some Persons who were Reputed to be Harbourers of Horse Theives and talk of Coming to Charleston to make some Complaints." [30]

The Regulator movement had begun. Not only had "justice" been executed without legal process, but the Backcountry had thrown out a threat, often to be repeated, of a descent upon Charleston. This menace to the planters became an ever-present reminder of Backcountry grievances. Persistent but seldom defined, it was therefore the more ominous.

The best answer the Governor and Council could make to the uprising was a proclamation which ordered the rioters to disperse and enjoined all officers to keep the public peace.[31] As yet Montagu knew of no "persons of consequence concern'd direct," but he had heard that 1500 men had "signed a Paper to support one another in Defiance, of the Civil Magistrates, and against the Laws of the Country." [32]

Probably only a few Charlestonians understood what was happening. Governor Montagu formed a new militia regiment in the

28. *S. C. Gaz. and C-J*, May 26, Aug. 4, 11, 1767; *S. C. and Amer. Gen. Gaz.*, June 5, Aug. 7, 14, 1767; *S. C. Gaz.*, Aug. 3, 17, 1767.

29. Council Journal, Aug. 10, 19, 1767. It was later to be remembered that this proclamation had had "very good Effects," and that several thieves had been brought to justice. *Ibid.*, June 12, 1770.

30. *Ibid.*, Oct. 5, 1767.        31. *Ibid.*

32. Gov. Montagu to Earl of Shelburne, Charleston, Oct. 8, 1767, P.R.O. Trans., XXXI, 422-24. Another early report of Backcountry "Associations" is in the *Va. Gaz.* (Purdie and Dixon), Dec. 3, 1767, under a Charleston date-line of Oct. 19, 1767.

Saluda region.[33] One of its officers was soon to be dismissed as a Regulator.[34] The Court of General Sessions in Charleston convicted Backcountry thieves and Regulators with a lack of discrimination that only made matters worse.[35]

On November 5, 1767, Governor Montagu, appearing before both Council and Assembly, asked legislation to "suppress those licentious Spirits, that have so lately appeared . . . and assuming the name of Regulators, have in Defiance of Government, and to the Subversion of good Order, illegally tried, Condemned and Punished many Persons." The next day both houses expressed their anxiety over the situation, and the Assembly asked the Governor for pertinent information and papers.[36]

Whatever the tendency to ignore Regulator grievances, it was sharply checked on November 7. For on this day the Remonstrance, a long, detailed, and highly eloquent protest and petition written by Woodmason, was presented to the Assembly over the signatures of four Wateree planters in the name of four thousand settlers.[37] Woodmason, who had prevailed upon the Regulators to "lay aside desperate Resolutions," [38] had prepared the fullest account of Backcountry grievances, major and minor, that the Regulator movement was to produce. In forceful language which sometimes became highly audacious, Woodmason lectured the Charlestonians on the duties they owed to the hordes of poor immigrants on the frontier.

The Remonstrance, backed by the threat of a Backcountry invasion of Charleston unless a redress of grievances was forthcoming,

33. *S. C. Gaz. and C-J*, Oct. 20, 1767.

34. Council Journal, Feb. 22, 1769.

35. *S. C. Gaz. and C-J*, Oct. 20, 1767; *S. C. and Amer. Gen. Gaz.*, Oct. 30, Nov. 13, 1767.

36. Commons Journal, Nov. 5, 6, 1767; Council Journal, Nov. 6, 1767. This is a very early use of the word "Regulator" in South Carolina.

37. Commons Journal, Nov. 7, 1767. See also pp. 191, 204, 213-33. Three days later, Gov. Montagu reported the "Petition" to the Board of Trade, Charleston, Nov. 10, 1767, P.R.O. Trans., XXXI, 423-24. The style and content of the "Remonstrance" are so clearly Woodmason's that, taken with his claim to authorship (p. 212), it has not been thought necessary to make a fuller analysis of the question.

38. See p. 28.

brought quick results. "The Situation of the Province makes it absolutely necessary that Courts of Justice should be established as speedily as possible," an Assembly committee notified its London agent, Charles Garth.[39]

Within four days of the presentation of the Remonstrance an Assembly committee reported in favor of a court system, a vagrancy act, and two companies of soldiers for three months to "Suppress and prevent disturbances" in the back parts. A committee was appointed to prepare a court bill, and the governor was asked to raise the two companies of soldiers.[40] It was no doubt as a further sop to Backcountry anger that some magistrates there, named by the four deputies who had presented the Remonstrance, were struck from the commission of peace as friends of the thieves.[41] The deputies themselves, Woodmason later reported, were "caress'd, and politely entertain'd in Town," given a copy of the votes of the Assembly, and upon their return home "Bonfires, and Firings, and every Demonstration of Joy, prevail'd hereon thro' the Country." [42] They would have rejoiced less had they foreseen the future.

The Backcountry "Regulation work" became temporarily official when the governor found it necessary to appoint leading Regulators as officers of the two companies of soldiers. The troops also consisted of Regulators, and many among them, as Woodmason stated, had been personally injured by the criminals: "Some in their Wives—Others in their Sisters, or Daughters—By loss of Horses, Cattle, Goods and Effects." The troops were commissioned as rangers, and after hearing a hortatory sermon from Woodmason began their three-month pursuit of the outlaw bands.[43]

39. Charleston, Nov. 13, 1767, Charles Garth Correspondence, Force Transcripts, 109-10, Library of Congress. Hereinafter cited as Garth Trans.

40. Commons Journal, Nov. 9, 11-13, 17, 1767.

41. Council Journal, Nov. 24, 1767. The four deputies also complained of the expense and difficulty of the trip to Charleston to obtain land warrants, and stated that in consequence many squatters took up land without warrants. They asked that back settlers be allowed to prove their rights to land before local justices of the peace. *Ibid.*

42. See p. 205.

43. Commons Journal, Nov. 17, 1767, Apɪ. 8, 1768. See pp. 279-80, 282.

Yet the crisis was far from over. The Regulators were incensed to discover that the court bill, which Governor Montagu signed on April 12, 1768, failed to provide for county, as well as circuit, courts. What was worse, the Assembly had inserted provisions in the act which made a disallowance by the Crown almost certain.[44]

Still another source of Backcountry anger was the continued arrest of Regulators for their illegal acts. Lieutenant-Governor Bull, who realized that such "persecution" was unwise, convinced Governor Montagu and Council to limit the number of Regulator convictions.[45] Such leniency would almost certainly have eased the growing sectional conflict had not a judge sent out new warrants for Regulator arrests without the knowledge of the attorney general.[46]

In May, 1768, Governor Montagu left the province[47] and Lieutenant-Governor Bull faced the consequences of the unauthorized warrants. As a result of these, Bull reported, several Regulators were convicted in Charleston: "This gave great alarm to Numbers as all who were present and aiding were equally Guilty: It then became a Common Cause and they being conscious of the rectitude of their Motives in what they had done, began to think their Numbers would defend them against such vexatious suits and the next step was to agree to oppose the officers who should go there to serve process."[48]

44. For progress of the court bill see Henry Laurens to John Moultrie, Charleston, Jan. 28, 1768, Laurens Letter Book, 1767-1771, 132-33; Laurens to Wm. Cowles, Charleston, Apr. 15, 1768, *ibid.*, 179-80; Council Journal, Mar. 21, 1768; Commons Journal, Jan. 15, Mar. 29-30, Apr. 8, 1768; Bull to Hillsborough, Charleston, July 18, 1768, P.R.O. Trans., XXXII, 14-18. A secondary account is in Smith, *S. C. as Royal Prov.*, 133-37.

45. Council Journal, Apr. 19, 1768.

46. Bull to Hillsborough, Charleston, Sept. 10, 1768, P.R.O. Trans., XXXII, 39.

47. Bull to Lords of Trade, Charleston, May 30, 1768, *ibid.*, 12.

48. Bull to Hillsborough, Charleston, Sept. 10, 1768, *ibid.*, 38-39. The Regulators may have promoted cohesion in their movements by seeing that many were "present and aiding" in their activities. A Regulator victim, John Harvey, stated that in September, 1769, he was chained to a sapling and whipped for an hour. Fifty different Regulators gave him "Ten Stripes" each until he had received 500 in all. Council Journal, Feb. 3, 1772. Five hundred lashes was evidently customary. See *S. C. Gaz.*, June 13, Aug. 15, 1768.

The plan took shape shortly after the April court sessions. In June, 1768, a "vast number" of delegates were reported to have met at the Congarees, "men of property" from as far away as the Peedee River. When the Peedee representatives returned home, wrote a correspondent from there, "they requested the most respectable people in those parts to meet on a certain day; they did so, and upon the report made to them, they unanimously adopted the *Plan of Regulation,* and are now executing it with indefatigable ardour." By this plan not only were evil-doers to be purged, but the jurisdiction of the Charleston court was to be denied over those parts of the province "that ought to be by right out of it." Writs and warrants from Charleston were to be served only "where, and against whom" the Regulators thought proper.[49] The same plan was presumably adopted by other parts of the Backcountry.

This denial of the authority of the Charleston court marked a new stage in the Regulator movement. Heretofore, the Regulators had meted out punishments without due process, in effect doing what they felt the Charleston court could not do. Now, however, they proposed to protect themselves from "persecution" by nullifying the jurisdiction of the court over them.

The government at Charleston was faced with the simple alternative of acquiescing in rebellion or opposing it. Even Bull, anxious to end the conflict, could hardly urge the first alternative. It was therefore inevitable that government and Regulators should meet in a series of head-on clashes of mounting seriousness.

As early as July, 1768, Charleston heard that a deputy of the provost marshal had been captured, disarmed, and mistreated when he attempted to serve writs against leading Regulators. When the unfortunate official reached Charleston with his story, the provost marshal was given a general patent of assistance and urged to enforce his processes to the utmost.[50]

Several days later a new incident was reported. A constable, with warrants of distress to serve on the property of Regulators,

49. *S. C. and Amer. Gen. Gaz.,* Sept. 2, 1768. See also *ibid.,* June 10, July 15, 1768; *S. C. Gaz.,* June 13, July 11, 25, 1768; Council Journal, July 5, 8, 1768, for continued activity among the Regulators.

50. *Ibid.,* July 29, Aug. 2, 1768.

summoned thirteen men to his aid. Near Marr's Bluff, on Peedee River, this group met a larger party of Regulators. A fight followed and, it was reported, some of the constable's party were killed and others afterwards whipped. All that part of the country was said to be the scene of riot and disorder.[51]

The Marr's Bluff affair became the "general subject of Conversation" in Charleston.[52] Bull assured the judges that he would do everything possible to bring the offenders to justice. He then issued two proclamations. The first commanded all peace officers and loyal subjects to suppress illegal activity. The second offered a pardon to all Regulators, except those involved in the Marr's Bluff affair, for acts committed before August 6, 1768, the day of the proclamation.[53] Charles Woodmason was among those to whom copies of the proclamation were sent. Anxious to restrain the Regulators from too excessive illegality, Woodmason dutifully tried to read the proclamations. He discovered that the people would not listen and finally did no more than send copies to Regulator meetings.[54]

Before Charleston knew that the proclamations were ineffective, Marr's Bluff became the scene of a second, even more revealing, incident. This time the provost marshal, Roger Pinckney, armed with warrants for the arrest of the principals in the first Marr's Bluff incident, set off for that place with Colonel G. G. Powell, who commanded the local militia. At Lynches Creek twenty-five militiamen put themselves under Powell, and at Marr's Bluff thirty-five more arrived. But when it was learned that the leading Regulator to be arrested, Gideon Gibson, was heavily guarded and could raise three hundred more men "in an hour," three captains and two lieutenants were summoned to bring twenty men each.

After Gibson first agreed, and then refused, to surrender, mat-

51. *Ibid.* For this encounter of July 25, 1768, see also *S. C. Gaz.*, Aug. 15, Oct. 24, 1768; Commons Journal, Aug. 15, 1770.

52. *S. C. Gaz.*, Aug. 15, 1768.

53. Council Journal, Aug. 2, 3, 5, 1768. The first proclamation is dated Aug. 3, and was published in the *S. C. Gaz.*, Aug. 8, 1768.

54. See pp. 57-60. Col. Richard Richardson in lower St. Mark's Parish wrote that the clemency offer "seemed to quiet the Minds of many" there. Council Journal, Aug. 19, 1768.

ters went from bad to worse for the provost marshal and Colonel Powell. The three captains and two lieutenants appeared with three hundred rather than one hundred men. Ominously, they stopped at some distance from their colonel. When Pinckney read his authority and Bull's proclamations and Powell explained why they had been summoned, the men "absolutely refused" to act. Gibson, they said, was "one of them" and had asked their protection. They then "said much" about their grievances, especially the lack of county courts and the exorbitant cost of law. Further conversations at a nearby house gained nothing. Colonel Powell felt humiliated and reported that if the Regulators had not still had "some faint regard" for him, they would have carried out a plan to abuse Pinckney. Powell offered to resign his commission.[55]

Defiance of the government by the Regulators became nearly complete shortly afterwards when the back settlers refused to pay their taxes. Their argument was suited to the times; they said that they should not be taxed without representation in the Assembly.[56]

By degrees the Regulators were formulating their aims. Their first activity had been in defense of their homes and their families. Now, as Lieutenant-Governor Bull saw, continued activity and discussion were producing a rationale for the movement: "It is natural when men thus circumstanced frequently Assemble to revolve in their minds not only the present Evils, but what may happen, and to trace the causes and the remedies of their Grievances, here the want of County Courts for distribution of Justice near their homes presents itself in the first place, with the present excessive Law charges, the increase of Vice and Immorality for want of Ministers to instruct and schools to cultivate the Minds of the Youth, and as the principal source of all that they have no Representatives in Assembly who know and can state their Grievances and can point out and urge effectually the proper Remedies, and because they are unrepresented they refuse to pay Taxes."[57]

The strength and determination of the Regulators had been

55. Col. G. G. Powell to Bull, Weymouth, Aug. 19, 1768, *ibid.*, Aug. 26, 1768. See also *S. C. and Amer. Gen. Gaz.*, Aug. 26, 1768.

56. Bull to Hillsborough, Charleston, Sept. 10, 1768, P.R.O. Trans., XXXII, 39.

57. *Ibid.*

made very clear by the two Marr's Bluff affairs. Anxiety grew among the coastal planters as rumors and "very alarming" stories came from the back settlements during August and September, 1768.[58] A report from Camden stated that twenty-five hundred or three thousand Regulators planned to go to Charleston, while about the same number would "hold themselves in readiness, in case they should be wanted." The invaders intended no injury to persons and wanted "only Provisions and Quarters till their complaints shall be heard." [59] The Regulators, as Henry Middleton explained, "give a good deal of uneasiness, and people in these lower parts seem to be much alarmed, and are apprehensive that such a formidable body of lawless people got together will not disperse themselves without doing mischief, and are fearful of the Consequences." [60] There was irony in the situation; the barrier to external enemies had itself become a threat.

At this time perhaps only Lieutenant-Governor Bull had arrived at the logical conclusion to be drawn from coastal weakness and Backcountry strength. He now outlined a policy of moderation for Lord Hillsborough: "I humbly apprehend, that the surest and only method of quieting the[ir] minds, is the treating them with moderation and their complaints with attention, and their Grievances with reasonable redress." The use of force was no substitute for justice and diplomacy, he wrote; it had proved impossible to raise the Backcountry militia (Provost Marshal Pinckney and Colonel Powell knew this well!), and the coastal settlements could not spare an adequate force from the work of policing their internal enemy, the Negro slaves.[61]

When Bull announced that an election would take place on October 4 and 5, 1768, for a new Assembly,[62] the Regulators showed that they too could be moderate. They now prepared for a descent upon the coast, but only to exert their political strength.

58. *S. C. Gaz.*, Aug. 8, 1768.

59. *Ibid.*, Sept. 12, 1768; *S. C. Gaz. and C-J*, Sept. 12, 1768.

60. Henry Middleton to Arthur Middleton, Goose Creek, Sept. 22, 1768, Joseph W. Barnwell, ed., "Correspondence of Hon. Arthur Middleton," *S. C. Hist. and Gen. Reg.*, 27 (1926), 110-11.

61. Bull to Hillsborough, Charleston, Sept. 10, 1768, P.R.O. Trans., XXXII, 40.

62. Council Journal, Sept. 15, 1768; *S. C. Gaz.*, Sept. 19, 1768.

In anticipation of the election two or three thousand men were reported to have met at the Congarees to plan a verification of parish boundaries.[63] Thereafter, the settlers themselves surveyed parish lines to establish their voting rights.[64] Then in early October the Regulators went to the polls, some of them riding one hundred and fifty miles or more to vote at the parish churches.[65] Although fearful inhabitants of the coast expected violence, there was none.[66] The Regulators elected some of their candidates, and only in St. Bartholomew's Parish were Backcountry votes refused by the church wardens.[67]

This great effort, however, accomplished nothing. The new Assembly was prorogued until the return of Governor Montagu in mid-November.[68] It reconvened almost simultaneously with the arrival of news that the Crown had disallowed the circuit court act.[69] Governor Montagu vaguely urged the Assembly to redress Backcountry grievances,[70] but a few days later he dissolved the Assembly because it had supported the circular letters from Massachusetts and Virginia relative to the Townshend Acts.[71] Without

63. *Ibid.*, Aug. 8, 1768. Henry Middleton wrote that the back settlers claimed that they would elect a majority of members of the Assembly and "it is possible they may effect it." To Arthur Middleton, Goose Creek, Sept. 22, 1768, *S. C. Hist. and Gen. Mag.*, 27 (1926), 110.

64. Bull to Hillsborough, Charleston, Sept. 10, 1768, P.R.O. Trans., XXXII, 37; *S. C. and Amer. Gen. Gaz.*, Sept. 30, 1768.

65. Bull to Hillsborough, Charleston, Sept. 10, 1768. P.R.O. Trans., XXXII, 37; Petition of John Lewis Gervais, Commons Journal, July 13, 1768.

66. *S. C. Gaz.*, Oct. 11, 1768.

67. St. David's elected Claudius Peques without a contest. The legality of the Backcountry votes that elected Moses Kirkland, Tacitus Gaillard, and Aaron Loocock was left by the church wardens of St. James Goose Creek to the Assembly to decide. Commons Journal, Nov. 17, 19, 1768; Petition of John Lewis Gervais, *ibid.*, July 13, Aug. 3, 1769; Gregg, *Hist. of Old Cheraws*, 169-71.

68. Henry Laurens to Mathew Robinson, Charleston, Oct. 19, 1768, Laurens Letter-Book, 1767-1771, 295; Bull to Hillsborough, Charleston, Oct. 23, 1768, P.R.O. Trans., XXXII, 58-59; *S. C. Gaz.*, Oct. 24, 1768.

69. *S. C. Gaz.*, Oct. 10, 1768; P.R.O. Trans., XXXII, 43-53.

70. Commons Journal, Nov. 17, 1768.

71. Montagu to Hillsborough, Charleston, Nov. 21, 1768, P.R.O. Trans., XXXII, 61; Commons Journal, Nov. 17, 19, 1768.

either a court act or an Assembly to write a new one, the Regulators were worse off than ever.

The despair of the interior settlers appeared in a petition from the Peedee River area. This petition, published in a Charleston newspaper, reviewed the causes of the Regulator movement, and urged that since the laws could not operate against "known villains" in the interior settlements, they should not be enforced against Regulators of "fair character" who had inadvertently broken the law. The release of one Mr. Miles, imprisoned in Charleston on the charge of having burned the house of "an infamous person," was asked. An undisguised threat followed: "Sorry should we be to meet with a disappointment in our expectations of Mr. Miles's release, for we feel the utmost reluctance to suffer any sort of violence to be used. * * * * * * This declaration your Honour [Lieutenant-Governor Bull] will admit not as the result of defiance in an insolent people, but as the distressing apprehensions of loyal subjects, conscious of a filial regard to your Honour, and a just respect for the publick peace." [72]

Yet even now, had Bull remained in executive charge, sincere promises of reform together with fair treatment might have weakened the Regulator cause. The back settlers were uneasy in their illegality and large numbers of them yearned for an executive pardon.[73] It was their misfortune that Governor Montagu could not see beyond the fact that rebellion must be suppressed.

In late February, 1769, Governor Montagu brought a Back-

72. *S. C. and Amer. Gen. Gaz.*, Dec. 12, 1768. As a preface to this petition, there is a letter addressed to the editor, date-lined Peedee, Nov. 28, 1768, and signed "P." The author of this letter states that the petition was to have been considered at "General Meetings" of the Congaree and Wateree inhabitants in order to present "one Memorial, containing the desires of the whole" to Lieutenant-Governor Bull prior to the November meeting of the Assembly. The pardon of Miles by Bull, "P" acknowledged, had made it possible to defer the other meetings. Both letter and petition are in a style which indicate they were very probably written by Woodmason.

73. Commons Journal, July 5, 20, 1769. Ten leading inhabitants of the Camden area stated that it was "the Universal wish of all parties" that an indemnity bill should be passed, for the people were "quite weary of living in the unsettled disunited precarious situation" that prevailed. Petition of Nov. 4, 1769, Council Journal, Nov. 8, 1769.

country magistrate, Jonathan Gilbert, to the Council chamber. Gilbert told how one I. Musgrove had been whipped and driven from his home by Regulators, and how he himself had risked his life to escape to Charleston. Gilbert named some of the leading Regulators, whereupon the Council decommissioned those among them who were magistrates and militia officers.[74] This act shattered the lenient, conciliatory policy of Bull, and in an atmosphere of hostility to the Regulators one of the Charleston judges, in collusion with the Governor, took a step which threw the back settlements into confusion and brought the province to the brink of war.

A bench warrant was issued for the arrest of twenty-five Regulators. The names were probably provided by Musgrove. This warrant was given for execution to one Joseph Coffell, a man in ill-repute in the Backcountry. The terms of his commission are not known, but Coffell claimed the rank of colonel, appointed Musgrove his major, and enlisted men, many if not all of whom were among the thieves whose activities had produced the Regulator movement. Thus prepared, Coffell's troops proceeded not only to arrest some Regulators, but to plunder the homes of settlers on Saluda River.[75]

Governor Montagu had apparently formulated his own policy. If coastal planters could not coerce the Regulators, perhaps the Backcountry enemies of the Regulators might do so.

Soon after the commission was given to Coffell, an incident happened that revealed with humiliating clarity the inability of the government to support its new agent in the Backcountry. On March 13, 1769, Governor Montagu showed the Council letters from Musgrove and others. These told how one Bossard, named in the warrant given to Coffell, had been captured. Eight Regulators who tried to rescue Bossard had also been seized. Musgrove's

74. Council Journal, Feb. 22, 1769; *S. C. and Amer. Gen. Gaz.*, Feb. 27, 1769. Three weeks later still other Regulators were deprived of their commissions. Council Journal, Mar. 13, 1769.

75. *S. C. Gaz. and C-J*, Mar. 26, 28, 1769; *S. C. Gaz.*, Mar. 23, Apr. 6, 1769; Council Journal, Mar. 13, 16, 22, 1769. The name of Coffell is variously spelled, and it is quite possible that the owner could not have chosen among the variations. It was to "Joseph Coffell," however, that the Assembly paid £107 for "Criminals." Commons Journal, Aug. 15, 1769.

party, however, claimed that it was surrounded by Regulators and could not bring the prisoners to Charleston.[76]

The question of how to escort the prisoners to the capital occupied Governor and Council for several days. The Light Infantry Company of Charleston was approached. They refused the assignment. Captain Owen Roberts and part of his Artillery Company were willing to go, but this force was thought to be inadequate. Provost Marshal Roger Pinckney was asked to accompany the troops. He declined and, when pressed, discovered a great many reasons why he should remain in Charleston. In desperation, it was finally decided to ask for British regulars.[77] But before anyone left, eight of Musgrove's men arrived in Charleston with five of the prisoners.[78] Their arrival may have convinced Governor Montagu that the dignity of the government had been maintained.

In the meantime, the Backcountry Regulators were gathering to confront Coffell and his troops, whose commission was not even known to exist.[79] Although prominent planters from the back settlements appeared before Montagu and the Council to testify to Coffell's bad character and the illegality of his behavior, it was nearly a week before Montagu agreed to disavow his activities. Montagu took the position that nothing should be done until Musgrove's prisoners were in Charleston jail.[80] Only then were three prominent Backcountrymen dispatched to inform the back settlements that the "illegal and arbitrary" acts committed by Coffell and his men were without authority.[81] The three men arrived at the Saluda River to discover the Regulators and the

76. Council Journal, Mar. 13, 1769.

77. *Ibid.*, Mar. 13, 15, 16, 1769.

78. *S. C. Gaz.*, Mar. 16, 1769; *S. C. and Amer. Gen. Gaz.*, Mar. 20, May 1, 1769; *S. C. Gaz. and C-J*, Mar. 21, 1769; Bull to Hillsborough, Charleston, June 5, 1770, P.R.O. Trans., XXXII, 263. The prisoners, poor Germans, were convicted but Bull obtained a pardon for them. Same to same, Charleston, Aug. 12, 1769, *ibid.*, 91-94.

79. *S. C. and Amer. Gen. Gaz.*, Apr. 3, 1769.

80. Council Journal, Mar. 16, 1769.

81. *Ibid.*, Mar. 22, 1769; *S. C. and Amer. Gen. Gaz.*, Apr. 3, 1769; *S. C. Gaz.*, Apr. 6, 1769.

troops under Coffell facing each other and ready for battle. Their intervention alone perhaps averted warfare.[82]

Backcountry anger was heightened by a coincidence of events. A new Assembly election had been called for March 7 and 8, 1769.[83] Frontiersmen, en route to their polling places in a second effort to choose representatives, had returned home without voting when they heard that Coffell's men were robbing and seizing their families. The belief arose that Coffell had been commissioned as a deliberate conspiracy to prevent the back settlers from voting.[84]

The total effect of Coffell's behavior was to provoke Backcountry fury to perhaps its highest point during the Regulator movement. According to Woodmason, the "Commotion" which arose was "not to be expressed—The People were about to march downward and destroy all the Plantations of those Gentlemen whom they thought in the Plot—And it was with difficulty they were restrain'd—They may thank the Writer of the Remonstrance for keeping of them Still." [85]

It was at this juncture that the Regulators decided upon an appeal for aid to the King and Parliament. They named as their delegates Woodmason and a Mr. Cary, but Woodmason refused the appointment and the mission did not take place.[86] Woodmason, however, was not inactive. He wrote a letter to one of the Charleston newspapers in which he denied the right of the Assembly to tax the unrepresented back settlers.[87] And he wrote the satirical advertisement of a "Cargo of Fifty Thousand Prime Slaves" to be posted in the Charleston Exchange.[88]

The collapse of Coffell's efforts marked a turning point in the conflict between coast and Backcountry. Never again was the government to attempt to coerce Regulators, while at the same time steps were taken to redress some of the Backcountry grievances. The reasons for this abrupt change in policy are not clear. Woodmason was convinced that fear of a Backcountry mission to ask

82. *Ibid.; S. C. and Amer. Gen. Gaz.*, Apr. 3, 1769. See pp. 208, 242-43.
83. *Ga. Gaz.*, Mar. 15, 1769.          84. See pp. 207-8, 242, 267.
85. See p. 209.          86. See pp. 209-10.          87. See pp. 260-62.
88. See pp. 256-59.

royal aid was responsible,[89] and he may have been right. The Backcountry refusal to pay taxes or to recognize the authority of the Charleston courts may have contributed.

Governor Montagu, who had made a hurried tour into the Backcountry, may have spoken from conviction when, in late June, 1769, he urged the new Assembly to pass a circuit court act.[90] During the following weeks, Governor and Assembly seemed almost to vie with each other for Backcountry favor as the court bill was debated. The Assembly implied that any slowness in inaugurating an act was the Governor's fault.[91] Montagu insisted that the Assembly meet all the Board of Trade's objections to the first, disallowed, act, and made it clear that the Assembly would have to answer for any failure to do so.[92] At last successful, the governor sailed for England on July 30, 1769, taking with him the new act for royal approval.[93]

Lieutenant-Governor Bull was again free to aid the interior settlements. He tried to interest the Assembly in the creation of new parishes in order to increase Backcountry representation.[94] And he largely inspired a bill, long discussed but never passed, to provide schools in different parts of the interior settlements.[95] A rumor that the school bill had passed the Assembly inspired Woodmason to compose a sermon of celebration.[96]

89. See p. 287.

90. Commons Journal, June 27, 1769; Committee of Correspondence of Assembly to Charles Garth, Charleston, July 7, 1769, Garth Trans., 162.

91. Commons Journal, June 30, 1769.

92. *Ibid.*, July 4, 6, 11, 14, 21, 22, 24, 26-29. For the constitutional struggle between governor and assembly see D. D. Wallace, *The Constitutional History of South Carolina from 1725 to 1775* (Abbeville, S. C., 1899), 27-31; Smith, *S. C. as Royal Prov.*, 135-39.

93. Committee of Correspondence of Assembly to Charles Garth, Charleston, July 29, 1769, Garth Trans., 164-65.

94. Commons Journal, Mar. 16, 1770, Jan. 23, 30, 31, Mar. 8, 1771; Wallace, *Hist. of S. C.*, II, 63-64.

95. Commons Journal, Jan. 30, Feb. 28, Mar. 3, Apr. 4, 5, Aug. 14, 1770; *S. C. Gaz.*, Mar. 15, Apr. 12, 1770; Bull to Hillsborough, Charleston, Mar. 6, 1770, P.R.O. Trans., XXXII, 203; J. H. Easterby, ed., "The South Carolina Education Bill of 1770," *S. C. Hist. and Gen. Mag.*, 48 (1947), 95-111; Wallace, *Hist. of S. C.*, II, 160-7.

96. See pp. 118-22.

In December, 1769, news arrived that the crown had approved the Circuit Court Act.[97] Although Bull proclaimed the fact the following February,[98] fulfillment was long delayed, for the act provided that it should not be effective until all the necessary jails and courthouses were built. Nearly three years were to pass before they were completed.

In the meantime Bull continued his efforts to heal sectional wounds. Regulator activity continued against the thieves, who had been scattered but were still troublesome.[99] Bull offered rewards for house robbers brought to Charleston jail,[100] a move clearly intended to reorient the Backcountry to Charleston as a center of justice. During 1770 and 1771 Bull pardoned large numbers of Regulators who were under indictment for having aided in the punishment of the "Rogues."[101] Still other Regulators were restored to office or commissioned as militia officers and magistrates.[102] Woodmason, delighted that six of the latter were

97. Garth to Committee of Correspondence, London, Nov. 20, 1769, Garth Trans., 177-78; same to same, London, Dec. 10, 1769, *ibid.*, 179-81; Hillsborough to Bull, Whitehall, Dec. 9, 1769, P.R.O. Trans., XXXII, 131.

98. Council Journal, Feb. 19, 1770.

99. Diary of Evan Pugh, Nov. 3, 1769; charge to grand jury, Charleston, Oct. 16, 1769, John B. O'Neall, *Biographical Sketches of the Bench and Bar of South Carolina* (Charleston, 1859), I, 398; Bull to Hillsborough, Charleston, Sept. 7, 1769, P.R.O. Trans., XXXII, 101; *S. C. Gaz.*, Apr. 5, 1770; Commons Journal, Feb. 15, 1770.

100. Council Journal, June 12, 1770.

101. Bull to Hillsborough, Charleston, June 5, 1770, P.R.O. Trans., XXXII, 262-63; Miscellaneous Records PP, 46-47, South Carolina Historical Commission.

102. See listing of James Mayson and John Savage as magistrates in the *S. C. and Amer. Gen. Gaz.*, Oct. 23, 1770. Eight leading Regulators were pardoned June 9, 1771, Miscellaneous Records OO S. C. Hist. Commission. Three of these, with other Regulators, were commissioned as magistrates in July, 1771, Council Journal, July 30, 1771. In his "Memorandum" on the Regulator movement, Woodmason says that the Regulators refused a general pardon because the lawyers could still "distress" them by private suits on behalf of Regulator victims: "At length Matters were reached on this Issue. The Principals of the Regulators were put into Commission of the Peace to effect that Legally, they before did Illegaly. The People enter'd into an Association for their Protection—Denouncing Personal Vengeance against any Lawyer, or Provost that should execute any Writs against them for Matters

Anglicans, preached a sermon in which he lectured the new justices on their duties.[103]

The construction of the jails and courthouses still lagged, probably because of the Assembly's anger that the newly appointed judges were Britishers rather than natives.[104] It was not until late May, 1772, that the Circuit Court Act was declared in effect,[105] and the courts did not actually open until November, 1772.[106] This event, which met the single greatest demand of the Regulators, took place after Woodmason, ill and discouraged, had left the province.

When the courts opened, former enemies discovered, to their astonishment, that their opponents were less fearful than they had imagined. Bull reported that the operation of the act produced "the most happy effects" in the interior settlements. Many men there had "conceived terrible apprehensions of the arbitrary behaviour of the Judges and the rapaciousness of the Lawyers," but the facts did not sustain their fears.[107] The judges and lawyers, for their part, returned from circuit to report themselves "astonished with the View of a fine Country, of whose Value and Importance they had before had very inadequate Ideas; and highly satisfied with the Reception they everywhere met, as well as the general Conduct of the Inhabitants,—who in those Parts where they are termed in a great Measure uncivilized, only want good Schools and School Masters, Churches and Ministers, and fit Mag-

---

transacted before that day—and banishment of the Country and Proscription of any private person that offer'd to molest, sue, or injure them. This Point settled—The Regulators permitted the Provost to serve all Writs of Debt &c. but no other till sitting and opening of the Courts, and this was done, in order to accelerate the opening of the Courts, and sitting of the Judges." Sermon Book, IV, [387-88].

103. See pp. 123-29.

104. Edward Savage, John Murray, and John Fewtrell to Hillsborough, Charleston, Jan. 23, 1772, P.R.O. Trans., XXXIII, 113-16; "Journal of Josiah Quincy," Mass. Hist. Soc., *Procs.*, 49 (1915-16), 450.

105. *S. C. Gaz.*, May 28, 1772.

106. *Ibid.*, Nov. 5, 1772.

107. Bull to Hillsborough, Charleston, May 15, 1773, P.R.O. Trans., XXXIII, 263.

istrates to render them as valuable a People as any upon Earth." [108]

The Regulator movement which thus ended on a note of mutual conciliation was only slightly related to the uprising which had troubled North Carolina during almost the same period. The North Carolina Regulators had appeared first,[109] and had probably both inspired and provided a name [110] to their counterparts in the southern province. And according to Woodmason, over 3,000 North Carolinians were prepared to help the South Carolina Regulators if troops were sent against them.[111] But beyond such loose ties as these, the two rebellions seem to have been unconnected.

The aims of the two movements were different. The North Carolina Regulators tried to "regulate" the local sheriffs, registers, clerks, and lawyers who, they complained, exacted illegal and exorbitant taxes, fees, and rents from them.[112] The Regulators of South Carolina, on the other hand, demanded the benefits of law and order, and their "regulation work" consisted largely of punishing and driving away the bandits who infested their settlements. Though the back settlers of both provinces had numerous and genuine grievances, there is little doubt that the South Carolinians had by far the greater provocation to rebellion.

Troops under Governor Tryon crushed about 2,000 North Carolina Regulators on May 16, 1771, at the Battle of Alamance. Quite possibly Governor Montagu might have attempted a similar feat in South Carolina had not that colony possessed an internal enemy too dangerous to be left unattended. The numerous slaves of Charleston and the coastal plantations served, all unconsciously, as allies of the Backcountry Regulators.

The writings of Woodmason and others show that the South Carolina Regulators blamed the lawyers, planters, and merchants

108. *S. C. Gaz.*, Dec. 10, 1772.
109. Possibly the first Regulator statement of aims appeared in June, 1765. See Archibald Henderson, "The Origin of the Regulation in North Carolina," *American Historical Review*, 21 (1916), 324-32.
110. "Memorandum" on Regulator Movement, Sermon Book, IV, [383].
111. See pp. 54-55, 250.
112. See *Col. Recs. N. C.*, VII, 249-50, 251-52, 699-700, 702-3, 722-28.

of the low country for their troubles.[113] Quite consistent with this accusation was their proposal to send Woodmason and Cary to England to ask King and Parliament for aid against their domestic enemies.[114] Antagonism to the coastal inhabitants was probably reduced by the Circuit Court Act, together with the other, lesser concessions to the back settlers. And after 1772 the constant arrival of new settlers, unacquainted with "regulation," further diluted Backcountry hostility.

Yet, after allowing for such interim changes, it is hard not to conclude that the Regulator movement in South Carolina contributed greatly to Backcountry Loyalism during the American War of Independence.

Upon the passage of the Intolerable Acts, and especially after the beginning of war with England, the revolutionary leaders of the Tidewater saw the arms-bearing frontiersmen in a new light. In July, 1775, the South Carolina Council of Safety commissioned William Henry Drayton and the Reverend William Tennent to go into the South Carolina Backcountry to "explain to the people at large the nature of the unhappy public disputes between Great Britain and the American Colonies." [115] Their task was a formidable one. During the years that succeeded the Stamp Act of 1765 the back settlers had been engrossed in their own struggle for freedom from tyranny. In consequence, they had not participated in the recurring struggles that had prepared the inhabitants of the Tidewater for war against England and for independence. Drayton and Tennent were now called upon to arouse within a few months a fear and hatred of England that had been maturing for ten years in older portions of the country.

The two men found their cause was far from popular. A man at Enoree hinted at complications in the Backcountry mind. There was, he wrote, a "wheel within a wheel," and there existed malice not only between back settlers, but between them and Charleston.[116] Dislike of Charleston was certainly present.

---

113. See pp. 250-51, 258, 262, *passim*.          114. See pp. 183, 209-10.

115. Order of Council of Safety, July 23, 1775, Gibbes, *Doc. Hist. of the Amer. Rev.*, I, 106.

116. Edward Musgrove to Drayton, Enoree, Oct. 14, 1775, *ibid.*, 203.

The interior settlers, Tennent discovered, had been taught that "no man from Charleston can speak the truth, and that all the papers are full of lies."[117] Another back inhabitant reported a rumor that men-of-war were to seize Charleston "if they would not submit to the stamp act [!] and all the other acts," at which news "they all seemed to be much pleased."[118] German settlers, fearful for their lands and unmoved by arguments based upon the rights of Englishmen, were particularly reluctant to join in revolution, and Drayton dismissed that "stiff necked generation" with the conclusion that "the Dutch are not with us."[119] Drayton especially feared certain powerful and popular Backcountry leaders, and he reported that some of them were "clearly of opinion they can beat the whole Colony." Without seizing a dozen of these men, he concluded, "our progress has been in vain, and we shall be involved in a civil war in spite of our teeth."[120]

Through argument, coercion, and force, the revolutionists made progress. Yet it was uphill work, for their summons to arms aroused little enthusiasm among settlers of the interior who were more accustomed to old and nearby enemies than to new and distant ones.

117. Journal of Rev. Wm. Tennent, Aug. 14, 1775, *ibid.*, 228.
118. Affidavit of Edward Morrow, Fair Forest, Sept. 9, 1775, *ibid.*, 168.
119. Drayton to the Council of Safety, King's Creek, near Enoree, Aug. 16, 1775, *ibid.*, 141. See also *ibid.*, 128.
120. Same to same, Lawson's Fork, Aug. 21, 1775, *ibid.*, 151, 153.

# The Regulator Documents:

## A LETTER TO AN ENGLISH FRIEND:

*"I now begin to be quite worn out,
and cannot go thro' the fatigues I've endured."* [1]

Parish of St. Mark. S. C.
March 26. 1771

Sir

After a long Silence I make bold to address You I met (as Yesterday) with the Bearers of these Papers on the Road to C. T. [Charles Town] and stay them a few Moments on the Path, just while I scrawl a few Lines to You—Indeed, I would, and should address his Lordship, but the Mens Haste admits not—I can

---

1. This long letter together with the six enclosures which follow the intervening "Remonstrance" comprise the Ful. Trans., S.C., Nos. 51-62. The original classification in the Fulham Palace was arbitrary, and the arrangement used here is that of the transcriber who followed the letter by the enclosures as they were numbered from one to six by Woodmason. The "Remonstrance," which was also enclosed with this letter, is Ful. Trans., N.C., S.C., Geo., No. 72. In this book it is presented after the letter, and before the other six enclosures, because it precedes them in chronological order. All these transcripts, like the others from the Fulham Palace in this book, have been checked for accuracy with the originals which are now on deposit in the Office of Church Commissioners in London.

There is nothing to show to whom this letter, together with the "Remonstrance" and the six other enclosures, was sent. From references in the letter to the Bishop of London and because these writings were eventually deposited in Fulham Palace, it is likely that the recipient was someone close to, and perhaps in the service of, the Bishop of London.

Some of the extensive notes appended to the "Remonstrance" and the other enclosures were probably written a year or two earlier than the letter. Where it has proved possible, these and the papers to which they refer have been more accurately dated in their place.

only therefore speak to You, a few Random Words—leaving what I have further for You, to be completed, when I can get Paper, as [I] have not been able to procure a Quire these 12 Months, through our Fools Resolves of Non-Importation.

By these People I transmit for Your private Information and Amusement—the famous Remonstrance, presented by the People to our Senate—which made so much Noise, and has caus'd such a Change of Measures, and Matters thro' this Province—Of which I am accus'd as being the Author—If so, there were 4000 Persons who sign'd, and witness'd to the Truths of the Contents, who intended marching in a Body to C. T. and delivering of it to the House. But the Lt. Governour hearing of it, wrote to me, desiring it might be deliv'd by Deputies in a constitutional Way —which was done—and a fair draught sign'd by the Deputies only, was presented—Whereby the People were dup'd—And the Remonstrance treated as the Act and Deed of only four impudent fellows, and not that of the People—This was a trick of the Lawyers.

You have also another Piece, wrote to spur forward the Establishment of Schools in the Back Country where I am—and for encouraging the planting of Wheat, Mulberry Trees, Vines, Olives, Apple and Pear Trees, Hemp, Flax &c. to set 30 M Idlers at Work. Which had Effect so far, as to subject the Author to ev'ry Degree of Resentment that could be devis'd against Him—The Physic was strong, and has operated; tho' the Body Politic does not as yet reap any Benefit.

You have several small Matters, that will tend to let You into the Light of Matters here, and how Public Concerns have been manag'd.

I shall give his Lordship an ample detail of the State of Religion and Ecclesiastical Polity in these Parts—Why I have not lately wrote his Lordship, has been owing to dread; lest my Letters should be intercepted before they reach him—for altho' we have a Post Office here Yet notwithstanding I have many of my Letters artfully taken up and suppress'd—which has brought on me many Vexations.

Soon after my Arrival here, I wrote his Lordship an Account of the Endemic Sickness that then prevailed, and how greatly the Clergy had been affected by it—This Letter [2] was seen, read, and examined by 50 Capital Persons, before ever sent over, and ev'ry Syllable was the strictest Truth, saving as to Mr. *Alexander*, who was not Dead, but lay Dying I put him among the Dead on the Assertion of 3 Reverend Gentlemen. However Mr. Alexander recovered—but the Dissenters made the Place too warm for him to stay, and he was oblig'd to go to the Northward—from whence I've not heard of Him.

His Lordship shewd my Letter to one Mr. Smith Rector of St Philip's C. T. This Gentleman wrote over a long Letter of Exclamation against me, attributing his ill Success in getting of Clergymen to fill the vacant Parishes, to my false Informations, and branding of the Province as a sickly Clime—This rais'd an horrid persecution against Me—and I was voted an Enemy to the Province—Unfit to stay in a Country that gave me Bread; for abusing, and depreciating it—So hard is it to speak Truth! But what if I had said, that some of those Gentlemen had been carried off by Poison, and did not lay down Life in a Natural Way? If I had so mention'd—it would not have been untrue tho' smother'd up, and hid from Public Notice.

It was urg'd to his Lordship, that I spoke an Untruth, when I said that there was never a Clergyman save my Self, on the No. Side Santee River, from that River to the Line, and from the Sea to the Mountains It was very true—It is true still—Where is there, or now is? Can any dare contradict this? Yet this Space contains the best half of this Province, and more than 2/3 of the White Inhabitants—And I here assert again and again that there is not one Episcopal Gentleman save my Self, in all this vast Distric—which contains the Parishes of P. [Prince] George P. [Prince] Frederick St. Davids, and St. Mark. Indeed, a Gentleman came out for P. Frederick and liv'd one Year—and Mr. Morgan [3] came out for St. Mark and liv'd a fortnight—All these are facts, as evident as the shining Sun and yet I've been abus'd, vilify'd,

2. See pp. 84-87.

3. A Thomas Morgan was licensed to South Carolina on May 29, 1769. Licensed to Plantations, Fulham Palace MSS., Office of Church Commissioners, London.

censur'd, and proscrib'd for speaking of Truths they wanted not to have divulg'd.

The various Scenes and Persecutions I've undergone shall be related to You at large, when I can get Paper to finish my Memoirs and shall then be transmitted, when [I] can find a safe Hand. I would not now have been in this Country only for sake of my Son, for whom I have projected several settlements that would have turn'd out advantagiously but have been travers'd in ev'ry thing, of ev'ry kind I've took in Hand—For being deem'd an Anti-American, I stand almost singly—You have the Occasion related, in Respect to my Soliciting to be a Stamp-Distributor— Before this I was greatly caressed, and ev'ry ones favriter. But this being discovered, I was deem'd (and am still) a private Spy and Correspondent of the Ministry—A faithless fellow—one that is a betrayer of the Country, and of the Rights and Priveleges of America—One in whom no Confidence is to be plac'd, and the like—Lord Bute never was more malign'd, or bespattered than I have been—The 120th Psalm could not be better apply'd by David than by my Self—for, as a private Person, I have many open and private Enemies to Encounter—As an Englishman, all the Herd of Scotch, Irish, and Americans—As a Patriot, and Supporter of the Rights of the People—All the Rich and Great Ones below—As a Christian, all the Vile profane Licentious Wretches around—As a Clergyman, all the Herd of Sectaries, and especially the Scotch Irish Presbyterians—bitter Enemies to the Church and the Establishment. As a Gentleman all the Rude, Impudent audacious Tribe among whom I live. And as the Trading Interest in these Back Parts is wholly in hands of a few Merchants who are all Presbyterians, I have their Enmity, thro' Jealousy, that I shall bring over my Son to carry on Trade here Nay, as a Minister, I have the Hatred of the Clergy—First, For reproaching them for their Indolence, Supineness, and Neglect of their Flocks—Of Religion—and the Interests of the Church— Secondly, Thro' the Great Pains and Travel I take, which is a Reproach to them—So that they cannot bear to hear my Name mentioned. Their Indifference in respect to the Sectaries, and giving up all things—Their Cringing and fawning to the Great

Ones—Their tameness in being subservient to the Will of the Mean Ignorant, Rich Individuals here—And their bowing down before the Dissenters, is what I never could, or will do or copy— They have carried their Compliansiance [sic] so far, as not even to preach against Popery on the 5th November [4] or to observe the Day—And I had complaint exhibited against me by the Dissenters for preaching on the 29th May.[5]

When Things will mend I know not—So far from having New Parishes, we have two that were made, annull'd from home— A Bill is in the House for making 6 new ones out of this large one I now am in, but it cannot pass—The Number of Members in the House is restricted—from Home—No New Members can be made—The Ministry want them to take from the Old, and add to the New—And this the lower Parishes will not assent too [6]— Mean while Religion and the Church, lye bleeding—Wounded ev'ry day—overrun with Sectaries, especially the New Light Baptists—who have broke up ev'ry Congregation I have founded— All the whole Back Country is now lost to the Church thro' want of Ministers and Churches. The article of Representation occasions all this. They blam'd the Regulators, as infringers of the Laws, and Insulters of Government And yet they acted the very

4. "Guy Fawkes' Day."

5. The 29th of May celebrates the day on which Charles II arrived in London from exile in 1660.

6. The crown demand that there be no increase in the total number of assemblymen was an almost insurmountable obstacle to Backcountry representation. The creation of St. Matthew's Parish in 1765 had been disallowed for this reason, whereupon the Assembly recreated St. Matthew's in 1768 with one member taken from the representation of St. James's, Goose Creek. St. David's was erected in the same year and given one of the two representatives of St. Mark's Parish. Acts to establish two new parishes, St. Luke's in Granville County and All Saints' in Craven County, were also disallowed in 1770 because their representatives would enlarge the Assembly. By this time crown policy was so clearly stated that the assembly bill of 1770-1771 to create six new parishes, with representatives in Assembly, would appear to have been an attempt to appease the Backcountry by the effort and to hope that the disallowance would be blamed on the English government. Board of Trade to the King, Nov. 21, 1770, P.R.O. Trans., XXXII, 358-59; Wallace, *Hist. of S. C.*, II, 63-64; Commons Journal, July 20, 1769, Mar. 13, 16, 1770, Jan. 23, 30, 31, Mar. 8, 1771.

same in Respect to G. Britain—The Back People never went half the length with them, as they took with the Mother Country. How things will be settled is uncertain—Many Plans are propos'd but none as yet adopted—They cannot on their own Principles, tax the People, without their being represented—And they cannot lay the Province out into Parishes and give them Churches and Ministers because G. Britain will not allow any greater Number of Representatives to be in the House than now are—Whereby Religion and the Church, are sacrific'd to Political Maxims.

I shall write Dr. Dodd, Mr. Broughton, Mr. Waring and other Gentlemen from Whom You will learn the true State of Religion here. We have now 12 Parishes vacant—Since my last to his Lordship We have buried the Gentlemen mention'd within—And this Mortality among the Clergy, I attribute to three Particulars—

First The Situation of the Parsonage Houses—most of which are built in the Old Style, on Edge of Swamps, in a damp moist Situation, which quickly kills all Europeans, not season'd to the Clime.

The Old Planters us'd this Method, in order to view from their Rooms, their Negroes at Work in the Rice Fields [7]—But this Method now is banish'd—The[y] find the bad Effects—and are all removing their Houses back into the High and dry Lands, remote from the Swamps.

The Gentry us'd annually to go off to some of the Northern Colonies for Change of Air—But they find it now rather too Expensive. One of our Dons (Benj Smith Esq) was last Year cast away,[8] he and family in going to Rhode Island—and many have left their Bones in these Places—They are therefore now thinking of their own poor despised Back Country, and are now flocking up

7. In a description of South Carolina written in 1763 it is said that the planters, more concerned with their fortunes than their health, built their houses near the rice fields or indigo dams. [Dr. George Milligen-Johnston], *A Short Description of the Province of South-Carolina* ... (London, 1770), in Milling, ed., *Colonial South Carolina*, 155.

8. The *Newport Mercury* of June 18, 1770, carried a story of a ship, chartered by Col. Smith of Charleston, being wrecked. Smith and his family escaped and arrived safely in Newport, but a mate on the ship was drowned. Carl Bridenbaugh, "Charlestonians at Newport, 1767-1775," *S. C. Hist. and Gen. Mag.*, 41 (1940), 47.

where I am, to build Summer Seats, and Hunting Boxes. Lands, not valu'd at a Shilling P acre three Years past, now sells for a Guinea—and is rising—And the Back Inhabitants, are (at last) carrying the Points they've so long labour'd for.

Court Houses and Goals are building—but the Article of Public Schools is postpon'd—except we will build a College in Charlestown.

The second thing destructive to the New Clergy, is, their living and constant residing and breathing one Medium of Air (to which I may add bad Water) Air, Hot and Moist in Summer—and Cold and Moist and thick in Winter—If they would sojourn now and then for a Week or two, up in the Back Settlements they might keep Health—But always moving in a very Narrow Compass—(not even going the Rounds of their own respective Parishes) cuts them off continually.

A 3d Circumstance is—The different Meats, Drinks, and Methods of Living to what they've been accustomed in England. All which (out of C. T. and its Environs) is diametrically opposite to their usual Methods—Where I am, is neither Beef or Mutton—Nor Beer, Cyder, or anything better than Water—These People eat twice a day, only. Their Bread, of Indian Corn, Pork in Winter and Bacon in Summer—If any Beef, they jerk it and dry it in the Sun—So that You may as well eat a Deal Board—And yet it costs me for this hard Living, at least 50 £ Sterling P ann. The intrinsic Worth of which is not so many Shillings.

You have among other Papers a Letter drawn up to be signed for to send to his Lordship, but I overruled it, till I see another Turn of Affairs—Also another Letter for the Parish of St. Mark which I suppressed for the same Reasons [9]—because they exaggerated Matters for the Parsonage stands so low, I cannot live in it—but reside twenty Miles above, on the Hills, for the Benefit of Air, from whence I ride down to the Church.

But the greatest Blow ever given me here, was thro' the Good Will of the People. They were determin'd to lay their Grievances at foot of the Throne, and send over Agents to London to His

9. The letter intended for the Bishop of London, together with that for the Parish of St. Mark, is missing from the Fulham Palace Manuscripts.

Majesty and both Houses of Parliament—To shew, That tho' these People below acted as they did with G. B. [Great Britain] Yet in their own Country, they practis'd those very Measures and Principles as they condemn'd, and railed against the Mother Country for. My Self and one Mr. Cary[10] was nam'd by the People for this Purpose—But this gave such an Alarm, that the People was promis'd ev'ry thing they could ask or desire, would they not execute this Plan—And they (foolishly) dropt it—relying on the fair Promises made them. But after they were lulled asleep, then they meditated Revenge against All whom they supposed put the People on such Measures. Several Gentlemen had their Military Commission took from them—Others put out of Office—and others struck out of the Commission of the Peace— Then they resolved to punish me, but knew not how—They got a Person to allege that I was a Drunkard—tho' its well known I hardly drink a Gallon of Liquor in a Year—and live for Months on Water. And to this, I had the Attestation of many Hundreds— I went to Town, and boldly look'd them in the face—and challeng'd any Proof to be made of the Charge—And desir'd to see my Accuser—but he was not produc'd and the Matter dropped —Meantime I received an Invitation to Maryland and prepar'd for my departure—But the People would not let me go—And petitioned that I should be removed to the Congaree Distric—to which I went—and stay'd 12 Months—Then the Vestry of this Parish press'd me to return here, and lay aside all thoughts of quitting the Province—to which I consented, on Account of the Number of Baptist Teachers which had lately appeared among them—Here I have been 12 Months, but intend not to stay, purposing to go higher up to the Parish of St. Simon and Jude (when established) by Invitation from these People—but if the New

10. This may refer to James Cary, a member of an English family in Camden. He was a justice of the peace for Craven County in 1770 and 1771 and was probably the Colonel James Carey of the loyalist "1st Regiment Camden" during the Revolution. *S. C. and Amer. Gen. Gaz.*, Oct. 23, 1770; Council Journal, July 30, 1771; Kirkland and Kennedy, *Historic Camden*, 104; E. Alfred Jones, ed., "The Journal of Alexander Chesney, a South Carolina Loyalist in the Revolution and After," Ohio State University, *Bulletin*, 26 (1921), 115.

intended Parishes be not rais'd, then I think to proceed to Virginia, and then for England—where I'd sooner be content with a Curacy of 30 £ p ann than the best Living in this Colony.

Indeed I gave our Vestry warning—and thought to have removed from hence last fall. I do not like the People—for I've [not] found one honest Man, or one Virtuous Woman among them. Which is an hard saying, but a true One. When I first came over, they advis'd me to Marry—A Circumstance I am wholly unfit for, as being both Old and Impotent for many Years past, thro' a fall received from an Horse, and a Kick received in the Scrotum. And this Incapacity for Nuptial Rites, was the Reason, that a Wife I had in England refus'd coming over to America, to live with the Man, who sacrificed all he had in Life, for her Benefit. I told our Vestry my Unfitness, which they laughed at as a Joke—And I courted two Ladies, and fairly told my Case—who declared they chose not to live as married Nuns—I then desired the Vestry to look out for Me—Our Vestry Sir consists of 9 Persons, all related too, and under controul of one Man. This Person nam'd a Relation of his—A Girl of about 28—Handsome and Agreeable—She received my Addresses—and we were engaged— But very luckily, in Interim, I learn'd, that my Fair One, had had a Lying in in Virginia before her Settlement here—and had no Nuns flesh about her—On which I dropp'd Affairs. And could not avoid reproaching my Vestry, for their Deception, and intended Delusion of me in so material an Affair—Whereon they wrote to England for a Minister in my Place, who is soon expected over [11]—tho' when he does come I know not what he'll do, or how live here—except he can fare as I do, which none but those long accustom'd to the People and Country can.

When I was bound Northerly, I received ample Testimoniums of my regular Life and Doctrine, to confute all Gainsayers—one

11. The Rev. Charles Martyn wrote to the Bishop of London that the vestrymen of St. Mark had authorized him to obtain a minister for that parish, and that he had obtained the consent of Thomas Walker to go there. In May, 1772, the Rev. Mr. Walker arrived in Charleston from London. The Rev. Charles Martyn to the Bishop of London, Feb. 1, 1772, Ful. Trans., N.C., S.C., Ga., No. 15; S. C. Gaz., May 28, 1772.

of which (from the then Vestry of this Parish) I make bold to enclose.[12]

I must beg Dear Sir of You, not to make any of my Letters or Papers Public—They are presented You only in a private Way from Gentleman to Gentleman—And nothing has been more hurtful to the Mother Country, than the House of Commons calling for Letters wrote from America, and their being afterwards expos'd and printed—Witness Mr. Hughes of Philadelphia, as to the Stamp Act—and Governour Bernard as to N. England [13]— It is this that has deterr'd me from writing to his Lordship—for as I am a suspected Person, I am narrowly watched—It is this that puts a Damp on ev'ry one this Side the Water, from throwing proper Lights on Things and Persons, and letting You know the Truth of Things. Unhappily for my Poor Back Country People, their Interest and those of the Inhabitants of C. T. have been thought incompatible tho' demonstra[ti]vely otherwise. They are quite connected—And this I have fully shewn—But there is an Old Leaven that still remains here—The Old Republican Spirit, that sent out the first Settlers of this Colony, is not yet extinguished, but appears now again. The Clergy here, do not exert their Rights, and tamely submit to ev'ry thing—While the Assembly assumes more and more Power continually. I could wish to see the Royal Prerogative more strongly asserted and supported. The Dissenting Influence entirely prevails and lately when I addressed those in Power to put a Stop to Presbyterian Justices of the Peace, Baptist Teachers—Itinerant Teachers of all Denominations from the Northward annually sent out here, and others, from marrying in my Parish, and that the Lieutenant Governour ordered an Information for to be fil'd in the Court of KB [King's Bench]. Yet it has not been done—We have but 4 or 5 Gentlemen at Council

12. The vestrymen and church wardens of St. Mark's Parish wrote that Woodmason had "taken Great Pains in discharge of his Duty," and that "his Converse and Carriage among Us hath been agreeable to his Function, and satisfactory to the Generality of People, as far as We know and believe." Letter of Recommendation of June 6, 1769, Ful. Trans., S.C., No. 50.

13. On Governor Francis Bernard and John Hughes, see Edmund S. Morgan and Helen M. Morgan, *The Stamp Act Crisis: Prologue to Revolution* (Chapel Hill, 1953), chs. 8, 14.

Board, 3 of whom are Dissenters—and the Majority of our House of Assembly are such as well as most of the Acting Magistrates.

I now begin to be quite worn out, and cannot go thro' the fatigues I've endured—Fatigues beyond whatever any Clergyman sustained, or undertook as yet in this Province—I've baptized above Two thousand Children Married some hundred Couples—and given (at least) 500 discourses in this my large Parish since here—And yet have not gone over one half of it, tho' have travell'd above 3000 Miles ev'ry Year since here—But I cannot say more—the Bearers hurry me, and will not stay one Moment—Pray lay me at feet of his Lordship with my best Respects and most Dutiful Honours, and hoping You'l excuse the Liberty here taken of this Address, I beg leave to subscribe my Self

Sir Your most obedient humble Servant, Charles Woodmason

### Clergy, deceas'd since my last Letters

Mr. Balsober—A Lutheran at Congarees
Mr. Copp—Johns Island
Mr. Thompson—Congarees or Broad River
Mr. Skeyne—P. [Prince] Frederic
Mr. Farmer—St. John's Parish
Mr. Crallan—Christ Church
Mr. McLeod— (Dis) [dissenter] James Island
Mr. Duncomb—Prince William
Mr. Wilton—Lecturer—**Charleston**
Mr. Gordon    (Dis) Ponpon
Mr. Baron—St. Bartholemew
Mr. Rae— (Dis) Williamsburgh
Mr. Gansendander    Orangeburgh
Mr. Amory—John's Island
Mr. Dawson—Johns Island
Mr. Gaston    (Dis) Waterees
Mr. Chiffelle—St Peter
Mr. Mc Clellan    (Dis) Black River
Mr. Morgan—of St. Mark
Mr. Alison    (Dis) Pedee
Mr. Fridereau—St. **Helena**
Mr. Evans—St. Bartholemew

Mr. Lloyd—
Mr. Drake   left Christ Church
Mr. Alexander   Prince William
Mr. Rowand   Congarees
Mr. Martin—St. Andrew
Mr. Hockley—St. John
Mr. Fayerweather   Prince George
Mr. Pierce—Dorchester

| Parishes filled— | Parishes Vacant |
|---|---|
| St. Philip—C. T. | Prince William |
| St. Michaels   C. T. | St. Helena |
| St. Andrew | St. Peters |
| St. James Goose Creek | St. Bartholowmew |
| St. James Santee | Prince George |
| St. John Baptist | Prince Frederic |
| St. John Evan. | Waterees |
| St. Thomas | Congarees |
| St. Matthew | Christ Church |
| St. Paul | St. Davids |
| St. Stephen | |
| St. George | New Parishes rais'd, but not |
| St. Mark | as yet establish'd |
| St. Andrew | All Saints |
| St. George | St. Luke |
| St. Stephen | St. Pattrick |
| | St. Bridget |
| | Queen Charlotte |
| | St. Simon and St Jude |
| | St. Albans |

Sir [14]

You have here enclosed the famous Remonstrance presented by my Parishioners to our Commons House of Assembly—Which tho' at first treated with Great Indignity and Contempt, at length prevail'd over all Opposition.

I annex to it, the Preamble of the Act they have got pass'd for

14. In spite of the new salutation, this would appear to be a continuation of the same letter.

Establishing of Courts of Justice [15]—which Act was not obtain'd but after vast Struggles—The Lawyers dy'd very hard and not till After making of the best Provision they could for themselves. This Preamble of the Law, evidences, that the Complaints of the People were not groundless—That they *really* suffer'd, and were greivously oppress'd and distress'd—And if their Enemies who thus oppress'd and distress'd them, Did, in this Public, authentic Manner acknowledge that these things were So, and thus confess'd to God and the World the Evils that their fellow Provincials labourd under—If thus much set down in the Law be granted— What remains behind, unnotic'd? Unredress'd? Even all that is contain'd in the remonstrance—Which is only an Enumeration (not an exageration) of Facts as visible as the Sun at Noon Day— And by this their Public Confession, and Redress of Part, they tacitly acknowledge the whole to be true.

As their Grievances are summ'd up under Heads I will just beg leave to Notice, what have, What has not been redress'd, or remedied.[16]

Request (1) Circuit Courts are granted—County Courts (or Quarter Sessions rejected—not yet in Force

The Old Counties are abolished—and the Province laid out into Six Districts.

The Plan adopted is quite distinct from any thing of the like Sort in Britain or America—It being a Maxim with these proud People, *Not to copy after others*—But to have some thing of their own, be it ever so absurd or ridiculous

Request (2) Not granted

———— (3) the former part granted—but not the latter—It would be giving up too sweet a Sugar Plumb.

(4) Not Granted—All Writs must be still returned to Charlestown which is an enormous Grievance and Expence.

15. The preamble of the Circuit Court Act does not appear among the Fulham Palace Manuscripts. An original copy of it, however, exists in the South Carolina Historical Commission Library in Columbia, S.C. The preamble makes clear the hardships to frontier inhabitants in having to attend Charleston court as witnesses, jurors, or parties to suits.

16. The following items refer to the twenty-three requests, or "Grievances," in the Remonstrance which follows this letter, pp. 230-33.

Not one Word, thought, or Deed, about Atachments, tho' an affair so absolutely necessary for the securing of Property that till granted No Trade—No Traffic can be well carried on

(5) Not yet thought off—or regarded

(6) Court Houses and Goals at six different Places are built— but not one House of Correction, as yet, in the Province—tho' most notoriously necessary, and loudly called for—But *Idleness,* is the Endemic Distemper of this Clime.

(7) Not as yet granted—Tho' Bills brought into the House time after Time for this Purpose—The Taverners, having greater Influence within, than the Country without Doors. Wherefrom travelling is 10 times more expensive than in England, and exceeding incommodious—You may travel better in Turkey Russia or Tartary, than in this Region

(8) Amended—But in a Loose and Vague Manner Nothing to the Purpose prayed for, but making Matters rather worse than better—But they would be said for to do something—Swine not thought off—And it is as yet indeterminate whether they are property or not as the Laws now are.

Request   (9) Agreed too—Executed but not yet published

          (10) Rejected

          (11) Agreed too in part—The Country being laid out into Six Parishes, tho' large enough for Sixty.

          (12) Not thought about

          (13)    Ditto

          (14) — Ditto

          (15) — Ditto

          (16) — Ditto

          (17) Granted.

And on this Head may be remark'd one Great defect of things here—Understand then, that Jurors are drawn by Ballot three Months previous to the Sessions—And their Names are publickly known (both Grand and Petit Jurors) where from a Man may bribe a Jury at his Will.

(18) Rejected—This article gave such offence—that they put all the Attorneys into the Commission, and struck out many Country Gentlemen.

(19) Granted—A Public School, for 20 Scholars, is order'd for ev'ry of the New Parishes

(20) Laugh'd at

(21) Amended.

(22) Ordered, in the General Survey of the Province

(23) Ridicul'd—On which, these Lines were fix'd on the State House.

### Inscription for the Statue of Mr. Pitt

> What Love to their adopted Sons
>   is by our Fathers' shown?
> We ask'd to taste the *Bread of Life* *
> And Lo!—they give—A *Stone!*

Great was the Uproar and Noise in the House, on Reading of this Petition—The Lawyers storm'd—Would vote it a Libel and Insult on the House. Moved, that the Deputies should be taken into Custody of the Black Rod Sent to Goal—That the Paper should be burnt by the Hangman, and the Like.[17]

But it was reply'd—Gentlemen—Here are the Deputies at the Door—Waiting to know your Resolutions—and what News they are to carry back to their Constituents—Do you know that this Remonstrance is sign'd by Four thousand Persons, in Name of Fifty thousand—And that these four thousand would have been now at that Door with this Paper, but thro' the Interposition and Address of your Lieutenant Governour (in whom the People repose Great Confidence) who desir'd ev'ry thing to be transacted Calmly and Quietly in a Constitutional Way. (Here the Deputies stepp'd in, and told them, that they came in behalf of the people—To be led either to Prison or to Death—They fear'd nothing—But bad[e] them take Care To do nothing Rashly. That they were Britons and not to be harrass'd or injur'd for asserting their Rights and Priveleges, or setting Matters and

* Administration of the Sacrament.

17. Three days after the reading of the Remonstrance, the four deputies sent a message to the Assembly in which they disclaimed any intention to have used "Language unfit for a Petition" or to have reflected upon the conduct of the legislature. Commons Journal, Nov. 10, 1767.

Things before them in a True Light—The Firmness and Intrepidity of these Men (be it spoken to their Everlasting Remembrance in the Annals of this Country, thô their Good Deeds may be forgotten) both soften'd and astonish'd the Vociferous Lawyers, and Haughty Demagogues.

The Remonstrance was Canvass'd—And at length nothing found exceptionable in it, but—the Word—*Infernal*.

They then proceeded to Votes—And gave a Copy of their Votes to the Deputies for to carry back to their Constituents—with assurance of their being pass'd into Laws.

They were caress'd, and politely entertain'd in Town—and departed with Joy and Gladness.

Bonfires, and Firings, and every Demonstration of Joy, prevail'd hereon thro' the Country.

But these Votes were never realized by those who made them.

And the People say, That they will never place Confidence again in those who so Notoriously break thro' *Public Faith*—For that once Violated—What dependance on Private Virtue?

This Proceeding, destroyed all the Harmony that was expected to take place from that Period, between the Upper and the Lower Inhabitants. The former would willingly have thrown themselves into their Arms, would they have embrac'd them as fellow Citizens and Protestants—But finding that they were only amus'd and trifled with—All Confidence of the Poor in the Great is [18] destroy'd and I believe will never exist again.

I would Note. That before these Deputies left Town, the House granted Two Companies of Rangers, for clearing the Country of Rogues—And these did their Work so Well, as to break Up the Combin'd Gangs of Villains—tho' not so fully as to secure many Individuals for Public Justice.

As the People found they could not rely on the public Faith— they strove hard to carry the Elections of New Members in some of the Parishes—and prevail'd—several Country Gentlemen being voted in on whom they could rely.[19]

This gave fresh Alarms—And it was a New Sight to see 1 M̶

18. Woodmason replaced "between the Upper and Lower Inhabitants is at present" with "of the Poor in the Great is."

19. For the election of October 4 and 5, 1768, see Introduction, pp. 178-79.

Men come 200 Miles to the field of Election whom they dream'd not off—And for the Rich fellows to be out voted.

Various Steps were taken on this Occasion, and some harsh Steps pursued to intimidate and fright the People.

They were told, that their actions were Rebellious—Contumacious—Insolent—Against Law—the Peace of the King—Insult on Government—Audacious—Impudent—Repugnant to Authority and what not—And some Gentlemen who were judged to be Advisers of the People, were deprived of their Commissions in the Militia and struck out of Commission of the Peace [20]—And ev'ry Step taken to preclude them (if possible) from being elected Members in the ensuing Assembly.

For this Assembly was not of Long Duration—the Law on which the Elections were founded not being approv'd off at home.[21]

Great Endeavours were us'd to find out the Writer of the Remonstrance. And it was easy to fix the Party—There being only one Clergyman in these Parts—and not *One* Single Person beside either capable of the Thing, or so well acquainted with Persons and Matters as Him.—Consequently 'twas his Work.

Private Resolutions were then taken to remove Him at all Events—an [as] an obnoxious Person—An ungrateful fellow—An Incendiary—for what Business have the Clergy with Temporal Matters. Let them stick to their Beads and Breviary.

The New Election came on [22]—Some thousands of People were on their Way down—and the Country hoped, that if they could not obtain a Majority, Yet have such Number of their own in the House, as to forward Matters in their favour—But all their Hopes proved abortive. A Scheme was set on foot, which threw the whole Country into a flame.

20. Some of the Regulators were struck from the commission of peace in February, 1769, shortly before the election. See Introduction, p. 180.

21. Woodmason is here in error. The Assembly to which he refers was dissolved in December, 1761, because a 1759 revision of the election law had been disallowed in England. See Wallace, *Hist. of S. C.*, II, 38. For the dissolution of Assembly of November, 1768, see Introduction, p. 179.

22. The new election for Assembly was called for March 7 and 8, 1769. See Introduction, p. 183.

For some days previous to the Election, A Warrant was obtain'd from one of the assistant Judges (an old, Weak, and ignorant Man) for to take up 25 Persons, on Suspicion of being concern'd in Riots and Tumults in the Back Country, and to bring them to Town, to give Security for their future peaceable Behaviour— With Power to take up likewise Any other suspected or reputed Persons guilty of any Outrages or Misdemeanours.

This Warrant was given to one of the Greatest Villains and Scoundrels in the Creation for to execute [23] who was sworn a Constable to that End but in a very private Manner.

This fellow (a common Robber, Thief, and notorious Rogue) goes among dispers'd Gangs of Thieves,[24] telling them that he had a Commission from the King to take up all whom he pleased that he judged disturbers of the Public Peace—That he was appointed a Colonel—Had power to make Officers, inlist Men— press Provisions and Horses, and to range the Country.

Hereon he collects together all the Rogues, whom the two Troops of Rangers had dispers'd—makes Captains Lieutenants and officers Forms a Camp—and with his Band of Ruffians, enters ev'ry House around, carrying off Horses, Meal, Corn, and Provisions, of all Kinds [25]—He did this the day after the People were gone down to the Elections—for this was the Scheme concerted by his Principals.[26]

The People hearing that their Houses were plundered—their Wives and Daughters carried Captives—and their Plantations broke up, in[s]tantly marched back again to secure their fami-

23. Joseph Coffell received the Bench Warrant. See Introduction, p. 181.

24. Coffell was reported to have enlisted at least a hundred men on the promise of £20 a month and a bottle of rum a day. Council Journal, Mar. 16, 1769; S. C. Gaz., Mar. 23, 1769.

25. Colonel William Thompson informed the Council that Coffell had imprisoned "Women and Children as well as men and going from House to House taking away their Provisions." Council Journal, Mar. 22, 1769. See, also, the testimony of Colonel Richard Richardson, ibid., Mar. 16, 1769.

26. In his "Memorandum" on the Regulator movement, Woodmason states that the thieves, at one time, called themselves "Friends of the Government." Sermon Book, IV, [376].

lies [27]— This was the Aim of those below—And hereby they carried the Elections in their own Way.

The freeholders who thus returned assembled together to Number of 500 Men well arm'd, and march'd to Camp of the Rogues, who were above 300 Strong—Bold and resolute—Each Side resolved to fight it out and give no Quarter. And had they been permitted, much blood would have been shed.

But some principal Gentlemen [28] rode post to Town to the Governour and acquainted Him with this Matter—who (pretending Ignorance) instantly [29] issu[e]d Orders for all Persons to disperse—revoking the Warrant of the Ringleader of the Rogues.

These Gentlemen came up with the two Parties, on Saludy River, just as they were drawn up in Array—each facing the other—and advancing to Fire—They threw themselves in between them: Proclaimd the Public Orders—and orderd all People to their Homes: However some of the Rogues were pursued, taken, and sent to Goal.[30]

The Damage done to the Poor Inhabitants by this Feat of Politics, was many hundred Pounds Sterling—They were stript of all their Winter Grain and Provisions—And many hundreds expos'd thereby to Hunger and Want, and which will be some

27. A letter from the Backcountry said that about seven hundred men planned to leave the Wateree River on March 18, and about the same number were expected from the Broad and Saluda Rivers, to oppose Coffell. The letter seemed to contain a threat. The "Right of the People is the Supreme Right" the author wrote, "and if something is not done ... the Consequence will be bad." Every "Man of Property" in the Backcountry was "a Regulator at Heart." *S. C. Gaz. and C-J*, Mar. 28, 1769. The style of this letter suggests that it might have been written by Woodmason.

28. The three men who intervened were Colonels Richard Richardson and William Thompson and Major Daniel McGirt. See Introduction, p. 182.

29. Actually, the Governor did not give such orders for some days. See Introduction, p. 182.

30. In another version, written many years later, Woodmason gives more details: "The Rogues retreated to Saludy River where the Country came up with them—Both Parties drew up in Battalia—and fac'd each other with presented Arms half the day waiting for the first Fire. Several Gentlemen pass'd between and assur'd the Regulators that the Rogues had a Bench Warrant to justify their Proceedings tho' they had greatly exceeded their Commission—so begg'd they'd not give the first Fire (as they were about to do) A Parley then ensu'd—and it was agreed to let the Rogues go off unmolested on Release

Years e'er they recover. The Principal Sufferers, were the poor Germans.[31]

But the Commotion which this rais'd in ev'ry Part, is not to be expressed—The People were about to march downward and destroy all the Plantations of those Gentlemen whom they thought in the Plot—And it was with difficulty they were restrain'd—They may thank the Writer of the Remonstrance for keeping of them Still.

But they could not be prevented from maltreating ev'ry Bailif that came into the Country to serve Process—They drove off many—and came to Resolutions of not suffering Process of any kind to be serv'd till Courts of Justice among themselves take place—In which Humour they still remain.[32]

And as they found themselves, only amused—Deprived of the Rights of Election—and prevented from having any Share in Public Matters they determined to send home Deputies, to the King, and to lay their Complaints at foot of the Throne.

Never could a more favourable Crisis happen—than this Period

of the Prisoners they had made, and delivery of some of the most notorious Villains—which was done." "Memorandum" on the Regulator movement, Sermon Book, IV, [377].

31. In his "Memorandum" on the Regulator Movement, written many years later, Woodmason is more detailed on the after-effects of the Coffell affair: "The plundered People went down in a large Body with their Clergy at their Head to complain of these Proceedings—But they obtained no redress, altho' many were totally ruin'd—The Governor and Council disown'd the Warrant and pretended Ignorance—The Justice only was blamed—and He found Means to get Clear of any Public Examination. But this was all Farce—for the Captain of the Banditti walk'd the Streets of C. T. [Charleston] publickly in Regimentals called himself Captain, married a Young Girl and went off the Province with his Booty—And his Personal Safety required it." Sermon Book, IV, [377-78]. In August, 1769, the Assembly granted Joseph Coffell £107 for "Criminals," probably payment for the arrest of Regulators. Commons Journal, Aug. 15, 1769.

32. The refusal to allow writs to be served in the Backcountry began as early as June, 1768. See Introduction, p. 175. In his "Memorandum" on the Regulator movement, Woodmason states that the provost marshal admitted that he had lost £1600 Sterling during the three years the Regulators forbade the serving of writs, and that as £10 Sterling "at least" attended each writ, the lawyers were deprived of about £16,000 Sterling. Sermon Book, IV, [388].

—for how would it have appear'd to the World, that Men who railed against General Warrants—Oppression—Tyranny Slavery—Chains, and what not And whose Mouths were continually Bawling, *Liberty! Liberty!* Coul'd be so notoriously guilty in Fact, and make others *feel,* what they only viewed in Speculation.

They pitch'd on their Poor Parson, and one Mr. *Cary,* a Gentleman of the Law, for to go for England, with Petitions to his Majesty—But the Parson declin'd the Commission as it would have involv'd him in great difficulties—And had he been hardship'd, it would have created as great a Stir on this Side, as Wilkes has done on Your side the Water.

The bare mention of such a thing, was alone sufficient to create him a Multitude of Enemies to those already prejudic'd against him—And now it was fully determin'd to rid the Province of him, and (if possible) with some Stigma the Gentlemen of the Law in particular vowing Revenge against him, so that it was almost dangerous to shew him Countenance.

Their Indignation was still raised higher, by a Piece that appear'd, called, A Modest Proposal &c.—Which shall be sent You Sir, when I can get time for to copy it—for I dare not trust it in any hand, lest it be made a State Engine against me.

The People would have exhibited their Complaints to the World, and drew up several Pieces to be inserted in the Gazette, but they could get *one* only publish'd—From that time the Press was shut against them, and they could get nothing publish'd The Printers said, *They dar'd not* being (as supposed) inhibited and afraid to affront the Commons House.

And herein appears in another Instance, the Equity and Impartiality of those who call themselves *Sons of Liberty* and who have made such Noise with the Words *Freedom Birth-Right—Privelege*—and Rights—*Liberty of the Subject* and such Sounds —And while they enjoy them in the fullest Latitude (and to great Abuse) Lord it over their fellow Provincials with all the Insolence of Human Pride, and Imperiousness of Arbitrary Law givers.

The severest Piece that was handed about, was, A Collection of Passages and Paragraphs from their own Speeches, Letters, and

Writings against Administration—The Country People in this Pamphlet turn'd their own Atirlery [*sic*] against themselves and they stood so Self Condemn'd, that not one of the Politicians could make reply—for the *Motto* was fully verified—*Out of thy own Mouth will I condemn thee*—I wish that I had it Sir to send You—but I will endeavour at it.

Ev'ry Artifice, Ev'ry mean Subterfuge (unbecoming Persons of Fortune and Character, and who too would be deemed Patriots have been made use off to evade granting Redress to the People or fulfiling the Promises made to them. To keep them in Humour The Governour took a Tour, and gave good Words—Still nothing was done. They would not so much as hear of *Public Schools*— but the Ridicule on that head bore so hard on them, that they came into it with a seeming Good Grace, That if a College was founded in the Town there should be Schools in the Country— The City Party to gain the one, were obliged to consent to the other.—So they are to have a College—Thus what small Matter is done, is obliged to be purchas'd at a Dear Rate.

The building of the Exchange,—Setting up Mr. Pitt's Statue Voting Money to Wilkes—Congress to New York, and other Charges the Public has sustain'd thro' these *Sons of Liberty* has not stood the Province in less than 20, ₥ £ Sterling, just to humour a few Noisey Bell weathers and Swaggerers, who bellow for Liberty, while they have already more than they make good use off—And what Profit has resulted to the Back Country? They had 50 Men given them for six Months to bring Rogues to Justice.

The Sums expended in conveying Offenders to Town—In Rewards for taking Highwaymen—To Constables—To Magistrates —To the Provost Marshal—To Officers of Justice—Goal and Conduct Money—To the Officers of the Court—and other Individual Expenses—if thrown together for only 5 Years last past—Would have built a Goal in ev'ry Parish but they seem'd afraid to set up such things in this Country as a Gallows or a Whipping Post, lest they scare Rogues away—Nor is their [*sic*] a pair of Stocks in the Province—A Pillory was never seen, till the late Chief Justice ordain'd that Punishment—And so remiss were they in punishing Offenders (who could always find Money to lighten their Punishments that this poor well mea[n]ing Gentleman took on him to see his Sentences duly executed which was one Charge of Insanity brought against him. But the Countenancing and Winking at Rogues—The fav[ora]ble treatment of them when taken—and their being let loose among the People, was fine Game and brought Excellent Profit to some few, who make Merchandize of the Bulk of Mankind—And it was a strange Scene to behold Felons, and honest Men who took and brought them to Justice, chained on the same Floor, only because they did not act quite agreeable to Law—How should they when the Laws were not extended to them—or that they received no Benefit from them? When the Magistrates were confederated with Rogues, and their prove [*sic*] assisting to their Escape, rather than Detention.

I could run on for an Age, but believe that have tir'd Your Patience, especially as You may think that I am out of my Proper Sphere—But Sir, if acting for the Good of Mankind in General The Right and Liberty of the Subject—the Relief of the Poor, the Needy the distress'd—the Stranger—the Traveller—the Sick and the Orphan—If the Advancement of Religion—Good of the Church, Suppression of Idleness, beggary, prophaneness, Lewdness and Villany—If banishing of Ignorance Vice and Immorality, promoting Virtue and Industry, Arts and Sciences, Commerce and Manufactures, and ev'ry Public Work, be Characteristic of a Christian I hope that I have not in drawing up the enclosed deviated from what my Great Master came into this World to establish—Glory to God Peace on Earth—and Good Will among Men—I shall hasten the other pieces—and remain Sir

Your most humble and obedient Servant Charles Woodmason P.S. You are desir'd to detach the Notes from the Remonstrance for obvious Reasons—they being design'd for your own private Use—You'l excuse my Haste and Inaccuracy—as I write this in a Cold, open, dark Logg Cabbin, in midst of Noise and People.

# The Remonstrance:

## "We are Free-Men—British Subjects—Not Born Slaves." [33]

COPY OF A Remonstrance Presented to the Commons House of Assembly of South Carolina, by the Upper Inhabitants of the said Province Nov. 1767

To

His Excellency The Right Honourable Lord Charles Greville Montagu; Captain General &c. in and over this His Majestys Province of South Carolina &c And

To

The Honourable The Members of His Majestys Council

And

To the Honourable Peter Manigault Speaker, and other the Members of the Commons House of Assembly

The Remonstrance and Petition of the Inhabitants of the Upper and Interior Parts of this Province on behalf of themselves, and all other the Settlers of the Back-Country.

Humbly Sheweth.

That for many Years past, the Back Parts of this Province hath been infested with an infernal Gang of Villains, who have committed such horrid Depredations on our Properties and Estates—Such Insults on the Persons of many Settlers and per-

33. Ful. Trans., N.C., S.C., Geo., No. 72. The "Remonstrance" and the notes appended to it are endorsed: "The Remonstrance presented to the Common's House of Assembly by the Upper Inhabitants—1767 And other papers relating to this Province." The "Remonstrance" was read in the Assembly on November 7, 1767. See Introduction, p. 172.

petrated such shocking Outrages thro'out the Back Settlements, as is past Description.

Our large Stocks of Cattel are either stollen and destroy'd—Our Cow Pens are broke up—and All our valuable Horses are carried off—Houses have been burn'd by these Rogues, and families stripp'd and turn'd naked into the Woods—Stores have been broken open and rifled by them (wherefrom several Traders are absolutely ruin'd) Private Houses have been plunder'd; and the Inhabitants wantonly tortured in the Indian Manner for to be made confess where they secreted their Effects from Plunder. Married Women have been Ravished—Virgins deflowered, and other unheard of Cruelties committed by these barbarous Ruffians—Who, by being let loose among Us (and conniv'd at) by the Acting Magistrates, have hereby reduc'd Numbers of Individuals to Poverty—and for these three Years last past have laid (in a Manner) this Part of the Province under Contribution.

No Trading Persons (or others) or with Money or Goods, No Responsible Persons and Traders dare keep Cash, or any Valuable Articles by them—Nor can Women stir abroad, but with a Guard, or in Terror—The Chastity of many beauteous Maidens have been threat[e]ned by these Rogues. Merchants Stores are oblig'd for to be kept constantly guarded (which enhances the Price of Goods) And thus We live not as under a British Government (ev'ry Man sitting in Peace and Security under his own Vine, and his own Fig Tree), But as if [we] were in *Hungary* or *Germany,* and in a State of War—continually exposed to the Incursions of *Hussars* and *Pandours;* Obliged to be constantly on the Watch, and on our Guard against these Intruders, and having it not in our Power to call what we possess our own, *not even for an Hour;* as being liable Daily and Hourly to be stripp'd of our Property.

Representations of these Grievances and Vexations have often been made by Us to those in Power—But without Redress—Our Cries must have pierc'd their Ears, tho' not enter'd into their Hearts—For, instead of Public Justice being executed on many of these Notorious Robbers (who have been taken by us at much Labour and Expence and Committed) and on others (who with great difficulty and Charge have been arraigned and convicted) We have to lament, that such have from Time to Time been *pardon'd;* and *afresh* set loose among Us, to repeat their Villanies, and strip Us of the few remaining Cattle Horses and Moveables, which after their former Visits they had left us.

Thus distress'd; Thus situated and unreliev'd by Government, many among Us have been obliged to punish some of these Banditti and their Accomplices, in a proper Manner—Necessity (that first Principle) compelling them to Do, what was expected that the Executive Branch of the Legislature would *long ago,* have Done.

We are *Free-Men*—British Subjects—Not Born *Slaves*—We contribute our Proportion in all Public Taxations, and discharge our Duty to the Public, equally with our Fellow Provincials Ye[t] We do not participate with them in the Rights and Benefits which they Enjoy, tho' equally Entituled to them.

Property is of no Value, except it be secure: How Ours is secured, appears from the foremention'd Circumstances, and from our now being obliged to defend our Families, by *our own Strength:* As *Legal Methods* are beyond our Reach—or not as yet *extended* to Us.

We may be deem'd too bold in saying *"That the present Constitution of this Province is very defective, and become a Burden, rather than being beneficial to the Back-Inhabitants"*—For Instance—To have but *One* Place of Judicature in this Large and Growing Colony—And that seated *not Central,* but *In a Nook* by the SeaSide—The Back Inhabitants to travel Two, three hundred Miles to carry down Criminals, prosecute Offenders appear as Witnesses (tho' secluded to serve as Jurors) attend the Courts and Suits of Law—The Governour and Court of Ordinary—All Land Matters, and on ev[e]ry Public Occasion are Great Grievances, and call loudly for *Redress* For 'tis not only *Loss of Time* which the poor Settlers sustain therefrom, but the *Toil of Travelling,* and *Heavy-Expences* therefrom arising. Poor Suitors are often driven to Great Distresses, Even to the spending their Last Shilling or to sell their *Only* Horse for to defray their traveling and Town Costs; After which, they are oblig'd to trudge home on foot, and beg for Subsistence by the Way: And after being Subpena'd, and then attending Court as Witnesses or as Constables, they oft are never call'd for On Trials but are put off to next Court, and then the same Services must be repeated. These are Circumstances experienc'd by no Individuals under British Government save those in South Carolina.

It is partly owing to these Burdens on our Shoulders, That the Gangs of Robbers who infest us, have so long reign'd without Repression: For if a Party hath Twenty Cattle, or the best of his Stallions stollen from Him, The Time and Charge consequent on a Prosecution of the Offenders, is equal too, or Greater than his Loss—As, *To Prosecute,* would make Him Doubly a Sufferer; And Poor Persons have not Money to answer the Cravings of *Rapacious Lawyers*—As proceedings at Law are *now* manag'd, it may cost a Private person Fifty Pounds to bring a Villain to Justice—And in Civil Cases, the Recovery of *Twenty Pounds,* will frequently be attended with Seventy Pounds Costs—if not Treble that Sum.[34]

When Cattle and Horses are Stollen, and the Thief is publickly known,[35] (at [*sic*] they will committ their Robberies openly at Noon Day) Persons who see and know of these Evils, are backward in making Information, as they thereby are certain to subject themselves to much Trouble and Expence, beside the Risque they run of being plunder'd themselves by the Rogues, in Revenge for Informing against them—And in Consequence of being subpena'd

34. Complaints about the high legal fees were old and not confined to the Backcountry. A petition of May 20, 1726, to the Council held that for the collection of debts not exceeding £30, fees as high as £60 were charged, and the lawyers would give no receipt. Petition in New-York Historical Society. Henry Middleton, writing of the grievances of the Regulators, said that their complaints of the "exorbitant and insupportable charges of the Law" were "most certainly well founded, for it is a grievance generally complained of, and which, I believe, everybody wishes to see remedied, except the dealers in the law themselves." Henry Middleton to Arthur Middleton, Goose Creek, Sept. 22, 1768, *S. C. Hist. and Gen. Mag.,* 27 (1926), 110. See, also, presentments of the grand jury, Oct. 21, 1741, Commons Journal, Dec. 3, 1741; G. G. Powell to Wm. Bull, Weymouth, Aug. 19, 1768, Council Journal, Aug. 26, 1768; *S. C. Gaz.,* Oct. 11, 1768; *S. C. and Amer. Gen. Gaz.,* Dec. 12, 1768; Bull to Hillsborough, Charleston, Sept. 10, 1768, P.R.O. Trans., XXXII, 39.

35. Many of the thieves were well known by sight and name and were listed in the newspapers. *S. C. and Amer. Gen. Gaz.,* June 5, 1767; *S. C. Gaz. and C-J,* July 28, Aug. 4, Oct. 20, 1767.

to attend the Courts of Charlestown, (under Great Disadvantages) they are often oblig'd to sell their Substance at half Value, to defray Road Charges, the Public having made no Provision on this Head—These long Journeys are often requir'd too at some *Critical Juncture,* very detrimental to the Poor Planter; who therefrom, will endeavour to avoid appearing against Rogues, when they are brought to Trial. From which Circumstances, many Rogues have been acquitted at Court for want of Evidence—The Trials of Others delayed—The Province (as well as In[di]viduals put to greivous Expence; And the Gangs of Robbers (here from Recruited and Spirited) have still reign'd without Controul, Ranging and plundering the Country with Impunity. We can truly say, they *Reign;* as by their Menaces, they intimidate many whom they have injur'd, from laying hold on, and bringing of them to Justice.

If we are thus insecure—If our Lives and Properties are thus at Stake—If we cannot be protected—If these Villains are suffer'd to range the Country uncontroul'd, and no Redress to be obtain'd for our Losses, All of Us, and our families must quit the Province, and Retire, where there are Laws, Religion and Government: For as the Laws now stand, It is of no Import to bind lawless profligate Persons to the[ir] Good Behaviour:—Reco[g]nizances are laugh'd at, because never put in Suit—Nor can be, but at the private Expence of the Suffering Party. Wherefrom, the Clergy, Magistratcy, and all in public Authority (who ought to be protected in Execution of the Laws, and honour'd in their Public Stations) are Insulted and Abused by Licentious and Insolent Persons without Redress.

The Trial of Small and Mean Causes by a Single Magistrate (a Wise Institution in the Infancy of the Colony) is now become an Intolerable Grievance partly thro' the *Ignorance* of some Justices, and the *Bigotry* and *Partiality* of Others. Individuals are rather *Oppress'd,* than *Reliev'd,* by their Decisions, for Persons are oft times saddled with Ten or Twelve Pounds Costs, on a Debt of as many Shillings, Thro' the Indolence, Connivance, or Corruption of several Justices, it is owing, that the Theives have gain'd such Strength and risen to such a pitch of Audacity—They well know, that if Warrants are issued out against them, that they will be slowly pursu'd: Or that they shall have timely Notice given them for to avoid the Officers: We could enumerate many flagrant Instances of this Sort [36]—But as ev'ry Complaint of this Nature from the Country have hitherto been disregarded, We can only close this Article with saying, That thro' the Venality of Mean Persons now in the Commission, *Contempt* instead of *Respect* is thrown on this so Honourable and Necessary an Office.

By poor Persons being oblig'd to travel to Charlestown to obtain Patents for Small Tracts of Land, or to renew their Warrants, His Majestys Kindness to his Subjects is defeated—As it causes Land to come as Dear, or prove as Expensive in Running out, as if for to be purchas'd. The same fees being paid on a Grant of Ten, as on one of Ten thousand Acres. The Like Grievance exists in Respect to the proving of Wills, or taking out Letters of Administration the fees on which are treble to what is charg'd at home, even tho' clogg'd with Stamps. When Effects of a deceas'd Party doth not exceed 40, or 50 £, half this Sum must be expended in Court fees—no distinction being made—It being alike the same, if the Effects are fifty, or fifty thousand Pounds. These are great Hardships on the Poor—especially as the fees now claim'd at the Public Offices, are double to what were

36. In a "Memorandum" on the Regulator movement, Woodmason was more specific on the "friends" of the thieves: "They had Spies in Pay in various Parts, and agents in most Places—Some to receive Goods and secret them— Others to give them Notice of Danger. On which Account they first well fee'd the Constables and inferior Officers—who either acquainted them of the issuing of Warrants that they might keep out of the Way—Or went a wrong Course after them—Or when in Custody let them escape and this oft with privity of the Magistrates, Who at length not only winked at them, but enter'd into Leagues, Confederacies, and Association with them—The first by way of Self Defence—On Promise that their Property should be untouch'd if they'd let them alone—The 2d Class, went Snacks with them, and received Presents—The third not only favour'd—but harbour'd protected and assisted them. All the Tavern Keepers were their private Friends for there they gamed revelled and spent their Booty. The Storekeepers were obliged to stand Neuter thro' fear of being plundered or privately took their Skins and other Goods at half Value, giving them Ammunition—Many of the Waggoners were their chief Instruments and Associates. They had private Houses of Resort filled with Whores who watched them all day while they slept." Sermon Book, IV, [ [365-66].

formerly demanded which merits the serious Attention of the Legislature.

As the Laws are now Modell'd, any malicious, malevolent Party, may arrest any Stranger, any Innocent Person, for any Sum whatever, without shewing Cause of Action, or making Oath of his Debt, or giving Security for joining Issue; Which often prevents Persons from getting Bail: for though the Debt or Ballance may not be Sixpence, yet the Sum alledged may be Six thousand Pounds. This intimidates Persons from becoming Securities, and subjects many to wrongful and Injurious Imprisonment; Whereby their Credit and Families are entirely ruin'd—Health impair'd—Lives sacrific'd, by lying in a Close and Stinking Goal!—Crowded with Thieves and Vagabonds! No Separation, No Distinction made of Paries, not hardly even of the Sexes—Who can boast of British Liberty, that is not safe one Hour from so dreadful an Oppression! A Stranger, or Vagrant in this Province, who can pay a Lawyer Ten Pounds, may at his Pleasure, or for his Frolic, send to Prison (at 200 Miles distance) the best Person here among Us, without his knowing on what Account or for what Reason And this in as arbit[r]ary a Manner, as in *France,* by a *Lettre de Chachet* [*sic*]—or in *Spain,* by Warrant from the *Inquisition.* Most sore are these Evils! Especially too when a poor Wretch who has inadvertanly broke the Peace, (for which in Britain, he would be order'd a few Lashes or a Small Fine, and be dismiss'd) Must lye five or six Months in this loathsome Goal amidst Theives and Robbers, in the Heat of Summer, and then afterward be discharg'd by Proclamation. Punishments ought to bear some Proportion to Trespasses—Nor should Small and Great Offences, be treated with equal Severity. To be confin'd six Months in Charlestown Goal at 2 or 300 Miles distance from Friends or Family, and to live in this hot Clime on Bread and Water is a far heavier Punishment, than for to be in the French King's *Gallies,* or a Slave in *Barbary:* And for persons to lye there Session after Session, for small Sums, or Petty Offences, is contrary to All Humanity. And more so (as We observ'd) When Persons of ev'ry Class, and each Sex are promiscuously confin'd together in a Space where they have not Room to lye; and no Distinction made between Offenders—but Theives and Murderers—Debtors to the

King—Offenders in Penal Laws, Vagrants and Idle Persons are closely huddled in one mixt Crowd.

When Persons are unwarrantably arrested by vexatious Pettifoggers, or Litigious Miscreants (as such will infest every Society) and *Bail* is given In this Case, should the Plaintiff discontinue, and refuse joining Issue, and drop the Suit, We apprehend (from the Sufferings of Many) that no Remedy at present lies for Relief of any innocent Person who is so treated, consistent with the Liberty of the Subject—But the Defendant must submit to 40 or 50 £ Charge and Loss—Or if He sue for Damages or Costs expended or for false Imprisonment after being Ruin'd and Undone, What Satisfaction is to be obtain'd against Insolvent Prosecutors?

By our Birth-Right, as *Britons,* We ought for to be try'd by a Jury of our Peers. This is the glorious Liberty of Free born Subjects—The darling Privelege that distinguishes *Britain* from all other Nations. But We Poor distress'd Settlers, enjoy only the Shadow, Not the Substance of this Happiness. For can We truly be said to be try'd by our *Peers* when few or No Persons on this North Side of *Santee* River (containing half the Province) are on the Jury List? The Juries of ev'ry Court are generally compos'd of the Inhabitants of Charlestown or its Environs: Persons, who never perhaps travell'd beyond Charlestown Neck: Who know not even the *Geography,* much less the Persons and Concerns of the Back Country. These determine Boundaries of our Lands, *without a View,* and decide on Matters of which they [have] no proper Conception. We think these Proceedings as absurd as if Affairs of *Shipping* and *Trade,* were to be settled by twelve Residents in our Woods, who never saw a Town, the Sea, or a Ship in their Lives.

Herefrom, the Lives and Properties of Us Back Settlers, may, *accidentally,* be affected, thro' the Judge or Jurors haveing no Personal Knowledge of Parties who depose in Court—Or of their *Quality* Estate, or *Character* they bear where they dwell—All Persons, without Exception, are now admitted to give Evidence, according to the Mode of their Profession and stand *Recta in Curia.* Now, as we are a mix'd People, and many *conceal'd Papists* among Us, (especially in the Disguise of *Quakers*) and as such are often admitted as Witnesses and Jurors, A wrong Verdict may often pass thro' this General Admission of Persons of all Countries Complexions and Characters being suffer'd to be on Juries, and so give Evidence without Distinction or Restriction.

Nor can We be said to possess our Legal Rights as Freeholders, when We are so unequally represented in *Assembly*—The South Side of Santee River, electing 44 Members, and the North Side, with these Upper Parts of the Province (containing 2/3 of the White Inhabitants) returning but Six—It is to this Great Disproportion of Representatives on our Part, that our Interests have been so long neglected, and the Back Country disregarded. But it is the Number of *Free Men,* not *Black Slaves,* that constitute the Strength and Riches of a State.

The not laying out the Back Country into Parishes, is another most sensible Greivance. This Evil We apprehend to arise from the Selfish Views of those, whose Fortune and Estates, are in or near *Charlestown*—which makes them endeavour, That all Matters and Things shall center there, however detrimental to the Body Politic, Hence it arises, That Assemblies are kept setting for six Months, when the Business brought before them might be dispatch'd in six Weeks—to oblige us (against Inclination) to chuse such Persons for Representatives, who live in or contiguous to *Charlestown;* and to render a Seat in the Assembly too heavy a Burden, for any Country Planter, of a small Estate, for to bear. From this our Non-Representation in the House, We conceive it is; That Sixty thousand Pounds Public Money, (of which we must pay the Greater Part, as being levy'd on the Consumer) hath lately been voted, for to build an *Exchange* for the Merchants, and a *Ball-Room* for the Ladies of Charlestown; while near *Sixty thousand* of Us Back Settlers, have not a Minister, or a place of Worship to repair too! As if We were not worth even the Thought off, or deem'd as *Savages,* and not *Christians!*

To leave our Native Countries, Friends, and Relations—the Service of God—the Enjoyment of our Civil and Religious Rights for to breathe here (as We hop'd) a Purer Air of Freedom, and possess the *utmost Enjoyment* of *Liberty,* and *Independency*— And instead hereof, to be set adrift in the Wild Woods among *Indians,* and *Out Casts*—To live in a State of Heathenism— without Law, or Government or even, the *Appearance of Re-*

*ligion*—Expos'd to the Insults of Lawless and Impudent Persons—
To the Depredations of *Theives* and *Robbers*—and to be treated
by our Fellow Provincials who hold the Reins of Things, as
Persons hardly worthy the Public Attention, Not so much as their
Negroes:—These Sufferings have broken the Hearts of Hundreds
of our New Settlers—Made others quit the Province, some return
to *Europe* (and therefrom prevent others coming this Way) and
deterr'd Numbers of Persons of Fortune and Character (both at
Home, and in *America*) from taking up of Lands here, and
settling this our Back Country, as otherwise they would have
done.

But whatever Regulations—Whatever Emoluments are offer'd
for the Embellishment or Benefit of the Metropolis, such are
readily admitted While We are consider'd by its Inhabitants (and
if they could, they would make Us) *Hewers of Wood,* and *Drawers
of Water,* for Service of the Town: Who treat Us not as Brethren
of the same Kindred—United in the same Interests—and Subjects
of the same Prince, but as if we were of a different Species from
themselves: Reproaching us for our Ignorance and Unpoliteness,
while they themselves contribute to it, and would chain Us to
these Oars, as unwillingly, that either Us or our Posterity, should
emerge from Darkness to Light, and from the Power of Satan unto
God. Their very Follies and Extravagancies would afford Us
Means of Knowledge and Refinement—What they Waste and
throw away, would lay for us the foundations of Good Things.
The Sums Trifled away in a Play House there, would have rais'd
Us Fifty New Churches; And the heavy annual Charges which
the Public is saddled with, attending the conveying of Prisoners
to Town—Summoning Juries, and other Incident Expences, together with Mr. Provost Marshalls and Mr. Attorney Generals
Bills, would if thrown together for these last Seven Years, have
defray'd the expence of building Goals and Court Houses in
ev'ry Parish of the Province, and all other Public Edifices. But
this is not comparable to the Damage done the Mother Country
and the West India Trade, by the Theives stealing of all our best
Horses, and then selling of them to Dutch Agents, for to be trans-
ported to the French Islands to work their Sugar Mills. Add to
this, The Depression of our Lands in Value—Prevention of their
Sale and Culture; Of any Improvements in Planting or Public

Works, thro' the Insecurity of All Property, by Incursions of the Theives—The Bad Character which the Back Settlements hath gain'd hereby (both in Britain and America) The Rise of Provisions thro' Loss of our Stocks of Meat Cattle—The Length of Time and Great Expence it will cost us to raise again a fine Breed of Horses—The Dread which Persons of Condition and Character entertain, even of their Persons should they travel among Us, (which deterrs them from sending of any Slaves for to improve their Lands in the Back Country, thro' fear of their being Stollen) Prevents their paying Us any Attention or Regard, or attempting any New Branches of Commerce, tho' excited thereto by the Society of Arts at Home: In short, the Dread impress'd on all Travellers, and which prevents Itinerants from visiting Us (and thereby making Cash to Circulate:) The Damp put on our Spirits through the disregards shewn Us by the Legislature (which has prevented, as beforesaid) many thousands from settling among Us, and lessening thereby the Weight of Taxes, and adding to the Increase of Provisions and Commodities for the Market—The drawing of Merchants and Mec[h]anics among Us, thereby lowering the present Exhorbitant Prices of Goods and Labour, and opening New Channels of Trade) All these, and other striking Circumstances, have been little thought off or consider'd in *Charlestown,* midst Scenes of Luxury and Dissipation.

Oppression will make *Wise Men,* Mad: And many sober Persons among us are become almost desperate in seeing the Non-Attention given to these and other Matters of Serious Concern, and which so nearly affects the foundation of Things. They seem weary of living (as they have done for Years Past) without Exercise of their Civil and Religious Rights, which they ought to share in Common with the Lower Settlements, and being deem'd and treated, as if not Members of the same Body Politic—For, can We vote for *Members* of *Assembly,* Or chuse *Vestry Men,* or elect *Parish Officers* when We have no Churches to repair too, or they are scituated, One, two hundred Miles from Us? Can *our poor,* be taken Charge off, when there hath been neither Minister, Church Wardens, or Vestry in St. Marks, or St. Matthews Parish for these three Years past? Nor either a *Church* built, or *Parish* laid out in any of the Upper Parts of the Province? Does not hereby a

Great and heavy Incumbrance fall on the *Generous* and *Humane?* On all who have *feelings for the Sufferings of others?* For the *Poor* the *Sick,* the *Aged* and *Infirm,* must be relieved and Supported in some Manner, and not left to Perish. What Care is, or can be taken of *Poor Orphans,* and their Effects (No proper Laws or Provisions being yet made on this Head?) Are they not liable to become the Pray [*sic*] of ev'ry Invader? Nor is here any Security to the Merchant or Trader who may Credit out their Goods, as Knaves and Villains may remove with their Substance unmolested into the Neighbouring Provinces, and there bid Defiance to their Creditors. Herefrom, No Credit can be given among Us—for no *Writ* can be obtain'd without going to *Charlestown*—No *Attachment* can be su'd out, but in *Charlestown*—and while these are preparing, Your Debtor has taken flight, and is quite out of Reach. And no *Marriage Licence* can be obtain'd but in *Charlestown*—And there ev'ry Person must repair to get Married, that would marry judicially and according to Law—for We have not Churches wherein to publish Banns, or Ministers to Marry Persons, Wherefrom, the Generality marry each other, which causes the vilest Abominations, and that Whoredom and Adultery overspreads our Land. Thus We live and have liv'd for Years past as if without God in the World, destitute of the Means of Knowledge, without *Law* or *Gospel, Esteem,* or Credit. For, We know not even the Laws of this Country We inhabit for where are they to be found, but in the Secretarys Office in Charlestown? The Printing a Code of the Laws, hath been long petitioned for, often recommended by the *Crown,* and delineated in the *presentments of Grand Juries,* as a Matter long wanting, and of the utmost Consequence: But like all other their Presentments, it lyes *totally unregarded.*

Of what Service have been—Of what Use are the Parish Churches of *Prince George, Prince Frederic* and *St. Mark,* to the Inhabitants of Williamsburgh Great and Little Pedee, Lynchs Creek, Waccamaw, the Congarees, Waxaws, Waterees, Saludy, Long Canes, Ninety Six, or Broad River! Places and Settlements containing Fifty thousand Souls? These Fabrics were plac'd where they are, to serve some Local Occasion, or particular Persons or Purposes; But are not (at least at present) of the least Benefit to the Back

Country: What Church can We repair too for Divine Service, nearer than *Dorchester* or *Charlestown?* Several Parishes being now destitute of Ministers, and no effectual Plan settled for their being properly supplied.

It is notorious, That thro' the Want of Churches and Ministers, New Sects have arisen, now greatly prevail, especially those call'd *New Lights.* Prophaneness and Infidelity abound—Ignorance, Vice, and Idleness prevail—And to the Great Indifference shewn by all Ranks to promote the Interests of Religion and Vertue, it is in Great Measure owing that such few Checks have been given to the *Villains* and *Outlaws,* who have devour'd Us. For, the Common People hardly know the first Principles of Religion: And so corrupt are their Morals, that a Reformation of Manners among them *in our Time* is more to be wish'd for than expected.

Thro' want of Churches and Ministers, many Persons go into the *North* Province, there to be Married, by Magistrates; Which hath encouraged many of our Magistrates (so venal are they) for to take on them also to solemnize Marriages—And this, without any previous Publication of Banns or any Sett Form, but each after his own Fancy, which occasions much Confusion, as they ask no Questions, but couple Persons of all Ages, and ev'ry Complexion, to the Ruin, and Grief of many families. Their Example have been followed by the Low Lay Teachers of ev'ry petty Sect, and also copied by *Itinerant* and Stragling Preachers of various Denominations, who traverse the Back Country, (sent this Way from *Pensylvania* and *New England,* to poison the Minds of the People)—From these irregular Practices, the sacred Bond of Marriage is so greatly slighted, as to be productive of many Great and innumerable Evils. For many loose Wretches are fond of such Marriages; On Supposition, that they are only Tempor[ar]y, or *Durante Placito;* Dissoluble, whenever their Interests or Passions incite them to Separate. Thus they live *Ad Libitum;* quitting each other at Pleasure, Inter-Marrying Year after Year with others; Changing from Hand to Hand as they remove from Place to Place, and swapping away their Wives and Children, as they would Horses or Cattle. Great Scandal arises herefrom to the Back Country, and Loss to the Community: For the Issue of such are too often expos'd deserted, and disown'd: Beggars are hereby multiplied—

Concubinage establish'd (as it were) *by Law:* The most sacred Obligations are hereby trampled on, and Bastardy, Adultery, and other heinous Vices become so common, so openly practic'd and avow'd as to lose the Stigma annex'd to their Commission: These are some of the Main Roots from whence the reigning Gangs of Horse Theives have sprung up from.

Through the Non-Establishment of Public Schools, A Great Multitude of Children are now grown up, in the Greatest Ignorance of ev'ry Thing, Save Vice—in which they are Adepts: Consequently they lead Idle and Immoral Lives: For, they having no Sort of Education, naturally follow Hunting—Shooting—Racing—Drinking—Gaming, and ev'ry Species of Wickedness. Their Lives are only one continual Scene of Depravity of Manners, and Reproach to the Country; being more abandoned to Sensuality, and more Rude in Manners, than the Poor Savages around Us: They will learn no Trade, or Mec[h]anic Arts whereby to obtain an honest Livlihood, or practise any Means of Industry; or if they *Know,* they will not *Practise* them. But range the Country with their Horse and Gun, without Home or Habitation: All Persons, All Places, All Women being alike to them: These are other deep Roots from which the Hords of Mullatoes and Villains we are pester'd with, have shot up: Whereas, had We Churches and Ministers, Schools and Catechists, Children would be early taught the Principles of Religion and Goodness, and their Heads and Hands, be employ'd in Exercises of the Manual and Useful Arts: Tradesmen would increase—Manufactures be follow'd up—Agriculture be improv'd—The Country wear a New Face, and Peace and Plenty smile around Us.

But in our present unsettled Situation—When the Bands of Society and Government hang Loose and Ungirt about Us— When no regular Police is establish'd, but ev'ry one left to Do as seemeth Him Meet, there is not the least Encouragement for any Individual to be Industrious—Emulous in Well Doing—or Enterprizing in any Attempt that is Laudable or public Spirited. Cunning; Rapine; Fraud and Violence, are now the Studies and persuits of the Vulgar: If We save a little Money for to bring down to Town Wherewith to purchase Slaves—Should it be known, Our Houses are beset, and Robbers plunder Us, even of our Cloaths. If we buy Liquor for to Retail, or for Hospitality, they will break into our dwellings, and consume it. If We purchase Bedding, Linen, or Decent Furniture, they have early Notice, and we are certain for to be stripp'd of it. Should We raise Fat Cattle, or Prime Horses for the Market, they are constantly carried off tho' well Guarded [37]—(As a small Force is insufficient for their Security). Or if we collect Gangs of Hogs for to kill, and to barrel up for Sale: Or plant Orchards or Gardens—the Rogues, and other Idle, worthless, vagrant People, with whom We are overrun, are continually destroying of them, and subsisting on the Stocks and Labours of the Industrious Planter. If we are in any wise injur'd in our Persons, Fame, or Fortune, What Remedy have We? What Redress can be obtain'd, without travelling Two hundred Miles to *Charlestown?* Where (thro' the Chican[e]ry of Lawyers—Slowness of Law Proceedings and Expences thence arising), We are *Greater Sufferers than before,* and only thereby add *Evil to Evil;* Nay, We have had, and daily do see, those very Horses and Creatures which have been stollen from Us, (and for which we have endeavour'd to bring Villians to Justice) We have seen these our Creatures sold before our Faces, for to raise Money to fee Lawyers to plead against us, and to save Rogues from the Halter. And what defence are the Laws (as they are now dispens'd) to Us, against such as are *Below the Law?* For in many Cases (as in branding and Killing of Cattle) Fines only being impos'd, and no Provision made for the Sufferer should the Injurer be a Vagrant, or Insolvent, incapable of paying the Fine—What Redress lyes in this Case? The confining of the Transgressor for six Months (at the private Expence of the Sufferer, beside his Charges of Prosecution) in the Commons Goal of *Charlestown;* Where it is as agreeable to Him to live an Idle Life, *In,* as *Out* of it; *Work* being the Article, he would avoid at any Rate, and We have not a Bridewell, Whipping Post, or Pair of Stocks in the Province—And the Workhouse of *Charlestown,* is only so in Name.

37. In newspaper articles the thieves were usually designated "Horse Stealers" or "Horse Stealers and Robbers." *S. C. Gaz. and C-J,* May 26, July 28, Aug. 4, 1767; *S. C. and Amer. Gen. Gaz.,* June 5, 1767; Bull to Hillsborough, Charleston, Sept. 10, 1768, P.R.O. Trans., XXXII, 38.

As the Back Country is now daily increasing by Imports of People from *Ireland,* and elsewhere (most of whom are very Poor) the Number of the Idle and Worthless must also increase, if our Settlements long remain in their present neglected State. Many of these *New-Settlers,* greatly repent their coming out here, to languish away Life in a Country that falls so very short of their Expectations; And the sober part of them, would more willingly return than remain here. They have indeed, *Land,* given them And may, with Industry, raise a bare Subsistence; But they are discourag'd from any bold Pursuits, or exerting their laudable Endeavours to make Improvements, thro' the Uncertainty, that attends Us all, i.e. Whether in the End, they may reap the fruits of their Labour—for such Number of Idle and Vagrant Persons from the Northern Colonies traverse and infest this Province, that if a Spot of Ground be planted (Especially with Fruit Trees for Cyder &c.) the Proprietor cannot be certain of gathering the produce, but may see it carried off before his face without Controul. So great is the weakness of Government in these Parts, that our Magistrates are weary of committing Persons to *Charlestown* for Petit Offences—And they have no Authority to inflict Punishments. It is therefore in vain for Us to attempt the laying out of Vineyards Sheepwalks, or Bleaching Grounds, as it would only be working for these Indolent, unsettled, roving Wretches.

Property being thus insecure, No Improvements are attempted —No New Plans can take Place—Nothing out of the Common Road can be executed, till Legislation is extended to Us. A Damp is now put on all spirited Endeavours to make Matters run in their proper Channel—And (shameful to say) our Lands (some of the finest in *America*) lye useless and unclear'd, being render'd of small Value from the many licentious Persons intermix'd among Us, whom We cannot drive off without Force or Violence.

But these our Lands would be of infinite Value and (in Time) the most desirable in the Province, were proper Regulations to take place, and Good Manners and Order be introduc'd among Us. Our Soil is not only fruitful, but capable of producing any Grain whatever. Our Vales and Woods are delightful Our Hills Healthful and Pleasant: This single Consideration merits the public Attention:—For, was the Country to be once clear'd of

Lawless and Idle People (or were they only for to be put under proper Restraint) Were Courts of Justice once establish'd—The Roads repair'd and Improv'd—Bridges built in proper Places and Travelling render'd safe and Commodious, We should no longer be pester'd with insolvent and licentious Persons from the Neighbouring Governments: Nor would this Province be the *Sink* (as now it is) of the refuse of other Colonies Such abandon'd Wretches would no longer seek Shelter or find Protection here; Nor set bad Examples to our rising Progeny: We should chase them away as *Beasts of Prey*. And was the Country once clear'd of such Vermin, it would induce Genteel Persons to *make the Tour of their Native Country* and not embark annually for *Rhode Island* or *New York* for the Benefit of—*Cool Air*—They may breath equal as salubrious on our Hills, And the *Specie* which is now carried out of the province by our travelling Gentry (*never to return!*) would circulate among the Poor Back Inhabitants, and quickly find its Way down to *Charlestown*.

We may be despised, or slighted for our Poverty, but Poor the Country ever will be, if it long remains in its present disorder'd State; as the few Persons of Property among us, must be oblig'd to quit their Farms, instead of their engaging of New Adventurers to sit down among Us. Were our Interests (which is the Interest of the Community) but properly attended too, and the Laws duly administer'd among Us, Our Industry and Application to raise Staple Articles for the Foreign Market would render this Province in few Years a most valuable Country, and one of the brightest Jewels in the Crown of *Great Britain*.

By our urging of these Particulars, and thus bringing them home to the Attention of the Legislature, We do not presume to reflect on or to censure the Conduct, much less to prescrible [*sic*] or Dictate to those in Authority; But We humbly submit our Selves and our Cause to the Wisdom of our Superiors—professing our Selves Dutiful and Loyal Subjects to His Majesty King *George*—True Lovers of our Country—Zealous for its true Interests, the Rights and Liberties of the Subject, and the Stability of our present happy Constitution in Church and State: We only enumerate *Plain* and *Glaring Facts* And all We crave is—The Enjoyment of those *Native Rights,* which as Freeborn Subjects

We are entituled unto, but at present are debarr'd off; And also the proper Establishment of Religion, and Dispensation of the Laws in the Upper Part of the Country All which our Petitions, We humbly beg leave (with the greatest Deference and Submission) to Sum up in the following Articles, Humbly Praying That the Legislature would be pleas'd to grant us such Relief as may be conducive to the Public Welfare—The Honour of the Crown—The Good of the Church, and the Peace and Prosperity of all His Majestys Leige People in this His Province.

With all due Respect, We humbly request

First) [38]    That Circuit or County Courts, for the Due and speedy Administration of Justice be established in this, as is in the Neighbouring Provinces.

2d)    That some subordinate Courts (to consist of Justices and Freeholders be erected in each Parish for the Trial of Slaves— Small and Mean Causes, and other Local Matters. And that (under the Governour) they may grant Probate of Wills, and Letters of Administration for all Effects under 100 £—Also To pass small Grants of Lands—Renew Warrants &c. (paying the Common fees—To prevent poor persons from travelling down to *Charlestown,* on Account of these, and other such Petty Matters.

3d)—That these Circuits or County Courts, may decide all Suits not exceeding 100 £ Currency without Appeal And that no *Nole Prosequi's* or *Traverses,* be fil'd against Informations made against Transgressors of the *Local,* or *Penal* Laws.

4th)    That the Clerk of the Circuit or County Court, may issue Writs, or Attachments for any Sum—All above 100 £ Currency to be made returnable to the Supreme Court in *Charlestown* and all under that Sum, returnable by the Sherif of each County to His particular Court—And that Justices of the Peace, or Clerk of the Court, may issue Attachments (as now they do Executions) for Sums under 20 £ Currency.

5th)    That the Poor Laws be amended, and some better Provision made for the Care of Poor Orphans and their Estates— Also of the Effects of Strangers Travellers and transient Persons dying within the Province.

38. See pp. 202-4 for Woodmason's comments upon how each of these requests was acted upon, or ignored, by the Assembly.

6th) That Court Houses, Goals, and Bridewells, be built in proper Places, and Coercive Laws fram'd for the Punishment of Idleness and Vice, and for the lessening the Number of Vagrant and Indolent Persons, who now pray on the Industrious—And that none such be allow'd to traverse the Province without proper *Licences* or *Passes*.

7th) That the Laws respecting Public Houses and Taverns be amended—and the Prices of Articles vended by them, for to be ascertain'd as to *Quality* and *Quantity*—And that none be permitted for to retail Liquors on the Public Roads, but such as can Lodge Travellers, and provide Entertainment for Man and Horse.

8th) That the Laws concerning the Stealing and branding of Cattle—Tolling of Horses—Taking up of Strays &c. be amended; That Hunters be put under some Restrictions, and oblig'd not to leave Carcasses unburied in the Woods; [39] And that some few Regulations be made in Respect to Swine.

9th) That the provincial Laws be Digested into a Regular Code, and be printed as soon as possible.

10th) That Gentlemen, who may be Elected as Members of Assembly—Commissioners of the Roads, and into other public Offices, be oblig'd to *Serve,* or *Fine.*

11th) That the Interior and Upper Parts of the Province, and all beyond Black River, be laid out into Parishes, or Chapels, Churches, and Parsonages be founded among them.

12th) That Ministers be provided for these *New,* as well as Vacant Old Parishes—and that some Method be devis'd for an immediate Supply of Parishes with Ministers on the Death, or Cession of Incumbents—Also for the better Care (than at present) of Vacant Churches and Parsonages.

13th) That the Salaries of the Country Clergy be augmented and some Provision made for their Widows, thereby, that Learned

39. In the outer circles of settlement the search for deerskins was an important activity. The Indian trade provided some of these, but white hunters swelled the quantity sent to Charleston for export. The deer hunters, at the end of the season, sometimes turned to the theft of hogs, cattle, and horses. See Bull to Hillsborough, Charleston, Oct. 4, 1769, P.R.O. Trans., XXXII, 108-9; Commons Journal, Jan. 7, 1768; Logan, *History of Upper S. C.,* 28-30. In August, 1769, a law was passed to restrict the dangerous activities of the hunters. See pp. 245-46 and n. 53.

and Goodly Men may be excited to come over to us, and not Profligates.

14th)    That all Magistrates, Lay Persons, and Itinerant Preachers and Teachers, be inhibited from Marrying And the Mode, and Authenticity of Marriages be settled: And that Dissenting Teachers be oblig'd to register their Meeting Houses, and to take the State Oaths, agreeable to the Statute (1 William and Mary) And that none but such settled Pastors be allowd' to teach or Preach among the People—

15th)    That some Expedient be devis'd for His Majestys Attorneys General to put Recognizances in Suit—And that he may be empower'd for to prosecute on all Recognizance's given for the Observance of the Provincial Laws.

16th)    That a proper Table of Fees be fram'd for all Ministers Ecclesiastical and Civil, to govern themselves by; And that the Length and enormous Expence of Law Suits be Moderated. This Province being harder rode at present by Lawyers, than Spain or Italy by Priests.

17th)    That Juries be impannelled from, and all Offences try'd in that County, wherein Crimes, Trespasses and Damages have been committed, or Sustain'd—Agreeable to *Magna Charta*.

18th)    That no Attorney be put into Commission of the Peace And that their Number be limited in the Commons House of Assembly.

19th)    That some Public Schools be founded in the Back Settlements for training up of the Rising Generation in the true Principles of Things—that so they may become useful, and not pernicious Members of Society.

20th)    That proper Premiums be annually distributed, for promoting Agriculture, the raising of Articles for Exportation, and establishing Usefull Arts, on the Plan of the Dublin Society, and that of Arts and Commerce in London.

21)    That the Statute for Limitation of Actions, and that for preventing frivolous and vexatious Suits, be enforc'd and Elucidated; And that the Liberty of the Subject, as to Arrests, and Wrongful Imprisonments, be better secur'd.

22)    That the Lines of the several Counties be run out from the Sea to the Cherokee Boundary—Also, that the Lines of Each

Old and New Parish be ascertain'd and known, that we may no longer wander in the Mazes of Supposition.

23) Lastly We earnestly Pray That the Legislature would import a Quantity of Bibles, Common Prayers, and Devotional Tracts, to be distributed by the Ministers among the Poor, which will be of far greater Utility to the Province, than erecting the Statue of Mr. Pitt.

The above Particulars are with the Greatest Deference and Respect, submitted to the Wisdom of the Legislature.

In the Name, By Desire, And on Behalf
of the Back Inhabitants, And Sign'd in
their Presence, By us their Deputies
Benjamin Hart [40]
John Scott [41]
Moses Kirkland [42]
Thomas Woodward [43]

Notes

Pardon'd) Their mentioning of this gave great Offence to the Executive Power: When Lord G. M. [Greville Montagu] came over, and Mr. B. [Bull] quitted, he set open the Prisons, as an Act of Grace, willing to conclude his applauded Administration with an Act of Mercy rather than Rigour—But in 3 Months, the Goal was again filled with these same individual atrocious Per-

40. A Benjamin Hart was among the petitioners from the Waterees who asked a pardon for the Regulators. Council Journal, Nov. 8, 1769.

41. John Scott was an early resident on the Wateree River. Meriwether, *Expans. of S. C.,* 102-3.

42. Moses Kirkland had come from the north to settle on Wateree Creek in 1752. He kept a small store and tavern and was accused of selling liquor to Catawba Indians. He later settled in the fork of the Broad and Saluda Rivers where he set up an important mill. During the Regulator movement, Kirkland was a leading figure among the Regulators. He wrote a violent attack upon Joseph Curry as one who tried to protect himself from Backcountry anger by a pretended conversion to Regulator principles. During the American Revolution, Kirkland became an influential Backcountry Loyalist. See *ibid.*, 136-37; Council Journal, July 29, 1768; *S. C. Gaz.,* Apr. 18, 1768.

43. Thomas Woodward was apparently an even more important figure among the Regulators than Kirkland. He figured prominently in the seizure of a deputy of Provost Marshal Pinckney. Council Journal, July 29, 1768.

sons, who, no sooner out of Prison but betook themselves immediately to repetition of their Old Offences and with greater
Cruelty than before—The first Objects of their Revenge, being
those who prosecuted them, and had before suffered by them.

At the 1st Session after Lord Charles G. M. in 1766, many of
these Rogues (before driven from the Northern Colonies) were
condemn'd But this Nobleman, willing to begin his Government (as his Predecessor concluded it) with Acts of Clemency,
pardon'd those Villains, who were again at Liberty to Rob and
Plunder, which they did in the Manner here set down—which
Account is far from being exaggerated. As the People could not
have Protection from the Laws, nor those in Authority Necessity
oblig'd them (First) to associate in families for mutual Defence—
But that Method proving ineffectual (as the Rogues would go in
Gangs of 15 or 20 Well arm'd) [44] The whole Country at length
rose in a Body, and drove the Villains—burning of their Cabbins
and Camps—taking away the Goods and Horses, and Young Girls
they had carried off. Many Battles were fought, and Persons
killed on both Sides—While the Government did nothing—
Silently look'd on—Publishing Proclamations—Some against the
Rogues—Others against the Mobb. The Rogues at length began
to Fire Houses likewise. This brought the Mobb to consider of
some Order in their Proceedings Who chose a thousand Men,
to execute the Laws against all Villains and Harbourers of Villains—These Men assum'd the Title of Regulators—They pull'd
down the Houses of all who had entertain'd, secreted, abetted,
and supported these Gangs of Theives Whipped the Magistrates
Who went Snacks with them in their Plunder, and protected
them.[45] Broke up the Brothels where they had their Nocturnal

44. At various times gangs of from twenty to fifty men were reported in
the forks of the Saluda River, on the Broad and Savannah rivers, and in the
Cheraws. *S. C. Gaz.*, Aug. 3, 1767, Oct. 3, 1771; *S. C. Gaz. and C-J*, July 28,
1767, Aug. 9, 1768; *S. C. and Amer. Gen. Gaz.*, June 5, 1767. One gang was
reported armed with rifle-barreled guns. *Ibid.*

45. Another description of Regulator activity appeared in a report from the
Peedee River section: "They [the Regulators] are every day, excepting Sundays,
employed in this *Regulation Work* as they term it. They have brought many
under the lash and are scourging and banishing the baser sort of people, such
as above, with unwearied diligence. Such as they think reclaimable they are

Revels, and where they us'd to carry, and deflower the prettiest Girls they could seduce or lay hold on [46]—All worthy of Death, they sent down to the Provost Marshal—All who promis'd amendment and were petty Rogues, they whipp'd—the Women they duck'd and expos'd [47] And at length securd and gave Peace to the Community Doing more in 3 Months, than the Executive Power had effected in twenty Years—and what (but for them) would never have been done.

We do not participate) Not any of the Back Inhabitants are on the Jury Lists—they must be tryed by Strangers Nor is any provision made for the Poor—for Roads—Bridges—or any one thing of Public Utility in their favour—The Local Laws in force, are almost antiquated—Calculated for Planters possessed of Slaves—and for the Meridian below—for the first Settlers of the Colony. Things are since greatly altered—wears another face—runs in other Channels—Yet these obsolete impracticable Laws, are all that these People could enjoy—Which (in other Words) is, having no Laws at all.

The Public having made no Provision) Provision hath since been made.

Recognizances) There being no Court of Exchequer—All Bonds and other Specialities, given to the Crown or Public are Matters of meer Form, and never put in Suit—but this Evil, hath since been partly redress'd.

May arrest any Stranger) Great Abuses of this Kind were

---

a little tender of; and those they task, giving them so many acres to attend in so many days, on pain of Flagellation, that they may not be reduced to poverty, and by that be led to steal from their industrious neighbours." *S. C. and Amer. Gen. Gaz.*, Sept. 2, 1768. Those who were whipped received five hundred lashes. *S. C. Gaz.*, June 13, Aug. 15, 1768.

46. Tipling-houses, hedge taverns, and private homes existed to entertain the thieves. See Council Journal, Oct. 5, 1767; Commons Journal, Jan. 7, 1768; Bull to Hillsborough, Charleston, Sept. 10, 1768, P.R.O. Trans., XXXII, 38. In Georgia, one Luke Dean was presented by the provincial grand jury "for keeping a disorderly house, and entertaining horse-stealers, and other persons of ill-fame; and also for entertaining and harbouring slaves." *Ga. Gaz.*, July 22, 1767.

47. In an account of Regulator activities "an infamous woman" was reported to have "received corporal punishment." *S. C. Gaz.*, June 13, 1768.

formerly practis'd but is now remedied—as an Affidavit must first go, and Course of Action be shewn.

Close and Stinking Goal) A Person would be in better Situation in the French Kings Gallies, or the Prisons of Turkey or Barbary, than in this dismal Place—Which is a small House hir'd by the Provost Marshall containing 5 or 6 Rooms, about 12 feet square each and in one of these Rooms have 16 Debtors been crowded—And as the Heat of the Weather in C. T. in Summer is almost intolerable, What must the Situation of Prisoners then be? They often have not Room to lye at length, but suceed each other to lye down—One was suffocated by the Heat of this Summer—and when a Coffin was sent for the Corps, there was no room to admit it, till some Wretches lay down, and made their wretched Carcasses, a Table to lay the Coffin on—Men and Women are crowded promiscuously—No Necessary Houses to retire too—The Necessities of Nature must be done by both Sexes in the presence of each other. And this shocking Confinement debarres unhappy Persons from receiving Visits from their Friends and Acquaintances prevents the Clergy of all denominations from visiting of Criminals, thro' fear of Infection [48]—And how terrible is the Reflexion, that many of these unhappy Persons are sent there, and are sufferers for Nothing? Arrested by those who owe to *them,* instead of their being indebted to others—Or confin'd for simple Assaults—for a smally fray occasion'd by Liquor, or in Passion—where they must lye 5 or 6 Months till Sessions—and when Sessions comes, then no Prosecutor. They are discharg'd by Proclamation—No Redress for this severe Punishment—Loss of Health—Strength—Fame—Credit—

48. In a memorial to the Lords of Trade, the provost marshal, Richard Cumberland, wrote that he was forced to hire a private house in Charleston for the prisoners, that "he understands from the representation of his Deputy, that he is thereby frequently reduced to the disagreeable necessity of confining them in such a manner as Humanity would otherwise forbid, and within such a Compass as in the Climate of South Carolina cannot but be productive of the worst consequences." [Received, Mar. 14, 1764], P.R.O. Trans., XXX, 124-25. Six years later, Lieutenant-Governor Bull recommended to the Assembly the building of a proper jail and gave similar reasons. Commons Journal, Feb. 21, 1770. See also *S. C. Gaz.,* Feb. 26, 1754; Presentments of Grand Jury, Oct. 17, 1764, in *S. C. Gaz.,* Nov. 12, 1764.

Complexion—Oft-times the Reason and Understanding—The Attorney General shews that [there] was just Cause of Commitment—and thus he is discharg'd paying of his fees! The dismal pictures that could be drawn of the Sufferings of Prisoners in this Place, would melt ev'ry Eye—affect ev'ry Heart, and exceed all we have related in the History of foreign Countries—Well might such Usage unknown to Free born Britons, set the People in a flame and make them loudly call on the Legislature for Redress—But the Members of this Body were all *Gallio's* and car[e]d for none of these Things—They enjoy'd their Claret Madera and Turtle, and the Cries of the Poor was deem'd Insolence and Impudence—How strange! this from Individuals, most of whom, 20 Years ago, were not worth 20 Shillings.

The Assembly however promis'd Redress. A Bill for Circuit and County Courts was brought in and read twice—The Lawyers took Care to put off the 3d Reading till all the Country Members were retir'd—and they had their own Junto—So in a thin House of 21 Members (19 Makes a House with the Speaker) which is a Matter .that requires Amendment and Notice of the Privy Council in England because Carolina Now is not the same Carolina as 50 Years past—But a New Country, and New People—And by Virtue of this defect in the Laws, 21 persons in this Government will bind posterity in Chains) In this thin House they rescinded County Courts and had the Bill pass'd for Circuit Courts only. To the great disappointment of the Expectations of the People, who now were convinc'd, that they could hope for no Redress of Greivances, but what they extorted—They were about to fly into Rebellion, and take to Arms—to plunder the Plantations of all the Members of the House, and pull down all the Houses of the Lawyers about their Ears—But a few sensible Minds, brought them to a better Sense of thinking and prevented their running into Outrages—This however did not prevent many Individuals from shewing their particular Resentments—for which they since have severely suffer'd.

Judge or Jurors have no personal Knowledge)
The Gross Ignorance of the Carolinian Gentry (indeed all in General in the Lower Settlements) of the Upper Country is so Great and Astonishing, as if related, would not admit of Belief.

Few among them ever travelled 50 Miles beyond Charlestown—and those who have only went the Rout of the Armies to the several Forts—knowing nothing of the Lands Settlements or People of the interior Parts—The very Council, and Clerks, and those in Office, know not one County from another—Grants of Lands in Craven County (the most Northwardly) have been made out for Granville Settlers, the most Southerly County, next Georgia—In the Public Proclamations, one Place has been set down for another—Justices of the Peace dead for Years, continued in Rolls of the Commission—They knew not even one Parish from another—and the Writer of this avers, that a Gentleman (now one of the Assistant Judges) being chosen Member for P. [Prince] Frederick Parish (only 60 Miles from Charlestown was taken aside by said Gentleman, and privately ask'd, Where the Parish lay? Their extream Ignorance was so Great, so asknowledged by themselves, that One of the principal Lawyers in the House moved, 'That before any Bill for Courts, Goals &c. be made, a Survey of the Province be made, that they might know their Routs &c. &c.—This was instantly agreed too—and 3000 £ Sterling voted for that Purpose—The Execution of this, was intrusted to a Member of the House (deeply indebted to Mr. Speaker) has been superficially executed. However it will serve as a Base for a more correct Edifice to be rais'd upon.

The Lawyers (We ought to say, The Spur Gallers, and Riders of this Country) made Motion, That wherever a Court House was to be, or should be built, there an House of Entertainment to be built likewise at the public Expense for their Reception—Which evidently shews, Of what Influence they have in the House, and how great their Ascendance over individuals, otherwise they never would have dar'd made so arrogant a demand.

However they took Care in the Bill for Courts &c. not to suffer—The Attorney General was allowed 200 £ Stg p Ann travelling Charges. This He thought insufficient (tho' he makes 700 £. Stg p an by his Post) And he retarded the Bill in the Privy Council of Britain till 'twas made 300 £ Stg P Ann which now is fixed—The Assistant Judges 300 £ Stg P Ann who never before had a Shilling and was an Honorary Post—The Clerk of the Crown secur'd to himself 300 £ Stg P ann for Life—and gave up his

Patent—The Provost Marshal compounded for 6000 £ Stg and surrender of his Patent (tho' 7 Years before he offer'd it for 2 M̶) And his Deputy secur'd the Sheriffship of Charlestown for Life— Equal to 500 £ Stg P Ann—But this is spoken partly on Information, tho (I believe) strictly true.

Meanwhile, the Chief Aim of the People was not attended too— For many Evils still remain—In all Suits as to Lands, they must still repair to C: T. [Charles Town] and how should C: T. Merchants know ought about Lands or their Boundaries? Thus the very material Articles which they wanted to be decided on the Spot is to be heard in France or Spain—For to contest about 50 Acres of Land and carry the Suit to C. T. (where only it can be decided) is more Cost than the Land is worth. And the Justices of the Peace have no Power to hear any Complaints as to Assaults, or Breach of the Peace—Wherefrom if a fellow, should give another only a Simple Box on the Ear—He is sent to Goal, there to remain 5 or 6 Months, beside paying all Charges As if One Months Impriso[n]ment were not adequate to the Nature, or Reparation of the Fault.

Sixty thousand Inhabitants) At least in the Back Country without Law, Gospel, or the least Advantage, of Civil or Religious Life—No Churches, Ministers, Schools, Order, Discipline No Roads Cut—Bridges built—Causeys made for them—But Strangers and Pilgrims they must execute ev'ry thing themselves— The People below will do nought for them—All which is owing to this Circumstance—There is but one Good Harbour or Port in this Country—where the Merchants are fix'd—which is Charlestown—altho Port Royal, is larger, deeper, and Safer—But it is too remote from the Back Country. Charlestown owes its Advantages, not to the Goodness of its Harbour, but its Centr[ali]ty to the Province, as being Equidistant from North Carolina on the one and Georgia on the other Side of it—This obliges the Back Country People to come to it—Not from Choice, but Necessity— Which the Charlestown Inhabitants are so sensible off That they will not mend a Road, or even a Bridge leading to the Metropolis for benefit of Commerce and Travellers but leave all things to be done by those who travel, as knowing that they must come to them for Goods, and can go nowhere Else—All things propos'd for the Good of the Back Settlers, has therefore all along met with the strongest Opposition from the Inhabitants of Charlestown [49] —Ev'ry one engaged as Promoters of Inland Commerce and Utility, have been proscribed as Public Enemies to the Province (i e Enemies to their Partial Interests, who would swallow all Things and Persons—Make ev'ry one Tributary to them—And who keep the Back Inhabitants in a State of Depravity Irreligion and Servility, to be dependant on them—that so they might tread on their Necks, and be Lords over them.

Poor Orphans) There is not yet an Orphan Law in this Province, wherefrom they are generally plunder'd and devour'd—No Law in respect to transient Persons dying here—or securing their Effects—This is all Booty And many other things of like Nature may be enumerated.

Nor is any Regulation yet made for Persons attending to obtain Warrants of Land—Things still remain as Usual—Ev'ryone must trudge to C. T. So that A Witty Planter once said He Hop'd that the assembly would lay a Tax on Urine and Ordure as Augustus did—And then ev'ry one when he needed, would go to C. T. to evacuate.

Dorchester) A Village 20 Miles from C. T.

New Sects) The Sectaries seeing the Insensibility and Reluctance of the Legislature to settle Churches and Ministers on Plan of the Establishment have been very Alert to settle themselves in ev[e]ry Hole and Corner where they could raise Congregations—Having built upwards of 20 Meeting Houses form'd Large Societies, and enter'd into strict Union for depressing of the Church, and preventing the Introduction of Episcopal Ministers—Great, and Successful have their Endeavours on this Head been—Not less than 20 Itinerant Presbyterian, Baptist and Independant Preachers are maintain'd by the Synods of Pensylvania and New England to traverse this Country Poisoni[n]g the Minds of the People—Instilling Democratical and Common Wealth

49. In a "Memorandum" on Circuit Courts, Woodmason states that the "heaviest Weight" thrown against them was from the inhabitants of Charleston "Who were apprehensive that County Courts, and Sessions, would prevent the Confluence of People to the standing and fix'd Courts there Established for the whole Province." Sermon Book, IV, [655-56].

Principles into their Minds—Embittering them against the very Name of Bishops, and all Episcopal Government and laying deep their fatal Republican Notions and Principles—Especially—That they owe no Subjection to Great Britain—That they are a free People—That they are to pay allegiance to King George as their Sovereign—but as to Great Britain or the Parliament, or any there, that they have no more to think off or about them than the Turk or Pope—Thus do these Itinerant Preachers sent from the Northern Colonies pervert the Minds of the Vulgar—Nor are the Quakers and other inferior Sects backward—they have too their travelling Missionaries—and many Romish Priests pass unnoticed to visit the Covert Papists under disguise of Quakers and New Lights.

The Drunkards [sic]—Moravians—and other Motley Sects, have also lately made their appearance this Way—All which never have happen'd had Churches been properly founded, and Ministers settled.

Such a mix'd Medley of Religions is hardly any where to be found as here—not even in Philadelphia, or Amsterdam.

Thro' want of Churches) Tho' there is a Law inhibiting all Lay Persons to marry under a Fine—Yet the Magistrates marry in Contempt of the Law—as do all the Sectaries in General.

Most of the Magistrates are Tavern Keepers—which occasions great Licentiousness and Prophaneness thro' the Country—for they are the Breakers and Pervertors of the Laws, instead of Conversators [sic].

Weakness of Government) This Expression in the Remonstrance gave great Offence but its a sad Truth. The Sceptic never yet touch'd these Parts—The Lenity of this Government surpasses Belief—And the Reins are held slack for Political Purposes, to draw People this Way.

After this Reflexion was thrown out by Back Inhabitants they were terribly harass'd, and made to know that they were not out of the Reach of the Rod of Power—Ev'ry Advantage against their Principals were laid hold on, to throw the Blame off from Government on them—Gentlemen in Commission of the Peace and in the Militia were dismiss'd without any Cause assign'd—Processes issu'd out against others, as Disturbers of the Public Peace And ev'ry Method taken to prevent any Gentleman of the Back Country being return'd as Member of Assembly—the most illicit and undue Arts were made use off to this End—In one Parish, A Gang of Negroes was arm'd and kept in the Bushes, to aid and assist their Owners, in Case of Emergency, while they by Noise and Uproar strove to intimidate the People from Voting—In another Parish A wrong Day was advertized even put into the Gazette— and thereby the Lawyers carried their Point—In another Parish, Great Tumult and Consternation arose—Bench Warrants against 25 Persons were issu'd for those Persons to be taken as they came downward to vote at the Election—These Warrants were given to a most abject and atrocious Villa[in] for to serve. He had private Instructions what to Do—While the Inhabitants were departed from their dwellings and gone down to Vote. He assembles a Gang of the Horse-Theives [50] to aid and assist him to secure Honest Men, for actually endeavouring to secure these Theives, and bringing them to Justice—This Gang of Rogues, under Pretext of being arm'd with Authority, enter'd into the Plantations and plunder'd all the dwellings of those Inhabitants who were gone down to the Election—seiz'd on their Wives, Daughters Cattle Horses, Meal, Provisions, and ev'ry thing that they could carry off. News of this flew downward which oblig'd 300 Men to return back to secure their families from Insults of the Rogues— and therefrom, the Election of a Country Member in that Parish was lost—And the Lawyers gain'd their Ends—But this only serv'd to aggravate their Sorrows—and caus'd a General Rising in the Country—6 or 700 Men well arm'd, turn'd out and march'd immediately after the Rogues,—Who hearing of their coming, collected their whole Strength, and drew up in their defence— About 600 in each Side—2 or 3 Lives only were lost [51]—The In-

50. A letter from the Backcountry termed Coffell and Musgrove "Banditti." *S. C. Gaz. and C-J*, Mar. 28, 1769. Another article, based on "letters from the Western settlements" stated that Coffell had "many returned horse-thieves and banditti in his retinue." *S. C. Gaz.*, Mar. 23, 1769.

51. "In this Rencounter but two Lives were lost. A Young Man coming over Broad River in a Canoo, row'd by two Negroes (in order to enquire the Cause of this Uproar) was shot at by the Rogues, and killed with one of the Negroes. He was a promising Youth and the Stay of his family—But his Parents could obtain no Justice, nor enquiry for this Blood—Nor a Warrant

habitants were resolute—well disciplin'd and march'd in Battalia
to the Camp of the Insurgents, who stood ready to receive them—
Nothing was wanting but the Word of Command for to Fire—
The Pieces of each Company were levelled and bloody Work
would have ensued, had not some Capital Gentlemen thrown
themselves in between the two Armies, and kept them at Bay—
A Parley was brought on—When some of the principal Rogues
were deliv'd up to Justice—The rest fled—Many of whom have
since been taken and executed. And this put an End to the Reign
of the Banditti, who never since have annoy'd the People
openly—But are all now pretty well subdued and the Peace of the
Country settled—

That the Salaries of the Clergy) The Town Clergy have 200 £
Stg P Ann Salary those of the Country 100 £ only—But by Reason
of the distance of the Back Country from C. T. and the great
difficulty and Expence of getting Articles from Town to the upper
Parts—A Clergyman may starve on his 100 £ Stg P ann as ev'ry
thing will cost him double the first charge ere he receives it. So
that a Back Country Clergyman may be said to enjoy only 50 £
Stg P Ann. if put on an Average with his Brethren: In the ancient
Law 25 £ Proclamation Money was allow'd for payment of the
Passage of ev'ry Clergyman over here—But by the Word [Procla-
mation] being omitted it is now chang'd into Currency—And a
Gentleman has only £3. 12 6 Sterling paid him, instead of fifteen
Guineas.—When a Gentleman dies, they'l pay his Widow only to
day of his Death, instead of the running 6 Months—The Law
says that their Salary shall commence from the day of the Ships
Sailing from England but now, its a favour if can get paid from
the day of Landing—The Vestries us'd for to grant Leave to Ministers, to take Journies for repair of their Healths &c. but now they
can't stir out of their parishes without asking Leave of the
House—No Provision made for their Widows—Should any Gentleman come over (suppose with a family) at Great Expence—
And a capricious Vestry or one Ruling Person among them (as

to apprehend any Person for it." "Memorandum" on the Regulator Movement, Sermon Book, IV, [378]. An article in the *S. C. Gaz. and C-J* of Mar.
28, 1769, states that a young man crossing in a canoe was shot and killed and
his Negro slave wounded.

there is always some swaggering domineering illiterate Bellweather in ev[e]ry Parish) should they reject Him—What has he to Do?—He cannot go back for want of Money—He has thrown himself out of Bread at home—and has it not abroad And thus is left on the World. This has been the Case, and Ruin of severals:—The least they can do, if they do not like them, is to pay freight of the Goods back, and replace them where they were before.

That no Attorney) The putting of Attornies into Commission of the Peace, for them to hear and determine Causes, has been attended with many Evils; for as they will take Bribes to pass Judgment—So when detected, their Plea is—That they took it as an Attorney for *Advice* not as a Magistrate to bias their Determination.

That the Lines) No County or Parish Lines are yet run—No Divisions mark'd but only on Paper—so that the People go on mathematically and those who live on the Borders, never pay Taxes or Toll—Muster—or serve any offices, as its impossible to ascertain to a Nicety, in what Distric they reside.

Partiality of Country Justices) As all the Magistrates take fees allow'd by Law, the dispensation of the Laws is in hands of poor and mean Wretches put into the Office to earn a Piece of Bread— So that no Gentlemen of Character or Fortune (tho' nam'd) do actually execute this Important Office—Wherefrom the Office is become Scandalous and Contemptible. The Dissenters in General are very fond to get into all kind of Offices—this of the Magistracy especially—so that they Lord it over the Poor Episcopalians.

Play House) While these Provincials were roaring out against the Stamp Act and Impositions of Britain on America, they were rioting in Luxury and Extravagance—Balls—Concerts—Assemblies—Private Dances—Cards—Dice—Turtle Feasts—Above all— A Playhouse—was supported and carried on. These People took from 60 £ to 100 £ Sterling, every other Night, for Months together—and carried away (or wasted) more Money, than would have built all the Churches, Public Schools—Goals—Bridges, and other Public Works that the Back Inhabitants wanted, and petitioned for.

The printing a Code) This has strongly been press'd on the Assembly from home—but never taken under Consideration till this Remonstrance awaken'd them—for it was not the Interest of the Lawyers, for the Laws ever to be publish'd—[52] They are still a Blank to ev'ry one—The House voted One thousand Pounds Sterling for a Compilement of the Laws which was undertaken by John R———e [Rutledge] Esq—but not yet printed—The Sum he demands for the Copies when printed, is beyond the Abilities of any to comply with.

No effectual Plan) The Indifference of these People as to Religion is very Glaring—The Wateree has been without a Minister, these thirteen Years—though a Salary fix'd—and no House or Habitation provided. Not a Chapel or House provided at the Congarees, tho' a Salary fix'd—So that a Minister has not where to lay his Head at these Places—All Saints and St. Luke have been laid out 3 Years—No Ministers—St. Davids 4 years No Minister Georgetown, but one (and that for few Months) in 15 years—Purrysburgh not one these 12 Years. Christ Church, not these 10 Years—and so of others—St. Johns Church was burnt down 12 Years past, and not yet rebuilt—St. Matthews begun on 5 Years past—the Shell up—St. Marks 12 Years past—Neither Church or Parsonage finished or habitable—and so of many others.

Branding and Killing of Cattle) The Laws hereon have been amended—Also those respecting Hunting[53]—but are still very

52. Josiah Quincy, visiting from Massachusetts, noted that the laws of South Carolina were not available in book form: "No wonder their lawyers make from £2000 to £3000 sterling a year! The rule of action altogether unknown to the people!" Mar. 8, 1773, "Journal of Josiah Quincy," Mass. Hist. Soc. *Procs.*, 49 (1915-16), 446-47. Charles Shinner charged that the lawyers in the Commons House of Assembly prevented publication of the laws in order to keep the people in ignorance of them. Commons Journal, May 27, 1767. For other complaints see: petition from Peedee, 1758, in Wallace, *Hist. of S. C.*, II, 50; presentments of grand jury, Mar. 20, 1765, *S. C. Gaz.*, June 8, 1765; presentments of grand jury, Oct. 16, 1765, *ibid.*, June 2, 1766; Council Journal, Oct. 29, 1765.

53. On August 23, 1769, the Governor consented to "An Act for the Preservation of Deer, and to Prevent the Mischiefs arising from hunting at Unseasonable Times." This act was declared necessary because of the "many idle, loose and disorderly persons, as well residents as non-residents in this Province," who killed deer for their skins, and left the flesh to attract beasts of prey dangerous to livestock. The killing of deer at night by light of torches

Vague—Idle, and insufficient—drawn up by those who know nothing of Things, or were ever in the Back Country—All Laws—All Acts, are calculated for the Meridian of Charlestown—and if they hit elsewhere, Well—if not others must make the best Shift they can.

Below the Law) The Country swarms with Vagrants—Idlers—Gamblers, and the Outcasts of Virginia and North Carolina—Nor can the Industrious obtain any Redress so that they are an heavy Clog on the Community—If You want to hire a fellow to Work, You'l not raise one for Money—But make a Dance, or a Frolic—and You'l see an hundred turn out.

Noli prosequi) Penalty of 50 £ is on all who presume to retail Liquer without Licence—A Licence costs 20 £—When Informations are made a Bill of 10 £ is given the Attorney General who files a Noli prosequi—So the Matter drops—And thus the Penal Laws are eluded, and render'd of no Account.

Bridewels) Not one as Yet ever thought off in the Province—Whereas Rogues Beggars—Strollers—and all Human Vermin, prey at large.

The above Notes are extracted from a Large Volume of Annotations on the Remonstrance, not as yet publish'd.[54]

---

also made the act desirable, for this practice led to the death of both people and cattle. The act forbade killing at night and set certain periods when deer hunting was illegal. *Stat. at Large of S. C.*, IV, 310-12.

54. This comment on the notes appears in Woodmason's own hand in the original in the Fulham Palace MSS. The "Large Volume" referred to is unfortunately lost.

# A Letter to Henry Laurens:

## "If We could be but calmly and tenderly heard." [55]

### Number 1

Extract of a Letter sent to Henry Laurens Esquire of Charlestown, by the Insurgents, who called themselves *Regulators.*

———— We are so oppress'd, by being deny'd the Liberty of the Press, or any Access to those in Authority That we are obliged to apply to You Sir, and to other humane Gentlemen, for favour and Protection; for we consider You as an Ornament to this Province—A Lover of Freedom and his Native Country As One uninfluenc'd by Party, unbias'd by Prejudice and of an disinterested Mind—The Country People regard You as a Friend, and Public Benefactor and do not forget past favours.[56] They hope, and believe, That as the *Gentleman,* You would extend the Blessings of Liberty, Learning, and Independance—That as a *Patriot,* You would promote Industry and the useful Arts—And as the *Chris-*

55. The letter to Henry Laurens is the first of six enclosures which Woodmason submitted with his letter of 1771 to an English correspondent. The letter and six enclosures are, collectively, Ful. Trans., S. C., Nos. 51-62. See p. 190 n. The letter to Laurens is not dated. However, it contains a complaint that the back settlers are denied liberty of the press. Thus it may have been written after March, 1769, when Woodmason's "Political Problem" was published, but his attempt to answer Christopher Gadsden's rebuttal was "Not suffered to be printed." See pp. 266-71.

56. Henry Laurens had been interested in the Backcountry since as early as 1761. He supported the circuit court act strongly, and denounced those who endangered its approval by the Crown in insisting that judges have tenure during good behavior instead of at the King's pleasure. See David D. Wallace, *The Life of Henry Laurens* (New York, 1915), 127-30. Laurens speculated in Backcountry land, and anticipated that the establishment of circuit courts would increase the value of his holdings. Laurens to Richard Oswald, Charleston, Apr. 27, 1768, Laurens Letter Book, 1767-1771, S. C. Hist. Commission.

*tian* (that shining Characteristic which absorbs all other Appellations) You would promote the Interests of Religion and Goodness, and plant the Moral Vertues in ev'ry Human Heart. Dart then (Good Sir) like the Sun, Your Influence on Us Poor Settlers. You have it greatly in your power to do Good, for many Talents are committed to Your Charge. Who that glories in the Title of Christian (as We know You do Sir) can partake of Divine Ordinances, and not at the same time Sigh at the thought that there are Ten Thousand in our Israel (Israelites indeed in whom is no Guile) who would gladly partake of these Heav'nly Benefits, and yet are debarr'd of them, altho' the Laws of Great Britain, and of this Province, give us indefeasible Right to Participation of them. Who can reflect on that universal Redemption purchas'd for Mortals by the precious Blood Shedding of the Son of God, and yet behold thousands of Souls involv'd in the grossest Darkness and Ignorance—No Churches, Schools, or Ministers—None to administer to them in Spiritual things, altho' there be ample Funds provided for these Ends. Who that bears the Name of *Protestant,* can hear these Divine Words—*Do this, in remembrance of me—Drink Ye* ALL of it, and at same Time be sensible, that a Multitude of his Fellow-Provincials, and Christian Brethren, ought, and would comply with this Injunction, and duly celebrate the Death of their glorified Saviour—and yet cannot—cannot—thro' the Worldly Wisdom of a few corrupt Minds.

Are we in a Popish, or Protestand Land, that We must be thus kept in Ignorance, not only of the Laws of the Land by which we are govern'd, and which we know not when we transgress (tho' are sure to be punish'd for it if found culpable) but also of the Gospel of Christ—Excluded from hearing the Word of God read or preach'd—debarr'd the Holy Sacraments (whereby 19/20 of our Children are Heathens)—May we not say that we are on the same Level with the Subjects of Spain and Portugal?

Do those who thus injure us, call themselves Free Men—Assume the Title of Sons of Liberty—and yet not consider, that we are also Free Born—British Subjects—Entitled to ev'ry Privelege they enjoy, Spiritual or Temporal. Why then are they withheld from Us?

Do such reproach Us with being Ignorant, Ill bred Irreligious,

Licentious, or Reprobate? At whose Door does this Charge lye? With us, who willingly would remove the Imputation, and emerge from this worse than Egyptian Darkness, or with those who would rivet on us these Chains, ever to remain (for them) in Irreligion and Depravity of Manners? Had they any Reflection— the least feeling—Were not their Hearts as Adamant and their Minds steel'd against ev'ry Sentiment of Public Virtue, and Humanity, they would not certainly have the Confidence to make these Reflexions—But the Imputation recoils on them—What excellent Officers would these Men have made under *Pharaoh,* to compel'd the *Israelites* to make Brick without Straw? We believe this to be the only Country in the World, where People pray, entreat, beg to be made Honest, wise, Virtuous and Industrious, and where their Superiors labour to depress and injure, their Bodies, and keep their Minds in a State of Servility and Insensibility.

If We could be but calmly and tenderly heard; To be treated with the Bowels of Love, and the Laws of Humanity (for if the Laws of the Land were extended to us, *We would be heard*) We should quickly disperse the Mists that now seem to cloud the Eyes of our Lower Settlers in respect to Us.—We could draw the Curtain and disclose many Scenes of Oppression not yet laid open to Public View—which if they had been duly attended too, the Word *Regulator,* would never have been heard. Sir—Let these Things sink deep into Your Soul—They must, and will penetrate the Breast of ev'ry Friend to Mankind—Such We esteem You to be, and are preswaded [*sic*], that You will not suffer Thirty thousand, in *Ninevah,* who know not their Right Hand from their Left, for to be sacrific'd as Victims, on the Altars of Venality Selfishness, and Corruption.

We are &c.

### Notes.

Liberty of the Press) They were obliged to send to Virginia, to have many Pieces printed particularly One, entituled The Groans of the Back Settlers.[57]

57. This work has never been found. However, it should be noticed that Woodmason does not explicitly say that it was ever printed.

Access)—Petitions from the Country were disregarded by the House—While the Governour and Lieutenant Governour were so pester'd with them, as to be out of all Patience.

It became Obnoxious to send down Petitions—Some who came with them were imprisoned as Disturbers of the Public Peace—After which No Persons would go to Town—which proved a great damage and Loss to those in Trade.

None could or would venture to draw Petitions for the People lest they should incur Resentment of the House. Wherefrom the People were obliged to go into N.C. to get Gentlemen there to write for them.

Above three thousand Men well arm'd, held themselves in readiness in N.C. to march into this Province to assist the Regulators, had there been any Troops sent against them—The Officers of the Regular Forces offer'd their Service,[58] but the Governour wisely declined them—and effected that by Mildness which Severity would not have compassed—

Humane Gentlemen) They wrote to many Gentlemen—but were disregarded and treated with Contempt—which only served to exasperate them. The within Letter is part of one of those which were sent to Town.

Altho' the Laws of Great Britain &c In 1734 or 36. Ten Townships were laid out by the Kings Orders Remission of Taxes for 10 Years to Settlers—Each Township was to be a Parish—and at 10 Years End, to send a Member to the Assembly—But these Injunctions never took Place. The Great people ran all the Good Land, and left the Rubbish to the Poor—The People who wrote this Letter [59] settled in some of these Townships under Vertue of this Grant of the Crown, and relying on having Churches and Representatives, but have had neither to this Day—So all their Labour and Travel has been of no avail.

Ample Funds) The Duties on Furrs, Skins, Rum &c. were first laid on, to raise Salaries for the Clergy, and strictly speaking be-

58. This may refer to Governor Montagu's intention to use regular troops to bring the Regulators, seized by Coffell's men, back to Charleston in March, 1769. See Introduction, p. 182.

59. This letter to Henry Laurens is clearly in Woodmason's style. He is apparently referring here to those under whose name it was sent.

long to the Church Fund. But a vast Surplus occurs ev'ry Year, which is turn'd over for other Matters, while the principal Ground for which they were originally granted, is not maintain'd

Worldy Wisdom) By some Stratagem, Instructions were procur'd from the Crown to the Governour Not to pass Laws for any New Parishes, except they would take Members from old Parishes, and give to the New Ones, so as that the No. of Members in the House should not exceed Fifty This was keeping the Game in their own Hands, and establishing Persons Members for Life—To this has been owing all the Vexations the Province hath suffer'd and Great Britain has felt the Effects of it—For they would not consent to part with any Members, so consequently the Back Country could not be laid out in Parishes at all but must remain in its present State.

Corrupt Minds) The People attributed all their Evils to some few Mercenary Lawyers and two or three Demagogues in the House—Some of these were never 20 Miles from C.T. Others were Dissenters and only out of Spleen to the Church of England, oppos'd the Building of Churches and Chapels, and establishing of Schools—and now that Schools are granted, it is dubious whether the Children shall be obliged to be brought up Conformists, or Not—The Matter is not yet settled—Nor is as yet the Qualifications of those who are to be Proffessors at the College —Only the Master is to be of the Church establish'd.

One Instance of what Power the Lawyers have in this Country (particularly in the Senate) is this—that when the Bill for establishing Courts of Justice was in Agitation, they mov'd, That wherever a Court House was built, there also a Grand House should be built for Reception and Accomodation of the Gentlemen of the Law, and them only—for to be by themselves and this at the Public Charge. While there was not a Good Road, nor a Bridge, nor a Church, or an Inn in the Country for the Inhabitants.

But this province from the beginning has always been in few Hands—It was settled long before Pensylvania—and see the difference, between a Land of Freedom, and a Land of Oppression— Carolina was little known, or thought off till 1728 when it became a Royal Government—for the Proprietors aim'd only at their own

Profit, not the Welfare of the People. But the Leaven is not yet Eradicated—Nor has one real disinterested Public-spirited Person, devoid of Party and Self-Interest, ever yet appear'd in this Country.—which greatly wants such a Phenix to give a New turn to Things.

# An Advertisement:

### "The pleasant Hills, Rising Grounds, and beautiful Prospects of the Back Country."

No. 2.

## Advertisement

Whereas a terrible Fogg has arisen within these few Years from the Rice Plantations, which greatly affects the Visual Nerves of the Proprietors, so that they cannot discern the pleasant Hills, Rising Grounds, and beautiful Prospects of the Back Country; Nor can (thro' the weakness of their Sight) find the Roads that would lead them to as fine Air and as sweet Water as is in America: And as through defect of this Organ, many Gentlemen and Ladies annually embark for Rhode Island and New York, in order to enjoy these Blessings Whereas would they move westwardly, they might not only partake of them, but from these Hills view the Turrets of Charlestown—These are to offer a Post Chariot and Sett of Horses, to any ingenious Oculist who can couch the Eyes of such Weak sighted Mortals, or to any skilful Naturalist who can dispel this Mist, so as to render the Back Country perceptible to the Gentry below.

## Notes

In vain hath the Society of Arts labour[e]d to set People here on making of Experiments, and turning some little of their Attention toward the Culture of Silk, Madder, and other Articles— They have no Turn of Mind this Way—Nothing but meer Necessity will incline them to any thing—While they can roll in plenty, and enjoy ev'ry Luxury at an easy Rate, they will run no Risques of making any Experiments. And yet these things would be Matters only of Meer Amusement—And no great Cost to any private

253

Hand—Indeed if the Public will pay, or give any Premiums, they may be induc'd to make Trial—But preserverance [*sic*], is not in the Composition of a Carolinian—They are Volatile—and quickly tir'd of attending the Process of any thing that is teidous [*sic*] or laborious in the Operation. The Assembly are very backward in giving Encouragement to any New Thing—Because they have been very often impos'd on—They having no Men of Genius among them who understand the Mathematics, or Principles of Philosophy. Herefrom, Projector *Stephens,* got 50 Guineas from them—and a low cunning, mean fellow, lately took them in for 500 £ Sterling for the Model (as he called it) of a New Machine for beating out Rice which was only the Model of one of our Lint seed Oil Mills in England—and copied from a Plate in the Universal Magazine. They have given 100 £ Sterling for setting up a Public Filature in Charles Town [60] which is thrown away, because not enough—They should grant a premium on all Cocoons, brought there which would set all our Young, Idle, lazy People to work—But they have granted a Bounty on Flour, and on Flax, rais'd and on thread spun, which is a thing of no Benefit—They have not got yet into the Method of making Green Tar or Potash, after so many Years Trial—altho' a Person offer'd to go to Sweden and Russia, and bring back the Process—They throw away many hundred Sterling annually at Horse Racing—It was propos'd to them, to put this Money into small Premiums to encourage Poor People to go on New things, so that all Hands might be employ'd, and none lye Idle—The Money sunk in a Statue to Mr. Pitt, and that given to Wilkes, if applied to planting of Orchards, or Mulberry Trees, or Vines, what a Benefit would it have been to their Posterity, and to the Mother Country. But this Money so applied, is quite contrary to the Sense of the People in General, who wish it had never been—but there are 3 or 4 in the House who sway the Members as they please.

The Lieutenant Governour (who is not only a Friend to the Country but to Mankind, and one of the best of Men) took a

---

60. On June 27, 1766, the Assembly voted £1,000, or about £140 sterling, to establish a silk filature in Charleston under the direction of the Rev. Mr. Gilbert. *S. C. Gaz.,* June 30, 1766. For other inventions see *Stat. at Large of S. C.,* IV, 30-31, 229-30; Sellers, *Charleston Business,* 150-51.

Tour this Summer upwards,[61] to shew others the Way, and has laid out a Hemp Plantation, by way of Encouragement to others—tho' not intended as any profit to himself.

Fine Air—Sweet Water The Air of Charles town is very moist—but grows better thro' their introduction of Sea Coal to burn,[62] which Ships annually bring over—However, with this help still Firing is very dear there—In Summer, the Air is extreme hot owing to its very low Situation, on a Sand Bank, on Verge of the Sea. The Water is very bad. No good Springs but at distance from Town—The Water makes the best Punch in the World, but the worst Tea. Multitudes go off the Province ev'ry Summer for fresh air—And when those who are *really Sick,* do so, they seldom reap Benefit—for going out to Sea, does not change the Medium—The Quality is the same—Whereas, would they but steer Inland, then they would breathe a very fine thin, and pure Air, replete not with Salene, but balsamic Particles, from the fine Woods and Waters of the Apalachian Mountains.

But nothing that can be said on this Subject can as yet induce them—Altho' we have found many hot Springs, and several Chalybeat Waters, that might be very beneficial to the Sick and Infirm—We cannot, as yet, prevail with any of the Faculty to take Journies to analyise these Waters—for here being nothing but Water for to drink—And no Accomodations for Travellers, Such as have spent their whole Lives, in feasting and High Living, can't bear the thoughts of keeping of Lent in the Back Country—as I am oblig'd to do thro' the whole Year.

61. This statement helps to date these notes on the "Advertisement." Lieutenant-Governor Bull made an extensive tour of the back settlements in May, 1770. Bull to Hillsborough, Charleston, June 7, 1770, P.R.O. Trans., XXXII, 279-80; Council Journal, June 12, 1770; *S. C. Gaz. and C-J,* May 8, 1770; *Ga. Gaz.,* May 16, 1770.

62. Dr. George Milligen-Johnston, in *A Short Description of the Province of South-Carolina,* wrote in 1763 that summer diseases were less frequent and milder in Charleston than in the country partly because of "a Thousand culinary Fires in the hottest Season to dry the Air." Milling, ed., *Colonial South Carolina,* 155. A visitor to Charleston in late 1764 made a similar statement. [Lord Adam Gordon], "Journal of an Officer in the West Indies who travelled over a part of the West Indies, and of North America, in the Course of 1764 and 1765," in Newton D. Mereness, ed., *Travels in the American Colonies* (New York, 1916), 397.

# *An Advertisement:*

## *"A Cargo of Fifty Thousand Prime Slaves."*

THE WITHIN Advertisement is drawn up in Manner of those commonly antecedent to a Sale of Negroes—It not being suffered to appear in the Papers, 'twas posted up at the Exchange and gave Great Offence to the Senators. It had the intended Effect To Gall, and Spur them, And as Satire ofttimes effects what Reason cannot, so this very Pasquil obtain'd what the Bible could not—It made many who before were indifferent to Things for to Interest themselves in behalf of the People—And altho' a Bill for Courts was pass'd and went home for the Royal Assent Yet the Lawyers prevented that being obtain'd for more than twelve Months, till the Salaries for the A———y G———l and others were settled to their Satisfaction.

The Governour being newly arriv'd, could have no perfect Knowledge of these Matters—To come at Truth, he took a Tour upwards among the People [63]—but mov'd with such Celerity, that none knew of his being in the Country, till he was long ret'd back to Town—

In the Land of Israel, when only one Woman (and her a Concubine) was ravish'd, a whole Tribe was cut off, because they would not execute Justice on the Ravishers—But here, Vile and Impudent fellows, would come to a Planters House, and tye Him—Lye with his Wife before his Face—Ravish Virgins, before Eyes of their Parents, a dozen fellows in succession.[64] Wherever

---

63. Governor Montagu toured the Backcountry in the spring of 1769. See Introduction, p. 184.

64. The Charleston newspapers went no further than to hint at Backcountry rapes. During a house robbery at Beaver Dam, it was reported, "Poor Mrs. Hayes, and her Daughter, a Child of about ten Years old, were not exempted

they heard of a Groaning, they would beset the House and lye with all the Women—At one House, they ty'd the Midwife to the Bed Post, and left the Poor Woman helpless, who, providentially was happily deliver'd—the fright effecting it. They carried off above twenty of the finest Girls of the Country into the Woods with them—and kept them for many Months, as their Concubines in Common among them—till they grew past Shame—and never could be brought back to a Life of Vertue when regain'd by their Friends.[65] They would put Irons in the Fire and burn the Flesh of Persons to make confess where they conceal'd their Money [66] —All the Merchants Stores were broke up—No Pedlars with Goods could travel—No Woman venture abroad—And numbers abandon'd their Habitations. Sixteen or Eighteen Persons (at times) lost their Lives, in Battle with these Villains:—And many Negroes (as well as Horses) were carried off—They penetrated, at length, to the Lower settlements and stole many Negroes. Even from one of the Council—And had they not so done, it was a Doubt, whether they would not have reign'd much Longer [67]— but when their own House was on Fire, they then thought on their Neighbours—Yet the Goodnatur'd Country People, pursu'd these fellows over the Mountains, and brought back their Negroes

---

from the Barbarity of those vile Miscreants, who treated them worse than the most Savage Indians: Void of every feeling of Humanity, after thus treating them, they took all the Cloathing belonging to these unhappy Victims." *S. C. Gaz. and C-J*, July 28, 1767.

65. "One of the Prisoners who was found not guilty by the Jury, with out going out of Court, was a Young Woman from Craven-County, under twenty Years of Age, indicted for stealing seventeen Horses. Her beauty and elegant Figure joined to the native Innocence visible in her Countenance, and the Strangeness of the Accusation, interested every Body in the Cause; her Council did her great Justice, and her acquittal was received with universal Satisfaction." *S. C. and Amer. Gen. Gaz.*, Feb. 5, 1771.

66. Reports of torture and cruelty by the thieves appeared in the press: *S. C. Gaz.*, July 27, 1765, Aug. 25, 1766, Aug. 3, 1767; *S. C. Gaz. and C-J*, July 28, Aug. 4, 1767; *S. C. and Amer. Gen. Gaz.*, Aug. 7, 1767.

67. In his "Memorandum" on the Regulator movement, Woodmason says that the planters were more willing to aid the Regulators when it became evident that the Backcountry thieves had stolen twenty or thirty of their slaves. It was thought they had run away, until they were brought back by the Rangers. Sermon Book, IV, [386].

to the Great People, hoping that this Instance of Regard would operate in their favour—But it signified very little.[68]

The Villains had their Confederates in ev'ry Colony [69]—What Negroes, Horses and Goods was stollen Southwardly, was carried Northerly—And the Northward—Southward—The Southward shipp'd off at New York and Rhode Island for the French and Dutch Islands—The Northward carried to Georgia [70] and Florida—Where smugling Sloops would barter with the Rogues, and buy great Bargains.

Our Senators treated all Representations of these things as Idle Tales—Nay, there were those who would assert there were not a thousand People in the Back Country—Ev'ry Complaint was adjudged Chimerical—Instead of attending to the Internal Concerns of their Country, and Welfare, Security, and Prosperity, and Trade of the Inhabitants They spent seven Years in wrangling and disputing about Politics and Priveleges, and the Concerns of Great Britain—and other foreign Matters.

No. 3.

Advertisement

To Be disposed off
On the Congaree, Saludy, Savanah, Wateree, and Broad Rivers
A Cargo of
Fifty Thousand Prime Slaves
(Remarkably healthy, and free from the Small Pox)
Lately imported from Great Britain, Ireland, and the Northern Colonies
In the Good Ship
CAROLINA
George Rex, Master,

68. Woodmason states that the Rangers lost by their venture, for their pay did not cover their expenses and they were not rewarded by Drayton, Parsons, or others whose slaves they returned. *Ibid.*

69. Reports from the Backcountry indicated a belief that there existed connections among the gangs from Virginia to Georgia, with meetings to plan operations and defense. *S. C. and Amer. Gen. Gaz.*, June 5, Aug. 7, 1767; *S. C. Gaz.*, Aug. 3, 1767.

70. Woodmason named Sunbury, Georgia, as one southern mart for stolen horses. Sermon Book, IV, [365].

In a short Passage of Ten Years—The Sale will begin on Monday the 17th day of April next [71]—Credit will be Given till—Public Good be preffer'd to Private Interest—

N.B. The above Slaves are sold for no fault—But they being stript of their Property by Theives and Vagabonds—Plunder'd of their Effects *according to Law,* by Mercenary Demagogues—and given up as a Prey to Vagrants and Outlaws, for to have their Throats cut—Their Estates rifled their families ruin'd—Wives insulted—Daughters deflowered, and their Properties sacrific'd and dispers'd—And not having any Courts of Justice where to lodge Complaints—Or proper Magistrates to whom to seek for Redress of Injuries—Or Rulers to notice their Greivances—Nor any Places for Public Worship wherein to implore the Divine Protection against, and Deliverance from these and other Evils, renders it absolutely necessary for the above Sale taking Place—

Public Spirit—Love of Country—Religion—Humanity—Charity Patriotism, and such *Old-Coin,* will be taken in Payment

> Its greatly to be hop'd, That the Gentlemen
> of the Long Robe, will attend, and buy away
> at the said Sale.

71. During the years of the Regulator Movement, April 17 fell on a Monday only in 1769. The reference is probably to the opening of the Court of General Delivery in Charleston, at which time it was anticipated that Regulators would be sentenced to punishment for their activity.

# *A Political Problem:*

*"Is it not Paradoxical, That the Frontier and Interior Inhabitants should pay Duties and Taxes."* [72]

No. 4

Congarees March 16. 1769

Mr. Crouch

I desire, thro' the Channel of Your Paper to state a Political Problem, and shall be oblig'd to any of Your ingenious Readers for a Solution.

### Problem.

The Colonists deny that any Power rests with, or is inherent in the British Parliament, for to levy Taxes, or impose Duties on them, without, or against their Consent, and for these Reasons

(1) That they are not, nor cannot be represented in the British Parliament

(2) That no British Subject whatever, ought to pay Taxes, or Duties of any Nature, to which he has not given Consent by his Representative in Parliament.

The Colonists have also exploded the Doctrine of *Virtual Representation*—And the above Reasonings have been adopted by the two last General Assemblies of this Province.

### Query (1)

As the Back Inhabitants were debarr'd from giving their Votes for Members of the Parishes in which they reside (being deem'd *Extra-Parochial*) How, and in what Manner are they, or can they be said to be represented in General Assembly And if not there

72. This letter, signed "SYLVANUS," appeared in the *S. C. Gaz. and C-J* of Mar. 28, 1769, though in a somewhat abbreviated form from that given here.

represented, With what Propriety can they be tax'd, or subjected to payment of inland Duties impos'd on Goods which they consume?

## Query (2d)

Is it not Paradoxical, That the Frontier and Interior Inhabitants should pay Duties and Taxes impos'd on them by their fellow Provincials, to which they have not given, or had their Assent requir'd? And with what Consistency can our Assembly exercise such Powers which they have pronounc'd Illegal But as they do exercise such Power, whence do they derive it, When they deny such Authority over themselves to be vested in the British Parliament?

## Query 3d

How can such Proceedure be reconcil'd with the above Reasonings, and Declarations of the Americans in their Disputes with Great Britain, or the Votes of our General Assembly?

## Notes

This was the only Piece which the Back Inhabitants obtain'd for to be inserted in any of the Carolina Gazettes—Mr. Gadsden (the Scriblerus of the Libertines) returned a Vague Answer— Granting the Facts acknowledging that the Inhabitants were refus'd Polling in St. Pauls Parish—and doubteless the Election would be declar'd Void—But he enter'd not into the Merits of the Cause, or investigated Matters—He knew that he should stand condemn'd—That his own Atirillery [sic] would be play'd off against him—He was aware of the Snare laid for him—For had he attempted any Justification, or Palliation of Things, An Answer to all he could say was ready drawn, extracted from his own printed Speeches and Epistles—He therefore only flourish'd off a little Declamation, To desire People to guard against Incendiaries—That this was a subtle Scheme, or Bait thrown out to divide them and make them take Umbrage at this Terrible Crisis when their Lives Liberties, Fortunes and all was at Stake ready to be swallow'd up by PlaceMen, Ministers, Pensioners, Commissioners &c. &c.

But the Piece had due Effect—The Election of St. Pauls was voted irregular—Yet no Censure pass'd on the Returning Officer —He had his private Cue—He did not act of himself, but by secret Directions.

Yet they jockey'd the Country People out of this Election afterward—effecting by Subterfuge and Fraud, what they could not openly avow.

For they put a Note into the Gazettes, that the day of Election would be on such a day of the Month—Which the Back Inhabitants rely'd on Whereas the Writs mention'd a Prior day— So that when the People came down in a Body to vote—Lo! the Election was past and Gone, Ten days—And all the Satisfaction they could obtain was, to be told, that it was an Error of the Printers—To such mean Arts had they recourse!

Nor have the People as yet been admitted to Vote—Many thousands are without the Parish Lines, which extend no further than Saludy River—beyond which, are as many freeholders, who annually pay Tax, as are below—Yet stand excluded from all Rights of Freemen, as to Provincial or Parochial Affairs, and in the same State as foreigners.

Lo! such are the Men who bounce, and make such Noise about Liberty! Liberty! Freedom! Property! Rights! Priveleges! and what not; And at the same time keep half their fellow Subjects in a State of Slavery; All that they set down under the head of *Apprehensions* from the Ministry—they now realize and execute over others—What they pretend for to fear, they make others feel—What they paint in Idea, the People experience in reality. And these very Scribblers, and Assembly Orators, who raise such on Outcry against Statesmen and Government, who ride, oppress, distress and keep under the lowest Subjection, half of the Inhabitants of this Province—Not caring who may starve so they can but eat—Who sink, so they swim—Who labour, and are heavy laden, so they can keep their Equipages. Their Throats bellow one thing—but their Hands would execute the reverse—they would fetter and Chain the Back Inhabitants, could they get them in their Clutches—And deprive them equally of their Civil Concerns, as they do of their Spiritual—These are the Sons of Liberty!—On Paper, and in Print—But we will never believe them

such. While they admit not their fellow Subjects to be represented—to give away their own Money—to consent to the Laws
of Government—To partake of Civil and Religious Rights And
to have Justice—the Laws—the Gospel—and sacred Ordinances
administred to others as well as to themselves.

# Christopher Gadsden Answers a Political Problem:

*"Such artful Insinuations and mischievous Catches."* [73]

Mr. Crouch,

I wish your Correspondent SYLVANUS had at least postponed his political Problem or Query, inserted in your last Paper, 'till he had seen whether the present Assembly would confirm the Church-Warden's Return (that may be made for aught I know) of Members for *a* Parish where it's Back Inhabitants 'have been denied the Liberty of voting,' because, in my humble Opinion, 'till such Confirmation from the House, the Query, so far from having any Dependance on, or connection with 'the Reasoning adopted by the two last Assemblies of this Province,' is altogether premature, and impertinent, and has the Appearance besides of coming from no Friend to those constitutional Liberties of the People, so well mantained by those Assemblies he mentions, in *Union with* those of ALL our Sister Colonies on this Continent, especially where it seems to be insinuated that this Denial was *general* 'at the late Election,' including as it may seem EVERY Parish extending to the Back Parts, not, as the Case really was, only at the Election of a *single* Parish.—What! because the Church-Warden or Wardens of *one* Parish (or suppose more) in the Province, may have acted improperly, (which has been, and will be, often the Case) is it *therefore* to be concluded the Assembly or whole Body of Representatives will do so too.—I do not know whom Mr. SYLVANUS may have conversed with since 'the

---

73. An answer to the "Political Problem" of Woodmason appeared in the *S. C. Gaz. and C-J* of April 4, 1769, and is ascribed by Woodmason to Christopher Gadsden. It is given here both for comparison with Woodmason's characterization of it and to show what Woodmason was answering in his "A Reply" which follows it.

late Election,' I am sure I have not been in Company with one Person in or out of the Assembly, but such as appeared concerned for what happened in *that Parish* Election, and made no Hesitation to declare, they looked upon it (if conducted as represented) to be illegal and void, to all Intents and Purposes.

It is to be hoped all such artful Insinuations and mischievous *Catches,* as well as every political *Legerdemain* whatever, to divide 'the Interior and Frontier Inhabitans' from those in the Towns and upon the Sea Coasts, and *from one another,* in order to set us by the Ears together, to divert us from the grand *Common* Concern, at this most momentous Crisis, not only of ALL the Inhabitants of this Province and their Posterity, but also of ALL British America, will be seen through before it is too late, and we are rivited in a Slavery beyond Redemption, and by far exceeding that of the Subjects of any absolute Monarch in Europe, who have but *one* Master to please, and he *at Home* with them, whereas we at this vast Distance shall have some Hundreds at least, if the late Measures are fixed upon us, and the Scriptures tell us no Man can serve TWO Masters.

*Yours, &c.* AMERICUS BRITANNUS.

Charles-Town, *April* 1, 1769.

# An Answer to Christopher Gadsden:

*"Have Patience—Have Patience! has for many Years been
the Prescription of our Political Quacks."*

## No. 5.

### A Reply to Mr. Gads[d]en's Answer to the Political Problem—
### (Not suffered to be printed)

Mr. Crouch

The Back Inhabitants agree in Sentiment with *Americus-Brittanus,* That it is better to have *"One"*, than *"Many Masters"* But as they would not be *"Rivetted in Slavery without Redemption"*—by far exceeding *that of the Subjects of any Monarch in Europe"* who have but One Master to please—which they have long undergone—If it be their Doom, still to remain—still to groan under many *"Political Legerdemains"*—and to be rul'd by *"Many* Task Masters—They would rather prefer *Foreign* than *Domestic* Servitude—To sweat for *Britons*—not for xxxx And to revere *"at a Distance"*, those *Rights* and *Liberties,* they stand entituled too, rather than *Tantalus* like, to view them near their Lip, yet prevented from tasting them.

The Proposers of the *Queries,* are as warm Friends to *Liberty,* and the *Constitution*—As ardent *Lovers of their Country; As* strenuous Advocates for the *Privileges and Interests of America* as *Americus-Brittanus* is, or can be—But they cannot without Concern, view *Self interested* and *Mercenary* Persons declaiming against *Oppression—Corruption—Venality—Ministerial Influence*—and continually harping on such Popular Topics, while these pernicious Weeds they so loudly doom to Reprobation— Are Nourish'd, Cultivated, and favour'd by themselves. All Measures of the British Parliament are view'd thro' a *Prism*—But their

266

own Matters are discoverable only thro' a Glass darken'd tho' it is to be hoped, that there will not be any Necessity of applying to any *Foreign Occulist,* to couch the Optics of those, *who will not see.*[74]

That the Back Inhabitants were openly *"denyd"* their Right of Voting for Representatives, in *"One Parish only"* may possibly be the Truth—But were not the Inhabitants of other Parishes prevented also from giving Suffrage? Was not *Coffel,* sent out with a Sham-Commission to disturb the Peace of the *Back-Country* at a *"Calamitous Crisis"* Were not the Parishioners of St. John's, St. James', and St. Andrews on the Road to these Churches, and oblig'd for to return (without Polling) for to defend their Effects and families from this *Commission'd Robber?* Does not this Proceedure amount to a Prohibition—Wherein is the difference between a Persons being *Overaw'd,* or *Circumvented* at such a Juncture? Of being prevented by *Military,* or *Civil* Execution?—But *Bobbadel* (so well vers'd in the Laws) can best resolve these Questions—and settle the Point, to whose Account, the Innocent Blood shed in these Tumults (rais'd by His Bench Warrants) ought to be plac'd.

Have Patience—Have Patience! has for many Years been the Prescription of our Political Quacks, to the Country People Their Patients have apply'd this Anodyne, till they are become Paralytic, and require more sovereign Remedies—Which if their own Doctors will not administer, they are determin'd to seek for Relief elsewhere—Lest they verify the Old Story—A Person in a Pleurisy desir'd Bleeding—His Friends run to an Irish surgeon, who answered that he was then very busy but begg'd them to have a Little Patience, and he would be with them—The Mans Agonies increase—Message on Message is sent to the Operator to quicken his Motions, or the Man would expire—His Reply still was—Have a little Patience—I'll be there presently—At length he comes—when they told him, they not now wanted him, for the Man was Dead!—What a Pity (says the Quack!) Arrah! had he had but Patience to have staid till I came, he might have been now alive!—

74. This is clearly a threat that the Backcountry will appeal to Parliament, if necessary, for a redress of grievances. See Introduction, p. 183.

## Notes

Of the Steps taken to keep back the Settlers from voting for Members of Assembly, I before spoke—As they had never been before admitted they now insisted on their Rights But as they exceeded the Lower Settlers in Number, and could thereby carry Elections, Ways and Means were devis'd to defeat their Intentions—And these Plans were executed; Some in one Shape, others in another.

The Words in Italic's are taken from Gadsdens Answers—where he says that the Ministry want to reduce the Americans to a worse State than those of any Absolute Monarch—By such inflammatory Pieces the Minds of the Ignorant have been greatly disturb'd; And yet this Son of Liberty *would*—and does use his utmost Endeavours to keep his fellow Provincials in a worse State of Servitude than the Subjects of France or Spain.

Political Legerdemain) The Term he gave the Queries—This nothing (says He) but a Political Legerdemain thrown out by some Agent of the Ministry to divide us at this Calamitous Crisis! What a Calamitous Situation Dear Charlestown art Thou in? One would think by this Writers Expressions That the Sword, Pestilence, and Famine were within thy Walls instead of the Peace and Plenteousness, that is ev'ry where seen within thy Palaces. But He forgets the Calamitous State of the Back Inhabitants, whom he would always keep in a State of Beggary.

Foreign Occulist) G———n [Gadsden] and others threw out Menaces, That sooner than submit to Laws impos'd by the British Legislature they would become Subjects of a Foreign Power—The Back Settlers retort on them and say, That sooner than be Subjects to a Junto in Charlestown, they will throw themselves under Protection of the British Parliament.

Bobbadel) A Name assumed by our Premier Assistant Judge,[75]

75. Rawlins Lowndes was born in St. Kitts, British West Indies. His father, Charles Lowndes, had emigrated to St. Kitts and had married the daughter of a planter. The family, in financial difficulties, moved to South Carolina where the father died when Rawlins was about 14 years old. The widow, before returning to St. Kitts, left the boy in the care of Provost-Marshall Robert Hall, who educated him at law. When Hall died, Rawlins Lowndes was given the

in a Pasquil wrote by him against Mr. Speaker,[76] whom he term'd Peter Pounce [77]—Mr. Speaker being a Gentleman of the Law—A Merry Paper Engagement was carried on between these two Members wherein they heartily expos'd and abus'd each other—The Justice branding the Speaker with Ambition and Prodigality—The Speaker bantering the Justice for his Ignorance, Pride, and Self-Sufficiency telling Him that he could [not] write a Sheet of Paper correctly—nor a Line of Grammar—that He was an Ass, and meer School Boy and deserved Whipping.

Vers'd in the Laws) He was originally a Parish Orphan Boy, nor knows his own Origin—Taken from the Dunghill by our late Provost Marshal—Made his Valet—then learn'd to read and write—Then became Goaler—Then Provost Marshal—Got Money—Married Well—Settled Plantations—became a Planter —A Magistrate—A Senator—Speaker of the House and now Cheif Judge.

Our other Judges—are—An old Broken Merchant who is totally ignorant of Common Sense [78]—A quondam Doctor of Physic—

---

vacancy until 1754, when he resigned to practice law. He was chosen to the Assembly from St. Paul's Parish in 1749, and between 1751 and the Revolution was repeatedly chosen a representative from St. Bartholomew's Parish. In 1766 he was appointed an Assistant Justice of the court. Hayes Baker-Crothers, "Rawlins Lowndes," Allen Johnson and Dumas Malone, eds., *The Dictionary of American Biography* (1928-36), XI, 472-73. In April, 1772, Lowndes was discharged from his position as Assistant Judge. *S. C. Gaz. and C-J*, Apr. 28, 1772.

76. Peter Manigault, a prominent South Carolina lawyer, was Speaker of the Commons House of the Assembly between 1765 and October, 1772. Mabel L. Webber, "Peter Manigault," *Dict. of Amer. Biog.*, XII, 234-35.

77. For the controversy between "Bobbadel" and "Peter Pounce" see *S. C. Gaz. and C-J*, Feb. 28, Mar. 7, 23, 1769.

78. Biographical information on the assistant judges during the period 1766-1770 is very scarce. Benjamin Smith, Daniel D'Oyley, and Robert Pringle were all assistant judges during this period, and all three were merchants. If the word "Broken" refers to health, rather than to financial standing as a merchant, Benjamin Smith may be the individual to whom Woodmason is referring here. Because of his ill health, Smith resigned as provincial Grand Master of the Free and Accepted Masons on January 4, 1768, and his obituary in the *S. C. Gaz.* of August 16, 1770, praises his patience in illness. A. S. Salley, Jr., "William Smith and Some of His Descendants," *S. C. Hist. and Gen. Mag.*, 4 (1903), 244-47.

who was originally a Scot[c]h Presbyterian Parson—Ejected for F———n — Turn'd Philosopher—then Practicioner in Physic— then Planter—and is now a Judge—He [His] looks rather denote him of the Tribe of Isaacher.[79]

Our 4th is—A Gentleman formerly Deputy Governour of the Island of St. Helena—A Shrewd cunning subtle Fox—A professed Deist—The greatest Mimic in Nature He'd take off Foot him- self—A proteus—can transform himself into any Shape or Colour—Can be any thing—Laughs at all Things Civil and Sacred—Is a Ridicule himself, and Ridicules all Mankind [80]— These Gentlemen make about 500 Guineas p Ann of their places— Amazing that the Crown do not send over some Friends of its own. The Cheif Justiceship is worth 1000 £ Sterling P Ann. Is now vacant—The Gentleman its offer'd too (who is a very able Lawyer and bright Genius) is a Friend of the Crown, but will not accept the Place, while such Assistants as the above are on the Bench. He thinks it a disgrace He would have Men of like Sense and abilities with himself for Compeers.[81]

79. Again (see preceding note) one can only guess at which of the three possible judges is referred to here. It may be Robert Pringle, who was born in Symington, Parish of Stow, County of Edinburgh, Scotland, in 1702, and emigrated to South Carolina about 1725 where he became a Charleston mer- chant. He was appointed an assistant judge of the Court of Common Pleas in 1760 and continued one until 1770. There is, however, nothing to show that he was ever a Presbyterian minister, philosopher, or physician. See Mabel L. Webber, ed., "Journal of Robert Pringle, 1746-1747," *ibid.*, 26 (1925), 21-30, 93-112.

80. This is a characterization of George Gabriel Powell. As a member of the Council of St. Helena, Powell was described as highly "artful" and quite "devoid of principle." When he was excluded from a share in some fraudulent political transactions, he denounced those who were profiting from it. His charges brought on an investigation by Capt. Robert Jenkins of "Jenkins' Ear" fame. Following a thorough reform by Jenkins, Powell became governor in 1741, and for two years engaged in the theft of money and provisions on his own account. In 1743, Powell was dismissed, investigated, and only allowed to return to England after he gave security to meet claims against him. Philip Gosse, *St. Helena 1502-1938* (Norwich, Eng., 1938), 176-77, 181-83. Powell was appointed assistant judge on Aug. 10, 1769, and replaced in 1772. *Ga. Gaz.*, Nov. 1, 1769; *Stat. at Large of S. C.*, I, 439.

81. William Wragg was consistently a loyal supporter of the British gov- ernment, and it was perhaps as a reward that he was offered the post of chief

Determin'd to apply for Relief elsewhere) An Intimation that they were resolv'd for to Petition the Throne—The Thought of this rous'd them instantly.

Altho' this Piece and the Queries was handed to the Press in as private and covert a Manner as possible, And ev'ry possible Endeavour taken to secrete the Writer, yet such a Chain of Inquisition was drawn out, that he was trac'd and they determined from that Instant to brand and Ruin him for Ever—He was term'd ev'ry thing that was Vile—pronounced an Enemy to America—To Liberty—A Spy of the Ministery An Agent of Hell—A Reprobate ungrateful Puppy Villain—Scoundrel—Rascal—Enemy to his Country, and what not.

---

justice in 1769. He refused the appointment on the grounds that his unwillingness to support nonimportation might be interpreted as a bid for just such a reward. McCrady, *Hist. of S. C.,* 468-69.

# A Letter to John Rutledge:

### "You call us a Pack of Beggars." [82]

### No. 6

This Copy of a letter sent to J. R. Esq. by the Regulators.

Sir

You say, that it is very Impertinent and Invidious for the Back Inhabitants to call themselves *Slaves,* When no People on Earth are in so great a State of freedom—and that they turn their Liberty into Licentiousness—And You ask with what Consistency or Propriety they presume to use the Word Slavery, in the Advertisement posted up at the Exchange.

You also say That our Legislature and Executive Powers have done for us all Services which we merit, or require, even beyond our deserts—and shewn us ev'ry possible Mark of Kindness and Goodness—but that we take too much upon us.

Whatever You in Town may fix as the Criterion of Things We, who *Know* and *Feel* where the Shoe pinches, can best determine. We think our Selves in a State of Servitude and those who are so, what other can they be denominated than Slaves?

You say, that a *Great deal* hath been *done* for us, and much more than We *Merit*—If so, then much remains *undone* (as I shall note presently) to bring us on the same Level (which You want not) the same foot with Your Selves.

Pray, are We not all Subjects of the same King? Fellow Protestants? Fellow Xtians? Fellow Britons? Of the same Blood and Origin? Are any of Your Descents, Greater, Nobler, ancienter,

82. This letter to John Rutledge was apparently inspired by the remarks of Rutledge upon seeing Woodmason's "Advertisement" relative to the sale of "50,000 slaves," which had been "posted up at the Exchange."

more reputable than ours? Many of You (tho' You abound in Riches) far ignobler; Have You more Virtue, more Religion More Goodness than Us?—Many, far less; Indeed You may be said to have more Learning, Politeness, Wealth, Slaves, and Lands but We speak of Intrinsic Worth—All we wish is, that You had better Hearts than we can boast; But what hinders that We be not your Equals in ev'ry Respect? Nothing but Your Pride Vanity, Selfishness, and Meanspiritedness—Had You any Seeds of Honour, Love of your Country, or Value for Mankind, You would strive, use Your utmost Endeavours, exert Your whole strength strain evry Nerve, to render all others around You, equally Easy Happy, Independant, Affluent, and genteel as Your-selves.

You call us a Pack of Beggars—Pray Sir look back to Your own Origin? Draw the Curtain up but for one twenty Years only, and View Persons as then, and now; It is a strange Succession of fortui-tous Causes that has lifted up many of Your Heads—Not Your own Wisdom or Virtue: Quite the reverse—But step back only to the beginning of this Century—What then was Carolina? What Charlestown? What the then Settlers (Your Ancestors)—Even such as We now are.

Will you pronounce that in 50 Years, our Posterity may not ride in their Chariots, while Yours walk on foot? Or do You fear it? It seems so by Your Conduct towards Us—Who would have dream'd 50 Years past that the Prussians should be now more than a Match for the House of Austria?

But We will put our Selves Sir into Your Hands; and as Your Genius and Capacity is allow'd to be as Great as your avarice Be pleas'd (for once without a Fee) to consider the following Queries —and then say, if the Term *Slavery*, be unapplicable to us.

(1) Is it not *Slavery*, for to travel 2, or 300 Miles, to sue for a Debt of 21 Pounds (3£ Sterling), and for to spend, six, nay ten Times that Sum, Law Charges, in Recovery of it? Exclusive of Time, Labour, Application, and Travelling Expences?

(3) [83] Is [it] not *Slavery*, for an Officer to come with a Writ

83. Note that through error Woodmason has numbered his first four com-plaints 1, 3, 2, 3. He also has two complaints numbered 14, so that the total number in the letter becomes twenty-six rather than twenty-four.

(like a Letter de Cachet) and force us *in a Moment,* from our Dwelling—Not give us a Minute to settle our Affairs, send for our friends—Compound the Debt, or look about us, but must be hurried in an instant 200 Miles down to C.T. there thrown into a stinking Goal, and lye many Months—While at same time, we know not the Party who arrests us—Or never had any Accounts or dealings with him—Or heard of Him—Or if any Connexions, possibly he may be ours, not we his Debtor—And all this we must suffer except we can raise Bail for 10 days—Then that Bail must surrender us in Town—where we must instantly go to Goal, if we cannot raise Special Bail—Which not one in an hundred can do in Town, where they are unknown And possibly not one in an hundred in the Country will be accepted should they ride 200 Miles down to Town with us—To Goal we must Go—And possibly after all this, the Party may discontinue—Never try the Cause—while we lye rotting in a filthy Dungeon—And after all this Suffering, and being put to vast Expence, We can have no Reparation—No Redress for such Usuage—The greatest Stranger in the Country who never saw us, may treat any one in this Manner; In England there is 24 Hours granted to the Party before he can be moved to Prison—but here, not a Minute? In [Is] nothis [not this] as great Slavery as if we liv'd in France?

2] Is it not Slavery, that when a Writ goes against me, I should oft times not know ought of the Matter—and Execution be awarded—That my Lands shall be seized and sold in C. T. unknown to me—and for Nothing—tho' of great Value—That my Slaves shall be taken and carried down there, and sold for not one tenth of their Value; Ev'rything I have took Possession off by the Provost Marshall And thus for satisfying a Debt of 100 £—I shall have Effects sold worth 1 M̶ 2 M̶ Pounds: Many Instances of which can be given.

(3) Is it not Slavery to be supenead to Court as a Witness, and travel 2 or 300 Miles—stay for days together in C. T. at great Expence—and never call'd on? The like when summon'd as a Juror—and in many other Instances!

(4) Is it not Slavery for to be imprison'd fetter'd arraign'd, put on Trail [*sic*] on Allegation or Information of some Villain, or by Malice of some Mean Justice of Peace—and no Prosecutor ap-

pear against me—No Prosecutor too be found to sue for false Imprisonment or to get any Redress for Loss of Liberty Credit Fame and Fortune? Yet this often happens to many.

(5) Is it not Slavery to travel 2 or 300 Miles to procure a Licence to be married or have Banns publish'd, or my Child Christen'd or to hear a Sermon, or receive the Holy Communion—? And as for Churching of Women—Visiting the Sick, Burial of the Dead, and other Spiritual Offices we are entirely destitute, there being neither Church or Minister among us.

(6) Is it not Slavery to travel 50, or 60 Miles to find a Magistrate, for to make a single Affadavit, or sue for a small Debt Or for to be sued before Magistrates, who never saw, or know any thing of the Provincial, or Common Laws?

7)—Is it not Slavery to ride such Lengths to appear as Evidence in some trifling nonsensical Suit, between two fools, about Matters not worth six pence While it shall cost me Ten Pounds Expence beside Loss of Time?

8) Is it not Slavery to ride 200 Miles to give my Vote for Election of Vestry Men—Church Wardens—Members of Assembly &c or to get any Parochial Business transacted?

9)—Is it not Slavery to be burthen'd with Vagrants—Poor Travellers Sick—Infirm—Aged Diseased, Lame Persons, Orphans and others who by Choice or Accident push or force themselves on me and whom it is impossible to remove without breach of the Laws of Charity, Humanity, and Christianity—There being no Workhouse—Hospital, Bridewell, or provision made, or the least Relief establish'd in these Parts for Objects of Charity, Paupers, Orphans &c.

10) Is it not Slavery to leave my Estate and Children behind me in hands of Executors and Trustees, who shall spend my Estate during the Minority of my Children—give them no Education—and when of Age, perhaps bring them in Debt? for Want of an Orphan Law?

11) Is it not Slavery for to be at the Time and Cost of 2 or 300 Miles to assist the Civil Officer, in conveying of Criminals to Goal?

12) Is it not Slavery for to be carried a Prisoner 200 Miles to C. T. there to lye in a filthy Prison for six Months at great

Risque, and often to Loss of Health and Life, and this only for a Simple Assault, in Drink, or Heat of Passion, not worth Cognizance? Or because I cannot find Surety for my better Behaviour.

13) Is it not Slavery to serve the Office of Constable—to be continually hurried about from one End of the Province to the other—To ride 100 Miles to serve a foolish Warrant? without any Allowance made—And to attend the Courts of Justice in C.T. for several days at great Expence? [84]

14) Is it not Slavery to serve the Office of Church Warden, and ride Circuits of 3 or 400 Miles to collect the Poor Tax, without any Allowance for so doing? And the same when appointed Collector of the Public Tax?

14) Is it not Slavery to be detain[e]d from Business 2 or 3 Months thro' want of Roads, Bridges, and Ferries—Or where they are laid out, for to ride 100 Miles about, to perform a journey of Ten Miles? Many Ferries being in private Hands—And no Attendance—And several of them fifty Miles asunder?

15) Is it not Slavery to live in continual Dread of Villains robbing of my House—stealing my Horses and Cattel—Ravishing my Wife and Daughters—(so that I dare not stir from home lest they should be expos'd Nor they travel abroad without a Guard) Just as if I was in a Country which was the Seat of War?

16) Is it not Slavery to be expos'd to the Insults of any Villain, or Vagrant, ev'ry Idle Rascal who will come to my House, and there stay and make free at his Pleasure, Nor I able to dislodge him thro' fear that if I affront Him, I shall have Horses or Cattle kill'd or Houses burn'd and therefore must bear such fellows Company, Insolence and Impudence perhaps Abuse—And no Redress for these Evils?

17) Is it not Slavery, to have the Articles which I consume, tax'd for the benefit of private Persons, and not the Public? Or to carry on Works of Splendor and Magnificence, in which I nor my fellow Public have the least Concern?

18) Is it not Slavery to have the Value of my Flour, and other

84. Country constables were ordered to attend the Court of General Sessions "at least once a twelvemonth, on pain of being fined." D. Campbell, "By order of the Chief Justice," Sept. 10, 1762, in *S. C. Gaz.,* Sept. 18, 1762.

Produce depress'd, and foreign Articles preferr'd to our own (equally good in quality if not better) and this to serve the Interests of a few only?

19) Is [it] not Slavery to see my Wife or Daughters Insulted, abus'd expos'd to the Ribaldry, Obscenity, Audaciousness, and Licentiousness of drunken idle, worthless scandalous abandon'd atrocious Profligates, Libertines and Lawless Persons, Who are without Habitation or Property, and can obtain no Redress. No Remedy for so great an Evil. Wherefrom No Woman whatever durst attend Musters—Races, Vendues or any Public Meetings— and are not secure even going to a Sermon?

20)—Is it not Slavery that I cannot be Master of my own House but that if I have a Wedding or Christianing or Birthday Dinner Or any set Entertainment for private Friends, that a Sett of Insolent Wretches shall intrude on my Premises—mix with, and affront my Company—Quarrel—Riot—Consume my Provisions and take what Liberties they please, with Impunity?

21) Is it not Slavery to be under Controul of Insolent Tavern Keepers where You are necessitated to Quarter at, in Your Travels, and to be expos'd to whatever Charge or Treatment they please for to Impose?

22) Is it not Slavery to be subject to the Impudence, Impertinence and Insults of Free Negroes and Mullatoe's, who greatly abound here? and who have taken Refuge in these Parts, from the No. Colonies—perhaps for Crimes committed there?

23) Is it not Slavery to be oblig'd to travel 200 Miles to C.T. there to give 2 or 3 Guineas to a Lawyer, for to know the Contents of such or such a Law, when the Laws say, that ev'ry Act of Assembly shall be Printed, and sent to ev[e]ry Parish Church? Are not our Laws locked up from us, as the Gospel is in Popish Countries?

24) Is it not Slavery to be without wise Magistrates—Without Religion—Without Laws—Without Police—Without Churches Without Clergy—Without Gospel—Without Sacraments—Without any to marry People—so that they marry each other—when and how they please—and separate and come together as they please wherefrom the Country is full of Whores and Bastards— And is it not Slavery for to have no Roads, Ferries, or Bridges—

And for poor People, who quitted their Native Land where they lived Easily and decently, for to come here to be Beggars—to be employ'd in cutting down the Woods and clearing Lands to raise Crops—and afterwards for to be obliged to cut Roads, to carry their Produce to Market—If any Peasants in Russia, Poland or Germany are in a worse State of Servitude than this, then Sir we will join You in that pious Wish You made in the House That the Back Country was at Bottom of the Sea.

# Injunctions to the Rangers:

## "You are to take these Free Booters and Desperadoes." [85]

Gentlemen

The present Audience is met to congratulate You, on opening the Important Commission Granted You by Government; For

85. Sermon Book, IV, [329-58]. Woodmason notes that this sermon was given "At Swift Creek, Wateree River Before Capt. Joseph Kirkland, and Capt. Henry Hunter, and their two Companies of Rangers." *Ibid.*, [364]. The Assembly had authorized two officers at £25 each, two others at £18 each, and two companies of twenty-five privates at £15 each per month for three months. Commons Journal, Nov. 17, 1767, Apr. 8, 1768. Woodmason's sermon probably took place in December, 1767, or January, 1768.

In his "Memorandum" on the Regulator movement, Woodmason gives more information on the character and accomplishments of the Rangers. When the troops were authorized, the question arose as to how and where they should be raised. The commissions could not be given to "the Rice Birds," for the thieves considered them cowardly and laughed at them. It was finally decided to offer the work to the Regulators. Those chosen to lead the Rangers, however, feared arrest should they come to Charleston, and the commissions were finally sent to Hunter and Kirkland.

The Rangers, continues Woodmason, were "brave Young fellows all men of Property." They chased the thieves through Georgia, both Carolinas, and into Virginia. Govey Black, a leading thief, was taken with sixteen others in North Carolina where they were hanged. Four or five others were killed in skirmishes. Some Negroes who had been stolen from William Henry Drayton were recaptured in Augusta County, Virginia, across the Blue Ridge, and some horses which belonged to the lawyer James Parsons were taken in Loudoun County, Virginia. More than 100 horses were recovered, and thirty-five young girls were returned to their families, "but they were grown too abandon'd ever to be reclaimed." In various encounters not a single Ranger was hurt or killed. Sermon Book, IV, [383-85]. A newspaper account gives further details: "Last Monday Week was brought to the Goal in this Town, by Mr. Thomas Woodward, the two following Horse-Theives, Ebenezer Wells, and Absolom Tilley, with four Negroes who had been stolen by some of their

279

Your taking those Steps by Legal Authority, which Necessity, and the Principles of Self Defence, forc'd You (and all of us) lately upon unauthoriz'd, and unempowered. The King has now drawn his Sword and put it into Your Hands for Protection of his Subjects in these Parts; and freeing the Country from a lawless Banditti, that has laid us all under Contribution—the Particulars of which are too well felt, for me to bring now before You. As Your Officers have requested me to give You a Word of Exhortation before You set out on the so long wish'd for Expedition, I shall from the Words of the Text, consider the Nature of the Kingly Office, and that of Your Commission under it. . . .

Your Commission is of a mix'd Nature Partly *Civil,* partly *Military.* You are to take these Free booters and Desperadoes, Alive if possible and deliver them to the Magistrates. But if they make resistance, and act either Defensively or Offensively, Then You are to treat them as Rebels—Outlaws, and an abandon'd Crew. And as You may be oblig'd to pursue them thro' many Provinces It was proper that You should be invested with the Character of the Kings Troops that Your March might not be impeded by delays in formal Applications to the Kings Courts.[86] For *Celerity,* is one Article of Your Commission. And You are stil'd *Rangers,* because Your Progress is not confin'd to any particular District.

. . . For when under Sentence of Death and saved from the

---

Gang, viz. Timothy Tyrrel, Govey Black, Christopher Marr, and others; three of the Negroes belonged to the Honourable John Drayton, Esq; and the other to William Williamson, Esquire. Mr. Woodward and five other Men set out after, and pursued them into Virginia, where they apprehended them upon New-River, near Colonel Chiswell's Mines." *S. C. Gaz. and C-J,* Mar. 8, 1768.

A company of South Carolina Regulators in late January, 1768, brought two captives and four stolen Negroes to Bethabara, the Moravian settlement in North Carolina. The captives and slaves had been seized in The Hollows, a section near the present town of Mt. Airy, N. C., and extending across the Virginia line. Adelaide L. Fries, ed., *Records of the Moravians in North Carolina,* I (Raleigh, 1922), 210 n., 377.

86. "It is thought unlawful to march the Militia out of the Province. When the King's service requires such a measure, troops are taken into pay." Bull to Hillsborough, Nov. 30, 1770, P.R.O. Trans., XXXII, 385.

Gallows by Clemency of a New Administration—they [the thieves] not [only] flew in the Face of Justice by returning again to their old Trade, but this with redoubled Vigour Cruelty and Villany. They added the Shocking Sin of Ingratitude to their former Crimes by spoiling those who were their Benefactors and Intercessors for them. They dealt treacherously with their Deliverers from an Halter—by robbing them at the very first Hour of deliverance and in the Sight of the Gibbet they escaped from.[87] And now the Sword is drawn against them for their demerits, and saith *Spare not.* . . .

Adultery and Fornication are gloried in, and practic'd in open Noon Day—The Almighty therefore permitted Your Wives to be ravished and Your Daughters Stollen, or deflower'd. Lying Cheating filching, Jockeying are made a Trade of, and He is accounted the cleverest fellow who is the best Trickster. Gaming and Gambling—Rioting and Drunkenness—Gambling and Wagering—Fighting and Brawling take up most of Your Time and Attention. No wonder then that Providence should punish You in Your own way, by such vile Instruments born and rais'd among Your Selves—Spawn of the Pillory and Whipping Post. They are really Plants of Your own Growth. Not one *European,* or Foreigner among them and what better fruit from such Trees could You expect than what You have received? . . .

But they would have met their Deserts long ago, had it not been fear'd that at the Gallows they would have told Tales of some Folk—And made Confessions, as would have affected the Hypocrites—the Venal—and the Receivers. They therefore were set

87. Woodmason here refers to a specific incident about which he gives other details in his "Memorandum" on the Regulator movement: "After laying 6 Weeks in Goal after the Sessions they [some captured thieves] were discharg'd —And to give a Proof of their Dexterity, and pay some Tribute of Gratitude to those Friends who had kindly interceded for their Lives, they took from a Pasture close by, and in sight of the Gibbet from which they had so often escaped, Two fine Horses belonging to one Mr. Parsons a Lawyer who had often pleaded their Cause for them and now had warmly interested himself in their favour; And toward Close of the Evening they seized four Negroes belonging to Jno. Drayton Esq. one of the Members of His Majestys Council, and Brother in Law to the Lieutenant Governour." Sermon Book, IV, [381].

adrift, in hope that they would have gone to some very great Distance. And this will still be the saving of many of them Whether You shew Mercy, or not. . . .

We are sensible that many Women and Girls are very deep in the foulest of Crimes, and Deeds of darkness not to be mention'd —And that they have been very Instrumental in aiding, abetting—Watching—Secreting—Trafficking and in ev'ry Manner supporting and assisting these Villains. While there are others who tho' now bold in Sin—Yet were either Stollen—debauch'd— trepann'd or forcibly made to take on with them. As many Females will fall into Your Hands, You will be very careful to distinguish rightly, in these Particulars.

From the Dispersion of the Gangs (many of which begin already to shrink) numberless Children of all Ages Sexes and Conditions must be thrown on the Public. Pity and Compassion will incline You to fall on proper Methods that they never more return to their Relations, lest their Minds be perverted, and We should see New Shoots of Thieves arise from the Old Roots. In this Respect it will be proper totally, and wholly to separate the Children from aged Persons, if they read them no Lectures of Revenge, or sow the Seeds of Malice or Vice in their Hearts. They should for ever be kept very wide asunder—Never more to see, or Converse with each Other.

As for the Elderly Persons, who have harbour'd Entertain'd, and Embolden'd these fellows, and taught them the Rudiments of ev'ry Vice, The Legislature doubtless will take some thought concerning them, by depriving them of their Lands and dwellings— Yet so as not to bring down their Grey Hairs with Sorrow, (tho it will be with Infamy) to the Grave. . . .

I know that many among You have personally been injur'd by the Rogues. Some in their Wives—Others in their Sisters, or Daughters—By loss of Horses, Cattle, Goods and Effects. But all these things must not be thought off—and should You come upon the Villains, You are not to vent Your rage against them so much for what You have suffered as for what they have made the Province suffer, and the Expence they have occasion'd to the Public. . . .

In the Act of Assembly that incorporated You, and in the Commission to Your Officers—Ye are call'd *Rangers*. A Term almost of Reproach among us, from the bad Conduct of those so stil'd in the last War. Who instead of protecting the Country, damaged it almost as much as the Enemy. Indeed, had they not behav'd so bad, the Indians would not. It is well known that this War originated from the Ill Conduct and Licentiousness of the Garrison of Fort Prince George to the Towns of *Keowee* and *Satochee*.[88] And it must also be infer'd, that the Indians rather acted defensively (in their way) than offensively for they could have done 50 times the Murder and Mischief than they did. And had the Rangers not been as Licentious as the Garrisons, the War might soon have been terminated. But after the withdrawing and return of the Regulars, These Rangers, instead of annoying the Enemy, fell to plundering of, and living at free quarter on the poor Scatter'd Inhabitants. The Forts into which they retir'd were fill'd with Whores and Prostitutes and there maintain'd at the Public Expence. The Stores were pillag'd to bestow Cloathing on them—They plunder'd the Settlers, and all others for Liquors Wasted the Ammunition and Provisions of the Troops, and there liv'd in an open, scandalous debauch'd Manner with their Doxies, instead of going on Duty. So that many complain'd That they sustain'd more damage from their Protectors than from the Enemy, as they stript them of the little the other had left and their prophaneness and Immorality was as Notorious, as their Debauchery—for they far exceeded the Kings Troops in all degrees of Wickedness. And notwithstanding all this Rioting and Wantonness—their Plunder—and High Pay, Yet (You know it) they all returned Poor and Penny less, with Shame and Contempt. But from the Known Vertue, Experience and Honour of these Worthy Officers under whose Command You are, I am morally certain that no such Complaints will ever arise against the meanest Individual among You, as Ye are all chosen Persons, and

88. Good relations between Fort Prince George and the Cherokee town of Keowee became strained when three young officers from the Fort assaulted three young Cherokee women whose husbands were absent on a hunt. The attack upon the women in their homes was repeated just before the beginning of hostilities: "In fact, the members of the garrison behaved with great hauteur and insolence toward all their Indian neighbors." Milling, *Red Carolinians*, 295.

of Estate and Credit. Therefore You'l act as becometh Gentlemen. Not when You have been kindly entertain'd in a Plantation, to make Waste, and do damage. To lye with the Negro Wenches and Servants To debauch the Daughters or pervert the Wife, or any other such ungodly Practices.

# The Regulators Praised:

## "All your Artillery was an Hiccory Switch." [89]

FROM WHAT has been said,[90] I hope none of my Auditors will imagine That I bring a railing accusation against them. Or hold up this Mirror for them to discover What they really Are. I am certain none can accuse You of Murder—For all Your Proceedings have been calculated for the Safety both of the Public and Individuals Not for Thieves—As all Your Attentions have been turned to the scouring the Country of such, and bringing them to condign Punishment, tho' they generally escaped it. As *Evil Doers,* and as *Busy Bodys* indeed You have stood Charged; But for why? Because you did, What was the Duty of others to Do, and they would not. You put the Laws into Execution. But it was without Authority—and because those trusted with the Execution of them, Were the known Violators and breakers of them. Companions of Theives—Receivers of Stollen Goods, and Confederate with all the Gangs of Villains that have infested the Back Country: You might have had resource to Arms and obtain'd by Forces what You could not by 20 Years Entreaty and Supplication Tho' You only demanded Your Birth Rights and Privileges as Britons and Free Men. But all your Artillery was an Hiccory

89. Sermon Book, IV, [456-62]. Woodmason notes that the sermon, from which the following extract is taken, was delivered in the Parish Church of St. Mark "on Occasion of the following Patriotick Persons (vulgarly call'd *Regulators* being put into the Commission of the Peace for Craven County vizt. Capt. Joseph Kirkland, Capt. Henry Hunter, Capt. Matthew Singleton, Mr. Robert Stark, Mr. Charles Culliat, Mr. Thomas Charlton All Members of the Established Church . . . ." *Ibid.,* [389]. The above men were commissioned magistrates in late July, 1771, and the sermon was probably delivered a month or two later. For another extract from this sermon see pp. 123-29.

90. Woodmason has earlier described the ideal magistrate.

Switch. You were without any Representatives in the Legislature—Not a Road established—Not a Church, Minister, or any Divine Ordinances. You liv'd as without God in the World with out Law, Justice, Religion, or the least Security of Property. The Protection of Government was not extended to You—So far from it, that it was deny'd. And Yet You bore all Your Share of Taxes—And the Public Edifices that do Honour to our Metropolis were rais'd cheifly by Impositions on Articles of Your Consumption. And yet You still laid Your Greivances before Your Superiors in a Constitutional Way—but without Redress. The Courts of Justice were not open to You—for You had none— You had neither Advocates or Intercessors—but Oppression and Destroyers—You were not Pragmatical for You could not get one Piece printed, Nor a Petition received read, or regarded. You could not hear God's Word, for the nearest Place of Worship was 200 Miles distant from any of Your dwellings—You could not obtain Redress for Wrongs—for the Courts of Justice were still farther off. *Oppresion* says *Solomon, will make even a Wise Man Mad.* And there was not a Species of Oppression that You did not sustain: Indeed, You were not consider'd as any Part of the Community—Not of an hundredth Part the Value—Not of any Estimation with their Negroes and Slaves.[91] And after a Patient Continuance in Well doing, You at length excited the Spirit of Britons, and insisted on Your Birth Right. The Protection of the Laws—the Administration of Justice—The Security of Property—A due Representation in the Legislature—And a Share in all Public Offices and Institutions. For tho' You are One hundred thousand Persons at least, Yet none of You were deem'd Worthy of being a Jury Man or a Magistrate (save a few Fanatics) or other, than Hewers of Wood and Drawers of Water, to a few Upstart Lawyers and Clerks in Office who have suck'd and prey'd on Your Vitals and would have made You their Pack Horses to future Generations. Instead of being counted Free Men,

91. "The rich folk below, consider'd the Back Country only as a Line of Outcasts they had plac'd there as a Barrier between them and the Indians for to ward off any Blows from them and their Negroes. While their Negroes were safe, the whole Back Country might go to the Devil for them." "Memorandum" on the Regulator movement, Sermon Book, IV, [371].

who had serv'd their King—brav'd Dangers—and on Credit of the Public Faith, settled this inhospitable Wilderness to make it a land flowing with Milk and Honey, and the Glory of all Lands (as it soon will be) You were thrown under ev'ry possible Discouragement. Ev'ry Obstacle laid in Your Way, to keep You as a Distinct People from the Lower Settlers and only as a Barrier between them and the Indians for Security of their Negroes and Plantations. Ye have nobly exerted Your Selves, and shewn Your Selves Men. Without disrespect to Authority trampling on the Laws, or Insolent to Government, tho' many little Errors have happen'd, and will happen in a mix'd Multitude. The Greatest Wonder Is, How such a Multitude have been restrain'd from not committing many Insolencies and Insults on their Enemies and Tyrants. As You were without Representation in Assembly, Your Cries could not be heard there—for all Ears were stopp'd. Then You nobly resolved to carry Your Complaints home, and lay them at the feet of Majesty.[92] The Sound of this awaken'd and affrighted Your Oppressors. They shook and trembled—What had been deny'd for 20 Years—Was instantly granted. Courts and Forums, and Prisons and Magistrates, and Judges, and Juries, and Roads, Bridges, and Public Works. One Day—One Spirited Resolution, effected what humble Petitions for 20 Years could not—Altho' there were Laws in Being (tho' unexecuted) that were effectual for Your Relief. The Crown approv'd all Your Proceedings. You were releas'd from the Calumies of Evil Doers and Busy Bodies by a General Pardon. And I have the Pleasure of seeing those here sitting in the Chair of Authority, who lately were almost proscrib'd as Enemies to the State and to their Country, Tho eminent for Your Loyalty to the one and Love to the Other. Indeed You were *Busy Body's*—Yet still, it was not in *other Mens Matters,* but solely in Your own. You indeed dictated to Government But it was, *What Things they had left undone* leaving them to Do, *What ought to be done* according to their Wisdom and Direction. Some Things still remain, to compleat Your being on the same foot with Your other Brethren provin-

92. Here Woodmason apparently refers to the proposal to send himself and a Mr. Cary to England to request Crown aid for the Backcountry. See Introduction, p. 183, and p. 210.

cials—The having this Country laid out into Parishes with Churches, Chapels and Orthodox Ministers, a New Jury List, and a proper Representation in the General Assembly. This Last You may depend on being debarred of for as long as possible—And without a Spirit of Prophecy, it may be foreseen, that this Circumstance will oblige You in few Years to recommence *Busy Bodys*. You have long been Ruled by a Junto of Your fellow Subjects, and been under an *Aristocratic* Government instead of a *Royal* and *Free:* And this Junto, as it has alway[s] had the Lead in all Public Affairs, will still hold fast the Rod, and make it prove to You a Rod of Iron, if not timely prevented by Your insisting to have Parishes, Vestries, A due Care of the Poor, and Internal Administration of Justice With a proper Attention to an easy Transportation of Your heavy Produce to Market; And not for the Public Treasure to be wasted in useless Works of Ornamental *Architecture* and Statuary, while the *Useful* and Profitable are wholly disregarded.

# Chief Justice Charles Shinner:

## "A Gentleman not of bright Parts, but of Tried Integrity." [93]

I DARE SAY while I have been saying this many among You call to Mind our late C[hief] J[ustice] Mr. S[hinner]. A Gentleman not of bright Parts, but of tried Integrity. Not of Shining Abilities but valuable Qualities. The Upright Judge—The sincere Friend—The Honest Lawyer, The worthy Man, and humble Christian.[94] He had his Weaknesses and Infirmities—But the Vertues of His Heart far outweigh'd the defects of his Head:— And Yet, Who was ever persecuted more for Righteousness Sake? Who ever was more vexed, defamed, Tormented? And by whom? By Ill Men—those who have kept You in Chains till now—And would have kept You *in everlasting Chains under Darkness till the Judgment of the Great Day,* had He not strenuously exerted himself in Your favour. To this Just, Humane Charitable Gentleman You are highly indebted for the Restoration of Your Rights and Priveleges You now enjoy; And for the procuring of them to You, he fell a Sacrifice to the Malice and Revenge of His and Your Enemies. They broke his Heart—And He very truly may be said to have dy'd a Martyr for the Liberties of the Back Country.

93. Sermon Book, II, [251-52]. Woodmason states that he gave the sermon, from which this extract is taken, at Flat Rock Creek, May 29, 1767; at the Parish Church of St. Mark, Nov. 4, 1770; at Elisha Dorsey's, and St. John's Chapel, Maryland, in 1773, *ibid.,* [258]. The first date is an error, for, according to the Journal, Woodmason was at Jackson's Creek on May 29, 1767, and Shinner did not die until February 27, 1768. The correct date is probably another month and day in 1768, or some time in 1769.

94. In a sermon, undated but after Shinner's death, Woodmason characterized him as "Mild, Tender, Compassionate, even to Softness, Never did He pass Sentence, but with Tears of Pity and Commiseration." Sermon Book, IV, [541].

In respect to Him You may discover to what Lengths Party Rage, Faction, and Clamour will carry the best of Men. In attempting to reform Proceedings at Law and pleaders at the Barr He took a Bull by the Horns, that gor'd Him to Death. And tho' He wanted not for Courage or Probity, Yet He was too feeble an *Hercules* to cleanse the *Augean* Stable, being a Stranger to his own Weakness. Had his Capacity been equal to his Will, He might have executed many Plans, for Your Interest, that now will never be revived. In short—In Him You've lost a most valuable Friend, and neither You or Me, will find such another therefore let us respect his Memory.

# Chief Justice Charles Shinner:

*"With great Reluctance and forebodings He embark'd with his family for Charlestown."* [95]

## Memorandum

CHARLES SHINNER ESQ. was a Gentleman of Ireland—Born (I think) in Limerick and bred to the Study of the Law in Dublin under some eminent Gentleman in that faculty. He was concern'd in a large Branch of Business at Limerick, where He lived in all that festive Hospitality, Freedom, and Generosity, so peculiar to the Gentry of Ireland. Here He shone for several Years—Beloved, Esteemed and Regarded: But by associating with the Nobility, and Gentry of larger Fortune than his own, He quickly exhausted his Patrimony. His Younger Days were spent in all that Idle Dissipation that marks the present Times. His Person was Tall, Robust, and not Inelegant. His Complexion Fair: Address Smooth—And Manners very graceful and Winning. No wonder He became a fav'rite of the Ladies, with whom He had many near Intimacies, and a strict Connexion with One most beautiful and engaging, of one of the best Families on the *Shannon.* By Her He had several natural Children that grew up to full Age, and were well Married. One of his Daughters visited Him at Charlestown. At length We find Him when about 50 Years of Age, a Barrister at Law and in some Employment in the

95. Sermon Book, IV, [519-28]. This "Memorandum" on Charles Shinner, precedes a sermon entitled: "A sermon drawn up for, and intended to have been delivered to the Settlers in the Township of Hillsborough, New Bordeaux and Londonburgh in South Carolina On Occasion of the Death of the Honourable Charles Shinner Esq. late Chief Justice of said Province." *Ibid.*, [517]. This "Memorandum" was clearly written many years after Woodmason's sojourn in South Carolina and contains errors both of fact and chronology. The early life of Shinner is probably based upon what Shinner had himself told Woodmason.

Court of Chancery and House of Peers in Ireland—In which Station He acquitted Himself with much Reputation, as His Fidelity and Integrity were unimpeachable and Conspicuous, and in the Light and Character of a Man strictly Honest in his Profession—Not to be Bribed or Bias'd: In whom the Greatest Confidence might be plac'd, and the utmost dependance placed—We find Him entrusted with the Writings and Concerns of a Long and teidous Law Suit of the Montagu Family litigated in the Court of Chancry in Dublin, and afterward removed by Appeal to the House of Lords in England—Betwixt London and Dublin We find Him going Ev'ry Session, carrying over Witnessess, Depositions &c. taking Interogatories—and performing all the Offices of a Dep'ty Master in Chancery.[96]

During these Journies We find Him the Sedate, and Moral Man—The Pious and Sincere Christian—Having seen much of Human Life, He heartily despis'd its Follies, and was weary of its Emptiness. We hardly find a more reform'd, or truly Religious Person. He ever was a strict Protestant: Would He have married into a Roman Catholic Family it might greatly have proved to his Benefit. But no Man more detested Popery—and few understood better the true Principles of Christianity. After living to be an old Batchelor He married a Young Woman in London. And at termination of the Law Suit, Lord Hallifax was so pleas'd with his Uprightness and Integrity, as to think that such a Man would Shine on the Bench as a *Judge* and prove a Blessing to Society. Accordingly, We find Him appointed to be Cheif Justice of the Province of So. Carolina about the Year 1760.[97] This was un-

96. A political attack upon Shinner, first published in *The St. James's Chronicle, or the British Evening Post*, Aug. 27, 1765, was reprinted in South Carolina. Without using his name it called him "An *Irishman* of the lowest Class" and the son of a tradesman, who had risen "*through a Series of those various Shifts and Changes which chequer the Lives of* NEEDY ADVENTURERS," to the respectable work of carrying bills, answers, and so on, between the law courts of England and Ireland. Having aided a lady in England who was engaged in an important Irish lawsuit, she recommended him to her brother who obtained him the appointment as Chief Justice of South Carolina. *S. C. Gaz. and C-J*, May 6, 1766.

97. Shinner was appointed Chief Justice in March, 1761. See Dunk Halifax, *et al.*, to the King, Whitehall, Mar. 17, 1761, P.R.O. Trans., XXIX, 50; at

solicited and unsuspected by Him. It surpriz'd, It griev'd Him: Well knowing, that He had neither Genius or Talents adequate to this Employ—and He foresaw at one View All the Evils and Troubles which afterward befell Him.[98] But He dar'd not refuse the Kindness of his Noble Patron, who too little knew the Situation of Affairs in America and the Temper of those People to whom He was consign'd. With great Reluctance and forebodings He embark'd with his family for Charlestown—taking with Him Two valuable and Sensible Gentlemen of the Law, to be his Support and Counsellors in all Emergencies with several faithful Domestics and followers But alas! the deadly Climate of Carolina swept them all off within three Years. While these Gentlemen lived, Mr. Shinner went on with Great Spirit, and supported his Station with Dignity and Applause. But when deprived of the Props that supported his Understanding—His Weakness of Judgment and Deficiency in Points of Law, and Judicial Matters, soon render'd Him Contemptible in the Eyes of the Carolinians, a Proud and Ignorant People. Having none to assist Him to repress the Insolence of the Lawyers, The Court was often disgrac'd by Disputes, Altercations, and Debates betwixt Him, the Barristers, and Crown Officers. To add to his Vexations, He had not one Assistant Judge to Succour, Advise, or Support Him. Those in that Post being very mean and Illiterate Persons, and a Burlesque on Magistracy. Nor was He less unhappy in his Political Capacity, than His Judicial. For He ever was oppos'd at Council Board by Mr. Beal, the Lt. Governour and other Members—who would thwart and oppose Him Right or Wrong, in all Things He proposed or engaged in for Service of the Crown—Good of the People, and Interest of the Church of England. Never had the King or Church so good an Advocate, So faithful a Friend, as was Mr. Shinner. Nor the People of Carolina ever so valuable a

the Court of St. James, Mar. 20, 1761, *ibid.*, 56; Sandys, *et al.*, to the King, Whitehall, Apr. 1, 1761, *ibid.*, 77. On May 6, 1761, Shinner was nominated as a member of the Council, same to same, Whitehall, *ibid.*, 100.

98. A few weeks after his appointment, Shinner was admitted to Grey's Inn. Any training he received here could not have been extensive, for he took up his work in South Carolina in 1762. See Wallace, *Hist. of S. C.*, II, 78-79, and note.

Patriot—For his whole Study and Labour was, To improve and enrich their Country by improving and extending its Natural Advantages. But these Public Benefits clashed with the contrary Notions—the Jobbs—the Contracts—the Self Interestedness of these Gentlemen. For as most of their Estates lay in or contiguous to C. T. Ev'ry thing propos'd for the Good of the Country was overruled as prejudicial to the Interest of the Metropolis. And nothing was ever done for Benefit of the Public by the then legislatures (as they then stood Modelled) but wherein something Peculiar or Beneficial resulted to C. T. consequently to Themselves. As the Parishes next to, and surrounding C. T. were compar[a]tively very small (tho Richer) than the Inland Parishes, Yet they sent treble the Number of Members—So that the Metropolis and 2 or 3 other adjacent Parishes, could alway[s] make a Majority, and divert the Public Money as they thought Proper. Mr. Shinner was determined to break this Junto and accordingly pointed out this Evil to Government at Home, And Plans for correcting it were sent over, but alway[s] baffled by the Arts and Cunning of the Republican Party—against Whom Mr. Shinner set his Face with great Steadiness—Consequently brought on himself all the Malice, Malignity, and Persecution of that Party.

Religion being wholly neglected and the Country overrun with an Numerous Herd of Wild Enthusiastic Sectaries more frantic than Bedlamites Mr. Shinner labour'd to get new Parishes laid out—Churches and Chapels built—Schools founded—Bridges built—Roads and ferries constructed, The Arts cultivated, The Culture of Tobacco Hemp Flax Cotton Silk, Vine, Madder &c. introduced and promoted. His Efforts to this End were Great and Laborious. Himself made Roads, Causeys, Bridges, Mills &c. for benefit of the Back Settlers. And he rais'd a Summer Villa 200 Miles from C. T.[99] to retire too in the Summer Heat and as a Prelude for others to follow, and not to go off their Country and spend its money annually in excursions to New York, Rhode Island, etc., etc. In these things He was joined by the Lt. Governour and one or two other. But the Merchants Traders Clergy

99. His home was apparently in the Waterees region. See Commons Journal, Apr. 9, 1767.

and Rich Planters all join'd together either to render abortive or [one word illegible] ev'ry Proceeding of this Nature. . . .

The famous Year 1765 now clos'd with passing the Stamp Act. As Government had made no Provision, or sent any Instructions over how Persons in Office should Act, in Case of Accidents: and as the Act was rejected Consequently all Things were thrown into Great Confusion. No Writs would be issued by the Cheif Justice without Stamps affix'd—The Session was open'd but no Business done—They hung the Stamp Master in Effigy Near the Court House in Sight of the Cheif Justice, who order'd the Constables to cut down the Gibbet, which they refused. He attempted it Himself, but was repuls'd and insulted. He then left the Court—and they libelled Him in Songs and Pasquenades—His Lady was then big with her third Child and near Delivery—The next Evening the Towns People rose in a Mobb and surrounded his House, demanding the Seal of Court. He refus'd—And stood arm'd in his defence After many threats (at which he was not intimidated) they ruin'd his Garden, broke his Windows, and did other Mischeif. Next day the Sons of Liberty made a Seal—and a Committee of them issued Writs and did all the Business of the Kings Court. This Assembly of the Mob so affrighted Mrs. Shinner as to throw her into Labour: She was brought to bed of a Son, and dy'd three days after.[100] The next Week he lost his eldest Son, and in about 3 Months, his little Daughter. Their Losses made great Impression on Him and sunk his Spirits already overpowered by the horrid Calumnies and Persecutions rais'd against Him. At length the Commons House of Assembly address'd the Governour to remove Him,[101] as a Person insufficient for his

100. Shinner credits the death of his wife to "mobs and frights about our House and her fear of my meeting some Misfortune abroad when I went out, and that every night we had some arms conveniently laid by the Bedside for fear of an attack upon our lives, this brought on her Labour before her time of which she died." Her death occurred on Jan. 7, 1766. "An Account of the Proceedings of the Chief Justice, Assistant Judges and Lawyers of South Carolina on the Stamp Act," enclosed in Montagu to Lords of Trade, Charleston, Aug. 6, 1766, P.R.O. Trans., XXXI, 130, 202.

101. On April 20, 1767, the Assembly, in an address to Governor Montagu, requested the suspension of Shinner; on May 3, Shinner gave his answers to the charges against him; on May 11, the Council unanimously recommended

Office, and of too weak Capacity for such a Trust.[102] The Governour being equally obnoxious to them, and being willing to keep his Place (which He had purchas'd) as long as possible lamely assented to suspend Him from the Bench till His Majestys Pleasure was known: But did not remove him from the Council Board. Soon after this Death depriv'd him of his little Motherless Babe: And this Stroke so affected Him, that He sunk under the Greifs and Troubles that lay Heavy on Him—Took to His Chamber and in about 3 Weeks dy'd of a broken heart.[103] Neither Religion or Philosophy availed to support Him. He lived not to hear that the Sentence of the Governor (to please the People) was confirm'd, and another nominated to succeed Him. Having no Relation, and dying Intestate—a fellow to whom he owed nothing administer'd his Estate—seized it into his Hands—Sold, and Spent it—None of his Friends or Kindred in G. B. or Ireland ever receiving a Shilling of all He left behind Him.

---

his suspension; and on the same day the Governor did as requested. Montagu to Lords of Trade, Charleston, May 12, 1767, P.R.O. Trans., XXXI, 326-27.

102. A committee of the Commons, in a long attack upon Shinner, charged that he was "wholly unacquainted with and ignorant of the Common Law, such Acts of Parliament as are of force here, and the Acts of Assembly of this Province," that he behaved in court with the "utmost Levity, Folly, Ludicrousness and Indecency." The report listed a number of acts by Shinner to illustrate his ignorance of the laws. Some of these could be understood in such a fashion as to sustain Woodmason's characterization of Shinner as kindhearted, for they appear to have been aid given to poor and unfortunate individuals. See Commons Journal, Apr. 9, 1767, and Shinner's defense, ibid., May 27, 1767.

103. Shinner died on February 26, 1768. Governor Montagu had received orders to dismiss Shinner the preceding day but, perhaps because of Shinner's imminent death, had not notified him. S. C. and Amer. Gen. Gaz., Mar. 4, 1768; Montagu to Hillsborough, Charleston, Mar. 25, 1768, P.R.O. Trans., XXXII, 7.

# ✝✝✝✝✝✝✝✝✝✝ INDEX ✝✝✝✝✝✝✝✝✝✝

# INDEX

*Note:* All places are in South Carolina unless otherwise indicated.